Islam, Politics
and the State

In memory of those men and women who
have given their lives and have
suffered to free Muslim society of
oppression and exploitation.

Islam, Politics and the State:

The Pakistan Experience

edited by
Mohammad Asghar Khan

Zed Books Ltd.

Islam, Politics and the State was first published by Zed Books
Ltd., 57 Caledonian Road, London N1 9BU, in 1985.

Copyright © Mohammad Asghar Khan, 1985.

Cover designed by Andrew Corbett
Printed by The Bath Press, Avon

British Library Cataloguing in Publication Data

Islam politics and the state : the Pakistan
    experience.
    1. Islam and politics — Pakistan   2. Pakistan —
Politics and government — 1971-
I. Asghar Khan, Mohammad
297'.1977'095491   JQ556

ISBN 0-86232-471-8
ISBN 0-86232-472-6 Pbk

US Distributor
Biblio Distribution Center, 81 Adams Drive,
Totowa, New Jersey 07512, USA.

Contents

Glossary

Ahadīth	—	plural of *hadīth*; sayings and traditions of prophet.
ahimsa	—	Hindu, Buddhist and Jainist philosophy; the law of reverence for and non-violence to every form of life.
Ahmadis	—	followers of Mirza Ghulam Ahmed Qadiani; a religious minority in Pakistan.
'ālim	—	literally, a learned man, generally used for a doctor of Islamic law.
al-Nās	—	people.
amīr	—	a person holding authority, a ruler, head of an organisation.
Ansārs	—	helpers; Medinan Muslims who helped the migrant Muslims in the Prophet's time.
Arya Samaj	—	a fundamentalist Hindu political organisation.
Ash'arites	—	followers of Abul-Hassan Al-Ashari. A Muslim religious sect which believed in determinism.
Bande-Matram	—	a patriotic hymn expressed in Hindu images.
bastis	—	habitations. Clusters of huts or dwellings.
batil	—	false (opposite of *haqq*, true).
bilād al makhzan	—	the country of the treasury.
bilād al sibah	—	the country in rebellion.
Brelavi	—	belonging to the Indian town Bareilly; belonging to the religious sect which adheres to the doctrine of Ahmad Raza of Bareilly; a conservative sect.
chādar	—	a sheet of cloth used by women in orthodox Muslim societies to cover their heads and bodies.
Deobandī	—	belonging to the Muslim religious seminary of Deoband, India; an orthodox sect which abhors superstitions attributed to the *Brelavī* sect.
dīn	—	way of life.
dīn-i-Ilahi	—	Mughul emperor Akbar's religious creed (1582 AD) aimed at uniting different religious communities of India. Now extinct.

dīnyāt	—	religious teaching
faqih	—	a person learned in *fiqh* (see below).
fatih	—	conqueror.
fatwa	—	a ruling by a jurist on the legality or otherwise of an action.
fiqh	—	literally, the exercise of one's intelligence to understand a matter, used for Islamic jurisprudence..
fiqhi Islam	—	*interpretations of Qur'ān and Ahadīth* as contained in the *fiqh* (jurisprudence) of medieval times.
fuqahā	—	plural of *faqih*, persons learned in *fiqh*.
hādīth	—	a tradition of the prophet.
haji	—	one who has performed the *hajj*.
hajj	—	annual pilgrimage to Mecca.
Harijans	—	literally, children of God; untouchables in India.
Hindu Mahasabha	—	a right-wing Hindu political organisation; aims at the establishment of a Hindu religious state in India.
Hijaz	—	region with which the beginning of Islam is associated, i.e. Medina.
hiyal	—	ruses to avoid a prohibition, such as that of interest.
ijmah	—	popular consensus.
ijtihād	—	the application of the mind to the verses of the Qur'ān and *Ahadīth* for applying them to particular situations or problems.
Ilahi hakoomat	—	the government of God.
ilhād	—	apostasy.
Imām	—	a religious leader.
islamiāt	—	Islamic religious studies.
jagirdari	—	feudal agrarian system.
jihād	—	literally, the utmost effort; a war in the cause of Islam.
kafir	—	one who refuses to believe in the unity of God.
Kafir-i-Azam	—	the great infidel, a term used to ridicule the title of *Quaid-i-Azam* used reverentially for Mohammad Ali Jinnah.
khalīfa	—	caliph, viceregent; owner of delegated powers to enforce the laws of God.
khilāfat	—	caliphate.
kissān	—	peasant.
kufr	—	disbelief; interpreted loosely as the act that

		renders a person outside the pale of Islam.
lailat ul qadar	—	the night of the beginning of the revelation of the Qur'ān.
madrassah	—	mosque school.
maktab	—	school of religious teachings.
majlis-i-amal	—	executive council.
majlis-i-shoora	—	consultative council.
mashaikh	—	religious leaders.
maumin	—	a true believer.
mihrab	—	elliptical part of the wall of a mosque from here the imam leads congregational prayers.
millat	—	community, religion, creed.
Mohammad-ur-Rasool Allah	—	Mohammad is the messenger of God.
Allah		
mudāraba	—	profit-sharing.
muballiqh	—	preacher.
muhalla	—	a small section of a town or city.
mujaddid	—	a person who restores Islamic doctrines to their pristine purity.
mujāhid	—	one who participates in *jihād* (see above).
mujāhideen	—	plural of *mujāhid*.
mujtahid	—	an authority on divine law who practises *ijtihād*, that is the search for a correct opinion and deduces the specific provisions of law from its principles and ordinances.
Mukti Bahini	—	Bangla for liberation army.
mulla	—	a theologist, a scholar, formerly an honorific applied to eminent scholars, now degraded to denote a person who is not so learned and is attached to a mosque.
mustazafeen	—	the weak ones.
Mu'tazilites	—	a group of Muslim philosophers who believe in man's free will and rationalism.
mutawalli	—	a custodian, a trustee.
muzāra'a	—	share-cropping.
nazmeen-i-salat	—	plural of *nazim-i-salat*, persons appointed by Pakistan's military government to exhort people to offer their prayers, five times a day in mosques.
Paisa Akhbar	—	name of a newspaper.
Pakhtun	—	or Pushtun, people of the Afghan race inhabiting mostly the North West Frontier Province of Pakistan.
pīr	—	literally an old man; teacher, master, a

		religious leader, a *Sūfi* (mystic) having a number of followers in a *khānqah* (monastery).
qadianis	—	see *Ahmadis*.
qazi	—	a judge; judge of a shariah court.
qest	—	equity.
Quaid-i-Azam	—	the Great Leader, a title used for the founder of Pakistan, Mohammad Ali Jinnah.
Ram Raj	—	raj or rule by Hindus in a Hindu state.
ribā	—	usury, interest, unearned income.
sadaqā	—	alms.
Sajjada Nashin	—	the successor to a spiritual leader, associated with his place of burial kept as a shrine.
salāt	—	prayer.
sangathan	—	literally, binding together. Hindu fascist movement.
Sharī'ah	—	social-religious law of Islam.

Preface

The contradictions between the egalitarian spirit of Islam and conditions in the Muslim World, the exploitation of the masses and the almost universal denial of human rights present the picture of a society which appears — the resurgence of Islam in some countries notwithstanding — to be in a state of stagnation, if not decay.

My years in detention since 1979 have provided me with an opportunity to reflect on the causes that have led to this state of affairs. During this period of forced leisure, I thought of writing on various dimensions of the problem. However, I soon realised that, because of the vastness of the subject and the lack of reference material at my disposal, it was not possible for me to tackle this task single-handed. I therefore decided to ask scholars with an enlightened and broad understanding of their subjects to help me in undertaking this work. I was very pleased to find those I approached enthusiastic in their response. My association with them has been unusual because I have not been able to meet them during the course of the preparation of this work. Our contacts have been mainly through correspondence undertaken despite the many obstacles that are a feature of today's Pakistan. This inevitably caused delays, and the editing of this book, without my being able to discuss the different chapters with their authors, was thus made more complicated. It is, I think, remarkable that in spite of the absence of these contacts, there is an identity of views of the different writers in their own disciplines on the main theme of this book. Another feature of this work is the contemporary nature of the writings.

I would like to express my gratitude to all those who would prefer to remain unnamed, who rendered valuable assistance in undertaking this study, typing the manuscript, checking the proofs and helping to put the book together. I hope that *Islam, Politics and the State* will be a contribution towards an understanding of the forces which have been at work in pushing Muslim society in general, and Pakistan in particular, towards its present state of cultural, political and economic backwardness and underdevelopment. It might also help to expose the coterie of exploiters — religious and secular — who abound in almost every Muslim state under the patronage of some dictator or the other.

MOHAMMAD ASGHAR KHAN

Introduction

by Mohammad Asghar Khan

Since the beginning of the 20th century when the process of decolonisation began, the Muslim World, which forms about one-sixth of the world's population, has been in ferment. As a result, countries from Morocco to Indonesia, where large Muslim populations are to be found, have been in a state of disequilibrium. Some of the trends in these countries are common to other postcolonial countries of the Third World. But there is, for want of a better term, an 'Islamic factor' prevalent in these countries which has contributed to the strains that these countries are experiencing. There is a thread of affinity which runs across national boundaries and geographical barriers, but there is also a diversity of experience — of language, history, tradition and culture — that provides a consciousness of their separate identity in the Muslim World spanning two continents and ten thousand miles.

A Muslim, according to the simplest definition, is one who submits to the will of God and believes in His book the Qur'ān and in His Messenger Mohammad ibn Abd Allah. Those who accepted this faith at some time during the past 1400 years passed their belief from generation to generation. A degree of common historical experience also provides a link between Muslims living as far apart as Jakarta and Rabat or Karachi and Tashkent. However, Islam is not ritualistic obedience to the creator alone, nor reverence and obedience to His Messenger without understanding the purpose and meaning of that message — a message that shook the world and created vibrations that continue to be felt to this day.

Born on Bedouin soil, among a people steeped in ignorance, superstition and strife, Islam brought a powerful message of justice, freedom and social equality to mankind. The message was simple, and it spread with amazing speed until by 712, barely eighty years after the death of the Prophet, it had reached Morocco and Spain in the west and India in the east. Muslim armies had marched through much of Europe and had reached Tours near Paris in 732. Yet by the time the third caliph, Uthman-ibn Affan, died in 656, the seeds of discord in Muslim society had been sown. With the death of the fourth caliph, Ali Ibn Abu Talib, Arab lands, the citadel of Islam, began to slide towards autocratic and monarchical rule. The stand taken by *Imam* Hussain at Karbala was the first major challenge to illegal authority and his martyrdom a lasting

1

invitation to *jihād* in the cause of righteousness. The example that he set has time and again been invoked by those struggling against tyranny, but Yazid's successors have also found their supporters throughout Muslim history. Many so-called *'ulamā* (religious scholars) who have provided support to autocrats have twisted religion to suit their masters, and there has been no dearth of hypocrites masquerading as religious scholars and divines. One such example is the *fatwa* issued in 1798 by the *'ulamā* of Al Azhar University in Cairo, the premier Islamic university in the world, in support of Napoleon Bonaparte when he invaded Egypt. The support of important sections of the *'ulamā* for autocratic rulers has inevitably led to exploitation of the masses with the attendant social and moral depravation of Muslim society.

In spite of this move of the Muslim World away from the original 'message', the initial momentum that this revolutionary religion created led to great discoveries in the fields of science, medicine, mathematics and astronomy. These discoveries, as well as the study and translation by Muslim scholars of Greek literature, brought light to Europe's 'Dark Ages' and sowed the seeds of the Enlightenment. Mohammad Ibn Musa al Khwarizmi, 780-850 (mathematics, algebra and geography), Abu Bakr Mohammad Zakariya Ali Razi, 865-925 (medicine), Mohammad Ibn Mohammad Ibn Yarkhan abu Naser Al Farabi, 870-950 (political economy and mathematics), Abdul Rahyan Mohammad Ibn Ahmed al Biruni, 973-1048 (mathematics), Abu Ali Ibn Hussain, known as Ibn Sina or Avicenna, 980-1037 (medicine), Omar Khayyam,[1] 1040-1124 (mathematics and astronomy), Ibn Rushd or Averroes, 1126-98 (medicine) and Ibn Khaldun, 1332-1406 (history) became household names in literary circles in Europe.

For the first 400 years, starting with the Qur'ān, reason and science reigned supreme, and the 'Islamic Renaissance' reached its pinnacle in the ninth and tenth centuries. While the light of learning lit by Muslim scholars was beginning to spread gradually in Europe, obscurantist and reactionary forces gained ascendency in Muslim capitals, and the spread of knowledge in the Muslim World was arrested. As Muslim lands began to be dominated by autocratic rulers and their henchmen, the feudal classes and an opportunistic clergy imposed an exploitative and retrogressive system that had little in common with the Islam of the Prophet. At about this time, the Muslim World underwent a traumatic experience from which it never really recovered. The sack of Baghdad by the Mongols in 1258 and their destruction of almost every institution of learning and research in Muslim Central and West Asia were blows with far-reaching consequences. Irrigation works, schools, colleges and libraries were destroyed, but more devastating than the damage to the economy and to these institutions was the paralysing effect on the intellectual milieu. Muslim society began to sink into ignorance and poverty, and social and religious schisms began to deepen. Originality and research were seriously impaired, and it was a long time before Muslim scholars could make any impact in the fields of learning and discovery. By that time, however, Europe had moved ahead in almost every field of human activity. A civilisation that had contributed a great deal towards the growth of Western culture and learning was never again able to regain its place of eminence in original research and scientific thought.

The advent of the 20th century saw the Muslim World in a pitiable state of helplessness. Almost all of it had been colonised by European nations, and there was not a single Muslim state that could be considered independent of foreign control in the true sense. Today, with most of these states having gained their 'independence', many of them find themselves economically and politically dependent on one or the other of the major powers. They are suffering from the effects of centuries of exploitation in which foreign powers, as well as their own exploitative classes, have played a part. Muslim history then is an association of diverse forces, spanning fourteen centuries since the advent of Islam. This period saw the birth of this great faith in its pristine glory, the early phase under the guidance and leadership of the four caliphs, its period of growth to distant lands, great strides in science and philosophy, the growth and consolidation of autocratic regimes and the role of a class of *'ulamā* in misrepresenting Islam, the colonisation of Muslim lands and then a gradual awakening of the Muslim masses.

Throughout this period of Muslim history, starting as early as the Prophet's time, there has been a struggle between progressive and reactionaries. Both have tried to interpret Islam in the light of their own understanding and often of their own interests. The interpretation of the Qur'ān and the *Ahadīth* has therefore not always been the same. With the passage of time these differences have grown, and the power of the state and of feudal interests has accentuated the divisions within Muslim society. Progressive thought has been opposed from the very beginning. Starting with the Prophet, who spread a message of equality and tolerance in the face of tremendous opposition from the class of exploiters of that time, everyone who has tried to emphasise the spirit of that 'message' has been opposed by vested interests. So-called *'ulamā* have let themselves be used for this purpose. They have been generous with the issue of *fatwa*s against anyone who has dared to oppose their obscurantist vision. Abu Dharr Ghifary (d.651), Syed Ahmed Khan (1817-96), Dr. Mohammad Iqbal (1876-1938) and Mohammad Ali Jinnah (1876-1948), who struggled for the emancipation of Muslims, were either branded *kafirs* (infidels) or abused for their progressive views. The great names in the sciences who gave the world a new dimension in reasoning and thought were likewise ridiculed by obscurantist *'ulamā*. Al Khwarzimi, the great mathematician who introduced algebra and authored the famous work *Surat ul Ard* (*The Shape of the Earth*) was branded a *kafir*. Al Razi, Al Farabi, Ibn Sina, Omar Khayyam, Ibn Rushd and Ibn Khaldun did not fare any better.

In modern times the opportunistic *'ulamā* of the Middle Ages have

3

been replaced by a class of so-called religious scholars whose vision unfortunately is no broader than that of their predecessors. They too wear intellectual blinkers and either fail to see reason or are ever willing to work for those whose aim is to exploit and suppress the people. This phenomenon prevails throughout the Muslim World, and whereas the West fought this battle and defeated obscurantists towards the end of the Middle Ages, the Muslim World has still to come to grips with this problem. This battle against ignorance and exploitation, which most of the Muslim World has yet to win, is made more complicated by the exploitation of religion by vested interests: monarchs, *mulla*s, dictators, usurpers and opportunists.

While these problems are to be found throughout the Muslim World, Pakistan appears to be well suited for a 'case study'. Geographically, it lies close to the Arab countries, Iran and Turkey to its west and Indonesia and Bangladesh to its east. To the north-west it has a common border with Afghanistan, which is close to the southern states of the Soviet Union with its large population of Muslim ethnic origin. Historically, Pakistan has been exposed to Arab and Iranian influences and has had trade and cultural contacts with the Arab world, Bangladesh and Indonesia. Culturally, it has been more exposed to Western influences than perhaps any other Muslim country. Economically, it is heavily dependent on Western aid and has a feudal-bureaucratic-military elite that, to the exclusion of the national bourgeoisie, is in a position to exploit the people. Politically, it is allied closely with the West, and its position in the East-West confrontation renders it particularly vulnerable. As a result of its historical and cultural past, it has a fairly large educated class, a developed judicial system — which it has inherited from the British — and an urban female population which has experienced at least one national election and is generally aware of its rights. Its *'ulamā* do not share a unanimity of views either on the interpretation of religion or on politics, and it has a tradition of political struggle on a national scale. Pakistan therefore is well suited for a study of different phenomena, many of which are common to other Muslim countries and are the result of various experiences that go back 1400 years and sometimes more.

Islam, Politics and the State comprises eleven chapters, which focus on contemporary social tensions and contradictions in the Muslim World, between modernists and progressives on the one hand and fundamentalists and reactionaries on the other, between the masses and the feudal elites, between enlightenment and obscurantism and between a living modern culture and mediaeval traditions. This tension is discernible on all planes — social, political, economic, cultural and intellectual. In almost all contemporary Muslim societies, the tradtional class of *'ulamā* tenaciously clings to the ideas and notions enshrined in mediaeval *fiqh* (Islamic jurisprudence) and has in general allied itself with those social classes which are embedded in the social systems of feudalism and capitalism. However, feudalism as a social relationship is being replaced by a higher social system: industrial capitalism, a pluralistic society and parliamentary democracy. This relatively new democratic and scientific culture is associated with the rise of social and natural sciences as well as with an increase in the social and political consciousness of the masses.

In addition to examining the overall political, social, economic and intellectual problems of the Muslim World, this book analyses in greater detail the problems of Pakistan. This has been done to underline the nature of the political economy of underdevelopment and dependence on the one hand and on the other to correlate different disciplines and areas in history, religion, politics, education, science and economics so as to develop an integrated approach for an understanding of the problem. While focusing attention on Pakistan, this examination highlights certain concepts and institutions which Muslim societies share as a result of their historical experience and as appendages of international monopoly capitalism. Thus, whether it is Pakistan, Indonesia, Turkey, Morocco or Egypt — although their specific problems may differ — their destiny as members of the poor Third World is the same.

Eqbal Ahmed in his chapter discusses the prejudices reflected in the works of Western orientalists. These prejudices and 'problems of perception' in their analysis of Muslim society, he argues, are the result of the nature of the fluctuations in the territorial, religious and cultural boundaries of Islamic civilisation with the West. He is of the view that as the process of decolonisation began, a change at least in thought appears to have started in the West. However, he explains that this welcome trend was overwhelmed by those with vested ideological interests, largely because of the Arab-Israeli conflict and Western support for the Israeli cause. The end of the colonial era therefore, he points out, did not produce a detente that could otherwise have been expected.

While discussing the relationship between religion and politics, Eqbal Ahmed argues that this phenomenon is not exclusive to Muslim countries but is to be found in other present day societies as well. In the United States, Israel and India for example, religion plays a significant role in the political process. However, in Muslim history, Eqbal Ahmed explains, there have been long periods when religion and state power have functioned separately. He is of the view that since 945, when the Buwayhid Prince Muiz al-Dawla Ahmed entered Baghdad and put an end to the Abbasid caliphs' dual role as temporal and spiritual leaders, power in effect has remained secularised almost for a thousand years.

A common theme running through the chapters by Eqbal Ahmed and Suroosh Irfani is the contrasting role of the *'ulamā* in different periods of Muslim history. The manner in which a large number of *'ulamā* have justified monarchical and autocratic forms of government by invoking religious injunctions is shown to be in sharp contrast to the non-conformist and anti-establishment role of certain sections of the Muslim intelligentsia. Thus, whereas Islamic injunctions have been relied upon by some *'ulamā* to confer legitimacy on authoritarian rule, Qur'anic verses and Prophetic traditions have been cited by others to exhort the people to rise against tyranny and oppression.

The modern progressive Islamic movement is discussed in detail by Suroosh Irfani with reference to contemporary events. He discusses the influence progressive Muslim thinkers like Shah Waliullah, Jamalud Din Afghani, Syed Ahmed Khan, Allama Iqbal and Ali Shariati have had on political movements in the Indian subcontinent and Iran over the last century. Suroosh Irfani explains that the antecedents of the progressive Islamic movement are to be found in the practice of the Prophet of Islam, whose revolutionary message transformed the lives of a people who were living under an oppressive social order. He discusses the role played in the Iranian Revolution by the *Mujāhideen-i-Khalq*, who are motivated by the revolutionary message of Islam articulated by their own theoreticians as well as by Dr. Ali Shariati. This tradition has been kept alive in the face of heavy odds, both in practice and in thought, by Muslims in different times and places. Whether it was a companion of the Prophet like Abu Dharr Ghifary, the grandson of the Prophet *Imam* Hussain, or a modern thinker like Dr. Ali Shariati, the revolutionary ideals of early Islam have inspired all those who have challenged both oppression and the illegitimate authority of the state.

A feature that is brought out in the chapters by Eqbal Ahmed, Abbas Rashid and Suroosh Irfani is the 'secular' nature of political movements and state power in Muslim society, notwithstanding the use of religious symbolism as a rallying point. Suroosh Irfani compares the Iranian experience, where the fundamentalist 'ulamā assumed power despite the role played by the *Mujāhideen-i-Khalq*, with the Pakistan Movement, where liberal and democratic Muslims secured power despite the opposition of the fundamentalist 'ulamā. Thus except for *Shi'a* Iran, where the 'ulamā along with the progessive Muslim intelligentsia have been in the forefront of political movements — constitutional (1905-9) or insurrectionary (1978) —, in *Sunni*-dominated areas such as Indonesia, the Indo-Pakistan subcontinent and Algeria and Palestine, popular movements for national liberation and democratic rights have been led by modernists. Fundamentalism in Muslim society, Eqbal Ahmed maintains is an aberration and is contrary to the political culture and historical tradition of Muslims. He is of the view that the limited but growing appeal of fundamentalist political groups in Muslim countries is a result of traumas of Muslim political life, in the absence of viable alternatives.

Omar Asghar Khan discusses the nature of the state in Muslim society in the context of the evolution of a centralised authority in the Hijaz as well as with reference to changes in the structure of state power which took place in response to changes at the socio-economical level. He argues that the revolution of a centralised authority in the Hijaz after the Prophet's migration from Mecca to Medina was a result of the peculiar social, economic and political conditions prevalent at the time and was not a part of the Prophet's mission. The intellectual implications of the transformation of the egalitarian nature of Muslim society into an elaborate bureaucratic structure, dominated by strongly entrenched vested interests, are examined by Ziaul Haque and Omar Asghar Khan in their respective chapters. They argue that the codification of *fiqh* took place in a monarchial-feudal period. It is therefore not surprising, they maintain, that protagonists of the status quo in many Muslim country refer to *fiqh* as codified during a feudal social order — besides the Qur'ān and *Ahadīth* as the sources for erecting as Islamic system.

Abbas Rashid discusses the differences between the formation of the nation-state in Europe and in the postcolonial world, of which most Muslim countries are a part. He points out that in Europe the formation of a strong centralised state followed the development of a national consciousness, which in turn was based on a common culture, language and ethnicity. In most postcolonial countries, however, the establishment by conquest, of a centralised state apparatus has pre-empted the evolution of a national consciousness. It is in this context that the question of ideology is discussed by Abbas Rashid. He argues that states, like individuals, need an ideology to give meaning to their existence. However, if the state is to allow for the development of a national consciousness based on the cultural, linguistic, ethnic and social characteristics of the different peoples inhabiting it, the ideology of such a state should take cognisance of the world view and thinking of the people who inhabit it. He explains that Islam is a central motif but not the only factor that goes into the development of Muslims' ideological framework, be they in Pakistan or in any other Muslim state.

Feroze Ahmed, in his chapter, discusses the manner in which ideology has been used to suppress the people, as has been done in the case of the less privileged 'nationalities' in Pakistan. In his opinion, slogans like 'Islam in danger' have been used as an opiate in the past, and the 'Ideology of Pakistan' is now being 'pushed down the throats' of the people of the smaller provinces. Akmal Hussain in his chapter discusses the failure of a fundamentalist Islamic ideology as a cementing force. He suggests that the state's interpretation of a religious ideology is seen by the people to sanctify the class interests of the ruling hierarchy and is a justification for repression.

It is pointed out by Abbas Rashid and Omar Asghar Khan that the Islam that is rooted in the popular mind has been popularised not by the orthodox *'ulamā* but by the *Sufis*, who were culturally and socially much closer to the masses. It would therefore appear that the projection by Pakistan's ruling hierarchy of a conservative and obscurantist Islamic ideology as articulated by the fundamentalist *Jamā'at-i-Islāmī* is likely to prove counterproductive.

The philosophy and the role of the *Jamā'at-i-Islāmī*, as well as its links with the military regime in Pakistan, therefore necessitate a close study of its religious and political thinking. This is why frequent references are made to it in this book, and in a chapter devoted to it, Zafaryab Ahmed

7

critically examines Maulana Maudood's theory of an Islamic state. In any democratic system in which the public is given an opportunity to express its choice, the *Jamā'at* cannot, in the foreseeable future, hope to come to power. In free and fair elections held in 1970, it fielded 150 candidates for the National Assembly of a united Pakistan and won four out of a total of three hundred seats. It is doubtful that it has added to its electoral strength since then. It has, however, been working systematically ever since Pakistan was created to infiltrate the important echelons of power in the state apparatus. The armed forces were given special treatment by the *Jamā'at*, and this investment paid off after 30 years when General Zia ul Haq staged a military coup in 1977. During Ayub Khan's era, in the early 1960s the *Jamā'at* was out of favour, and its early converts in sensitive branches of Pakistan's armed forces and the administration conducted themselves with the necessary degree of caution.

During Yahya Khan's two-and-a-half year rule, the *Jamā'at-i-Islāmī*, for the first time, entered the corridors of power and collaborated fully with the military regime in its military action in East Pakistan. In spite of having suffered a crushing defeat in the 1970 elections, it assumed responsibility for advising and supervising the 'Islamisation' of East Pakistan and for providing *razakārs* (volunteers) to assist the military in its operations there. After Yahya Khan's exit, the *Jamā'at* was in opposition to Zulfikar Ali Bhutto's government and moved close to the martial law regime as soon as the People's Party's government was toppled. Having experienced a period of co-operation with the military, during Yahya Khan's martial law, it felt at home with the military regime of Zia ul Haq, who had been a long-standing convert to the *Jamā'at's* philosophy. They were therefore able to establish a rapport with the military regime without any loss of time. In fact since the *amir* (head) of the *Jamā'at* was not, unlike other political leaders, placed in detention when the military assumed power in July 1977, it would be reasonable to assume that the rapport was already there. The *Jamā'at* soon moved into the martial law government and deeply infiltrated the departments of state. Today it is represented by its trusted men in some key policy-making institutions and those organisations that influence public opinion, such as the Islamic University, Islamabad; the Institute of Policy Studies, Islamabad, headed by Professor Khurshid Ahmed, a prominent leader of the *Jamā'at-i-Islāmī*; the Pakistan Institute of Public Opinion; the Pakistan Television Corporation; Radio Pakistan; the National Press Trust; universities and colleges; *zakāt* and *hajj* committees; and *salāt* committees. Two of the important functions of these people are to act as agents of the government and to project the thinking of the *Jamā'at-i-Islāmī*. It is therefore able to influence the thinking and policies of the military government, which appears to be moving systematically towards implementing the *Jamā'at's* policies and religious philosophy.

So long as Zia ul Haq remains in control of Pakistan's affairs, therefore, the *Jamā'at-i-Islāmī* will continue to provide the ideological guidelines for the military regime. After his exit too, the armed forces, which include fairly substantial elements in the officer corps who are opposed or have not been converted to the *Jamā'at*'s religious and political philosophy, will find it difficult to move back to the neutral position they once enjoyed. The doctrinal infiltration of the *Jamā'at-i-Islāmī* in the armed forces is now fairly deep, and its cessation can now come about only by either revolutionary changes in the country or by a gradual process of depoliticising the armed forces. It is a realisation of the dangers inherent in this situation that has led to frequent references to the *Jamā'at-i-Islāmī* in this book and to a closer examination of its thinking than it would otherwise merit.

Abbas Rashid and Omar Asghar Khan both point out that the lack of attention paid by progressive forces to the liberal-progressive traditions of Islam and their failure to keep in view the cultural framework of the people while elaborating politico-economic programmes have meant that fundamentalist organisations like the *Jama'at-i-Islāmī* have, by default, had a field day. The *Jamā'at* has therefore been able to define its concept of an Islamic ideology, almost unchallenged, in its various dimensions. Since the military regime of Pakistan has been converted to the *Jamā'at-i-Islāmī*'s model of an Islamic state as elaborated by its chief theoretician, Sayyid Abul Ala Maudoodi, it is important to understand the nature and implications of Maulana Maudoodi's model. Omar Asghar Khan argues that, by misrepresenting Qur'ānic verses and the *Ahadīth*, the *Jama'at-i-Islāmī* has tried to legitimise an authoritarian state aimed at upholding the status quo. Akmal Hussain and Zafaryab Ahmed in their chapters discuss the manner in which the *Jamā'at-i-Islāmī* functions as a political organisation, its philosophy, and its relationship to the military establishment. Akmal Hussain also examines changes in the sociology of the officer corps of the Pakistan armed forces that have taken place since Partition and their political implications.

In conformity with its philosophy of capturing power through infiltrating various institutions and organs of the state, the *Jamā'at*, with the support and sympathy of the military regime, has over the last few years managed to infiltrate and influence the bureaucracy, educational institutions, media, trade unions, police and armed forces. Abbas Rashid, Zafaryab Ahmed, Akmal Hussain, Pervez Hoodbhoy and Nayyar argue that the Islamisation of the country's institutions therefore bears a strong imprint of the *Jamā'at*'s Islamic model. Islamisation appears to have been undertaken to secure a future for a regime that depends on terrorising the public on the one hand and securing the support of obscurantist and reactionary sections of the population on the other. Punitive measures like public floggings are therefore common, and the legal code has been changed, by virtue of which, besides other things, women have been deprived of their fundamental rights.

It is as a part of these policies of the military regime, explain Pervez Hoodbhoy and Nayyar, which are designed to ensure its perpetuation, that the educational system of the country is being altered. The most far-reaching effect of this is the manner in which the history of Pakistan, as taught in schools and colleges, is being rewritten. They explain that while a number of history textbooks portray the *'ulamā*, a large section of whom actively opposed the Pakistan Movement, as the genuine leaders of the independence movement and the creators of the state, the democratic nature of the movement and the role of the common people are consistently played down. Obscurantism in the form of a reactionary ideological framework has come to pervade the curricula prepared by the government under the guidance of the *Jamā'at-i- Islāmī*, not only in the arts but in the sciences as well. The ideological constraints in the way of the development of a rational and scientific attitude are discussed by Pervez Hoodbhoy in another chapter, and he argues that a scientific attitude cannot take root without allowing the spirit of free enquiry to develop. The sorry state in which scientific institutions find themselves today, not only in Pakistan but also in most other Muslim countries, is, he emphasises, a result of the absence of a conducive ideological, social and political environment. It is pointed out by Hoodbhoy that in contrast to the present state of decay that Muslim society finds itself in, the sciences, philosophy and literature flourished in the Muslim World some nine or ten centuries ago. Muslim civilisation, it has been noted, was at its peak when acquisition of knowledge was not impeded. However, the tolerance and encouragement shown by liberal Muslim rulers such as Al Mamun were short-lived.

The persecution of scientists and philosophers by the ruling elite, who felt threatened by the spirit of free enquiry and rationality, is a sad chapter in Muslim history. Although there have been, since then, spurts of intellectual activity in various periods and parts of the Muslim World, based on scientific and rational thought, never again has there been that official patronage and social sanction that was witnessed during the years of the Islamic 'Enlightenment'. Mercifully, the spirit of free enquiry bequeathed to Muslims by scientists and philosophers like Ibn Sina, al Biruni, Omar Khayyam, Ibn Rushd and Ibn Khaldun has not been obliterated despite efforts to do so by the obscurantists. And although a conducive environment for realising the scientific potential is lacking, the urge to move forward is strong among sections of the Muslim intelligentsia.

Besides a discussion of the Islamisation of education and science in Pakistan, problems related to the Islamisation of society, politics and economy are discussed by Ziaul Haque and Omar Asghar Khan. In this context Ziaul Haque discusses the different meanings of Islam. Changes in the socio-economic structure of Muslim society lead him to categorise Muslim history into the revolutionary Islam of the Prophet, 'feudal Islam' which replaced the Islam of the Prophet and the rightly-guided caliphs, and 'bourgeois Islam' of the contemporary era. He points out that it is 'feudal-bourgeois Islam' that forms the basis of the ruling class' Islamisation policies in Pakistan. He explains that it is their endeavour to legitimise the prevailing exploitative socio-economic structure — a structure which is based on the coexistence and interaction of tribal, feudal and capitalist modes of production.

While discussing the Islamisation policies of the military regime in Pakistan, Ziaul Haque argues that the introduction of so-called interest-free banking and *mudāraba* (profit and loss sharing) has nothing to do with Islam. These institutions and practices which predate the advent of Islam are emphasised by Pakistan's military regime, and those practices that relate to the feudal-capitalist era of Islam are adopted as the basis for Islamising the economy. The egalitarian practice of early Islam in abolishing the institutions of *ribā* (usury) and *muzāra'a* (share-cropping or ground rent) is, it is pointed out by Ziaul Haque and Omar Asghar Khan in their respective chapters, conveniently ignored by the ruling classes. Claims of the military regime in Pakistan regarding the elimination of interest are, it is argued, nothing but eye-wash. On the other hand, the practice of *hiyal* (ruses to avoid the prohibition of interest), which has been widely practised in different times and places throughout Muslim history and is also a feature of the present-day Muslim World is, Omar Asghar Khan states, used to get round the prohibition of *ribā*.

Pervez Hoodbhoy, Ziaul Haque and Omar Asghar Khan examine the social implications of the religious fanaticism that has been unleashed in Pakistan in recent years. Besides the negative effects on scientific and economic development, the more glaring consequences have shown up in a number of social tragedies. Humiliating punishments like public flogging of men and women, killings in the name of Islam, clashes between *'ulamā* belonging to different sects, violence in the precincts of holy places, and an unprecedented increase in brutality against women in a society where there is official and legal sanction for discrimination against them are some of the social implications of 'Islamisation' in Pakistan which have been discussed in a number of chapters.

Akmal Hussain examines the interaction between Islam, politics and the state, in the context of the historical forces that led to the emergence of the state of Pakistan. While discussing the nature of the state, its structure in relation to the political and economic power of the ruling classes is explained. The militarisation and bureaucratisation of the political process and the nature of the economic, social and political crisis confronting Pakistan are also examined. It is argued that this crisis can be resolved only by the subordination of the military and the bureaucracy, institutionally, to the political process. The centralisation of state power in the hands of the military-bureaucratic oligarchy, he explains, has resulted in a crippling burden on the economy and a feeling of deprivation among the smaller provinces.

Feroz Ahmed in his chapter argues that as a result of the high-handed approach of Pakistan's ruling hierarchy in dealing with the democratic demands of the smaller provinces, there has been an intensification of nationalist consciousness among the 'oppressed nationalities'. This has been especially true for the Sindhis, whose struggle for their democratic rights within a truly federal Pakistan is discussed at some length in the course of this work. In his discussion of the contemporary unrest in Sind, Feroz Ahmed examines on the one hand the historical development of a 'national self-image' among the Sindhis and on the other the 'insensitivity and ruthlessness of Pakistan's rulers' in dealing with their aspirations. He notes that in order to impose centralised authority on the peoples of Pakistan, Islam has been used to justify the denial of ethnic, linguistic and cultural distinctions which are a feature of multinational states like Pakistan. Ever since the debate on the constitution in the Constituent Assembly and the Objectives Resolution of 1949, the demands of the smaller provinces, it is pointed out by Zafaryab Ahmed, have time and again been rejected by terming them as contrary to the spirit of Islam, which is explained by the self-styled 'defenders of the faith' to be synomonous with centralised authority.

The work ends with a discussion of Pakistan's geopolitical options in the wake of the Soviet invasion of Afghanistan, the Iranian Revolution, the United States' interests in Pakistan's military establishment and the domestic political situation. There is also a discussion of the national security implications of Pakistan's adherence to an aggressive fundamentalist and doctrinaire Islamic ideology. Both the internal and external responses that could be evoked by such reliance are examined. It is argued that Pakistan's problems — some inherited and others acquired — are such as could endanger the survival of the country as an independent state. On its ability to rid itself of some of its self-created shibboleths will, it is argued, depend its future.

References and Notes

1. Known to the West by the translation of *Rubaiyat* by Edward Fitzgerald and by his *al Tarikh al Talali* (a solar calendar).

1. Islam and Politics

by Eqbal Ahmed

Problems in Perception

In writing about Islam and politics, one faces special difficulties. The field of Islamic studies, strewn with ancient potholes and modern mines, is dominated by apparently different but actually complementary adversaries — the 'traditionalist' *'ulamā* and the 'modern' Orientalists. Their methods are different; so are their intentions. Yet, with few exceptions, both tend to view Islam's relationship to politics in fundamentalist and textual terms. Both emphasise the absence of separation between religion and politics in Islam. Both hold an essentially static view of Islam and interpret change and innovations produced by social and economic forces as impingements on establishments, therefore ordained, religious standards. Both treat the most creative periods of Muslim history — that is, the Umayyads in Spain, the Mughuls in India, the Safavids in Persia — as deviations from the norm. The interplay of the Westerners' academic orthodoxy and the *'ulamā*'s theological orthodoxy has set the terms of prevalent discourse on Islam.

A second problem concerning perceptions and prejudices should be noted. The Islamic civilisation is the only one with which the territorial, religious, and cultural boundaries of the West have fluctuated for fourteen centuries. Islam's relationship with the West has been continuous frequently intimate, and marked by protracted and violent confrontation and fruitful, though often forgotten, collaboration. During the century that followed the prophethood of Mohammad, the dramatic expansion of Islamic dominance occurred largely at the expense of Christendom. Subsequently, the West and Islam remained locked in a relationship of antagonistic collaboration that included seven centuries of Muslim rule in Spain, an unsuccessful invasion of France, and an inconclusive occupation of Sicily. The long and bitter confrontation during the Crusades, and later the Ottoman domination of the Balkans, further solidified in the West the adversarial perceptions and menacing images of Islam and Muslims. Even the Prophet Mohammad and the Qur'ān were not spared several centuries of vilification and abusive misrepresentation. In turn, mediaeval Muslim writers misrepresented and misjudged Judaism and

13

Christianity. However, because Islam venerates biblical prophets as predecessors of Mohammad, their polemics fortunately stopped short of vilifications *in extremis*. To the Eastern world's credit, the 'mediaeval canon' of Christian discourse on Islam (up to the 18th century) has been admirably documented.[1]

This unique history of the West's encounter with a non-Western civilisation undoubtedly left on both sides a heritage of prejudice and resentment. Yet, in this pattern of hostility, there were periods of accommodation. While our cultures were traditional, agrarian and mediaeval, there existed a structural symmetry between them which accounted for a degree of equality in the exchange of ideas as well as of products. Winners and losers manufactured and used the same weapons, traded in comparable goods and debated on familiar intellectual premises. There was a certain congruence of class interests and shared attitudes among aristocrats, craftsmen, traders, scholars. The commonality of outlook between Saladin the Great and Richard the Lion-hearted is known to almost every Muslim and Christian child even today. Students of European and Muslim history can recall numerous such examples. But the symmetry which had formed the basis for both intimacy and antagonistic collaboration between Islam and the West disappeared in modern times. Nothing in the past was as damaging to Muslim-Western understanding as has been the structurally unequal encounter of traditional, agrarian/pastoral Muslim societies with the industrial and capitalist West. Its many ramifications include, as we shall presently see, modern Islam's peculiar, disjointed relationship to politics.

A dramatic reversal in the relationship between the Muslim World and the West began with Napoleon Bonaparte's invasion of Egypt in 1798 and the establishment of British dominion over Mughul India during the 18th and 19th centuries. It ended with the break-up of the Ottoman empire, which was the last of the Muslim empires, and the colonisation by European countries of virtually all of the Muslim World from East Asia to West Africa. It was a traumatising development for the Muslims. This was not merely due to the fact that for the first time in the confrontation between Islam and the West they were the colonised, not the colonisers; rather, this latest encounter of Islam with the West was felt as a deeply dehumanising and alienating experience. Modern imperialism was unique in history in that it was a complex and highly integrated system in which preindustrial and pastoral civilisations were either destroyed (as was the case with the great civlisations of the Western hemisphere) or subjugated (as were the countries of Asia and Africa) to serve the needs of the mercantilist and industrialising Western metropoles. The legitimising principles of this system (that is, the white man's burden, the *mission civilisatrice* or the manifest destiny) were based on the assumption of the inferiority of 'native' peoples, their lesser existence, and their diminished humanity. Devaluation of the colonised civilisation, debasement of its cultural heritage, and distortion of native realities have been part of the moral epistemology of modern imperialism. These were important elements of the 'corporate institution' which Edward Said and others have recently analysed as 'Orientialism'.[2]

As the process of decolonisation began, the Western need to justify domination over the 'natives' was lessened. A certain detente in the organised libel against Islam and Muslims was expected. The expectation was credible, given the growth of ecumenical sentiments in the United States and Europe and the ease in communications provided by technological development and international exchange. After centuries of interruption, the possibility had reappeared that Western scholars and their Muslim counterparts would begin to recognise and reassess the limitations and biases of their intellectual work and to examine critically but positively the meaning of the Islamic experience in history and society. The trend that emerged between the world wars, first in France, then in Britain and the United States, suggested that a change in this direction had started. In France, the works of Louis Massignon encouraged the rise of a 'revisionist' school which included scholars of Islam such as Jacques Berque, Maxime Rodinson, Yves Lacoste, and Roger Arnaldez. In Britain and the United States, their counterparts were to be found in H. A. R. Gibb, Wilfred Cantwell Smith, and Norman Daniel. Unfortunately, this welcome trend was overwhelmed by those with vested ideological interests.[3]

Far from producing detente in the postcolonial era, the Cold War and the Arab-Israeli conflict added to the Western discourse on Islam an element of manipulation and malevolence. Cold War academic functionaries and pro-Israeli Middle East 'experts' have rendered difficult an appreciation of contemporary Muslim problems. These include distortions, misrepresentations and libels, not mere criticism. Critical writing needs to be distinguished from racial and ideological hostility. There is a desperate need for critical analyses of the Muslim World's contemporary predicament. From Morocco to Syria, from Iraq to Pakistan and Indonesia, Muslims are ruled by armed minorities. Some describe themselves as socialist and democratic, others as Islamic; yet others as Islamic socialist, and democratic. Nearly all Muslim governments are composed of corrupt and callous elites more adept at repressing the populace than at protecting natural resources or national sovereignty. They are more closely linked to foreign patrons than to the domestic polity. The recent rise of fundamentalist, neototalitarian Muslim movements is an aberration, not a norm, in Muslim history. However, it is predicated upon the failure of the current regimes and the absence of visible and viable alternatives. These are hardly the times for expert praise and paeans. But critical scholarship is the opposite of heartless and opportunistic employment of expertise.

It is a nemesis of biased scholarship that the societies and systems it serves ultimately suffer from its distortions. An understanding of Muslim politics and the anguish and aspirations of Islamic, especially

Middle Eastern, people has slipped beyond the grasp of most 'experts'. Hence, historic trends toward major developments, such as the outbreak of an epoch-making revolution in Algeria, an Arab military rebound in October 1973, or Anwar Sadat's dramatic and disastrous *demarche* for peace, went unnoticed until events hit the headlines. In 1978, big men in the United States, from Jimmy Carter to Walter Cronkite, were surprised by the failure of the experts to perceive the revolutionary process in Iran, which had been long in the making. The failure, nevertheless, was as predictable as the Iranian Revolution. The Shah was deemed a friend of the United States as well as of Israel; he was 'modern', anti-Islam, and generous to the experts. Foremost Iranian experts explained the Shah by distorting Iran and its history. Thus Professor Leonard Binder, a distinguished professor at the University of Chicago wrote:

> Here is a nation, Iran, that has not ruled itself in historical times, that has had an alien religion (Islam) imposed upon it, that has twisted that religion (*Shi'ism*) to cheat its Arab tormentors, that can boast of no military hero . . . that has been deprived by its poets and mystics of all will to change its fate.[4]

Professor Marvin Zonis, another well-known expert on Iran, found the 'kingly grace' of the 'Shahanshah' (King of Kings) towards

> foreign scholars . . . both courageous and laudable . . . the monarch's control over the internal situation is at its zenith. It is undoubtedly true that no Iranian ruler, however, exercised as much power or commanded as responsive a political system as does Mohammad Raza Pahlavi in 1974, 'urban guerrillas' and censorious foreign critics notwithstanding.[5]

Examples are nearly as numerous as experts. Superficially trained, attached to disciplines and methods in flux, governed by the preferences of governments and foundations, and lacking empathy with the *objects* of their study, the area experts of the postcolonial era have all the limitations of conventional Orientalists but few of their strengths.

A historically rigged intellectual tradition, then, continues to dominate Western perspectives on Islam. Its impact on Muslims too has been considerable. It has made the traditionalist *'ulamā'* more obdurate and closed to new methods of critical inquiry. It has led educated Muslims to neglect substantive contributions of Western scholarship to theological ideas and historical interpretation. Above all, it has stunted the creative and critical impulses of modernist Muslims by activating their defensive instincts.

In writing about Islam for a largely Western audience, a Muslim faces hard choices between explanation and exploration. One's instinct is to explain the errors, deny the allegations, and challenge the overwhelmingly malevolent representations of Muslim history, ideals, and aspirations. For a century, since Syed Amir Ali wrote *Life and Teachings of Mohammad,* most modernist Muslim writers have, to varying degrees, surrendered to this instinct.[6] There is a certain poignancy to their effort, for these colonised, Western-educated Muslims were desperate to communicate to the West, in Western terms, pride in their devalued culture, distorted history, and maligned religion. For their labours, they have been dubbed Islam's 'Apologist' school. Thus, another vast body of contemporary literature on Islam merely symbolises the futility of corrective and defensive responses to the Orientalists' representation of Islam. This is reason enough to resist giving in to this urge.

Relationship between Religion and Politics

It is commonly asserted that in Islam, unlike in Christianity and other religions, there is no separation of religion and politics. In strict textual and formal legal terms, this may be true. But this standard generalisation is not helpful in comprehending Muslim political praxis either historically or contemporaneously. In its most fundamental sense, politics involves a set of active links, both positive and negative, between civil society and institutions of power. In this sense, there has been little separation, certainly none in our time, between religion and politics anywhere. For example, Hinduism played an important role in the ideological and organisational development of the Indian national movement. Mahatma Gandhi's humanitarian and idealistic principles of passive resistance and non-violence drew on Hindu precepts like *ahimsa.* The Mahatma was challenged by fundamentalist religious parties like the *Arya Sama'j* and the *Hindu Mahasabha* and died at the hands of a Hindu fundamentalist political assassin. In South-east Asia, including Vietnam, Buddhism and Buddhist institutions have been a potent force on both sides of the political divide.

In the United States, where the two major political parties have become increasingly indistinguishable on the basic issues of war and peace, the Christian churches have emerged as the primary platforms of political discourse, disputations, and even militancy. The political activism of Christians in the United States ranges widely from the right-wing Reverend Jerry Falwell's Moral Majority through the centrist liberalism of the National Council of Churches, to Dorothy Day's populist humanism and Father Daniel Berrigan's militant pacifism. In Latin American countries — including Argentina, Chile, El Salvador, and Brazil — government sponsored assassination squads have been carrying out their murderous missions in the name of preserving Christian values and virtues. On the opposite side, bishops are killed and nuns are raped for their advocacy of justice and democracy.

As for Judaism, we have witnessed its full-fledged politicisation with a fundamentalist ideology successfully staking out its claims to Palestine on the Bible's authority. The Bible is still being invoked to justify the expansion of Israel into 'Judea and Samaria' (that is, the West Bank and Gaza) and further dispossession of Christian and Muslim Palestinians from their ancient homeland. Since the outcome of the struggle for power in revolutionary Iran remains uncertain and since in Pakistan a self-proclaimed 'Islamic' dictator rules in isolation, Israel and Saudi Arabia must be counted as the two truly theocratic states in the Middle East. Both have a contradictory existence: one as an 'Islamic' monarchy, the other as a sectarian 'democracy', whose Christian and Muslim subjects are treated, under law, as second-class citizens. Given these facts, it is obviously tendentious to ascribe to Muslims, as media commentators and academic experts so often do, a special proclivity to engage in religiously motivated politics.

In a narrow perspective, the relationship of politics and religion may be discussed in terms of the links between religion and state power. In this sense, separation between state and religion has existed in the Muslim World for at least eleven of Islam's fourteen centuries. The organic links between religion and state power ended in 945 when a Buwayhid prince, Muiz al-Dawla Ahmad, marched into the capital city of Baghdad and terminated the Abbasid caliph's dual role as the temporal and spiritual leader of the Islamic nation. For a time, the caliph served in various parts of the Muslim World as a legitimising symbol through the investiture of temporal rulers — sultans, amirs, and khans — among them, successful rebels and usurpers. The Buwayhids, who ruled over Iraq and Fars as amirs, kept the caliphate in subjection for 110 years until they were displaced in 1055 by Tughril, the Seljuk warrior. In 1258 the Mongols sacked Baghdad, killed the caliph and his kin, and terminated the Abbasid caliphate, which had been for two centuries a Merovingian cipher. Although the caliphate was revived and claimed — at different times in various places, by a variety of rulers — it never quite mustered the allegiance of a majority of Muslims. Power, in effect, remained secularised in Muslim practice.[7]

One is generous in dating the effective separation of religion and state power from the Buwayhid intervention of 945. The fundamentalist *'ulamā* take a somewhat more conservative view. They believe that no Muslim state has been Islamic since the accession to power of the Umayyad dynasty in 650; to them, the Islamic state effectively ended with the first four caliphs who had been companions of the Prophet Mohammad. However, the minority *Shi'ite 'ulamā,* who believe that legitimate succession belonged only to the blood relatives and descendants of the Prophet, definitely do not regard two of the four caliphs ('Umar and 'Uthmān) as legitimate rulers. The orthodox *'ulamā's* rejection of the Islamic character of Muslim states after 650 is based primarily on three factors. The first concerns the presumed impiety of all but a few exceptional rulers (that is, 'Umar Ibn Al-'Azîz, 717-20). The

18

second relates to the historic prevalence of secular laws and practices in Muslim statecraft. The third involves the actual fragmentation of the Islamic World into multiple political entities — historically, sultanates, emirates, khanates, sheikdoms, empires, and now, republics. All theologians agree on principles of a single *'umma* (Muslim nation) and a single caliph (or *imam*) as essential to a truly Islamic policy governed according to divine laws and the example of the Prophet.

Lacking all three conditions of the ideal Islamic polity, Muslim peoples have for more than a millennium accepted as legitimate the exercise of state power by temporal governments, as long as they observe the basic norms of justice and fair play and rule with some degree of consent from the governed. This generalisation applies also to the overwhelming majority of *'ulamā* and local religious leaders. In fact, the most renowned theologians of Islam — that is, al-Māwardi (947-1058), al-Baghdādî (d. 1037), al-Ghazzālî (1058-1111), and Ibn Jamà'a (1241-1333) — have developed a large body of exegeses to justify, explain, and elaborate on this historic compromise between the Islamic ideal and Muslim political realities. Thus, as in all religious communities, there is a repository of millennial traditions in Islam that tend to surface most forcefully in times of crisis, collective stress, and anomie.[8] Times have rarely been as bad, as stressful or as disorienting for the Muslim peoples as they are now. Hence, all the contrasting symptoms associated with deep crises of politics and society — rise of religious fundamentalism, radical and revolutionary mobilisation, spontaneous uprisings and disoriented quietism — characterise Muslim politics today.

A fusion of religion and political power was and remains an ideal in the Muslim tradition. But the absence of such a fusion is a historically experienced and recognised reality. The tradition of statecraft and the history of Muslim peoples have been shaped by this fact. The many manifestations of this reality are important in comprehending the Muslim polity. A few of these need to be mentioned here. As a religious and proselytising mediaeval civilisation, the Islamic *'umma* evinced a spirit of tolerance towards other faiths and cultures that has been rare in history. It is important for us to acknowledge — for the sake of historical veracity as well as for a desperately needed reinforcement of non-sectarian and universalist values in Muslim civilisation — that non-Muslims, especially Christians, Jews, and Hindus, have been an integral part of the Islamic enterprise. In the precolonial period, Muslim law and practice reflected a certain separation and autonomy of religious and social life along confessional lines. Admittedly, there were also instances of excesses against and oppression of the non-Muslim population under Muslim rule. Yet the greatest achievements of Islamic civilisation in science, philosophy, literature, music, art, and architecture, as well as statecraft, have been the collective achievements of Christians, Jews, Hindus, and others participating in the cultural and economic life of the 'Islamicate'. In fact, the most creative periods of Muslim history have been those that witnessed a flowering in the collaborative half of our ecumenical relationships. This secular fact of Muslim political praxis, from Indonesia and India through the Fertile Crescent and Egypt to Spain, is generally neglected in the writings both of the *'ulamā* and the Orientalists. Yet it is more relevant to understanding Islam's relationship to politics than the antics of any current 'Islamic' political leader.

Throughout history, Muslims, like other people who live in complex civilisations, have evinced paradoxical tendencies in relation to politics. In dissident movements, Islam has sometimes played a crucial role by galvanising group support for opposition leaders around a reformist and often puritanical creed, attacking the corruption and profligacy of a ruling class. The latest case in point is *Ayatollah* Khomeini's Islamic government in Iran. An early example is the austere movement of Ibn Tūmart, which in the 12th century gathered enough support in North Africa to displace the Almoravid dynasty in Morocco and Spain. A later example is the puritanical *Wahhabi* movement of the 18th century, which gained tribal support in the Najd, especially of the tribe of Saud, and thence spread to the Arabian peninsula. In power, such reformist movements have betrayed a proclivity to softening and secularisation. The Almohad, for example, patronised the rather secular and speculative Philosophical School including Ibn Rushd, known in the West as Averroes (1126-1198).

On the other hand, the Muslim community has resisted state sponsorship of a creed or even a school of religious thought. Thus, two of the greatest Muslim rulers encountered popular resistance when they unsuccessfully attempted to sponsor an official creed. The Abbasid caliph, al-Mamūn (786-833), son of Harun al-Rashīd (of the *Arabian Nights*!) and founder of the House of Wisdom in Baghdad (where many of the translations and commentaries on Greek works were completed and later contributed to the European Renaissance) adopted the Mu'tazilite's doctrines as official creed. This rationalist school of religious thought in Islam was beginning to flourish when it received the sponsorship of the state. At the time, the caliphate was in its prime. Resistance to it mounted rapidly in the Islamic community. It was thus that the Mu'tazilites acquired the dubious distinction in Muslim history of engaging in the first significant practice of repression on theological grounds. Similarly, Akbar the Great (1542-1605), the most illustrious of the Mughul emporors in India, met with widespread resistance from his Muslim subjects when he promulgated his own electric creed *Din-i-Ilahi* (1582). Fortunately, Akbar was sceptical and open-minded enough to refrain from forcing his eccentric, ecumenical creed on the populace.

Contrasting Trends in the Politics of Islam

Historically, the *'ulamā* as a class prospered and played a conservative role as mediators between political power and civil society, much like the clergy in Christendom. During the first two centuries of Islam, a significant number of theological scholars adjured any identification with power, declining to serve even as judges. Thus, *Imām* Abū Hanifa (d. 767), founder of one of the four schools of *Sunni* Islamic law, was flogged for refusing the judgeship of Baghdad. In later years many served as legal advisers to governments and as judges. The institution of *waqf* (private and public endowment of property to mosques and schools which were invariably administered by the *'ulamā*) and the *'ulamā*'s role as educators and as interpreters of religious law, insured for them a lucrative and prominent place in society next to the military and bureaucracy. As a class, therefore, they betrayed a certain bias in favour of stability and obedience to temporal authority. Thus, al-Māwardi, al-Baghdādî, and al-Baqillani — great theological authorities to this day — held that an unjust and unrighteous ruler should not claim obedience and that the community would be justified in transferring its allegiance to a contender. However, they opposed rebellion and civil war. The great philosopher-theologian, al-Ghazzāli — the equivalent in Islam of Thomas Aquinas — and his successor Ibn Jama'a invoked the doctrine of necessity to counsel that public tolerance of even a bad ruler was preferable to anarchy and civil strife. Professor Anwar Syed has rightly concluded that the theologians 'endorsed the secularization of politics in return for a pact of mutual assistance between the government and the *'ulamā*.'[9]

Recognising their historical role as well as their present discontent, most contemporary Muslim governments have tried various schemes that offer a modicum of security and status to the *'ulamā*; in almost all instances they have been successful in co-opting the clerical class. It is noteworthy that the most iconoclastic of contemporary Muslim rulers — Habib Bourguiba (b.1903) of Tunisia — has encountered the least resistance from the *'ulamā*. This is so not only because he has enjoyed considerable popularity among the masses as the liberator of Tunisia, but also because, unlike Kemal Ataturk (founding father of modern Turkey) or Mohammad Raza Khan (1877-1944, founder of the Pahlevi dynasty in Iran), Bourguiba did not attempt to suppress forcibly religion and traditional Muslim institutions. Rather, while instituting modernist reforms, he allowed the *'ulamā* a certain visibility and status as religious leaders.

The political quietism of the *'ulamā* has not been shared by all sections of the Muslim intelligentsia and by no means by the majority of the Islamic community. There has, in fact, been a perennial tension between the moral imperatives of Muslim culture and the holders of power. It is difficult to recall a widely-known Muslim saint who did not collide with state power. Popular belief may have exaggerated the actual confrontations with contemporary rulers of men like the Persian saint Mevlana Jalaluddin Rumi (1207-73) — best known to the West as the founder of the mystic order of 'whirling dervishes' — the Indian, Khwaja Muinuddin Chishti (1142-1236), and the Moroccan saint, Sidi Lahsen Lyusi (1631-91). But in this case, popular belief is the more significant indicator of political culture. It is equally important to emphasise that in each instance the collision was not incidental, a mere adding of lustre to the growth of a legend. Rather, it was a principal landmark in the making of a saint, in distinguishing the exceptional Muslim from the ordinary. In this conception of sainthood there is an admission, on the one hand, of the difficulty of achieving the alignment of piety with power and an affirmation, on the other hand, of a Muslim's obligation to confront the excesses of political authority.

The political culture of Islam is, by and large, activist and insurrectionary. Scholars have described the Muslim heartland from Pakistan to Mauritania as lands of insolence. Historically, rebellions have been as endemic here as were wars in Western Europe, and the target of insurrection has often been the state's authority. Until recently, all but a few Muslim polities were typically divided between what the Maghrebis ('Western' Arabs of North Africa) aptly named *bilad al sibah* (the country in rebellion) and *bilad al makhzān* (the country of the treasury). There are exceptions to the rule, but normally, both popular rebellions and dynastic movements of opposition have been led by temporal figures. When involved in dissident politics, religious figures and groups were generally associated with the mystical schools, that is, with the pietist and populist, rather than the orthodox, theological tradition in Islam. However, as with state power, Islam has played a certain role in the legitimisation of revolt. If the state-oriented *'ulamā* cited religious injunctions against disobedience and contumacy, rebels too invoked the Qur'ān and the Prophet's traditions, calling upon Muslims to struggle (*jihad*) against tyranny and oppression.

An explanation for the perennity of the insurrectionary strain in Muslim societies lies, at least partly, in the fact that wherever Islam took hold, it had its origins in a counter-tradition, a dissident point of view. In many regions such as North Africa and Central Asia, the spread of Islam was dialectically linked with social revolt. In other places, such as the Indian subcontinent, Islam's egalitarian precepts and emphasis on social justice (both widely violated in practice) offered an escape to the disinherited from the harsh realities of oppression. In its exemplary form, Islam is a religion of the oppressed. Hence, to this day it retains a powerful appeal among the poor and oppressed throughout the world. It is currently the most rapidly growing faith in Africa and the East Indies. In the black communities and prisons of the United States, too, Islam has a significant presence. Even in independent India it is still finding new converts among the *Harijans* (literally, 'children of God', Gandhi's preferred name for the untouchables). The religious and cultural force of Islam continues to outpace its political capabilities.

Historically, then, the Islamic community has lived in separate polities ranging from tribal societies to modern republics. These secular political entities have been ethnically, linguistically, and often religiously diverse. They have been subject to constant change brought about by the dynastic challengers and popular insurrections and, occasionally, by somewhat religiously motivated reformist movements. Given its heterogeneity, observers of the Muslim World are impressed by the evidence of unity in Islamic peoples' cultural, social, and political life. There is evidence also of a strong Islamic affinity across territorial and linguistic divides. This sense of solidarity has been based not merely on religious beliefs and practices but on a shared consciousness of history and a commonality of values. In this respect, the Islamic civilisation was and, to a lesser extent remains, inherently political. The values and linkages that defined the unity of the historically diverse Muslim community have been political in the deepest sense of the word. It should suffice here to mention only a few factors that produced, over the centuries, the patterns of unity-in-diversity — what scholars have called the "mosaic" of the Muslim cultures.

Unity in Diversity

For centuries a complementary tension, creative in its impact on society and individuals, had existed between particularist and universalist loyalties and *loci* of Muslim political life. Typically, a Muslim held two sets of identity: one — immediate, social, and spatially particular; the other — historical, ideological, cultural, and global. Almost all Muslims lived in intensely community-oriented societies which, paradoxically, eschewed isolation. The paradox had a political dimension. The interests and demands of local authority — that is, the extended family, tribe, city, guild, and ethnic or linguistic group — in principle competed with the universal expectations of the 'umma, the vast Islamicate, that is, the worldwide community of people who embrace the teachings of the Qur'ān and practise Islam. The stability and quality of Muslim life had depended on the extent to which these two identities were reconciled. The achievement of such a reconciliation had been a preoccupation of politics in Islamic civilisation. Its attainment was by far the greatest accomplishment of civil society in the Muslim World. The processes by which this was achieved included a certain decentralisation of power, a toleration of differences, and a pluralism in religious and cultural life. Thus, while the 'umma was one and was ideally united, its diversity was presumed. Rather, it was honoured and extolled, for indeed it was the sign of God's mystery and creativity (Qur'ān, 30:22). Also, the prophets had declared 'differences within the 'umma to be a blessing'.

A complex web of laws, activities, and institutions had contributed to the development of a common identity and culture in the Muslim World. A shared system of law, education, aesthetics, and religious organisations (especially religious fraternities or mystical orders) had assured the growth and continuity of a unifying ethos that cut across the political, ethnic, and linguistic boundaries of the Islamicate. For example, the divided and diverse *'umma* was assured a certain structural unity by a common adherence to the laws of the *Shari'ah,* which were based on the Qur'ān, the *Sunnah* (traditions of the Prophet), and *ijmah* (consensus of the community). Typically, the *Shari'ah* served less as a guide to governmental conduct than as a regulator of societal relationships — of property, business transactions, marriages, and public morals.

For centuries, Muslims from the Pacific to the Atlantic Oceans were not merely born and buried according to similar rituals; more importantly, they were likely to be punished for crimes or failure to honour a contract, to have a grievance redressed, to settle a property dispute, to get married or divorced, and to make business transactions in accordance with similar, though not always identical, laws and codes of conduct. Similarly, the educational system of the Muslim world was based on a shared tradition of jurisprudence, philosophy, mathematics, ethics, and aesthetics. Hence, it was not uncommon for jurists and scholars to serve in more than one country in a lifetime, for artists and architects to live and work in various kingdoms, for elites to intermarry across political boundaries, for nomadic tribes to move from one ruler's domain to another. The passport was inimical to the spirit of the Islamicate. The phenomenon provided the framework for a sharing of values, the growth of an extra-territorial ethos, a source of collective identity.

This state of affairs lasted until the 18th century, when Western imperialism started to 'territorialise' the Muslim world. Thereupon began its parcelling out into colonies and spheres of British, French, and Dutch influence. The differences and hostilities of European nation-states came to be mirrored in Muslim lands. For the first time in its long and eventful history, Islamic civilisation began to be defined by reference to another. Neither its wars nor peace, neither prosperity nor sufferings were of its own making. A people habituated to a history of success were reduced to serving another's history. The myriad links which had assured Islamic culture its unity-in-diversity were severed. Its fragmentation, institutionalised in multiple ways, was completed by the creation of highly centralised, 'independent' nation-states, governed by postcolonial military-bureaucratic elites, each a disfigured copy of its colonial predecessors. The 'mosaic' of Muslim culture was destroyed. The remarkable continuity which, over centuries of growth and expansion, tragedies and disasters, had distinguished Islamic civilisation was interrupted. This change, labeled 'modernisation' by social scientists, has been experienced by contemporary Muslims as a disjointed, disorienting, unwilled reality. The history of Muslim peoples in the last one hundred years has been largely a history of groping — between betrayals and losses — towards ways to break this impasse, to somehow gain control over their collective lives, and to link their past to the future.

Crisis of Muslim Society

In discussing the role of religion in contemporary Muslim politics, four points should be emphasised. First, the contemporary crisis of Muslim societies is without a parallel in Islamic history. Second, throughout the 19th and 20th centuries the role of Islam in politics has varied by time and place. Third, the evidence of continuity with the patterns of the past has been striking. Fourth, in the 1980s, there is a trend toward the growth of fundamentalist, neototalitarian Muslim movements. The phenomenon is contrary to the political culture and historical traditions of the Muslim majority. The still limited but growing appeal of the fundamentalist parties is associated with the traumas of Muslim political life and the absence of viable alternatives to the existing state of affairs. A brief discussion of these points follows.

When a civilisation reaches a point of fundamental crisis and perceptible decline, we see three responses: restorationist, reconstructionist, and pragmatist.

The restorationist is one that seeks the restoration of the past in its idealised form. This is the thrust of fundamentalism, of such movements as the Muslim Brotherhood in the Arab world, the *Jamā'at-i-Islāmī* in Pakistan, the *Sharekat Islam* in Indonesia, and the Islamic government of postrevolution Iran. So far, these have been minority movements in the Muslim World. Without exception, they have failed to attract the majority of workers, peasants, and intelligentsia. This was true even in Iran, where the shift toward the current fundamentalist ideology began *after* the seizure of power.

The reconstructionist is one that seeks to blend tradition with modernity in an effort to reform society. This is the thrust of the modernist schools which have, intellectually and ideologically, dominated the Muslim World since the middle of the 19th century. The most influential writers and thinkers of modern Islam — Jamaluddin Afghani, Shibli Nomani, Syed Ameer Ali, Mohammad Abduh, Mohammad Iqbal, Tahir Haddad, among others — have belonged to this school of thought; in political life their influence had been considerable until the rise of military regimes in many Muslim countries. This was true also in Iran, where until after the Shah's fall no significant group of *'ulamā* had openly challenged the eminent *Ayatollah* Naini's formulation in support of the democratic and constitutionist movement (1904-5), a position that was endorsed by the leading theologians of the Shi'a sect of Islam. For five decades, successive generations of Iranian religious leaders had reaffirmed this position. During the 1977-78 uprising against the Shah, all the politically prominent clerics of Iran, including *Ayatollah* Khomeini, claimed to favour a pluralistic polity and parliamentary government. The first appointment by Khomeini of a social democratic government with Dr. Mehdi Bazargan as prime minister seemed to confirm this claim. Above all, it should be noted that the mobilisation of the Iranian

Revolution toward Islam had been the work of such lay Muslim intellectuals as Dr. Mehdi Bazargan, Jalal Alî Ahmed and Abul Hasan Bani Sadr. The most important populizers of Islamic idealism were Ali Shariati, a progressive layman, and *Ayatollah* Mahmud Taleqani, a radical religious leader. Although *Ayatollah* Khomeini had been an important opposition figure since 1963, he was far from being the central figure he became in 1978. In January 1978, as the revolution began to gather momentum, the Shah's regime did Khomeini the honour of singling him out for its most publicised and personal attack. From this point on, he became the counterpoint to the hated but central figure of the Shah. An explanation of his meteoric rise to charismatic power lies in the complex character of Iran's disorganic development, which lent one of the objectively most advanced revolutions of history a millenarian dimension.

The pragmatist denotes an attitude of viewing religious requirements as being largely unrelated to the direct concerns of states and governments and of dealing with affairs of state in terms of the political and economic imperatives of contemporary life. The regulation of religious life is left to civil society and to private initiatives. This approach has not been opposed by the reconstructionist school of intellectuals. As discussed earlier, it parallels the historical Muslim experience; as such, it is accepted both by the masses and the majority of the ʿulamā. Thus, wherever popular attitudes have been tested in open and free elections, pragmatist political parties and secular programmes have gained overwhelming victories over their fundamentalist adversaries. In this realm of real politics one finds the resonances of the historical patterns discussed earlier. A few examples follow.

The paradoxical historical pattern involving, on the one hand a preference for the temporal exercise of power and for a this-worldly political exchange and, on the other hand, popular vulnerability to religious symbols and slogans in times of social stress and collective anxiety, is replicated in modern times. Thus, throughout the 20th century, the political heroes of the Muslim world, the liberators and founding fathers of contemporary Muslim nations, have been secular and generally Westernised individuals. For example, Kemel Ataturk (1881-1938), founder of modern Turkey, Mohammad Ali Jinnah (1876-1948), founding father of Pakistan, Ahmed Sukarno (1901-70), first president of Indonesia, Gamal Abdul Nasser (1918-70), second president of the republic of Egypt, Habib Bourguiba (b.1903), of Tunisia, and the Seven Historic Chiefs of the Algerian Revolution, are regarded as the most popular and decidedly historic Muslim leaders of this century. The movements and political organisations they led were secular and were heavily influenced by modern, largely Western, ideas. Today, the most popular movement in the Arab world, the Palestine Liberation Organisation, claims a 'secular and democratic' polity as the basis of its programme: two of its three most prominent leaders are Christians.

By contrast, religious sectarianism is being most aggressively displayed in the Near East by two exclusionary ideologies and movements, the Phalangists and Zionists — one Maronite Christian, the other Jewish. Their shared antipathy to the secular, democratic, and universalist ideal underlies the ironic alliance between Israel and the Phalange, that is, between the Jewish state and the first fascist movement to make a successful bid for power in the post-World War II period. This same phenomenon also explains, perhaps, the fact that in the Occupied Territories Israeli authorities have been particularly harsh on the Christian population, and in an effort to destroy the unity of Christian and Muslim Palestinians, the government of Israel has been encouraging the growth of fundamentalist Muslim groups in the Occupied Areas, allowing them considerable freedom to organise. This freedom is denied to the ecumenical and secular Palestinian nationalist movement.[11]

Another historical pattern repeating itself in our time is the resistance to state-decreed religion in the two countries where an official version of Islam is being imposed on citizens by the state. In Iran, thousands of people have been executed and jailed for their opposition to *Ayatollah* Khomeini's Islamic regime. Significantly, the Iranian resistance today is made up primarily of former activists and supporters of the opposition to the Shah. It includes the youthful *Mujāhideen* movement, influenced by Islamic radicals *Ayatollah* Mahmud Taleqani and Dr. Ali Shariati; the followers of Abul Hasan Bani Sadr (first president of Iran after the revolution); the nationalists who had previously supported the constitutional regime of Prime Minister Mohammad Mossadegh; and many disillusioned former supporters of *Ayatollah* Khomeini. Were they to be given the freedom of choice, a majority of Iranian people would probably rid themselves of the fundamentalist tyranny in favour of a pluralistic and democratic regime of the sort the Iranian revolution, including the leaders of its Islamic wing, had promised them. In Pakistan, there is a certainty that if General Mohammad Zia ul Haq were to fulfil his promise of a free election, the secular political parties would win it by an overwhelming majority — a certainty which has led General Zia to violate for more than six years the solemn promises he made to hold free elections within ninety days of his coup d'état.

Colonial Encounter and the Trauma of Muslim Life

The centrality of Muslim peoples' predicament lies in the nature of their latest encounter with the West. The colonial encounter was unique in that it entailed the transformation of land and labour into commodities, in the literal capitalist meaning of the word. Inevitably, it caused the erosion of economic, social, and political relationships which had been the bases of traditional Muslim order for more than a thousand years.

Unlike capitalist development in the West, in the Muslim World it

27

occurred under foreign auspices for the benefit largely of the metro-politan power. Hence, it involved uneven change. Consequently, the vast majority of Muslim people still live in structurally archaic and increasingly impoverished societies, but they are organically linked with the modern and industrial metropolitan world. They are the men and women — *mustazafeen*, the weakened ones — for whom the Algerian and Iranian revolutions had the strongest appeal. Germain Tillion, a French anthropologist who worked among the Algerians, has described them as

> living on the frontiers of two worlds — in the middle of the ford — haunted by the past, fevered with the dreams of the future. But it is with their hands empty and their bellies hollow that they are waiting between their phantoms and their fevers.[12]

The trauma of Muslim life today is augmented by the fact that the resource-rich, strategically important heartlands of Islam are still subject to conquest and colonisation. For the Palestinians, the era of decolonisation opened in 1948 with the loss of the greater part of their ancient homeland. Now, they are being systematically dispossessed of its remnant, the West Bank and Gaza. In Lebanon, the refugees who fled in 1948, mostly from Galilee, are being terrorised in Israel's pursuit of its policy of 'dispersion'. Jerusalem, a holy city and touchstone of Arab cultural achievements, has been unilaterally annexed, as have the Golan Heights. Since the creation of the United Nations, only three of its members have lost territories without being able to regain them. All three were Arab states. Only at the cost of betraying others and of isolating itself from its Arab/Islamic milieu did Egypt reclaim in 1982 the territories lost in 1967. Now Lebanon has joined the list of occupied countries; its ancient cities — Tyre, Sidon, Nabatiyyeh — are ruins. Beirut, the cultural capital of the Arab World, became the first capital city in the world whose televised destruction was watched by the world week after week. No Arab, no Muslim government budged except to suppress popular support at home. Their lucrative business with the United States — the sole sustainer of Israel — continued as usual. Never before had the links between wealth and weakness, material resources and moral bankruptcy been so tragic. Never before in the history of Islamic peoples had there been so total a separation of political power and civil society.

In the breach there is a time bomb. When the moral explosion of the masses occurs, it will undoubtedly have reference to the past. But its objective shall be the future. The past is very present in postcolonial Muslim societies. That it is a fractured past invaded by a new world of free markets, shorn of its substance and strength, incapable of assuring the continuity of communal life does not make it less forceful. Its power derives from the tyranny of contemporary realities and the seeming absence of viable alternatives. For the majority of Muslim peoples, the experienced alternative to the past is a limbo — of foreign occupation and dispossession, of alienation from the land, of life in shanty-towns and refugee camps, of migration into foreign lands, and, at best, of permanent expectancy. Leaning on and yearning for the restoration of an emasculated and often idealised past offer one escape from the limbo; striking out, in protest and anger, for a new revolutionary order is another. Occasionally, as in Iran, the two responses are merged. More frequently, they are separated in time but are historically and organically linked. Hence, in our time, religiously-oriented millenarian movements have tended to be harbingers of revolution.

The 'hopes' that underlie popular support of religious movements in our time, Islamic or otherwise, are not really of the 'past'. The slogans and images of religio-political movements are invariably those of the past, but the hopes that are stimulated by them are intrinsically existential hopes induced and augmented by the contemporary crisis, in this case, of the Muslim World. The often publicised ideological resurgence of Islam (social scientists and the American media spoke as much of 'resurgent' Buddhism in the 1960s) is a product of excessive and uneven modernisation and the failure of governments to safeguard national sovereignty or to satisfy basic needs. In the 'transitional' Third World societies, one judges the present *morally*, with reference to the past, to inherited values, but *materially* in relation to the future. Therein lies a new dualism in our social and political life; inability or unwillingness to deal with it entails disillusionment, terrible costs, and possible tragedy. One mourns Iran, laments Pakistan and fears for Egypt.

References and Notes

1. See Norman Daniel, *Islam and the West: The Making of an Image* (Edinburgh: The University Press, 1958).

2. Edward Said, *Orientalism* (New York: Pantheon Books, 1978).

3. For a discussion of this question, see Stuart Schaar, 'Orientalists in the Service of Imperialism,' *Race and Class* 11 (Summer 1979).

4. Leonard Binder, *Iran: Political Development in a Changing Society* (Berkeley: University of California Press, 1962), pp. 61-2.

5. Marvin Zonis, 'The Political Elite of Iran: A Second Stratum?' in *Political Elites and Political Development in the Middle East*, ed. Frank Tachau (New York: Halsted Press, 1975), pp. 212-3.

6. Syed Ameer Ali, *Life and Teachings of Mohammad or the Spirit of Islam*, 3rd ed. (London: W.H. Allen, 1899).

7. I owe this and the following points to Anwar H. Syed, *Islam and the Dialectic of National Solidarity in Pakistan* (New York: Preager, 1983), Chapter 2.

8. The literature of millenarian movements is quite extensive. A few basic works are as follows: Vittorio Lanternari, *The Religions of the Oppressed* (New York: Knopf, 1963); N. Cohn *The Pursuit of the Millenium* (London: Secker and Warburg, 1957); S.L. Thurpp, ed. *Millennial Dreams in Action:*

Comparative Studies in Society and History, supplement II (The Hague: Mouton, 1962).

9. Anwar H. Syed, *Islam*, Chapter 2.

10. See James Kritzeck and William H. Lewis, eds., *Islam in Africa* (New York: Van Nostrand-Reinhold, 1969). On the appeal of Islam among poor blacks in the United States, see the very powerful *Autobiography of Malcolm X* (New York: Grove Press, 1965); Archie Epps, ed., *Speeches of Malcolm X at Harvard* (New York: Morrow, 1968); E.U. Essien-Udom, *Black Nationalism: A Search for Identity* (Chicago: University of Chicago Press, 1962). Relatively little is known about the continuing conversion of untouchables to Islam. For a brief description and references, see *World View: 1983* (New York: Pantheon, 1983), pp. 113-4.

11. For example, due to property expropriations and repression, in Jerusalem alone the Christian population had been reduced from 25,000 in 1967 to 7,000 in 1980. Similarly, Palestinian Christians constitute a disproportionate number of political prisoners in Israel.

12. Germaine Tillion, *Algeria: The Realities* (New York: Knopf, 1958).

2. The Progressive Islamic Movement

by Suroosh Irfani

'Religion in its most advanced forms moves from the individual to society'
(Iqbal).[1]

Introduction

Since the late 1970s, Islam has emerged on the world political scene with
dramatic effect: the revolution in Iran demolishing 2500 years of
monarchy; the seizure of the Kaaba, the holiest place in Islam, by Muslim
militants; the assassination of Sadat; the Afghan resistance in the form of
a 'holy war' against the Soviet-backed regime in Kabul; the suppression
of Islamic opposition to Hafiz Asad's regime in Syria, culminating in the
Hama massacre; and the bloody spate of executions and assassinations
following the fall of former President Bani Sadr of Iran on 20 June 1981 —
these are among the more powerful examples of Islam in political action.
However, decades before the current turmoil in the Muslim Middle East
drew the world's attention to Islam and its potential for political action, a
new state was created in the name of Islam when Pakistan appeared on
the map of the world as its first Islamic republic on 14th August 1947.

As with the Iranian Revolution during 1978-79, the Indian Muslims
had invoked Islam in the 1940s as a rallying banner to express themselves
politically. Their struggle was motivated not by the desire for a theocratic
state to be ruled by Muslim divines, but by socio-economic ideals and the
right to develop their cultural identity and spiritual life as a free and
independent nation.

However, ever since the liberal, progressive, and lay Muslims raised
the demand for a separate homeland for Indian Muslims and led the
struggle for Pakistan, despite opposition from several 'ulamā-led Islamic
organisations and members of the professional clergy, a bitter controversy has raged on Islam in the political and socio-economic process
between the progressive and liberal Muslims, on the one hand, and
members of the 'ulamā and the clergy on the other. In a sense the
Pakistan Movement could be viewed as a forerunner of many Islamic

movements today which invoke Islam for achieving political power and socio-economic objectives. It also incorporates many of the contradictions which characterise various Islamic movements in present times. It would therefore be misleading to attribute to these movements a monolithic Islamic ideology in the political, economic and social realms. Indeed, a common denominator of contemporary Islamic movements — that is, movements which invoke Islam to legitimise their quest for securing political power — is their disagreement about the methodology of the struggle, its socio-economic objectives and the manner in which these goals are to be achieved.

Two Categories

Broadly speaking and at the risk of oversimplification, one could place the tendencies characterising various Islamic movements into two general categories: traditional (conservative, fundamentalist) and progressive. There are of course other varieties of political Islam. Islam may be used with the explicitly expedient goal of keeping unrepresentative regimes in power, or, in some cases with some quantum of conviction and self-righteousness, for delegating absolute governmental authority to hereditary monarchies. In such instances, the majority of '*ulamā* have invariably supported those in power, from either conviction, sheer opportunism, or a mixture of both. Then there is the purely secular approach to politics, as for example in Turkey, where religion is confined to the personal realm and spared from being dragged into politics by a plethora of competing 'Islamists' wielding the magic wand of *fatwa* (religious decree) for warding off their political opponents by branding them 'un-Islamic', 'deviants', 'hypocrites', or 'communists'.

As for our 'traditional' and 'progressive' categories, although both stress the ideal of 'true Islam' and the need for adhering to its pure spirit, there are many significant aspects in which they differ. According to the traditionalist view, if Muslims recapture the zeal of the early believers, they will in some vague and predestined way unshackle Islam and allow it, according to its own logic, to transform their politics as well as other dimensions of their lives.[2] In some instances, the traditionalists tie up the return to the indigenous cultural heritage to a militant and total rejection of all that is foreign and Western. In other cases, the rule of the divines and the legists is deemed to be inseparable from the establishment of an Islamic state. In present-day Iran, for example, the supreme power in political, economic, and military matters rests with the *wilayat-i-faqih*, the 'jurisconsult', who in this case happens to be *Imam* Khomeini, and, in his absence, a three- to five-member supreme council of high ranking *Shi'a* divines. The progressive Islamic movement, on the other hand, has evolved independently of the traditionalist Islam of the '*ulamā*, the dogma of theological schools and the insistence that the text of the Qur'ān is literal, uni-dimensional and static. Politically, the progressive Islamic movement is anti-imperialist, and, in the economic domain, its opposition to capitalism and the exploitative system on which capitalism rests is unequivocal. It believes that Islam as an ideology can mobilise the Muslim masses by its appeal to social justice and the challenge it poses to the status quo.

Clearly then, in talking about Islam it becomes necessary to point out 'which' Islam and 'whose' Islam; whether political rulers use Islam as the opiate of the people or whether the masses invoke it as 'the cry of the oppressed'.[3] Furthermore, there is a tendency on the part of some progressive Muslims to believe that a cultural revolution within Islam (or a redefinition of Islamic religious thought) is to precede or be contemporaneous with radical change in the social and economic life of the people, with the interpretation of Islamic law being no longer the exclusive prerogative of the *'ulamā*, as demonstrated by Colonel Qaddafi in Libya. By emphasising the Qur'ān as the direct source of legislation, Qaddafi has eliminated the role of *imam*s and the *'ulamā*. He attacked the Islamic jurists (*fuqahā*) who had 'distorted' Islam through their interpretation, first because of their *tazzamut* (strict rigidity in interpreting religion) and second because as human beings they were the product of the human societies in which they lived. They were no more important than any Muslim, for Islam established a direct relation between man and God and did not require any intermediary. As Qaddafi puts it, 'the holy Qur'ān is in the Arabic language, and we can comprehend it ourselves without the need for an *imam* to interpret it for us'.[4] Shah Waliullah, the greatest Muslim reformer of India, probably had this argument in mind when he took the revolutionary step of translating the Qur'ān into Persian in order to make its message accessible to a larger Muslim audience in 18th-century India. Qaddafi's interpretation of Islam, therefore, is not new and original. In fact, it seems he has been influenced by the legacy of Islamic reformers like Syed Jamal-ud-Din Afghani, Mohammad Abdu, and Shakib Arsalan.[5] But what distinctly strikes one as original about Qaddafi is his comprehension of the movement of history and the spirit of the time — his belief that the present era is a turning-point in history, marking the great awakening of the masses. Qaddafi has demonstrated that the masses for him include both men and women marching together as a force shaping social evolution and national history.

This chapter, however, limits the scope of the historical development of the progressive Islamic movement to the Indo-Pakistan subcontinent, the extension and evolution of the movement in Iran, and the relevance and implications of the revolutionary Iranian experience of the progressive Islamic movement for Pakistan.

Beginnings of the Movement

In the Indo-Pakistan subcontinent as well as in Iran, the development of a progressive Islamic movement can be attributed to Syed Jamal-ud-Din Afghani, the 19th-century Muslim reformer and political activist, and more specifically in India to Shah Waliullah. Shah Waliullah sowed the seeds of such a movement in the Indian subcontinent through his sustained emphasis on the necessity of exercising *ijtihād*, the principle of reconstruction and renewal in Islamic thought. An enlightened Muslim endowed with a sociological imagination, Shah Waliullah was well ahead of his time because of his comprehension of the principle of change in the ever-evolving human society. This realisation brought him to the important conclusion that the legists of the past had lived, thought and developed their *ijtihād* (interpretation of Islamic law) under social and psychological conditions that were far removed from those under which future generations of Muslims were to live. Consequently, there was no room for blindly following the edicts of past legists because the social conditions and the level of consciousness under which past interpretation had evolved had become redundant or irrelevant at a subsequent stage of historical development. However, in a more immediate and political sense, the progressive Islamic movement can be linked to Syed Jamal-ud-Din Afghani, whose penetrative insight into the history of Muslim thought made him a 'link between the past and the future'.[6]

The central ideological concern of the progressive Islamic movement is to redefine Islam in the light of modern knowledge and scientific advancement — the level of contemporary consciousness — a task that requires the contemporary Muslim intellectual 'to rethink the whole system of Islam without breaking away from the past'.[7] The mainstay of the progressive Islamic movement therefore lies in its approach to the Qur'ān, which is dynamic and creative, as opposed to the static and literalist approach of the traditional *'ulamā*. It is in this sense that the progressive Islamic movement stands for the 'rethinking' and the reconstruction of religious thought in Islam. Iqbal believes that Afghani fully realised the importance and immensity of this task because of his broad vision, intellectual maturity, and rich life experiences.[8] It was with Syed Jamal-ud-Din Afghani (1839-97) that the transformation of Islam from a traditionally held religious faith into an anti-Western political ideology began to take shape.[9] He strove to make Islam the mainspring of popular solidarity. His political activity and teachings combined to spread among the intellectual and official classes of Middle Eastern Muslims 'a secularist, meliorist, and activist attitude towards politics'.[10] Being the practical extrovert, Afghani helped organise and disseminate such tools of modern political action and education as the political-ideological journal, the leaflet, the secret political society, all of which have been important in changing the face of the Muslim World.[11] Afghani also stressed the need for parliamentary and constitutional reforms for curtailing the power of autocratic governments. However, his political activism and his flair for practical action left him with little time and energy for organising Islam as a system of belief and action in a comprehensive ideological framework, a task which Afghani's contemporary, the leading Muslim intellectual of the time, Syed Ahmed Khan (1817-98), had initiated. Syed Ahmed sought to expound Qur'ānic thought in the light of modern scientific knowledge through a rationalistic approach to the Qur'ān.

Syed Jamal-ud-Din Afghani vs. Syed Ahmed Khan

Like Afghani, Syed Ahmed also aimed at the reform of Muslim regligion by invoking its original spirit and replacing the antiquated system of Islamic jurisprudence by progressive laws, where considerations for the general well-being and uplift of the people and demands of the time were to have 'preference to the literal text of the revelation'. Neither Afghani nor Syed Ahmed Khan stressed strict Qur'ānic or early Islamic laws, nor did they generally support the traditional *'ulamā*. Both of them were primarily concerned to show that Islam was compatible with reason, freedom of thought, and other modern virtues. Being open to new ideas, they were not concerned with reimposing or reinforcing the Islam of the past.[12]

The crucial difference that made Afghani an unforgiving critic of Syed Ahmed was Afghani's stress on Islam 'as a force to ward off the West', against Syed Ahmed's loyalist approach to the British rulers in India. This difference arose from the differing order of priorities which the two Muslim reformers had set for themselves. For Syed Ahmed Khan, the primary issue was to combat the backwardness of Indian Muslims in the social and educational fields — an undertaking that was inseparable from Islamic reform — hence Syed Ahmed's untiring efforts for presenting Islam as a religion that was rational and compatible with science and which urged believers to pay attention not only to the word of God, but also to the work of God. In this sense, it was perfectly 'Islamic' for Muslims to ponder the work of God-nature and the scientific laws that governed all existence. In Syed Ahmed's scheme of things, immediate political struggle against the British had little relevance in view of the social and intellectual stagnation of the Muslims. In a way, his pre-occupation with the educational uplift of the Muslims was perhaps a reaction to the glaring contrast of Muslim backwardness in educational, economic, and scientific domains with the West at the international level and with the Hindus at the local level. It was Syed Ahmed's conviction that Muslims would never rise without weeding out superstition and an archaic mode of religious belief through science and education. Furthermore, another reason for his appeasing approach towards the British rulers lay in the situational antecedents of purely subcontinental relevance. In the aftermath of the 1857 rebellion against the British, which was generally believed to be Muslim-inspired because the British had replaced the Muslims as rulers of India, Muslims were discriminated against in all spheres of public life. Chaudhry Mohammad Ali has vividly portrayed the picture of Muslim desolation and decay in the decades following the events of 1857: 'the Muslims felt too proud to co-operate with the victor, too sullen to adjust themselves to the new circumstances, too embittered to think objectively, and too involved emotionally with the past to plan for the future'.[13] Hindus, on the other hand, were forging ahead in all fields. Trade had been largely in Hindu hands even under Muslim rule, and because they took avidly to English education, ways were opened to them in careers in law, engineering, medicine, teaching, and journalism. A new middle class arose in India, consisting almost entirely of Hindus, which assumed leadership of the India that was taking shape under British rule.[14] To quote just one example, in 1878 there were 3,155 Hindus as against only 57 Muslims holding graduate and post-graduate degrees.[15]

Syed Ahmed saw clearly the state into which the Muslims had fallen and the long and difficult ascent they had to undertake. He believed that the *realpolitik* of the time was for Muslims as a first step towards cultural, educational, and material progress to establish mutual trust between themselves and the British. This was to be followed by the reform of the Muslim educational system, of religion, and of the approach to Islam and the Qur'ān, and the education of Muslims in contemporary issues. The politics of resistance, as preached by Syed Jamal-ud-Din Afghani, the roving rebel, had to give way to an alliance of expedient acquiescence with the British. The sustained efforts of Syed Ahmed Khan in his Indian constituency had steady and productive intellectual results. In 1877, he succeeded in establishing the first Muslim college at Aligarh along modern educational lines. In the years to come, several colleges on the Aligarh model sprouted in different parts of India with Syed Ahmed Khan's college graduating to a university. Aligarh Muslim University became the crucible of awareness for Muslims of India — a conscious-ness-raising centre that played an indisputable part in the struggle for Muslim identity and its logical consequence, Pakistan.

In comparing Syed Ahmed with Afghani, one could perhaps say that the latter was as one-sided in devoting his energies to politicising Islam as Syed Ahmed had been apolitical in respect of Islamic reform. Moreover, Afghani was sceptical about positive religions and held an evolutionary view of religion. His belief that a simpler prophetic religion was useless for less advanced people, and a more rational, reformed religion was what the masses needed later as they became more evolved, overlapped with some of Syed Ahmed's ideas.[16] Therefore, his attacks on Syed Ahmed's religious world view could be seen as a political manoeuvre for political ends, motivated mainly by an irrepressible rancour against the articulate Syed Ahmed for not combining his religious reform with armed insurrection against the British. Thus, at one stage in his life, much of Syed Jamal-ud-Din's energy was consumed in combating Syed Ahmed's school of thought. Indeed, in his zeal for demolishing the basis of Syed Ahmed's movement, Afghani did not hesitate to launch his rhetorical attacks from the position of the traditional 'ulamā. Afghani wrote

Refutation of the Materialists during his stay in India from 1880-82, a book whose direct and immediate aim was to attack the ideas of Syed Ahmed Khan. His Paris-based journal, *al-Urwa al-Wuthqa*, accused Syed Ahmed of openly casting doubt on Islamic dogma, weakening Muslim cohesion and resistance to the British, inviting people to reject religion and erasing in them the traces of religious and patriotic zeal.[17] Quite obviously, the attack was not on Syed Ahmed Khan's rationalism, reformism, and scant orthodoxy, all of which Afghani shared. It was against Ahmed Khan's belief in co-operation with the British rather than in nationalist opposition, and his willingness to borrow as much as possible from the British, which for Afghani was a threat to the Indian Muslim heritage.[18] That Afghani was being unfair and uncharitable in his wholesale condemnation of Syed Ahmed Khan as 'irreligious' is borne out by the lifelong commitment and devotion which enabled Syed Ahmed to accomplish both immediate and long-range objectives that proved to be of incontrovertible strength for the Muslims. Moreover, the perceptive yet pragmatic Syed Ahmed was well aware of the revolutionary, democratic and egalitatian spirit of Islam, in which he ardently believed. This is evident in his letter to an English friend:

> I have firm faith in Islam, which teaches radical principles, is against personal rule and accepts neither limited monarchy nor hereditary government, but approves of an elected president. Nor does Islam allow the concentration of wealth.[19]

On the intellectual front then, Syed Ahmed's mission was to emphasise the rational, secular, and scientific dimension in Islam and educate Muslims along modern lines, in order to enable them to comprehend the objective and secular correlates of the religious and spiritual dimension and to incorporate these principles in their society and life. As for Afghani, much of the contradition in his writings and stance on the intellectual and political levels could be attributed to the conflict between acknowledging the urgency for adopting Western techniques while refusing to be identified with the West. Moreover, given Afghani's characteristic temperament, his approach, unlike Syed Ahmed's, aimed at achieving quick political gains for the Muslims, rather than cultivating in them the awareness and preparedness for a drawn out struggle for their political and economic emancipation.

Reconciling Contradictions
Regardless of the antipathy and rancour Syed Afghani harboured against Syed Ahmed, it was the fusion of the two tendencies these men represented in Islam — one political, the other intellectual — that laid the ideological foundation for a progressive Islamic movement. Indeed, as it turned out, Syed Ahmed's programme did not differ in essentials from that of the chief disciple and expounder of Syed Jamal-ud-Din Afghani,

the great Egyptian reformer Mohammad Abdu. Abdu's programme for Islamic reform was based on the following four points:[20]

1. Purification of Islam from corrupting influences and practices;
2. Reformation of Muslim higher education;
3. Reformation of Islamic doctrine in the light of modern thought;
4. Defence of Islam against European influences and Christian attacks.

Syed Ahmed Khan's emphasis primarily lay on the second and third of these points.[21] The progressive Islamic forces that were later to emerge differed in the methods and extent of emphasis given to the above points. To varying degrees, these issues remained the overriding concern of progressive thinkers like Mohammad Iqbal, Khalifa Abdul Hakim, and Ghulam Ahmed Pervez in Pakistan. In Iran they were pursued by Mehdi Bazargan's Liberation Movement as well as by Dr. Ali Shariati and the *Mujāhideen-i-Khalq*, the revolutionary Islamic forces in the Iranian Revolution. Shariati and the *Mujāhideen-i-Khalq* blended the purification of Islam from corrupting influences with a clearly defined struggle against imperialism and its socio-political ramifications in the Muslim World. The two became a potent ideological force, challenging the monopoly of the traditional *Shi'a* theologians erected along an intricate pyramidal structure of religious hierarchy with the final authority vested in the grand *ayatollahs*.

As has been pointed out, in the Indian milieu, a sustained reformatory assault on the scholasticism of the theologians was started much earlier by Syed Ahmed Khan and reached a high point in the writings of Iqbal. Syed Ahmed's reform was to shift the traditionalist approach determined by customs and attitudes of Arabia before the 11th century to an approach that was more in keeping with the rationalism of 19th-century Europe.[22] From Syed Ahmed's viewpoint, there was nothing unusual about his approach. He regarded it as an extension of al-Ghazzali's method, the 11th-century theologian who maintained that every school of thought among Muslims interpreted the Qur'ān rationally in the light of its time. Perhaps one could regard Syed Ahmed's approach as an unorthodox offshoot of that of Shah Waliullah, the 18th-century reformer who set the pace for the dynamic approach to Islam in India.

Shah Waliullah and the Reassertion of *Ijtihād*

In a fundamental way, Shah Waliullah (1703-62) can be said to have founded modern Islam in India. He himself believed that he was the *fatih*, the inaugurator of a new era, or one whose arrival coincides with a scientific age and who holds the key to mysteries of the coming era.[23] Waliullah asserted his claim as a *mujaddid* of his age, the one who presents or restates the law in a form which, while remaining in conformity with its original basis, is suitable to new conditions arising from the changes of time.[24] A theologian and a *Sufi* mystic who claimed he was in direct spiritual communion with the Prophet, who guided and instructed him, Waliullah thought of society in sociological terms.[25] Religious injunctions, he maintained, were to be observed not necessarily because they were divine in origin but because of the benefits they could confer both on the individual and society. The purpose of Islamic commandments was social. Such a view had its precedent in Ibn Khaldun, the renowned Muslim historian. However, given Waliullah's popular standing as a *mujaddid* and a scholar of high standing, who had unravelled fresh avenues of knowledge regarding social evolution and the psychological and spiritual advancement of human beings, he provided a broad base upon which later thinkers could build, both in theological and secular directions. It is perhaps in this sense that Iqbal has referred to Shah Waliullah as the first Muslim to have felt the urge of a new spirit.[26]

Evolution and Change

The idea of continuous change and development or evolution remains the basis of Waliullah's discussion.[27] According to Waliullah, 'the individual and his society, as well as humanity in the aggregate, inclusive of human institutions and customs, evolve and develop through a particular order of progress'.[28] Waliullah's ethical principles have a close relation with psychology and sociology. His ethics deal not only with particular people in particular conditions or particular times but also with humanity at every stage of its evolution. According to his system, ethics are relative, in the sense that no perfect and absolute form can be determined for the whole of humanity at all stages and times.[29] His studies of different societies and customs at different times led him to the conclusion that every age has its own spirit and conditions that are products of the previous history of the people. To illustrate his thesis, Waliullah compares the history of humanity and its societies with that of an individual human being. As the individual passes through the various stages of life (e.g. childhood, youth, old age), being governed in each stage by different rules of conduct, in the same way the rules governing various societies change with the change of times. 'Indeed, the forms of useful customs vary with the times and with the general behaviour of people.'[30] Even righteous traditions remain suitable and useful customs (*al-rasm al-salih*) so long as they serve their purpose. For there might come a time during the process of social evolution and change in circumstances where these same righteous traditions may cease to serve their original purpose or begin to hinder the welfare of individuals or of society as a whole. The same traditions, then, become harmful customs.[31] Explaining the relativity of righteous tradition further, Waliullah holds that every righteous tradition has reformative and progressive effects on the people and society, so long as it is practised by the right kind of people at the *right time* and in the *right situation*. The same customs may turn out to be harmful and destructive if they are practised out of place and time. Thus, for example, the institution of slavery and the traditions and precedent set for the humanistic treatment of slaves by Islam would be totally redundant and irrelevant in the modern age. Redundant and outdated customs fall into the category of those customs which have become harmful though they were beneficial originally. Also belonging to this category are righteous customs which are practised with such extremism or exaggeration that one develops undue attachment to them or practises them at the cost of neglecting other customs or duties. Waliullah believed that slavish adherence by theologians to the opinion of mediaeval jurists endangered social evolution. He wanted the theologians to look for the pure religion in the Qur'ān itself and apply the Qur'ān to their own time and circumstances. This of course could involve by-passing the mediaeval jurists. Since Waliullah realised that a changing society could not forever be bound to old rules and values, he emphasised the need for *ijtihād* in legal matters as a means for restoring the purity of Islam. A *Sufi* of the *Naqshbandi* order, Waliullah preached that every age must seek its own interpretation of the Qur'ān and the traditions.[32] Indeed, one of the major causes of Muslim decay, he believed, was rigid conformity to interpretation made in other ages. In this respect, he did not differ much from Sheikh Ahmed of Sirhind (1562-1624), his more orthodox predecessor, or from Mohammad ibn Abd al Wahab in Arabia, who also considered blind following of mediaeval authorities to be an element of weakness in Islam.[33]

Islam is a universal religion, but it is one that was presented to the world in an Arabic pattern. Since it was not possible for any religion to develop in a vacuum, religious traditions were presented in a particular cultural pattern — in this case, Arabic — but it did not mean that Islam was forever tied to Arabic customs and procedures. In different cultures, the pure religion would be expressed in different ways.[34] This aspect of Waliullah's thought was seized upon by Iqbal (1876-1938) in his effort to develop a dynamic concept of Islam. Commenting on Waliullah's approach, Iqbal noted that the law revealed by a prophet takes special notice of the habits, ways, and pecularities of the people to whom he is specially sent. For building up a universal *Sharî'ah*, the Prophet accentuates the principles underlying the social life of all mankind and applies them to concrete cases in the light of the specific habits of the people immediately before him. The *Sharî'ah* values (*ahkam*) resulting from this application (e.g. rules relating to penalties for crimes) are in a sense specific to that people, 'and since their observance is not an end in itself, they cannot be enforced in the case of future generations'.[35] The task for Muslims was to systematically distill from Qur'ānic texts, most of which were specific responses to concrete historical situations, those general or universal ethical principles which have relevance to the changing conditions of life at any given stage in its historical development.[36] This was a clear call to *ijtihād*, the right to reactivate the principle of reconstruction and renewal in Islamic thought, by conceding to individual judgement on religious issues. To most traditionalist theologians, the individual scholar had no such right. The last word on the subject had been said by the end of the 10th century, and since then, the 'gate of *ijtihād*' had been closed.

Extending Frontiers

Shah Waliullah could thus be credited with expounding the dynamic and evolutionary approach to the Qur'ān that inevitably widens the scope of *ijtihād*. He also worked for minimising the importance of differences of interpretation in the details of *fiqh*. Since none of his followers had his dynamic outlook and creative insight, they were unable to project Islam as a progressive and evolutionary movement on the social and spiritual planes. The founding of the theological school in Deoband by some of Waliullah's devout disciples was an attempt to institutionalise his living and vital ideas by turning them into static statements of another dogma. However, the sparks of consciousness of Shah Waliullah's creative outlook had generated and inspired many, among them Syed Ahmed Khan, the free-thinking rationalist and the unorthodox offshot of this outlook, as well as Iqbal. In the years that followed, Allama Ubaid ullah Sindhi, a *Sufi* well-grounded in the essence of Waliullah's works, spent a lifetime in propagating his teachings. Syed Ahmed Khan applied his independent judgment not only to legal matters but to the Qur'ān itself.[37] For Iqbal, *ijtihād* represented the principle of movement in the structure of Islam. Liberating Islam from its mediaeval shackles required first of all liberating *ijtihād* from restrictions that had grown around its application. For Iqbal, these restrictions were artificial and extraneous to Islam, because during the early days of Islam, *ijtihād* was practically synonymous with opinion. It was later that it developed a restricted meaning: the opinion of only those claiming for themselves a special right to form such judgements. As Iqbal saw it, this increasingly narrow definition of the term was the result of three factors: the activity of conservative thinkers, the appeal of aesthetic Sufism, and the destruction wrought by the Mongols. In the first place, the conservative thinkers felt their position threatened by the early rationalist movement (*Mu'tazila*) in Islam, which they invoked Islamic law to suppress. Reacting against the rigid outlook of the conservative *'ulamā* and the legists, the Sufis went their own way, attracting and absorbing the best minds in Islam. As a result, the Muslim state was left in the hands of mediocrities, who 'found their security only in blindly following the schools of Muslim law'.[38]

The final blow, according to Iqbal, was inflicted by the Mongols, who sacked Baghdad in 1258 and destroyed the centre of Muslim intellectual life. To meet this threat and to conserve what remained, traditionalist *'ulamā* resisted, contrary to the practice of early Muslims, all innovations in Islamic law.[39] Further, noting the dynamic and mobile spirit of Islam, Iqbal states from that about the middle of the 1st century to the beginning of the 4th, no less than 19 schools of law and legal opinion appeared in Islam:

> This fact alone is sufficient to show how incessantly our early doctors worked in order to meet the necessities of a growing civilisation. With expansion, conquest and consequent widening of the outlook of Islam, these early legists had to take a wider view of things and to study local conditions of life and habits of new peoples that came within the fold of Islam. In their efforts at interpretation, these legists gradually passed from the deductive to the inductive attitude.[40]

Iqbal therefore declared the closing of the door of *ijtihād* 'pure fiction', suggested partly by the emergence of legal thought in Islam and partly by that intellectual laziness which, 'especially in the period of spiritual decay, turns great thinkers into idols'.[41] If the *'ulamā* upheld this 'fiction', modern Islam was not bound by this 'voluntary surrender of intellectual independence'.[42] Did the founders of one school ever claim finality for their reasonings and interpretations?[43] Iqbal's answer to this question is clear: 'never'.[44] Iqbal therefore found the claim of progressive Muslims to reinterpret the foundational legal principles of Islam in the light of their own experience and altered conditions of the comtemporary world to be 'perfectly justified'.[45] Restating the premise of Shah Waliullah, Iqbal held that in view of the Qur'ānic teaching that life is a process of progressive creation, 'it is necessary that each generation, guided but unhampered by the work of its predecessors, should be permitted to solve its own problems' in accordance with the level of its consciousness and the demands of the time.[46] Viewed from this perspective, the Qur'ān for progressive Muslims became a response to the need for conscious direction of society and history.

Qur'ānic Dynamism
As Iqbal put it, the Qur'ān had now to be read as a book which throws light on the birth, growth, and death of nations. In the history of revealed literature, the Qur'ān is probably the first book which spoke of people as a living organisation obeying certain definite laws.[47] Qur'ānic dynamism is the natural response to the growing complexities of a mobile and broadening life. Iqbal believed that his lectures on the reconstruction of religious thought in Islam were not the last word on the subject, but were meant to be signposts to a dynamic and creative Islamic approach. As he put it in the introduction to his lectures, with the passage of time, new points of view necessitating fresh interpretations of principles were bound to arise. Such principles were only of academic interest to a people — the rigid *'ulamā* — who had 'never experienced the joy of spiritual

expansion', but they were vital forces in the life of progressive Muslims.[48] The static approach to Islam was retrogressive because 'to have a succession of identical thoughts and feelings is to have no thoughts and feelings at all. Yet such is the lot of Muslim states today', Iqbal remarked.[49] 'They are mechanically repeating old values.'[50] Iqbal hoped that Muslim scholars, following ibn Khaldun, would be inspired by the realities of experience and not by the scholastic reasoning of jurists who lived and thought under different conditions of life. It was in this sense that Iqbal admired the Turkish nation which had 'shaken off' its 'dogmatic slumber'.[51] Iqbal felt that Turkish intellectuals were right 'to tear off' from Islam the hard crust that had immobilised an essentially dynamic outlook on life in order to rediscover the verities of freedom, equality and solidarity on which to rebuild the moral, social and political ideals of a progressive Islamic society. However, after the death of Iqbal, any significant and sustained effort in this direction remained more or less localised.

Mujāhideen-i-Khalq and the Revolution in Iran

It was not until 1978 that this approach to Islam emerged with renewed vigour and as a decisive factor in the Iranian Revolution that demolished 2500 years of monarchy in Iran. At the intellectual level, it was represented by Dr. Ali Shariati, the French-educated historian and sociologist, and the *Mujāhideen-i-Khalq*, the urban guerrilla organisation of progressive Muslims who gave concrete expression to revolutionary Islamic ideals through their revolutionary action. From 1963 to 1977, the progressive Islamic movement made a great leap forward during 14 years of intense intellectual and revolutionary struggle which Shariati and the *Mujāhideen-i-Khalq* had to wage against the heaviest odds. While Shariati was primarily engaged in propagating and developing a revolutionary Islamic idiom, the *Mujāhideen-i-Khalq,* most of whom were inspired by Shariati's lectures and writings as well as by teachings of *Ayatollah* Taleqani, Mehdi Bazargan and their own theoreticians, was dealing with the more challenging task of blending radical Islam with revolutionary action. The Qur'ān became for the *Mujāhideen* a book 'that emphasized deed rather than idea'.[52] By the time the popular and democratic movement of the Iranian people was underway, progressive Islam had attained a firm ideological foundation.

The inability of the traditional, often obscurantist, clergy to transform Islam from a dogma into a dynamic revolutionary ideology, its failure to comprehend this necessity, and its opposition to progressive Muslims were major factors in alienating the intelligentsia from Islam. Through this unconscious strategy, the traditional formalist clergy had been remarkably successful in perpetrating its monopoly on Islam, to Islam's detriment. In this sense, the *Mujāhideen-i-Khalq* represents the first attempt by any Islamic organisation to challenge the clergy on ideological grounds. By relying on Islam as a revolutionary ideology capable of meeting the strategic and tactical needs of organised revolutionary struggle, the *Mujāhideen* reintroduced Islam as a force against imperialism, despotism, exploitation, and religious hypocrisy, which they believed to be the major obstacles to man's social and spiritual evolution. Drawing their inspiration from religious figures like Hazrat Ali and Abu Dharr Ghifary, the radical companions of the Prophet, as well as from revolutionary struggles of the 20th century in Russia, China, Algeria, Cuba and Palestine, the *Mujāhideen-i-Khalq* surged ahead as a major political-social force accelerating the cultural revolution within Islam. Perhaps for the first time in modern history, progressive Islam posed a challenge to Marxist movements in Iran, in particular among the students and intelligentsia. Because of the cultural and emotional background that the *Mujāhideen*'s ideology already enjoyed in an Islam milieu, the reformed concept of Islam which Muslim modernists like Mehdi Bazargan and his Liberation Movement had provided in the 1960s, the the revolutionary redefinition of Islam that Shariati was contemporaneously developing, the *Mujāhideen*'s movement received a firm thrust. Moreover, the emergence of the *Mujāhideen-i-Khalq* organisation in 1965 was not an overnight development the the logical product of a painstaking process of intellectual and spiritual evolution in Islamic religious thought. The founding members of the *Mujāhideen-i-Khalq* were young university graduates associated with the Liberation Movement who felt they had outgrown the reformist level of Bazargan's movement and had entered a dimension where Islam was revolutionary and called for decisive action. It was the *Mujāhideen*'s rapidly growing popularity among socially aware and educated young Iranians, both inside the country and abroad, which perturbed not only the Pahlavi regime but the traditionalist clergy as well. The regime had not succeeded, despite its secret police, torture apparatus and firing squads, in liquidating the *Mujāhideen*. To destroy the sympathy and support the *Mujāhideen* had mustered, the regime's propaganda against the *Mujāhideen* branded them variously as 'apostates', 'terrorists' and 'Islamic Marxists'. In presenting itself as the true custodian of the *Shi'a* faith, the Pahlavi regime was supported by the overwhelming majority of the clergy. A group of clergymen even issued a religious decree to the effect that the *Mujāhideen* were not Muslims. For the *Mujāhideen* these accusations were inevitable in the perennial battle of religion against religion. The dimension of this conflict, however, reached grotesque proportions when, instead of the Pahlavi regime, Khomeini's regime became the arch-enemy of the *Mujāhideen* shortly after the Shah was overthrown, bearing testimony to Shariati's statement that 'religious despotism is the most oppressive and pernicious form of despitism in human history'.[53]

Like Syed Ahmed Shaheed, the first Muslim revolutionary in India to lead the armed struggle of Muslims against internal despotism during the first quarter of the 19th century, the *Mujāhideen-i-Khalq*'s *jihād* against the 'invincible' Pahlavi regime was far more spectacular than it was immediately successful. Syed Ahmed Shaheed was an Indian *Sufi* warrior whose emphasis on armed struggle distinguished him from other Sufis of his time. Likewise, the *Mujāhideen-i-Khalq* consisted of regenerated and socially aware young Muslims, mainly college students, distinguished from all Muslim groups and Islamic organisations in the Shah's Iran by their actual presence and involvement on the field of social and political struggle against a ruthless dictatorship. It was in this atmosphere, where arrest by SAVAK meant endless torture, imprisonment, and execution, that the *Mujāhideen-i-Khalq*'s ideology continued to evolve — a factor that helped give their ideological efforts a certain precision and clarity not to be found in other revolutionary Islamic literature of the time.

Ideological Foundation

One of the earliest ideological tracts of the *Mujāhideen*, later published as a booklet, is called *The Dynamism of the Qur'ān*.[54] It lays down the ground for the overall world view of the *Mujāhideen* on various ideological issues. According to this tract, which was in secret circulation during the *Mujāhideen*'s years of clandestine activity since the early 1970s, dynamism is the general characteristic of all evolutionary phenomena. Being the opposite of inertia and stagnation, dynamism refers to the capacity a phenomenon possesses for change and transformation. Through this capacity for evolutionary transformation, a phenomenon is enabled to make adaptations and adjustments to changes in environment, thereby both preserving and continuing its existence. Were the Qur'ān devoid of this quality, it would have remained a static collection of archaic verses and words that lacked the living vibrancy to transmit creative guidance to the changing human situation. Following Shah Waliullah, the *Mujāhideen* argued that the scholasticism of theologians and their exegesis performed under specific conditions of the past had infected Qur'ānic interpretations with inadvertent — or expedient — distortions. It was in anticipation of this problem that Hazrat Ali once remarked that a time would come when nothing would remain of the Qur'ān except the words written on its pages, for Muslims would cease to realise that it was the living word of God with the potential for a creative dialogue with, and adaptation to, the spirit of the age. In the 20th century, Islam as viewed by the *Mujāhideen* had become integrated with feudalism and capitalism, a potential weapon for deployment by imperialism against progressive forces and social evolution, and a prisoner in the rigid and prejudiced minds of bigoted, compromising and semi-literate clergy. As a result, the meaning and implications of liberating Islamic ideas had become warped, their dynamic impetus lost. Thus, for example, whereas the pioneers of Islam had thought of *tawakkul* (complete reliance and trust in God, who created the universe with a purpose) as an invincible incentive in their evolution-affirming struggles, later Muslims invoked it to justify their sloth, lack of initiative and indifference to revolutionary endeavour.[55] The same passivity had been injected into Islamic terms like *sabr* (patience and detachment in the face of mundane turmoil and trials by keeping faith in the purpose of the Creator) and *taqwa* (an attitude of revolutionary renunciation, self-control and discipline born of the awareness of the movement of history, from the seen to the unseen). These terms had been woven into a protective cocoon within which Muslims were kept, in order to blunt their concern with socio-economic and political realities and to preserve the status quo. The challenge facing socially aware contemporary Muslims therefore was enormous. They had to tear into shreds this 'idol', the deathly cocoon of dogma, in order to release the true spirit of Islam — a task that would of necessity bring them into a head-on collision with the protectors of the old order. But such had been the course of history and of the idol-breaking tradition of Hazrat Ibrahim, which represents, as a model and a tradition, the strategic nexus of the *Mujāhideen-i-Khalq*'s ideology.

Sunnat-i-Ibrahim (Abrahamic Traditions)

The nucleus of revolutionary Islam, its redefinitions and concepts such as 'sacrifice' and 'armed struggle' against 'idols' (retrogressive forces that inhibit the social and spiritual evolution of the individual, the masses and society) emanates from Hazrat Ibrahim, the prophet of God. For the *Mujāhideen-i-Khalq*, Abraham's story is the story of the unitary and integrative ascent of man. It is the story of freedom and liberation, of history as it unfolds towards the ideal unity of humanity, based on consciousness of divine unity (*touhid*). The *Eid-i-Qur'bān*, or festival of sacrifice (which Muslims the world over observe at the conclusion of the annual pilgrimage to the Kaaba, the House of God, in order to keep alive the memory of Abraham and his ordeals during the evolution of his consciousness), is for the *Mujāhideen* the international path of revolution and sacrifice.[56] Its philosophical exposition in a dynamic framework would help in understanding the *Mujāhideen*'s opposition to *Ayatollah* Khomeini and his system of *wilayat-i-faqih*, rulership of the jurisconsult, which equates the position of the jurisconsult (in this case, *Ayatollah* Khomeini), an ordinary mortal, with that of the infallible *imam* for all practical purposes.[57] For the *Mujāhideen*, Abraham is 'the friend of God', his agent on earth and the symbol of the idol-breaking tradition.

This tradition is not confined to a specific point in past history but needs to be carried forth throughout history against the changing forms of the idols of the times by 'Abrahams of the age'. Abraham's story, therefore, is a vital theme, and, as an archetype, quite familiar: when Abraham rises to prominence in his society, the ruling powers and the religious establishment feel threatened with extinction. They mobilise the people against Abraham, using the slogan that he is trying to destroy their religion and is a threat to the people's faith. The rulers and their collaborators — the false men of religion running the religious show — arrest Abraham and put him on trial. The rulers try to capitalise on the people's ignorance, their prejudices, and instinctive conditioned allegiance to outmoded traditions and customs prevailing as a matter of habit, in order to crush Abraham, the revolutionary. They invoke their religion and sentence Abraham to death on the ground that he has deviated from the community's religion, its popularly held beliefs and norms, and has insulted their religion by insulting their idols. (At other periods in history, these 'idols' can be the religious dictators, the military men, or the state.) However, when Abraham fearlessly steps into the fire, it becomes a bed of flowers. But Abraham has to pass though even more tortuous tests to become a symbol for freedom-loving people of all times. He is ordered by God in a dream to sacrifice his son, Ismail. The rest requires Abraham to forego all attachments, human sentiment and attraction to any thing or person that might slacken his commitment to the ultimate cause, which as we shall see has a direct bearing on the masses at the social and spiritual levels. (Note the relativity of ethics and values in Islam, a point first raised by Shah Waliullah and which Shariati has discussed at length in his works.) It is only after Abraham has inwardly agreed to undergo the trial and has psychologically and emotionally prepared himself to sacrifice what is most dear to him that he is absolved of making the sacrifice. His total devotion and commitment to the ultimate cause qualifies him to build the house of God for the people. The most meaningful lesson of Abraham's ordeal is that God did not want Ismail to be sacrificed but wanted Abraham to sacrifice *his* Ismail, his most cherished attachments and feelings at an emotional and psychological level.[58]

The purpose of the pilgrimage, then, is to develop in man total commitment to a suprapersonal cause, the ultimate value in the face of which all other considerations pale into insignificance. Thus the pilgrimage, as the *Mujāhideen* see it, is a multidimensional experience. It is a

symphony which begins with the soft circumambulations of the Kaaba and reaches its climax in the roaring blood of sacrifice. Before the stage of sacrifice, the pilgrim was prohibited from causing any injury in any form to others or to himself, or even to plants. Now the revolutionary pilgrim must shed blood. At the moment when the search for reality and gnosis is about to be lost in idealistic symbolism, reality, stark, hard, and bloody, comes into the forefront and reveals the message of the rites of the 'sacrifice'; that a real struggle against the 'idols' — the forces of evil, oppression, despotism, and reaction — is not possible without sacrifice. Unafraid, fearless and in step with Abraham, we must go to war against those idols (Satans) who have today donned the cloak of religion and declare themselves to be custodians of our faith. Despite their proclamations that they are safeguarding the citadel of Islam, these Satans are safeguarding their own interests under the slogan of Islam. They have become a party to the imperialist Satan.[59]

Abraham's story, conclude the *Mujāhideen-i-Khalq* in their treatise, is not merely the story of a single individual or a historical prophet. It is the story of history. The Abrahams of today are those who fearlessly sacrifice their fondest attachments and possessions and in doing so are liberated from the insidious tendencies of exploiting others and dominating them. Without the readiness for sacrifice, nothing would remain of existence except decay and destruction. Sacrifice, then, means selflessness, the passage for realisation of freedom and unity, a prologue to revolution. Evolution, a slow and gradual process, does not proceed without a sudden forward thrust, without revolution, when the requisite conditions have been constellated. And revolution is not possible without sacrifice and selflessness. One has to die before one dies, by transcending and sublimating the cravings of the self-seeking ego, in order to life in unifying folds of eternal love. Sacrifice is the passage from 'nothingness' to 'being', the gateway to freedom from fear and anxiety, to liberation and perfection. And the true significance of sacrifice lies in qualitatively reliving Abraham's experience, for 'Allah has spoken the truth, therefore follow the religion of Abraham, the upright one' (3:94). For Ali Shariati, the *Mujāhideen-i-Khalq* were the followers of the religion of Abraham, the upright one.[60] After Mohammad Hanif-nejad, the 27-year-old founder of the *Mujāhideen-i-Khalq*, and his four comrades were executed by the Pahlavi regime's firing squads in 1971, Shariati in a moving elegy recorded his belief about what the emerging *Mujāhideen* stood for, with Mohammad Hanif-nejad portrayed as a symbol of Abrahamic tradition:

> O you who are committed to creating equity on earth, Muslim *mujāhid*s who emanate from the community upright by nature, who experienced love during *tawaf* [circumambulation of the Kaaba during *hajj*, Muslim pilgrimage], and engaged in struggle [*sa'y*, a stage during *hajj* re-enacting the search and struggle of the Prophet Ismail's mother, Hajar, for water in the desert] and attained consciousness and self-consciousness to comprehend the meaning of Prophet Ismail's sacrifice — you are the carriers of the liberating message of *touhid* from Abraham, the message of the Qur'an, wielding the sword of Ali, and bringing as souvenir a vessel filled with the life-giving water of Zam Zam.[61]

As a measure of revolutionary commitment and selflessness, sacrifice, for the *Mujāhideen-i-Khalq*, is irrevocably connected to the social dimension, as is implicit in the Muslim pilgrimage to Kaaba, the House of God. It was after his experience of sacrifice that Abraham was commissioned by God to build the House at Mecca — a house that is a symbol and a model for the collective house of mankind, as confirmed by the Qur'ān: 'Most surely the first house appointed for men is the one at Makkah, blessed and a guidance for the nations' (3:95). This house has no owner, except God, and it is the house of all the people, shared equally by all: 'The sacred mosque we have made equally for all, for the dweller therein and for the visitor' (22:25).

The Kaaba, then, is the house of equality and freedom, a model for the collective house of humanity where people liberated from the noose of prejudice, discrimination, oppression and exploitation would live to realise their self-actualising potential. It is a house where all contradictions are resolved and humanity lives in the classless spirit of devine unity that forms an integral experience of the pilgrimage. The great challenge for contemporary 'Abrahams' lies in the degree to which they are able to translate this ideal into the real by striving for creating a *touhidi* classless society. With the dawning of insight into life's purposive movement, the *Mujāhideen* see no reason why one should desist from wholeheartedly committing one's life to the collective and social uplift of the people and continuing the 'idol'-breaking mission of Abraham by smashing the changing faces of idols which in one form or the other have stood in the way of social and spiritual liberation.

Ali Shariati and the New Wave of Consciousness

To many, Dr. Ali Shariati (1933-77) is the epitome of the intellectual dimension of the progressive Islamic movement. All the progressive and revolutionary tendencies for the intellectual, socio-economic, cultural and political emancipation of the Muslim masses that fired the imagination of reformers and activists during the past centuries find articulate expression in much of Shariati's work. During his lectures at Hosienieh Irshad, an Islamic centre at Tehran that he used as a platform for propagating his views from 1968 to 1972, he pointed out to his listeners that contemporary Iran was at a stage of development similar to that of pre-Reformation Europe. Consequently, political reformers needed to learn from Luther and Calvin, take up tasks appropriate to their environment and always keep in mind that the *Shi'a 'ulamā*, unlike the mediaeval European clergy, enjoyed a great deal of influence over the city bourgeoisie as well as over the urban and the rural masses.[62] But this did not mean that only the *'ulamā* were qualified to lead a social and national revolution meaningfully. He was influenced by the organised armed struggle against the Pahlavi regime that began in 1971, and particularly by the *Mujāhideen-i-Khalq* movement. Shariati supported the armed struggle of the *Mujāhideen* and propagated its message in some of his most memorable and moving lectures. Many of his students later became members of the *Mujāhideen* organisation.

Shariati often stressed that the return to true Islam would be led not by the *'ulamā*, but by the progressive *rushanfakran* (intelligentsia). In his book *Return*, he argued that the Islamic 'Renaissance', 'Reformation', and 'Enlightenment' would be brought about more by the intelligentsia than by the traditional clergy. In his *Mazhab Ali'yeh Mazhab* (Religion Against Religion), he claimed that in the modern age the intelligentsia was the true interpreter of religion. In *Chah Bayad Kard?* (What is To Be Done?), he insisted that progressive intellectuals were the genuine exponents of dynamic Islam. Similarly, in a pamphlet entitled *Entizar* (Expectations), he argued that scholastic learning could remain in the hands of the theologians but that true Islam belonged to Abu Dharr, the *Mujāhideen*, and the revolutionary intelligentsia.[63]

The logic of Shariati's arguments clearly threatened the whole legitimacy of the clergy. For if revolutionary Islam was the only true Islam, then scholastic Islam was false Islam, and revolutionaries, even if unacquainted with *fiqh*, were better Muslims because of their selfless struggle than the conservative *'ulamā* with their verbal reservoir of Islamic learning.

The twofold revolution Shariati envisaged — one national, the other social — was therefore to be carried forth by the intelligentsia

> because it is the intelligentsia that can grasp society's inner contradictions, especially class contradictions, raise public consciousness by pointing out these contradictions, and learn lessons from the experience of Europe and other parts of the Third World.[64]

Having thus charted the way to the future, it was for the intelligentsia to guide the masses through the dual revolutions. But the intelligentsia's estrangement from both Islam and its revolutionary dimension was a major factor in postponing a popular, grass-roots revolution in many Muslim countries. Much of Shariati's concern was therefore directed at focussing the attention of the intelligentsia and the educated youth on Islam as a revolutionary ideology. Given his exposure to sociology, history, and the history of revolutionary struggles in the 20th century, Shariati presented Islam in an idiom that his audience understood.

The Methodology of the Prophet's Revolution

To bring Islam to the forefront of socio-political struggle in an ideological framework, and to inject it as a dynamic force in the life of the individual and society, Shariati suggests using the method that he believed the Prophet Mohammad had used for effecting social change and inner transformation among people. This method was different and distinct from other approaches — the conservative, the revolutionary, and the reformist. For Shariati, conservatism was a method used by formalists and guardians of traditions. It was employed by those who sought to preserve the outworn customs and superstitions in society because they believed themselves to be the society's guardians. The conservative clings to the outmoded customs of the past because 'his logic tells him that if we changed the customs of the past, it is as if we have separated the root from the tree'.[65] For the conservative, therefore, social relationships that had become enmeshed with customs and the existing social structure were sacred vestiges of society. Opposed to conservatism was revolutionarism, which viewed the retention of outdated customs and relationships as tantamount to social stagnation. For the revolutionary, it was necessary to make a sudden break with the forms, customs and relationships which had become chains clamped to the body and spirit of the people. The supposedly middle way between the above two approaches was reformism, with its emphasis on changing social conditions gradually. But such an approach was not feasible in practice, because the long period of time required by the reformist approach allowed internal and external enemies to gain strength and destroy the objectives reformists hoped to attain through gradual change.

The method of the Prophet, however, was different from the above three methods — he kept the form of a custom, but changed its meaning in a revolutionary way.

> The Prophet preserves the form, the container of a custom which has deep roots in society and to which people have gotten used from generation to generation, but he changes the contents. He changes the spirit, direction and practical application of this custom in a revolutionary, decisive and immediate manner.[66]

Shariati thought that the Prophet's method had the positive characteristics of all the other methods. Among the many examples Shariati cited to illustrate the Prophet's method was *hajj*, the annual pilgrimage to Mecca. Before the Prophet Mohammad, the circumambulation of Kaaba was a glorified form of idol worship loaded with ancester worship and superstitions. While the Arabs performed the pilgrimage for idol worship, they believed that Abraham, the Friend of God, had built Kaaba, the house where they kept their idols. According to Shariati, it was revealed to the Prophet of Islam to take the form of the *hajj* ritual and change it into 'the largest, most beautiful, and deepest rite founded upon the unity of God and oneness of mankind'. Through his revolutionary approach which retained the mould and form of the ritual but revolutionised its meaning, the Prophet, according to Shariati, took the rite of the pilgrimage of idol worshipping tribes and changed it into a custom 'completely contrary to, and opposite of, its original use'. This was a revolutionary leap, marking a shift in consciousness and in the way one apprehended things. As a result of this method, the Arab people did not have to undergo the anguish of having to dispense with historically rooted and emotionally valued traditions and rituals. Rather, 'they sensed the revival and truth and cleansing of their eternal customs'. They could, thus, easily move from idol worship to the other end of the spectrum:

unity. Although this method was more sudden and unexpected than any cultural or intellectual revolution, society was not aware of the fact that the building and foundations of its idol worship had been torn down. 'This leap, this social method, found within the traditions of the Prophet is a revolution within a custom which preserves the outer form but changes the content.' Shariati believed that the Prophet's method was the only method which the clear-minded intelligentsia could effectively use for bringing about change and transformation in modern Muslims and their society. 'It is with this method that one can reach revolutionary goals without forcibly bearing all the consequences of a revolution and without opposing the basis of faith and ancient social values'. The great advantage of this method was that through applying it, one did not remove oneself from the people. Being a firm believer in the traditions of his culture, Shariati realised that it was not possible to inject ideas from other cultures which had no organic roots. By applying the methodology of the Prophet in his own society, Shariati was able to redefine 'the basis of the belief of his people as well as his society's perception of itself'.

Following the Prophet's method, Shariati attributed to *hajj* a symbolic significance with social and political implications in a contemporary idiom. As Shariati saw it, *hajj* was a magnificent ritual for tuning man's consciousness to the frequency of a permanent revolution and for propelling man and society on the evolutionary path of growth towards perfection. There was a definite social and political component to *hajj* in addition to its spiritual significance. For instance, the ritual that required the pilgrims to hit three idols with stones during a stage in *hajj* was viewed by Shariati as having a crucial symbolic significance for the present. He saw these three idols as capitalism, despotism, and religious hypocrisy. *Hajj* was an objective expression of the oneness and unity of mankind, of a classless and harmonised humanity striving together toward sublime value. The challenge for the Muslim was to translate the *touhid* subjectively experienced during *hajj* into working principles and objective realities in one's life and society by keeping constantly in mind the significance of the experience and renewing it through recollection of God: 'Who created you from a single soul' (Qur'ān, 4:1). *Hajj* was an exercise where one trained oneself in the Abrahamic tradition to become the destroyer of reactionary forms and outmoded relationships in one's society. When standing at Abraham's position (*maqam-i-Ibrahim*, a stage during *hajj*):

> you promise God that you will fight to save people from being burned by the fire of oppression, ignorance and reaction. During the battle for people's liberation (*jihād*) throw yourself in the fire to save other people. Live the way Abraham did and be the architect of the Kaaba of faith in your times. Help people to step out from the swamps of stagnated and useless lives. Awaken them from their stupor so that they refuse to suffer oppression in the darkness of ignorance.

To strive truly in the way of God and way of the people, one had first to achieve *taqwa*, that is, 'train oneself in becoming a responsible rebel by becoming genuinely involved in the problems of the people'. For it was not possible to achieve *taqwa* 'by becoming a monk and isolating oneself from people'. However, it was no easy task to become a *mujāhid*, a striver in the path of God and the people, without facing immense hardships and staggering odds:

> The way of righteousness, the road toward Allah, may never be approached without practicing devotion, self-denial, transpersonal generosity (*isaar*), captivity, torture, exile, pain, endless danger, even the firing squad. This is how one may walk with the people and step in the direction to approach Allah.[67]

Shariati applied the Prophet's methodology to the problems of society, history, and man's growth and development, thereby developing a sociology, a philosophy of history, and an anthropology (or evolutionary psychology) in the Islamic tradition. The foundation of all this work rests on *touhid* (divine unity) as a world view. For Shariati, belief in *touhid* has its social, material, and human implications. It lays down the infrastructure for the unity of mankind, for the integration of social classes, and for the unity of creation in the universe. Applied to the social plane, the simple logic of *touhid* is that if God is one, humanity must become one to reflect the unity of God in the unity ojf mankind. Shariati's conception of man, society and history is evolutionary, dynamic, and dialectical. He views man as a combination of opposites and a dialectical being. The contradiction between the two poles within him — his lowly, animal and base tendencies and his quest for sublime values, for transcending his situation and urging him towards absolute perfection (God) — creates the permanent evolutionary oscillation in man. Thus man is torn between the two forces within him pulling in opposite directions, towards baseness (mud) and towards absolute perfection (God), . Because of his dual nature, man is subject to a certain form of deterministic evolutionary movement. God is absolute will and consciousness. Man is a manifestation of God's will and is continuously evolving towards God. Religion is a means for this evolutionary movement, not an end in itself. As for history, it is the story of man's becoming. Whereas man is born of the inner battle between 'mud and spirit' and 'Satan and God' in Adam, history begins with the battle between Cain and Abel. The war within Adam is subjective; that between Cain and Abel is objective. History, like man, is a dialectical movement. The contradiction in history begins when Cain (representing private ownership and the agricultural system) kills Abel (representing the age of primitive communism). Abel, the herdsman, is killed by Cain, the landlord. With this, the age of common ownership of sources of production in nature (the age of hunting and pastoralism) and the spirit of brotherhood and true faith are destroyed. It is replaced by the age of agriculture, private ownership, religious hypocrisy and violation of other people's rights. Before the struggle between Cain and Abel began, private and monopolistic ownership of natural resources, for instance of water and earth, was non-existent. Everything was equally available to everyone.

Shariati's concept of sociology is also derived from the Qur'ān and other Islamic sources. As he views it, only two forms of societies are possible — the society based upon *touhid*, belief in divine unity, and the society based upon *shirk*, ascribing partners to God (polytheism). Opposed to *touhid* as a world-view is the world-view based upon *shirk*. A leitmotif in Shariati's works stresses the point that the difference between the two world-views (*touhid* vs.*shirk*) is no simple difference — for the battle of history, religion in various forms of *shirk* has justified social *shirk* i.e., divisions in society, whether economic, moral, or racial, whereas *touhid* throughout history has been fighting against the world-view of *shirk* and the social divisions and hierarchies born of this world-view. The battle of history, therefore, is the battle of religion against religion. Shariati believes that 19th-century intellectuals were right in their belief that religion had played the role of a narcotic, for they had seen religion to have always been used as a tool by the ruling classes for justifying their oppression and exploitation of the people. But these intellectuals, Shariati noted, failed to distinguish between the world-view of *shirk* and the world-view of *touhid*, an error in which modern intellectuals persist to this day.[69]

Ideological Commitment and Social Action

According to Shariati, Islam brought the greatest revolution in the social and spiritual history of man by changing the direction of religious energy from the 'hereafter' to the 'here and now'. Through a thematic analysis of Qur'ānic chapters. Shariati demonstrated that the dominant theme, accounting for three-quarters of the Qur'ān, dealt with society and life, natural and material phenomena, and thought, reflection and belief. Furthermore, only two of the 114 chapters in the Qur'ān dealt with religious rituals.[70] Social commitment, consciousness, and choice were therefore central to the individual's role in Islam. The Qur'ān was a continuum between people and God, enjoining that service to people was service to God. Man's evolutionary growth and the development of his personality were possible only through social struggle. By withdrawing from life it was possible to make a philosopher, a poet, or an ascetic, but not a Muslim. Hence, Shariati insists that to become a true Muslim, one must direct all one's energy, will, and blood to the path of growth and evolution of human society by fighting against oppression, exploitation, and ignorance of the masses. In the socially aware and conscientious individual, ideological commitment was an expression of this intrinsic sense of responsibility and yearning for higher values. Given this inner tendency and universal urge, the Muslim youth on the path of awareness had to face a peculiar dilemma. Having rejected the stagnant facade of a formalist Islam, the youth had two choices: either to opt for modernism by incorporating the consumer-oriented model of Western capitalism in their imperialist-backed society or to accept Marxism with its materialistic philosophical basis. Neither of these options could really serve the interest of Muslims. Moreover, both imperialism and Marxism would not countenance the emergence of Islam as a progressive revolutionary ideology, though for entirely different reasons. Imperialism was opposed to revolutionary Islam because it feared losing its markets and its exploitive control of Muslim societies, whereas Marxism could oppose revolutionary Islam for fear of losing its ideological basis among revolutionary forces in a predominantly Muslim Third World.

Shariati's main criticism of Marxism was directed against the Marxist premise that gave a purely materialistic dimension to the struggle against exploitation and to class contradictions. Shariati believed this over-emphasis on materialism was unnecessary, that the struggle against capitalism and the class system should have formulated its philosophy of history not by rejecting religion but by linking itself up with the struggles of the prophets, because 'without religion, it is not possible to have true socialism for creating a classless society'.[71]

Progressive Islam and Socialism

There appears to be almost no difference between Iqbal and Shariati on this issue. Iqbal wished to see a revolution in Islam similar to the Bolshevik revolution but with a spiritual basis. Expounding this idea further, Khalifa Abdul Hakim, acknowledged to be 'the most authoritative and faithful disciple of Iqbal', states that,[72]

> the Islamic *'umma* also wants to undergo a revolution more or less similar to the one that occurred in Russia, but the motive for this revolution should be Islam, not atheism. In fact, the spirit of *touhid* should be the motive force for the entire revolution.[73]

For Iqbal, socialism was admirable as it had 'most successfully accomplished the task of demolishing redundant customs and institutions. The religion it foreswore deserved to be rejected'.[74] According to Iqbal, if socialism had eliminated monarchy, aristocracy, and capitalism, it had done the right thing, because together, these dehumanising practices had downgraded the stature of man to a level lower than that of an animal. But achieving welfare in terms of food and housing was not the sole purpose of human existence, the stages of human evolution being infinite.

When viewed in its historical perspective, socialism, however, had an irrevocable weakness. Since socialism is the product of the materialistic struggle of the West and is born of the view that existence has no reality apart from the material nature, it linked the quest for a just economic social order in material life with atheism. For Iqbal, this was unnecessary, for an egalitarian revolution need not necessarily have any relation to a purely materialistic philosophy of atheism. Nevertheless, Iqbal held that 'the Bolshevik Revolution could be linked with Islam' because such an economic system was identical to the Islamic spirit.[75] For Iqbal, as for Shariati and the *Mujāhideen-i-Khalq*, if the correct belief about God and the human spirit were incorporated in socialism, then 'socialism becomes Islam'.[76] Khalifa Abdul Hakim also makes Iqbal's position on the issue of private ownership unequivocal; Iqbal agrees with the Muslim socialists and communists that 'the earth is created by God, and it has the same standing as water and air on which none can claim personal ownership'.[77] From the above, one can draw the unambiguous conclusion that Iqbal is a Muslim socialist. While Iqbal might not have specifically advocated a 'classless' society, the egalitarian spirit is unmistakable in his works.

For Iqbal, the religious ideal of Islam is organically related to the social order. The rejection of the one involves the rejection of the other. Islam did not content itself with the mere enunciation of a fundamental principle. It applied that principle to concrete life and showed the ways as to how it should work. 'It gives Muslims the ideal of a state as a socialistic and democratic structure.'[78] However, as pointed out earlier, Islam's socialism is different from Marxism as it does not accept dialectical materialism as the ultimate reality and a substitute for God.[79] This is the divide which distinguishes the progressive Islamic movement as it stands today (Iqbal, Shariati, Taleqani, *Mujāhideen-i-Khalq*) from Marxism. However, Iqbal was attracted by several Marxist teachings 'insofar as they exemplified Islamic social principles'.[80] He cited the Soviet Union as proof that some Islamic social principles could be applied in modern times:

> From the behaviour of nations it appears to me that the rapid progress of Russia is not without gain. Perhaps at this time it demonstrates the truth that is hidden in the phrase, 'Say: the surplus.'[81]

'Say: the surplus' refers to the Qur'ānic verse which Iqbal often cited: 'and they ask thee what they should spend (in the cause of social welfare): say: the surplus' (2:219). Iqbal's socialism is rooted in Islam's social teachings based on Islamic principles of equality and brotherhood. For Iqbal, the idea of human unity in Islam is 'neither a concept of philosophy, nor a dream of poetry. As a social movement, the aim of Islam was to make the idea a living factor in a Muslim's daily life and thus carry it towards further fruition.'[82] This fuller fruition, for the *Mujāhideen-i-Khalq*, is to be found in their classless society where belief in divine unity — *touhid* — forms the basis. Shariati also argued that the Prophet's intention was to establish not just a monotheistic religion but a *nizam-i-touhid* (unitary society) that would be bound together by public virtue, by the common struggle for 'justice', 'equality', 'human brother-hood', public ownership of the means of production, and, most significant of all, by the burning desire to create in this world a 'classless society'.[83]

The central theme in much of Shariati's work is that Third World countries such as Iran need two interconnected and concurrent revolutions: a national revolution to end all forms of imperial domination and revitalise the country's culture, heritage, and national identity; and a social revolution to end all forms of exploitation, eradicate poverty and capitalism, modernise the economy and most important of all, establish a 'just', 'dynamic' and 'classless society'.[84] The Islamic concept of equity or *qest* features prominently in the works of Shariati, as it does in the writings and speeches of Taleqani, the progressive *ayatollah* whom the Shah had thrown in prison for collaborating with the *Mujāhideen-i-Khalq*. For all these progressive forces, *qest* is the central economic and social concept leading to an egalitarian society. According to Taleqani, *qest* means giving everyone the right that is his due and returning to him the fruits of his labour and thought. It means the negation of exploitation of man by man, 'the vilest and meanest of all phenomena that have emerged in history'.[85] Taleqani also dealt explicitly with the stand of Islam regarding secular or communist revolutionaries who had staked their lives in the struggle for the uplift of underprivileged people, to bring equity and justice in society and not to make any personal gains. He said that

> the problem of equity is of such great importance in religion and in Islam that the Qur'ān places the murderers of even those persons who have nothing to do with religion, yet are fighting for the cause of equity, in the same category as the murderers of the prophets.[86]

Taleqani supported this contention by quoting from the Qur'ān the relevant verse:

> Those who veil the verses of God, those who unjustly kill the Prophets and also unjustly kill those who have risen for equity, promise them a painful agony (*Al-Imran* 20).

Elaborating this theme further, Taleqani points out that those who are familiar with the interpretation of the Qur'ān are aware that in the above verse the murder of those persons who have risen for establishing equity points to a group other than the prophets — that is, to a people who had not heard or grasped the call of the Prophet:

> Such people are not to be accused, for, nevertheless they are moving on the path towards equity. They have risen for actualizing *qest* (equity. The Qur'ān ranks their murderers with those who murder prophets. It has warned their

murderers of a painful doom. This is the liberating truth of Islam since its first days.[87]

Talewani reiterated the standpoint of progressive Muslims vis-à-vis Marxist revolutionaries during a meeting with a Cuban delegation:

> We have common ideas with the Marxists in negating exploitation and imperialism, and for safeguarding freedom. What we do not accept is the primacy given to materialism (by the Marxists). We believe in the primacy of God. We believe in the primacy of *conscious* and creative origin. For us, the Cuban Revolution is a magnificant revolution. In fact, any revolution in any part of the world which is against injustice, despotism, and imperialism, is in our view an Islamic revolution.[88]

Shariati, the Marxists and the Clergy

While imperialism and class inequalities were denounced as society's main long-term enemies, two additional issues also became the targets of many of Shariati's polemics. The first was 'vulgar Marxism', especially of the 'Stalinist variety'; the second was conservative Islam, notably the clerical variety that had been propagated by the ruling classes for over twelve centuries in order to stupefy the exploited masses. Thus many of Shariati's controversial works deal precisely with Marxism, particularly the different brands of Marxism, and with clericalism, especially its conservative misinterpretation of *Shi'ism*.[89]

It is significant that in his polemics Shariati did not resort to the stock argument that the clergy invariably used against the left: that Marxists were atheists and *kafirs* (blasphemers) and consequently, amoral, corrupt, sinful and wicked. On the contrary, in discussing Marxism, he argued that what defined a true Muslim was not possession of a subjective faith in God, the soul, and the hereafter, but rather the willingness to take 'concrete' action for the truth:

> Examine carefully how the Qur'ān uses the word *kafir*. The word is only used to describe those who refuse to take action. It is never used to describe those who reject metaphysics or the existence of God, the soul, and resurrection.[90]

It was to stress this premise that the opening sentence of Iqbal's magnum opus, *The Reconstruction of Religious Thought in Islam*, says that 'the Qur'ān is a book which emphasises deed rather than idea'.

Insofar as Muslims and Marxists were concerned, just as it was possible for Muslims to learn and benefit from science, so they could learn from Marxism for achieving and interpreting their Islamic objectives and ideals:[91]

> Why should it not be possible for Islam to gain from the revolutionary experience of other peoples, of other schools of thought, in pursuing its

ideological direction, and for achieving the objectives its ideology envisions? To the extent that such an approach is scientific and evolutionary, to that extent it is Islamic.[92]

However, the perceptive Shariati in his ideological encounter with many Iranian Marxists could not fail to notice the dogmatic attitude of many of the ardent followers of Marx. Their rigidity and one-dimensionalism were comparable to that of the clerical monopolists in self-centredness and a desire to monopolise scientific socialism. For Shariati, opposition to economic exploitation, class polarisation and capitalism represents the common interests of the majority of people and emanates from the burning quest for freedom among socially aware, conscientious and committed individuals. Therefore, to restrict the right to struggle for an egalitarian society to a particular brand of materialistic ideology is to be as narrow-minded and prejudiced as the high priests of various religious sects, with each sect being convinced that only those who adhere to its particular mode of belief, ritual and principles are truly human and 'the chosen', the rest being 'infidels', or 'deviants' heading for hell, and therefore, 'fit for execution'.[93]

Since revolution was not the sole prerogative of any particular philosophy, world-view, or group, no one had the right to impose a universal ideological monopoly on revolutions. While advocating a return to Islam, Shariati frequently criticised the traditional *'ulamā* in order to differentiate himself from conservative, clerical Islam:

> It is not enough to say we must return to Islam. We must specify which Islam: that of Abu Dharr or that of Marwan the ruler. Both are called Islamic, but there is a huge difference between them. One is the Islam of the caliphate, of the palace, and of the rulers. The other is the Islam of the people, of the exploited, and of the poor. Moreover, it is not good enough to say one should be 'concerned' about the poor. The corrupt caliphs said the same. True Islam is more than concerned. It instructs the believer to fight for justice, equality and elimination of poverty.[94]

Shariati accused the *'ulamā* of becoming an integral part of the ruling class, of 'institutionalising' revolutionary *Shi'ism*, and therby betraying its original goals. He also blamed them for failing to continue the work of reformers such as Syed Jamal-ud-Din Afghani. He spoke out against their demanding 'blind obedience' from their congregations, retaining a 'monopoly' over religious texts, and preventing the public from gaining access to true Islam. He claimed that the clergy refused to look ahead and instead looked back at some mythical 'glorious age' and treated the scriptures as if they were fossilised, scholastic parchments, rather than an inspiration for a dynamic revolutionary world outlook.[95]

Islam vs. Islam

Through his first-hand experience and dealings with the clergy, Shariati discovered and revealed the destructive nature of religious reaction and discussed and analysed its insidious effects on the cultural, political, economic and ideological dimensions as a historical process. His penetrating insight enabled him to develop a new framework and delineate the features of religious reaction: deceit and manipulation (*tazvir*) were potential components of economic expediency in the face of economic power (*zar*); coercive intimidation (*zur*) was a correlate of economic exploitation (*estesmar*), an ignorance born in closed minds at the mass level (*estehmaar*), a potential ally of despotism (*estabdad*). His detailed descriptions and analysis of religious reaction revolve around the above concepts. He developed this new terminology because he felt compelled to 'open a new account' for religious reaction, which derives its power and legitimacy by attributing to itself divine sanction and a supramaterial status and by maintaining a symbiotic relationship with 'earthly rulers', entrenched despotic and exploitative powers. In a candid letter to his wife written after Hosienieh Irshad was closed by the combined efforts of SAVAK and the clergy, Shariati referred to the 'high priests' of religious power:

> They have huge reservoirs of stupidity, ignorance and prejudice at the disposal of their deceit, cunning, and treachery, the pulpits and the *mihrab*s and thousands of admirers and preachers who look up to them, and the huge material support of Zionism, and the genius of imperialism and the CIA at their back.[96]

His direct interaction with members of the clergy during the four years of his work at Hosienieh Irshad was an eye-opener. In a letter to his father, Shariati wrote:

> Although I have been brought up in a religious environment since my childhood, and I have grown among religious people doing religious work, nevertheless the situation was such that I never got the opportunity of living with the *mullas* — we were merely neighbours of the *mullas* and their particular environment, not residents under the same roof. But now I am facing them directly, and I have seen them without their pretentions and in their natural dealings. I have become aware of their intense degree of selfishness, ignorance, ruthlessness, heartlessness, lying, and greed for the material. They are prepared to do anything, any treachery, and will join hands with anyone where their personal and group interests are concerned. Every day which passes reveals more clearly their grotesque face . . . their treachery and betrayal are unparalleled and of a type that even the mercenary agents of the Shah's interrogation and torture apparatus would be ashamed.[97]

But Shariati's condemnation by the grand *ayatollahs*, the clerical leaders and their rank and file did not give rise to despair. If anything, it merely confirmed that he was on the right path:

> What gives [us] hope and indicates that [our] path is right is the fact that these condemnations and conflicts are not a product of misunderstandings or personal differences or clash of personal or private interests. The real cause is the difference and contradiction between two modes of thought, two paths, two forms of works. One is a form heading towards decay and condemned to obliteration, the other is a form which is destined to be born and grow because of the spirit of the time and in conformity to the needs of the milieu. This is the reason why they [the traditional clergy] despite all their religious paraphernalia, the sacred signs and titles that they have stuck to themselves, their organised establishment, and the support among the common masses, will become more and more helpless, despised, and rejected. The more that they try [to preserve their hold], the more they will sink in the swamps of their destiny.[98]

On the opposite side, facing this decaying religious form, is the true religion:

> Reaction views it with murderous eyes, imperialism and its alert agents are frightened of its growth, the official intelligentsia conditioned by its own traditional mould attacks it just because it is a religion, and the common masses view it with estrangement, even thinking it to be *kufr*. The establishment knows that this new-born child will become a Moses to-morrow, and so, the pharaoh (political power), the *mullas* (religion of the establishment) and the *mala* (fat-bellied capitalists) would try and go after it and uproot it. But despite all this, Divine Providence has willed that the new stirrings of life, although in a minority, will prevail over the majority. This it has been in the past, so it will be this time.[99]

The outspoken Shariati repeatedly emphasised that in Muslim lands, the way towards liberation was through liberating Islam from the claws of the professional clergy, 'a distinct group who had imprisoned Islam by monopolising it'.[100] Whether consciously or unconsciously, this group was linked to the 'ruling powers', 'the dominant class', and 'capital'. Ever mindful of the potential of the traditional clergy for leading people astray, Shariati prayed: 'God! Don't let my faith in Islam and my love for the Prophet and his family make me a party to the merchants of religion, the oppression of fanaticism, and the hirelings of reaction.'[101]

Although Hosienieh Irshad was closed and Shariati was arrested to spend 600 days and nights in solitary confinement before being able to escape to London, he was confident that the future belonged to dynamic Islam. The zeal and commitment that he had observed among the educated youth of Iran flocking to his lectures, and their revolutionary action stemming from a progressive Islamic ideology that had by now crystallised in the *Mujāhideen*, convinced Shariati that Islam had broken out of the prison walls of the professional clergy:

> Since the time Islam has come out from the monopoly of the clergy, since that moment I am convinced that Islam has reached a crucial state [in its history]. Islam has found selfless fighters and true lovers from among the lay generation. They have passionately experienced Islam, the spirit of the time, and the direction of history. Today we see that they are changing the history of Islam at a planetary level [by wresting it from the asphyxiating grip of the clergy]. With the death of our official [formal] clergy, Islam will not die.[102]

Shariati compared the daring action of young and regenerated revolutionaries, fighting against despotism and reaction, to the inertia of the fossilised scholars crouched over escapist treatises in the secluded corners of their theological seminaries:

> Half a dozen conscious, socially aware, and conscientious high school students have far more worth than a large number of 'titled', 'turbaned', 'respectable', 'revered and ostentatious believers'. For the latter end up in meaninglessness and dogma, whereas the former kindle the sparks from where the flames of illumination, evolution, and revolution rage. Islam began with these flames, and its reconstruction would also begin with them.[103]

Conclusion

Despite a strong ideological framework and powerful political organisation, the progressive Islamic movement in Iran failed to secure political power. Instead, power gravitated into the hands of the *Ayatollah* Khomeini, better known to his followers as '*imam* of the '*umma*' (leader of Muslim people) and the clergy that support him. In this sense, the Iranian experience poses a sharp contrast to the Pakistan Movement, where liberal and democratic Muslims secured political power despite two factors: 1) opposition of Islamic political organisations led by '*ulamā* who were known political scholars; and 2) the absence of a well-articulated ideology. The movement for a separate homeland for Muslims in India, although mainly fired by religious sentiment and expressed in an Islamic framework, remained, nevertheless, secular in its objectives. Pakistan was not meant to be a theocracy, a religious state ruled by the '*ulamā*. This was a point about which there was no ambiguity, and it was clearly stated by Mohammad Ali Jinnah, the creator of Pakistan, in a speech during the height of the Muslim struggle for Pakistan: 'What are we fighting for? What are we aiming at? It is not for a theocracy, nor for a theocratic state.'[104] But if that was so, then what about religion?

Religion is there, and religion is dear to us. All the worldly goods are nothing to us when we talk of religion, but there are other things which are very vital, our social life, our economic life, and without political power how can you defend your faith and your economic life?[105]

Thus, for Mohammad Ali Jinnah, the relationship between social emancipation, economic strength, political power and religion was in no way contradictory. A few months after the creation of Pakistan, Jinnah repeated that 'Pakistan was not going to be a theocratic state, to be ruled by priests with a divine mission'.[106]

The misgivings about the nature of a theocratic state ruled by religious divines, which Mohammad Ali Jinnah had intuitively felt, Ali Shariati had experienced through his first-hand knowledge of an encounter with Iran's vast and hierarchical religious establishment. His description of a theocratic regime, therefore, is more lucid. For Shariati, a theocracy is a regime wherein members of the religious hierarchy occupy political and governmental positions (i.e. positions of power both in the party and the government):[107]

Theocracy means the rule of the clergy over the people; the natural effect of such a government is despotic oppression, because the clergy believes itself to be the vicegerent of God and the legitimate authority for implementing what it believes to be God's commands on earth. In such a state, people have no right to express themselves, criticise, or disagree and oppose the clergy. A religious scholar self-righteously believes himself to be a religious authority, just because he happens to belong to a religious apparatus and not because of the people's view and popular endorsement. Therefore, if such a person attains power, he would be an irresponsible ruler because he does not hold himself accountable to the people.[108]

Such a state of affairs would inevitably result in the creation of the most terrible form of despotism, oppression, tyranny, and personal dictatorship, because the spiritual ruler 'believes himself to be the Shadow of God and His representative on earth'.[109] Given such a suprapersonal position, the religious dictator

controls the life, property, and honour of the people. He shows no hesitation in committing any transgression and violation, for he sees in them the will of God. In addition he believes those who oppose him are people who are 'accursed by God', lost and deviants, 'untouchables' and the 'enemies of God and religion', who have 'no right to be alive'; any punishment or tyranny to which such 'dissidents' are subjected is viewed by him [the supreme religious ruler] as God's justice.[110]

Given the social and religious milieu of the traditional religious establishment in Iran, with an organisational network, power, and influence of *Shi'a* divines among the common masses, Shariati's prognosis of a theocratic regime appears realistic enough for Iran. The Islamic regime in Iran has used its interpretation of theocracy in the concept of the *wilayat-i-faqih* for vesting the supreme and absolute authority of the state in the person of *Imam* Khomeini and in his absence, in a successor senior *ayatollah*, or a supreme council of divines (*fuqahā*). The function of the *faqih* presupposes powers far superior to those of any modern ruler, since they practically involve not only sweeping political, judicial and legislative powers, but also, contrary to what Khomeini initially declared, spiritual prerogative.[111]

Article 110 of Iran's Islamic Constitution confers on the *wilayat-i-faqih* (or the Council of Divines) powers to appoint and dismiss the supreme commanders of the armed forces and the commander-in-chief of the Islamic Revolutionary Guards, to declare war and peace, to approve the suitability of presidential candidates, and to dismiss the president of the republic with due regard to the interest of the country. The presidency and the parliament, although directly elected by the people after approval of presidential candidates by the *wilayat-i-faqih* and the screening of the candidates for the parliament after their 'Islamic' credentials have been ascertained, are subordinate to the office of the *faqih* or the Council of Divines. The Islamic government in Iran believes that opposition to it system is tantamount to waging war against God and His emissary, a crime that must be punished by death. The Iranian regime has demonstrated its willingness and ability to confront its opponents and critics by practically carrying out this punishment. For example, after the outbreak of street demonstrtions protesting the dismissal of Bani Sadr from the presidency on 20 June 1981, *Ayatollah* Moussavi Tabrizi, chief prosecutor of the Islamic Republic, made the following declaration in a Friday prayer congregation:

> Anyone who opposes this system and the just *Imam* of the Muslims [Khomeini] must be killed. If such a person is arrested, [he or she] must be killed, and if wounded, further wounds must be inflicted to the extent that he [or she] is dead. Anyone who refuses to obey the just *Imam* and opposes the [present] system must be given the death sentence.[112]

The above declaration was repeatedly broadcast on the Iranian radio and television and published in the local press. Other religious officials of the Islamic Republic have also stressed the illegality of any challenge to the position of the *faqih* as a revolt against 'divine sovereignty'.[113]

However, for progressive Muslims, an Islamic state has an altogether different meaning, diametrically opposite to that espoused by the Iranian *'ulamā*. Broadly speaking, from their progressive Islamic perspective a state based on the *touhidi* concept has two basic qualifications:[114] 1) it is not based on (mere) force and domination; and 2) it aims at achieving ideal principles in human society. These criteria make the divide between a secular and a 'dynamic' state based on the *touhidi* concept rather nebulous. However, with *touhid* forming the spiritual basis of Muslim society, and given that 'the essence of *touhid* as a working idea is equality, solidarity, and freedom', the state, from the Islamic standpoint, becomes 'an endeavour to transform these ideal principles into space-time forces'.[115] In other words, *any state* striving to realise the ideals of equality, freedom, and solidarity in human society, is a state based on the *touhidi* concept — 'call it a secular state if you please',[116] because 'all that is secular is sacred in the roots of its being'.[117] A state cannot be Islamic in the sense that 'it be headed by a representative of God on earth who can always screen his despotic will behind his supposed infallibility', as Iqbal had unequivocally emphasised and as Ali Shariati and Mohammad Ali Jinnah had feared.[118]

References and Notes

1. M. Iqbal, *The Reconstruction of Religious Thought in Islam* (Lahore: Sheikh Muhammad Ashraf, 1977), p.1.

2. J. P. Piscatóri, ed., *Islam in the Political Process* (Cambridge: Cambridge University Press, 1983), p.3.

3. Ibid.,p.4.

4. Asaf Hussain, 'Qaddafi's Desert Revolution', *Islamabad Daily Muslim*, 21 March 1982.

5. Ibid

6. M. Iqbal, *Reconstruction*, p.97.

7. Ibid.

8. Ibid.

9. N. Keddie, *An Islamic Response to Imperialism* (Berkeley: University of California Press, 1983).

10. Ibid.,p. 35.

11. Ibid.

12. Ibid., passim.

13. C. Muhammad Ali, *The Emergence of Pakistan*, Research Society of Pakistan (Lahore: University of Punjab, 1973), p.7.

14. Ibid.,p.7.

15. R. Gopal, *Indian Muslims: A Political History* (Bombay: Asia Publishing House, 1959), quoted in C. Muhammad Ali, *The Emergence of Pakistan*, pp. 7-8.

16. N. Keddie, *Islamic Response*, p.14

17. Ibid., p.71

18. Ibid., p.67.

19. Altaf Hussain Hali, *Hayat-i-Javed* (Lahore: Ain-i-Adab, 1966, reprint of 1902 edition), quoted in C. Muhammad Ali, *The Emergence of Pakistan*, p.9.

20. H. A. R. Gibb, *Modern Trends in Islam* (Chicago, 1947), p.33, quoted in Freeland Abbott, *Islam and Pakistan* (Ithaca: Cornell University Press, 1968).

21. F. Abbott, *Islam and Pakistan*, p.147.

22. Ibid., pp.125-6.

23. A.J. Halepota, *Philosophy of Shah Waliullah* (Lahore: Sind Sagar Academy, 1975), p.5.

24. Ibid.

25. F. Abbott, *Islam and Pakistan.*

26. M. Iqbal, *Reconstruction.*

27. A. J. Halepota, *Shah Waliullah.*

28. Ibid., p.146.

29. Ibid.

30. Shah Waliullah, *Hujjat Allah al Baligha,* Vol. I (Cairo, AH 1352), quoted in A.J. Halepota, *Shah Waliullah,* p.136.

31. A. J. Halepota, *Shah Waliullah,* p. 135. Also see Dr. Ali ·Shariati *Zaminay-i-Shenakhat-i-Qur'ān* [Context for Understanding the Qur'ān] (Tehran, 1979), in which the working of this principle in the text of the Qur'ān has been demonstrated. The reader should note that for many works by Dr. Shariati and by the *Mujāhideen,* bibliographical details are incomplete. Most of these works have been published in pamphlet form, and the information that exists about these works has been given.

32. A. H. Halepota, *Shah Waliullah.*

33. I.H. Qureshi, *'Ulemā in Politics* (Karachi: Ma'raf, 1972).

34. F. Abbott, *Islam and Pakistan.*

35. M. Iqbal, *Reconstruction,* p. 172.

36. F. Rahman, *Islam and Modernity: Transition of an Intellectual Tradition* (Chicago: Chicago University Press, 1982).

37. F. Abbot, *Islam and Pakistan,* pp. 150-1.

38. M. Iqbal, *Reconstruction.*

39. F. Abbott, *Islam and Pakistan,* p.166.

40. M. Iqbal, *Reconstruction,* p. 165.

41. Ibid., p. 178.

42. Ibid.

43. Ibid., p. 168.

44. Ibid.

45. Ibid.

46. Ibid.

47. Ibid.

48. Ibid., p. 162.

49. Ibid.

50. Ibid.

51. Ibid.

52. Ibid., p. 1.

53. A. Shariati, *Bazgasht Bay Kodam Khishtan?* [Return to which Self?] (Tehran, 1980), p. 263.

54. *Mujāhideen-i-Khalq, Dinamism-i-Qur'ān,* (Tehran, 1978).

55. *Mujāhideen-i-Khalq, Isaar, Jehād, Shahadat* [Selflessness, Revolutionary Struggle, Martyrdom] (Tehran, 1978).

56. *Mujāhideen-i-Khalq, Falsafa-i-Eid-i-Qorban* [Philosophy of the Festival of Sacrifice] (Tehran, 1980).

57. See Hamid Enayat, 'Iran: Khumayni's Concept of the Guardianship of the Jurisconsul' in J.P. Piscatori, *Islam in the Political Process,* p.168.

58. A. Shariati, *Hajj* (Ohio: Free Islamic Literature, 1977).

59. *Mujāhideen-i-Khalq*, *Falsafa-i-Eid*, p. 11.

60. Iqbal had anticipated the dynamic meaning of the Abrahamic tradition in his powerful verse: 'This age is in search of its Abraham, the world has become a house of idols [static, retrogressive forces], smash it with the message of *touhid*.'

61. A. Shariati, quoted in *Mojahed*, June 1984, p.28.

62. A. Shariati, *Rasalat-i-Roshanfekr Barayi Sakhtan-i-Jame'eh* [The Intelligentsia's Task in the Construction of Society] (Sodon, Ohio, 1979), p. 6, quoted in E. Abrahimian, 'Ali Shariati: Ideologue of the Iranian Revolution', *MERIP Reports*, January 1982.

63. Ibid., p. 28.

64. Ibid., pp. 19-20.

65. A Shariati, *Fatima is Fatima*, trans: Laleh Bakhtiar (Tehran: Shariati Foundation and Hamdami Publishers, 1980), p. 63.

66. Ibid. p. 65.

67. See Suroosh Irfani, *Revolutionary Islam in Iran: Popular Liberation or Religious Dictatorship?* (London: Zed Books, 1983), pp. 112-23.

68. Ibid.

69. A Shariati, *Touhid Va Shirk* [Monotheism and Polytheism] (Tehran, n.d.).

70. Suroosh Irfani, 'The Spirit of Islamic Revolution', *Pakistan Times*, 9 June 1979.

71. *Doktar Shariati* (Tehran: Shariati Foundation and Hamgam Publishers, 1979), p. 106.

72. Mohammad Osman, '*Iqbal aur Khalifa Abdul Hakim*', *Daily Jang* (Lahore), 30 January 1982.

73. K. A. Hakim, *Fakr-i-Iqbal* (Lahore: Institute of Islamic Culture), p.252; M. Osman, 'Iqbal aur . . . '.

74. K.A. Hakim, *Fikr*, p. 250.

75. Ibid., p. 20.

76. Ibid., p. 250.

77. Ibid., pp. 246-7.

78. K.A. Hakim, *Islamic Ideology* (Lahore: Institute of Islamic Culture, 1952), p. 242.

79. Ibid.

80. J. L. Esposito, *Voices of Resurgent Islam* (New York: Oxford University Press, 1983), p. 185.

81. Ibid., p. 185.

82. M. Iqbal, *Reconstruction*, p. 141.

83. A Shariati, *Islamology*, Lesson 2, p. 101, quoted by Abrahimian, 'Ali Shariati', p. 26.

84. Ibid.

85. *Ayatollah* Taleqani's public speech at Baharistan Square in Tehran, 21 July 1979, quoted in Suroosh Irfani, *Revolutionary Islam*, pp. 146-7.

86. Ibid.

87. Ibid.

88. S. Irfani, *Revolutionary Islam*, documents Taleqani's interview with a Cuban delegation on 4 August 1979.

89. E. Abrahimian, 'Ali Shariati'.

90. A. Shariati, *Islamology*, Lesson 13, pp. 7-8, quoted in E. Abrahimian, 'Ali Shariati'.

90. A. Shariati, *Islamology*, Lesson 13, pp.7-8, quoted in E. Abrahimian, 'Ali Shariati'.

91. A Shariati, *Collected Works*, Vol. 23, p. 115, quoted in *Mojahed*, June 1984.

92. A. Shariati, *Collected Works*, Vol. 23, p. 109, quoted in *Mojahed*, June 1984.

93. A Shariati, *Collected Works*, Vol. 4. pp. 357-8, quoted in *Mojahed*, June 1984.

94. A Shariati, *Islamology*, Lesson 13, pp. 14-5, quoted by E. Abrahimian, 'Ali Shariati', p. 27.

95. Ibid.

96. 'The Generation of Revolution and the Certain Death of Reaction', *Mojahed*, June 1984, p. 14.

97. Ibid.

98. Ibid.

99. Ibid.

100. A. Shariati, *Jahat-Giri-Yeh-Tabaqati-Der Islam* [Class Direction in Islam], p. 134, quoted in *Mojahed*, June 1984, p. 28.

101. A. Shariati, *Collected Works*, Vol. 7, *Niyayesh* (Tehran, n.d.), p.108.

102. A. Shariati, *Collected Works*, Vol. 10, p. 130.

103. A Shariati, *Zamine-Yeh-Shenakht-i-Qur'ān*, p. 12.

104. Quaid-i-Azam Mohammad Ali Jinnah's speech at the conclusion of Muslim Legislators' Conference in Delhi, 11 April 1946, quoted in Fatahyab Ali Khan, 'Objective of the Pakistan Movement', *Islamabad Daily Muslim*, 4 May 1984.

105. Ibid.

106. Quaid-i-Azam Mohammad Ali Jinnah's broadcast talk to the people of the United States of America about Pakistan, recorded in February, 1948, quoted in F. Ali Khan, 'Objective'.

107. A. Shariati, *Collected Works*, Vol. 22, p. 197, quoted in *Mojahed*, June 1984.

108. Ibid., p. 18.

109. Ibid.

110. Ibid.

111. Hamid Enayat, 'Iran: Khumayni's Concept', p. 178.

112. *Kayhan* 29.6.1360 (Iranian calendar).

113. See the statement of Hujat-ul-Islam Sani'i, member of Supreme Council of Guardians, in *Ettela'at*, Mordad 1360 (Iranian calendar) 31 July 1981, quoted in Hamid Enayat, 'Iran: Khumayni's concept', p. 180.

114. Iqbal, *Reconstruction*, p. 155.

115. Ibid., pp. 154-5.

116. K.A. Hakim, *Islamic Ideology*, p.243.

117. Iqbal, *Reconstruction*, p. 155.

118. Ibid., pp. 154/5.

3. Pakistan: The Ideological Dimension

by Abbas Rashid

Ideology and the Nation-State

The 'need' for an ideology arises out of man's compulsive striving to give some sort of structure and meaning to his experience.[1] Beyond life's apparent uncertainty and chaos he seeks some sort of scheme, a plan, an order. Ideology provides man with the means to do so by giving him approved models of action, goals, ideals and values and, in the case of an ideology based on a religious world-view, helps him come to grips with such important existential features of human life as birth, death, suffering, evil, etc. At the same time, however, in contradistinction to a more 'secular' ideology a religious ideology is unlikely to contain an elaborate blueprint with specific instructions about the structuring of society's economic and political systems. Whether it is grounded in a more secular or a more religious terrain, at the level of the individual, an ideology helps to explain. Such an explanation may seek to mystify or to demystify; it may seek to raise consciousness by rescuing reality from 'facts', or it may provide instead a false consciousness. At the level of society, ideology has its 'binding' function. [2] Its significance depends on the degree to which it can bind effectively.

The nation as a necessary basis of the state is a relatively recent development which owes its emergence to the Industrial Revolution and the middle class's consciousness of itself as a class and its struggle for ascendancy. Before the French Revolution the nation was only incidental to the state. There was no particular significance attached to the correspondence between the political boundaries of a state and the cultural boundaries of a nation. With the nation, as a self-conscious entity, becoming central to the state, a strong nation became a *sine qua non* for a strong state. And what constituted a strong nation? Any number of factors were supposed to lend strength to a sense of nationhood. These included a common language, shared history, ethnic ties, etc. Eventually, however, the decisive factor was subjective and psychological. A people formed a nation when they thought themselves one. This is where ideology with its binding function becomes critical. It provides a nation the 'self-consciousness' of being one and thereby impels it to acquire the framework of a political state. It also sustains in a nation-state the conviction that the nation as a concept continues to define the collectivity circumscribed by the edifice of the state. In the case of most Third World countries, the issue is somewhat further complicated by their colonial experience, as a result of which they are often state-nations rather than nation-states.[3] Unlike the West's experience, where national consciousness preceded the development of a strong and centralised political state, the bonds which could tie a colonised people together were, at best, not allowed to develop and, at worst, subverted where they did exist.

This was not a conspiratorial matter. It was merely the logic of colonialism at work. Consequently when these colonised societies emerged as independent political states it was often the result of a *negative* nationalism directed at the oppressing colonial power. But it still meant that in a positive sense nationalism remained weak, and the nation, if it could be called that, remained fragmented, with loyalties defined at the subnational level, i.e., at the level of the region or province — the territorial unit where the 'community of culture' defined an authentic as opposed to a wishful state of affairs. In most cases, therefore, the post-colonial state in the Third World was not only overdetermined in relation to the nation but was multinational to boot. The fact that such states were often multinational implied that there existed within them a plurality of cultures. In fact, culturally autonomous groupings which were subjected to the colonial process and were kept from developing ties of trade, language, travel etc. with contiguous areas came to acquire in many cases virtually the self-consciousness of a national people. In other words, they now felt the urge to acquire for themselves the political framework of the state. Hence, the transition from a plurality of cultures to a plurality of nations. It was the consensus of a 'national' plurality that the state needed for its strength.

Without the consensus of the nation in which the state is grounded, it is merely a brittle political edifice that soon becomes dependent for its perpetuation on violence within and benefactors without. It is important, though, for any ruling elite, however narrow its objectives, to keep the use of force to a minimum, for it has its own disruptive dynamic. One solution is to *disarm*, in an ideological sense, a large section of the population. This is to be achieved by appearing to conform to values that people cherish, particularly those at the upper end of the scale of cherished values; so that when in Pakistan, for instance, a government is seen to be more 'Islamic', it may well be able to afford being less democratic (a value slightly lower down the scale). It is always possible to show, of course, that Islam need not mean an absence of economic advancement or democratic rights, but at the *popular* level the ruling elite will attempt to curtail such exposure, whenever necessary, through its virtual monopoly of the means of mass communication (not to mention the use of the coercive powers at its disposal). In this way a state ideology of *popular disarmament* can serve for relatively long periods the purposes of a ruling elite which has no mandate from the nation it rules. Any attempt at a sustained popular mobilisation in such circumstances must equally take into cognisance not only the universe of people's cherished values but the latter's ranking as well as their relative state of 'activation'. For if we were to consider, for analytical purposes, democracy, nationalism and Islam as distinct cherished values, then any one of these may be chosen as the mainstay of the state's ideological offensive, and the more 'active' value would represent the terrain of the ideological confrontation. Structurally, then, ideology has two sets of constituent elements, the 'inherent' and the 'derived'.[4] The former is based on factors like historical experience, folk memory, oral tradition, etc., while the latter pertains to a more structured corpus of ideas derived from an external source (through books, speeches, etc.). There is, of course, no hard and fast dividing line between the two, for what are derived ideas to one generation may be inherent to the next.[5] To the extent, however, that derived and inherent ideas can be seen as distinct, derived ideology can become acceptable at a popular level only if it is not seen to run counter to the inherent. And when the nature of this fusion is not mechanical it is likely to leave both sets of constituents in considerably altered form.

All this is not to suggest that the realm of ideas and values is operative independently of the material conditions in which it is rooted. But it is to argue that the former is not a mere 'reflection' of the latter but is in constant and dynamic interaction with it. Otherwise it would be possible simply to wait for a change in material conditions to bring about an appropriate change in ideology. This of course leaves unresolved the problem of how people will be mobilised to change the material conditions. Gramsci is among those who recognised the relatively autonomous nature of the ideological factor. 'To the extent', he argues, 'that ideologies are historically necessary they have a validity which is "psychological"; they "organise" human masses and create the terrain on which men move, acquire consciousness of their position, struggle, etc.'[6] Furthermore, there is room in his formulation 'for those less structured forms of thought that circulate among the common people, often contradictory and confused and compounded of folklore, myth and day-to-day popular experience; these count among what he calls "non-organic" ideology'.[7]

The recognition of Islam by the Indian Muslim elite, as a cherished value central to the inherent ideology of the Muslims of the subcontinent, dates from the War of Independence of 1857. Islam's consequent effectiveness as a frequently used rallying-cry succeeded in conveying the impression that it was the sum total of their inherent ideology. The impression seemed to survive even when patently 'extra-Islamic' factors should have been discernible, as in the movement among Indian Muslims to acquire a nation-state for themselves. While 'inherent' Islam was crucial to the enterprise, it should be equally obvious that the 'derived' idea of nationalism was no less so. Territorial nationalism with its roots in 18th-century Europe has very little to do with the concept of the *'umma* prescribed by Islam. Over time, however, the derived had become the inherent, and a large number of Indian Muslims responded to the call for Pakistan without any sense of unease over this apparent inconsistency. Not only, therefore, did the elite, despite its frequent use of Islam, remain unaware of the dynamic between the 'derived' and the 'inherent', but it was also unable, consequently, to continue consciously the process of 'deriving'. In other words, it did not see as its task the elaborating of a 'positive' ideology, grounded in the 'inherent', cognisant of the evolution and change in material circumstances and people's aspirations. In a negative sense, the birth of Bangladesh is an obvious by-product of this failure. Islam was not made an issue in the Bangladesh movement and presumably retained, therefore, its eminence as a cherished value. Among the beliefs that had become 'inherent' and were activated by the leadership were those related to pride in the Bengali language and culture and suspicion of the 'foreigner' (which West Pakistan came to be seen as) exploiting Bengal and being responsible for its misery. Similarly, in West Pakistan, the peasant's inherent belief that he had a right to own a small piece of land contributed significantly to the PPP's success at the polls.

Whereas the Pakistan People's Party (PPP) regime showed little interest in *elaborating* into a positive ideology their loosely structured polemic, proposed economic remedies and affirmations of the faith, the present military government has devoted itself to the task with remarkable zeal. Of course, the nature of a regime is also indicative of the kinds of interests its elaborated ideology is likely to serve. An assessment of this factor as well should therefore determine whether civil society should support or counter a particular ideological formulation.

'Defining' the Muslim Identity in India

After the war of 1857, people like Syed Ahmed Khan and Amir Ali, in calling upon Muslims to strengthen the bonds of community, were not doing anything very different from what others like Shah Waliullah had done before. Ever since the disintegration of the emprie under Aurangzeb, Muslims had been urged to rally more than once. In order to rehabilitate Islam (or to secure the interests of Indian Muslims) Shah Waliullah had gone as far as to invite Ahmed Shah Abdali to rid India of the scourge of Marhattas. There had been the movement of the *mujāhideen* led by Syed Ahmed Brelavi dedicated to the establishment of an ideal Muslim state in the North-West Frontier (then part of the Sikh empire). In Bengal the *Faraizi* Movement led by *Haji* Shariatullah had similar aims. In both cases deterioration in the economic position of the Muslim peasantry had meant renewed interest in 'building' Islam in some insulated enclave. In theory, freedom from religious encroachment was being sought. In fact, the freedom to benefit materially was implicit. Thus, a century before the creation of Pakistan two miniature Muslim states almost emerged in the same Muslim majority areas which were later to constitute Pakistan. Equally, however, we should not forget that Muslims fought against Muslims in India with no less determination than was demonstrated against non-Muslims, whether it was Babar against Lodhi or Nadir Shah's reign of terror against the inhabitants of Delhi. In other words, for Muslim kings and emporors, religion often took second place to the imperatives of dynasty and empire.

However, the events of 1857 themselves contributed to the sharpening of the contours of a 'Muslim' identity. Two factors were mainly responsible for this. Firstly, given the sources and the pattern of the uprising, those who bore the brunt of British vengeance happened to be Muslims. Secondly, influential Muslim leaders like Syed Ahmed Khan in the wake of the mutiny made a conscious effort to denigrate its methods and stress its futility. They advocated instead a closing of the Muslim ranks and complete loyalty to the British. In his quest to consolidate an all-India Muslim identity, Syed Ahmed Khan deemed it essential to deny the existence or validity of any ethnic or regional ties to which an Indian Muslim might adhere, as shown in a speech delivered at Meerut on 16 March 1888:

> As regards Bengal, there is, as far as I am aware, in lower Bengal a much larger proportion of Mohammadans than Bengalis. And if you take the population of the whole of Bengal, nearly half are Mohammadans, and something over half are Bengalis.[8]

So clear was Syed Ahmed about this distinction that he could quite let himself go when he was referring simply to 'Bengalis'. Referring to the possibility of competitive examinations in India in a speech, he remarked:

> Think for a moment what would be the result if all appointments were given by competitive examination. Over all races, not only over Mohammadans but over rajas of high position and the brave Rajputs who have not forgotten the swords of their ancestors, would be placed as a ruler a Bengali who at the sight of a table knife would crawl under his chair.[9]

Thus, the 'authoritative' definition of a Muslim emanating from north-central india abstracted from the identity of the Muslim inhabitants of various regions in India the validity of their specific heritage, not least because Muslim notables in these parts did not refine themselves territorially. They saw themselves as Mughuls, Syeds, etc. — claiming descent from the conquerors.[10]

The matter was not limited to ethnicity. Language, if anything, was a prior victim. Around the 1860s Hindi was already being actively promoted as the sole appropriate language for the Hindus of northern

India to the extent that Babu Shiv Prasad, an Urdu writer, started pressing the Hindu members of Syed Ahmed Khan's Scientific Society to replace Urdu by Hindi as the language for the society's transactions. Apparently, Hindu speakers of Hindi were also among the chief opponents of Syed Ahmed's plans for a Muslim university. Slowly, therefore, from such beginnings, the idea gained ground that the defence of Urdu was a *sine qua non* for anyone in India calling himself a Muslim, and thus was Urdu tied inextricably, in the minds of many, with the concept of an Indian Muslim identity.

The process evolved into not just a denial of the language favoured by the Hindus of northern India but simultaneously of much that was indigenous in the identity of the Indian Muslim. This fact was enthusiastically picked up by Hindu revivalists like Chatterjee. In response to Hali's *Mussadas* [The Ebb and Flow of Islam] published in 1879, Chatterjee in 1882 wrote about Urdu in his *Annandmath* [The Abbey of Bliss]:

> A language and literature which came to base itself upon the ideology which denied upon the soil of India the very existence of India and Indian culture could not but be met with a challenge from the sons of India, adherents of their national culture; and that challenge was in the form of highly sanskritised Hindi.[11]

Thus, the closing inwards of communities along the lines of Hindu and Muslim was increasingly a matter not just of religion but of language and culture as well.

What had been different in the inherent ideology of the two communities thus assumed greater significance, and exclusivism emerged as a central factor on both sides. Reacting to the partition of Bengal (1905), even a moderate like Aurobindo Ghose could write in a *Bande Matram* editorial:

> The groundwork of what may well be called the composite culture of India is undoubtedly Hindu. Though the present Indian nationality is undoubtedly composed of many races and the present Indian culture of more than one world civilisation, yet it may be admitted that the Hindu forms its base and centre . . . and the type of spirituality that it seeks to develop is essentially Hindu.[12]

If Muslims took such sentiments to mean that *their* spirituality or what was 'inherent' to them was to be reconstituted in a Hindu framework, the prospect, regardless of their class or region, could not have been one they welcomed. This is not to say that class and regional differences were not important.

The material condition of Muslims in different parts of India was characterised by a great degree of unevenness:

> In upper India the Muslims were in a strikingly different position. The north-western provinces and Oudh had been *centres* of Muslim power since the end of the twelfth century. Here the community was a minority of some 13%, but as a whole it was more influential, more prosperous and better educated than its coreligionists in other provinces of British India . . . a far larger proportion of the community lived in towns, and of the rural Muslims many were landlords, whereas in Bengal the typical Muslim was a poor peasant.[13]

The elite, however, continued to gain strength among Muslims for two basic reasons. It found a receptive audience because its message adhered to the framework of a shared inherent ideology. Second, while its efforts may seem hypocritical in some ways (e.g. recommending land reforms in Bengal where the landlords were mostly Hindu but not in the north-west provinces where many large landowners were Muslims), they did manage to foster a degree of general Muslim identification with issues like lack of education, discrimination in employment, inadequate political representation, etc. Thus while their use of Islam may have been subjectively opportunistic, it was nevertheless effective given the context. The element of opportunism, of course, need not be understated. In 1910 Lady Minto wrote as follows in her diary:

> The Aga Khan arrived to stay with us today. He seems to have had a triumphal progress through India amongst the Muslims. He says that the only real way to appeal to the feelings of natives is by means of the superstitions of their religion, and consequently he has instructed the priests in every mosque to issue a decree that any Mohammadans who incite to rebellion or go about preaching sedition will be eternally damned.[14]

Within the Muslim community, in contrast to this Westernised Muslim elite, the other group which struggled to attain a position of leadership was that of the orthodox religious leaders (not entirely conservative in their politics), who regarded the credentials of the former to lead the Muslim *'umma* with contempt. There were those who like Maulana Shibli Nomani, Mohammad Ali Jauhar and Abul Kalam Azad, who shared with the generally orthodox community of *'ulamā* the belief that the Muslim League was nothing more than a bunch of loyalist toadies. They were referred to by Azad, for instance, as 'those heretics and hypocrites who during the last forty years had co-operated with the Satans of Europe to weaken the influence of the Islamic caliphate and Pan-Islam' and who had 'paralysed the Muslims'.[15] They felt equally strongly about being Indian nationalists as being Pan-Islamicists. At the end of the First World War, therefore, when they were instrumental in launching the *Khilāfat* Movement, they invited the Hindus to join them, an offer readily taken up by the latter. They were thus able to forge meaningful links with the wider Indian nationalist movement even though the cause they espoused had little to do with India itself. It nevertheless provided a handle for a large number of Indian Muslims to get into stride as a clearly anti-British movement, which the League, till then, neither was nor cared to be. For the urban Indian, the institution of the *khilāfat* had some significance, but in the countryside the word *khilāfat* was probably understood as *'khilāf'* (against) the British, and people rallied to the movement on that basis too. At the popular level, in other words, these leaders were perfectly acceptable as long as they were seen to be espousing an active anti-British political creed and, significantly, at this point no great concern was shown for the fact that people like Jinnah stood apart from, and disapproved of, the movement. Undeniably the *Khilāfat* Movement had struck a responsive chord in a wide range of Muslims, whatever their understanding of the nature of the struggle. The reasons for its failure are therefore instructive. The leadership relied on the existence of a widely-held cherished value of Indian Muslims — preserving the caliphate in Turkey and getting rid of the infidel British rulers. While the movement did mobilise people, it acquired 'local' grounding and became vertically stratified.

The *Moplah* Rebellion in Malabar, the *Kissan* Movement in UP and other localised outbreaks of communal violence reflected the appropriation of the ideological framework for the pursuit of local ends.[16] In the Malabar district, for instance, the Muslim peasant community of *Moplah*s happened to be suffering at the hands of mostly Hindu landlords. Tenancy reforms had been a long-standing demand. The mobilisation inspired by the *Khilāfat*, therefore, soon degenerated into anarchic violence with Hindus being looted and murdered, desecration of Hindu temples and forced conversions. *Khilāfat* flags appeared, and *'Khilāfat* kingdoms' were proclaimed. The Hindus as a consequence started the *Shuddhi* and *Sangathan* Movements, which in turn provided the incentive for Muslims to step up their activities in the *Tabligh* and *Tanzim* Movements.[17] These movements, seeking to proselytise and consolidate Hinduism and Islam respectively, undermined considerably the basis for Hindu-Muslim unity built up around the *Khilāfat* Movement initially. The transnational framework within which the *Khilāfat* leadership tried to implement Islam politically was inappropriate for the time. In the 20th century, increasingly, the operative realm for ideology and religion would be the nation-state. It was, in fact, the immediate consequence of a letter to the Turkish prime minister sent by the Aga Khan and Syed Amir Ali that Mustapha Kemal (who was looking for an excuse) summoned the National Assembly, stressing the need to 'cleanse and elevate the Islamic faith, by rescuing it from the position of a political instrument'.[18] Indian Muslims were called British agents, and Amir Ali, along with the Aga Khan, were referred to as 'heretics', presumably on the grounds that they were *Shi'as*.[19]

In India itself the widening divide between the two communities had been politically institutionalised when the Indian Councils Act of 1909 gave constitutional recognition to separate electorates (for Muslims and non-Muslims). While the *Khilāfat* Movement in the 1920s is often seen with some justification as the high point of Hindu-Muslim amity before Partition, this coming together seemed to take place on the basis of a tactical rapprochement between the leadership of the two communities rather than as a result of a deeper and therefore more resilient ideological accommodation. Increasingly, aspects of the inherent ideology of the Indian Muslims were highlighted and invoked in ways that would leave the Hindu community outside the pale. Maulana Mohammad Ali, it was alleged, had in one of his speeches gone so far as to offer help to the Afghans if they were to invade India (and drive out the British).[20] The fact that such an allegation could be made against the most prominent leader of the *Khilāfat* Movement is itself indicative of the tension and undercurrents which continued to inform the movement. On their side, the Hindus did not do much better. Even though leaders like Gandhi put their full weight behind the *Khilāfat* non-co-operation movement, the mobilisation of the Hindu constituency was based on an exclusivist 'Hindu' idiom in which the Muslims had no place, nor was it possible for them to identify with it. The exclusivist populism of mem like Chatterji and Tilak was in many ways continued by Gandhi despite his obvious desire to co-operate with the Muslims within an Indian framework. Jawaharlal Nehru once remarked:

> Even some of Gandhiji's phrases sometimes jarred upon me — thus his frequent reference to *Ram Raj* as a golden age which was to return. But I was powerless to intervene, and I consoled myself with the thought that Gandhiji used the words because they were well-known and understood by the masses. He had an amazing knack of reaching the heart of the people.[21]

It is interesting to note that, while Nehru finds Gandhi's vocabulary jarring, he objects — being a good 'liberal' — to the fact that it is religious but not to its exclusivity. The 'masses' and the 'people' he is referring to as having been reached by Gandhi are obviously Hindus, for surely *Ram Raj* could have had no evocative content for an Indian Muslim.

It should be added that for the communities to be mobilised at all a set of conducive material conditions existed at the time:

> In 1918 the monsoon had failed disastrously, and famine prevailed in large parts of India well into 1919. The prices of foodgrains soared, as did the cost of other necessities. The world-wide epidemic influenza added to the miseries of the hunger-weakened populace and claimed untold numbers of lives. Government measures to cope with the shortages, including restrictions on the export of foodgrains, the import of surplus rice and wheat, and public famine relief works, came too late to prevent unrest.[22]

The Founder's Perception

The two communities, however, remained unsuccessful in evolving a resilient ideological basis for sustained and joint political activity, and the behaviour of Congress governments after the 1937 elections further intensified the perception among Muslims in various parts of India (Congress ministries had been formed in seven out of the eleven provinces) that in independent India the enforcement of a Hindu framework was inevitable.

Of course the idea of a separate state for the Muslims of India had already been presented in some detail by Mohammad Iqbal in his presidential address at the annual session of the Muslim League in 1930:

> I would like to see the Punjab, North-west Frontier Province, Sind and Baluchistan amalgamated into a single state. Self-government *within* the British empire or without the British empire, the formulation of a consolidated north-west Indian Muslim state appears to me to be the final destiny of the Muslims at least of North-west India.[23]

Iqbal recognised with remarkable clarity that the basis for such a state had to lie not simply in Muslim majority areas but in Muslim majority areas in India which were geographically and therefore culturally contiguous. This is why Bengal, where the greater number of Indian Muslims lived, was conspicuously absent from his formulation. 'The life of Islam', he contended, 'as a cultural force *in this country* very largely depends on its centralization in a specified territory.'[24] The defining characteristic of Iqbal's state was therefore autonomy, not sovereignty, as is clear from his phrases such as 'within the British empire' or 'as a cultural force in this country'. Equally, Iqbal's formulation in the address, regardless of how he comes through in his poetry, makes it clear that the inherent ideology shared by Muslims in terms of Islam is a necessary but not a sufficient basis for the autonomous Muslim state he envisions. Thus, while the poet in him has no hesitation in unifying the Muslims of *Cheen o Arab* (Arabia to China) the political philosopher prescribes a homeland only for the Muslims of North-west India, thereby recognising the specificity of cultural configurations which could equally be defined as Islamic.

Those, therefore, who had accepted Islam and made it a part of their inherent ideology had not by this transformation arrived at a world-view which was identical with that of Muslims everywhere else. Nor had they by virtue of this development committed themselves to a particular *political* framework. The political framework, in Iqbal's consideration, could be the British empire or an independent India. There could be one autonomous Muslim state in the north-west, or there could be a number of such states throughout India, and, further, Iqbal categorically dismissed the possibility of 'religious rule' in such states. Though never explicitly stated, Iqbal appears to have envisaged the coming together of the different autonomous Muslim states as they *consciously* elaborated Islam in an unreservedly *Indian* context. This is the 'Muslim India within India' that Iqbal talks about, and his concept is not theocratic but cultural.[25] As Iqbal said, Hindus should not 'fear that the creation of autonomous Muslim states will mean the introduction of a kind of religious rule in such states'.[26] On the contrary, he sees such development as giving Islam 'an opportunity to rid itself of the stamp that Arabian imperialism was forced to give it, to mobilise its law, its education, its culture, and to bring them into closer contact with its original spirit and with the spirit of modern times'.[27]

Thus, for Iqbal, the oneness of either the *'umma* or the Indian Muslims was a desirable end, never an assumption. He considered the differences among Muslims living in different parts of India as significant with regard to the constituent units of his proposed autonomous state. He could, presumably, foresee the possibility of these differences being rendered non-antagonistic within a progressive Islamic framework which could convincingly protect and promote the legitimate rights and interests of the constituent units. That others too may have held somewhat similar views at the time is indicated by the fact that the well-known Lahore Resolution adopted by the Muslim League in 1940 did not even mention Pakistan, saying that the north-western and eastern zones of India should be grouped to constitute 'independent states', in which the constituent *unit shall be 'autonomous and sovereign'.*[28]

Clearly, therefore, the Pakistan that came into being in 1947 exceeded the hopes and expectations of the Indian Muslim leadership, even though Jinnah was to refer to it as 'truncated and moth-eaten'. The force of circumstances impelled Jinnah to fight for the best possible Pakistan in terms of territory, population, resources, etc. For him the Islamic nexus was a point of departure and the Islamic polity an ideal. The Indian Muslims had a right to a homeland in which they could pursue their lives as Muslims *unencumbered* and constantly strive in so doing to realise the ideals postulated by Islam. Though Jinnah was preoccupied with the task of acquiring this homeland, he was never unconscious of what remained: 'We shall have time for a domestic programme and policies but first get the government. This is a nation without any territory or any government.'[29] Nor was he unaware of the limitations of the League as he exhorted his constituency to 'vote for a Muslim League even if it be a lamp post'.[30] And as he desperately tried to put together an election-winning coalition, the imperative of presenting a powerful Muslim front forced him to recognise the interests of those whom he might otherwise have entirely dismissed. As he once said, 'the Muslim camp is full of those spineless people, who, whatever they may say to me, will consult the deputy commissioner about what they should do'.[31]

To the extent that Jinnah himself conceived of Pakistan in an Islamic context, his perception rested on Islam viewed as a broadly defined set of regulating principles, an ethos which the Muslim nation inherently possessed and sought to incorporate into its socio-economic fabric:

Islam was not only a set of rituals, traditions and spiritual doctrine. Islam is a code for every Muslim, which regulated his life and his conduct — all aspects: social, political, economic, etc. It is based on the highest principles of honour, integrity, fair play and justice for all. *One God, equality and unity are the fundamental principles of Islam*[32]

It is not difficult to discern the imprint of Iqbal's thought in such statements of Jinnah, though of course the former was much more articulate in dealing with matters ideological. Of the Two-Nation Theory he remarked as follows as early as 1930:

A community which is inspired by feelings of ill will towards other communities is low and ignoble. I entertain the highest respect for the customs, laws, religious and social institutions of other communities . . . Yet I love the communal group which is the source of my life and my behaviour and which has formed me as what I am by giving me its religion, its literature, its thought, its culture, *and thereby recreating its whole past, as a living operative factor, in my present consciousness.*[33]

Indeed, inherent ideology can come close to being so defined, and in their own ways, having recognised its significance, both Jinnah and Iqbal provide evidence of the centrality of this concept in their formulations.

The success of the Muslim League at the popular level, however, was not entirely the result of the prospect it held out for securing the past as a living factor for the Muslim community. It was, certainly, as much a matter of securing the future. And this aspect corresponded to the other critical dimension of ideology, i.e. positive or derived ideology, which addresses people's felt material needs. Apart from Iqbal's and Jinnah's declarations with regard to a just and progressive society, the very idea of an autonomous or independent 'Muslim' state (in the popular mind) subsumed within it the concept of social and economic justice. At the regional level, too, the position of the League was often articulated in progressive terms. For instance, nationalisation of key industries figured prominently in the Punjab Muslim League's manifesto drafted under the influence of Danyal Latifi, a well-known radical. The manifesto recommended a ceiling on land holdings, progressive taxation involving the imposition of additional taxes on large landowners and nationalisation of banks. In Bengal, the general secretary of the provincial Muslim League, Abul Hashim, was also radical in his approach to socio-economic issues. G. M. Syed, who had been the president of the Sind Provincial Muslim League from 1943-45, held similar views and had been extremely critical of Sind's landowning elite.[34]

While popular sentiment responded to such ideas, which seemed to extend those of Iqbal and Jinnah, Islam was also being put to an entirely different use by the landowning elite of the Punjab, for example. In order to consolidate their traditional feudal hold on politics in the province, many politicians felt that being an average run of the mill Muslim was not enough, and so they proceeded to elevate themselves to the status of divines. A '*mashaikh*' committee of the Muslim League was formed, and virtually overnight an embarassment of '*pirs*' and '*sajjada nashins*' appeared on the political horizon of the province.

> Khan Iftikhar Hussain Khan of Mamdot was described as Pir Mamdot Sharif, Sirdar Shaukat Hayat Khan as *sajjada nashin* of Wah Sharif, Malik Feroz Khan Noon of Darbar Sargodha Sharif and Nawab Mohammad Hayat Qureshi as *sajjada nashin* of Sargodha Sharif and to top it all, the secretary of this committee, Mr. Ibrahim Ali Chishti, was designated *Fazil-i-Hind sajjada nashin* of *Paisa Akhbar* Sharif.[35]

It is no wonder then that people like G. M. Syed had this to say about the Muslim League and its use of Islam:

> Do not forget that Islamic society actually in existence is that in which the religious head is an ignorant *mulla*, and spiritual leader an immoral *pir*, the political guide a power-intoxicated feudal lord and whose helpless members are subjected to all the worldly forces of money and influence. If the really important question about the abolition of the *jagirdari* and *zamindari* system crops up . . . what would not a rich *jagirdar* . . . do to use his influence as also that of the *mulla* and the *pir* to resist this threat to what is essentially an immoral and un-Islamic cause?[36]

Within days after Partition, in his unaugural speech to the assembly, Jinnah indicated his concern at such blatantly self-serving use of Islam by down-playing its role in the affairs of state. He said, 'You may belong to any religion or caste or creed — that has nothing to do with the business of the state'.[37] It is unlikely that Jinnah at this late stage considered Islam unimportant, all of a sudden. More than anyone else, he must have realised that the *raison d'être* for Pakistan was a fair and just society striving to conform to the highest Islamic principles, but equally he believed that the route to this end was not through a maze of stultifying theocratic institutions and duplicity. Such goals had to be achieved in his day and age through the harnessing of the consent and energy of the millions whose backing and support had made Pakistan possible.

The Muslims of India had voluntarily come together as a state. By definition, they had an Islamic ethos. The state was not required to make them into what they already were. It could only end up lending its machinery and power to manipulation if it acted on this premise. And unfortunately, despite Jinnah's efforts, it proceeded to do so. In his zest to bind the nation together at the grass-roots level so that among other things it could better resist encroachments from the bastions of institutionalised religion and feudal politics, Jinnah may have been persuaded to overlook the significance of the extra-Islamic features of the shared inherent ideology, i.e., those aspects that the provinces did not share.

These included language, pre-Islamic cultural norms, music, etc. Any Muslim society would be expected to possess features predating the advent of Islam, whose content was not intrinsically anti-Islamic and which could, therefore, continue as before. Language is a prime example of a factor which may be neutral vis-à-vis Islam but which contributes significantly to the totality of an inherent ideology.

To say, therefore, that Islam was a paramount factor in the inherent ideology of those who opted for Pakistan is not at all to say that it did not also contain other factors which were significant but not shared. Locally specific factors which could be seen as extra-Islamic but by no means antagonistic to Islam (and therefore prized and cherished by the people) were increasingly viewed with suspicion and distrust. Thus Jinnah's exhortations calling for a total identification with Pakistan and urging people to forego the consciousness of being Punjabis, Sindhis, Baluchis, Pathans and Bengalis, though well-intended, provided fertile ground for the subsequent use of Islam to quash the autonomy of the provinces in the interests of 'greater unity'.[38] There is no doubt that Jinnah, had he lived, would have recognised the legitimacy of the dissatisfaction that had started building up around these issues even during the first year of independence. He had the wisdom to recognise when his policies were out of line with the popular will and also the courage to correct himself. After all, the 'ambassador of Hindu-Muslim unity' had evolved into the founder of Pakistan.

Religious Orthodoxy vs. Uncertain Liberalism

In all the different Muslim states that exist today, the 'received word' has been articulated differently given the specific conditions prevailing in a particular time and place. The result, obviously, cannot be the creation of some sort of monolithic Islamic empire but the emergence of socio-political entities which are nevertheless, in some significant way, informed, if not inspired, by the ideal of Islam. In the case of Pakistan, the very project as understood at the popular level was closely associated with Islam. This is not to deny the complexity of factors at work, material or otherwise, but to suggest that formulation of ideals is of critical significance in the context of any society. And, in the case of Pakistan the dream had been contoured in an Islamic mould, or in the words of W. C. Smith, 'The popular aspiration for a new and better social order had been cast in an Islamic form'.[39] Given the nature of the enterprise, it was unfortunate that those who assumed responsibility and power in practically all the fields of national activity, from the bureaucracy and army to the arts and education, were not competent to provide any leadership in the critical realm of ideology.[40] Nor, indeed, were they conscious of any real need to do so. Their major concern in this area appears to have been to keep those from attaining a significant voice in the life of the nation who had so strenuously opposed its creation — the *'ulamā*. The ruling elite did realise that its focussing on Islam during the time of the Pakistan Movement meant that they were now vulnerable to the conservative initiatives of this group, of whom by far the most astute was Maulana Maudoodi. From having consistently attacked Jinnah, the Muslim League and the very idea of Pakistan, he had by May 1947 aligned himself appropriately for laying a claim to leadership in the new scheme of things. At a Pathankot gathering Maulana Maudoodi commented:

> It is almost settled now that our country will be divided and partitioned. A portion of it will be handed over to the Muslim majority, and the other will be dominated by a non-Muslim majority. In the first region we will try to awaken and guide the popular will to base the foundation of our state on the law and constitution which we Muslims consider divine. Our non-Muslim brethren should, instead of opposing this ideal of ours, allow us this opportunity to work it out and see for themselves how far in contradiction to a secular, irreligious, national democracy, this God-worshipping democratic caliphate, founded on the guidance vouchsafed to us through Mohammad, proves a blessing for the inhabitants of Pakistan and to what extent for the whole world.[41]

Indications such as these of the shape of things to come perhaps led Jinnah to overstate his case, as in his forceful declaration in his inaugural address to the Constituent Assembly:

> We are starting with the fundamental principle that we are all citizens of one state. We should keep that in front of us as our ideal. And you will find that in the course of time Hindus will cease to be Hindus, and Muslims will cease to be Muslims, not in the religious sense because that is the personal faith of the individual, but in the political sense as the citizens of one nation.[42]

Jinnah could possibly have added that they will continue to be Hindus and Muslims in a cultural sense. For this was an aspect of the new state that the Westernised elite tended to ignore. They felt that a less 'Islamic' Pakistan would automatically transform itself into a more liberal one. They mistook their own position of relative strength in Pakistani society as evidence of a popular deep-rooted partiality towards Western liberalism. This was a major error. Where they needed to articulate Islam in ways that would render it adequate to confront the real problems that the Muslim nation faced in the middle of the twentieth century — of disparity, hunger, disease, illiteracy, etc. — they were sidelining it into an exclusively personal realm. Instead of elaborating Islam's secular and liberal content, they were substituting for it a Western, Eurocentric liberalism informed by hundreds of years of Christian tradition, a liberalism rooted in its own specific past, having its own martyrs and heroes, its own cherished values, a particular view of the world and, not least, its own ethos.[43]

On the other hand, the average traditionalist also had no idea about how Islam could be presented in a *positive* ideological formulation, i.e. how to extrapolate from the religion of Islam the structure of an economic and political system that could be implemented in Pakistan. Maudoodi, however, was by no means 'average'. Recognising the nature of the opportunity, he proceeded to apply himself to this end, occupying a significant position in the effort to provide the specifics of an Islamic state — a goal that the Objectives Resolution adopted by the Constituent Assembly in March 1949 appeared to accept. Of course, the substance of what Maudoodi proposed was illiberal and undemocratic in the extreme, but there was no denying the 'systematic' aspect of his formulation.[44] And this was critical, although it did not have overwhelming appeal at the mass level. However, precisely because it was systematic it would prove to be a powerful instrument, even in the hands of a few, in times of general uncertainty and confusion over the *raison d'être* of Pakistani society and the goals it had meant to pursue. The significance of Maudoodi's work is reflected not in the heights of political success which he or the *Jamā'at-i-Islāmī* could manage to scale but in the extent to which it relocated the ideological centre of gravity. Perhaps the first major indication of this reorientation was provided by the Punjab disturbances of 1953. Soon after Pakistan's inception, the *Majlis-i-Ahrar*, another orthodox religious party which had opposed Pakistan's creation, started demanding the expulsion of the *Ahmadi*s from the pale of Islam. The *Jamā'at* and other smaller (though similar) fry played an active role in the All-Pakistan Muslim Parties Convention held in Karachi and the All-Muslim Parties Convention held in Lahore in January 1953. The court of enquiry set up by the Punjab government pointed out 'that throughout one representative or the other of the *Jamā'at-i-Islāmī* kept attending the meetings of *Majlis-i-Amals* (executive councils) of Karachi and Lahore'.[45]

The purpose of the enterprise was clearly the wresting of the ideological initiative (the objective being political gain), for the *Ahmadis* were far too few in number to pose any real threat to the mainstream Islamic tradition that most Pakistanis shared. It would, however, be unfair to suggest that only the orthodox sectarian elements like the *Jamā'at* were seeking political gain. The Chief Minister of the Punjab — the Western-educated Daultana — was also not averse to a little political expediency. In the context of his role in the disturbances, the Munir Report states that the

> situation had tremendously improved by the imposition of a simple ban, inadequate as it was, but was allowed to deteriorate by an attitude of complete indifference to what the *Ahrar* or the *'ulamā* said or did after July 1952. On the contrary it was encouraged by the Chief Minister's public utterances supporting the view that the *Ahmadis* were not Muslims.[46]

Of course, it was not entirely a matter of opportunism where the Westernised ruling elite were concerned. Along with the rest of the society they had simply not addressed themselves to the task of formulating a liberal response to such initiatives — which could be traced back to 1948 and the murder of Major Mahmud in Quetta after an anti-*Qadiani* public meeting.[47] As the Munir Report explains, 'on coming to know of this gruesome murder, the intelligence bureau drew the attention of the provincial authorities to the secret activities of the *Majlis-i-Ahrar*'.[48] It is inevitable then that the response, when it did come, was not in the form of a popular countermobilisation along liberal-democratic lines but in the form of army action and the imposition of martial law in Lahore (for the first time in Pakistan's history). From being concerned exclusively with the defence of Pakistan's geographical frontiers, the army had taken its first step towards becoming an arbiter in the realm of ideology. The lack of any dynamic linkage between the ruling elite and the large mass of the people stood badly exposed despite, or because of, the fact that the army was able to bring the situation under control within a matter of hours:

> Physically the government was able to suppress the riots, but ideologically it was disarmed. The political leaders were essentially men of liberal modernist views, who in discussion with Europeans would have eagerly refuted any suggestion that Islam was an intolerant or obscurantist religion. But when faced with obscurantism and intolerance in practice they lacked the self-confidence to tell the people that the *'ulamā* were misrepresenting Islam.[49]

However, what was true of 'liberal' politicians did not necessarily apply to the entire liberal spectrum, and the enquiry commission, composed of two liberal judges, did an admirable job of highlighting the incongruencies and internal contradictions in the views of those belonging to the orthodox religious establishment who were held to be the authorities on matters of religion and ideology. In this sense perhaps the anti-*Ahmadi* agitation *was* recognised as a warning signal inasmuch as the exhaustive work of the commission could be seen as an effort to discredit the *'ulamā* and counter their efforts at misrepresenting Islam. It called for strong measures:

> Nothing but a bold reorientation of Islam to separate the vital from the lifeless can preserve it as a world idea and convert the Mussalman into a citizen of the present and future world from the archaic incongruity that he is today.[50]

The Liberal Response

The politicians, however, seemed to understand the import of this observation in relatively mechanistic terms. The way out, they felt, was to appease the *'ulamā* by going along with their recommendations wherever their own interests were not threatened while denying them any real share in legislation or decision-making. The 1956 constitution, in fact, is a classic example of this kind of lip service and manoeuvring and reflects, on the one hand, the need to project an Islamic orientation and, on the other, the intent to deny it substance. The desire to keep the *'ulamā* from assuming a position of any political significance may have been a primary motivation, but the means they adopted to achieve this end showed the limitations of their political style. However much they identified themselves with the values of Western liberalism and democracy, their elite politics faithfully reflected the inequities and inequalities of the prevailing system in which the greater mass of the population was neither trusted nor taken into confidence. Instead of confronting the orthodox views of the *'ulamā* in a serious and systematic manner and at a popular level, the constitution was adorned with a number of Islamic directives and principles as a concession to the views of the *'ulamā*. The constitution stipulated, for instance, that the head of state should be a Muslim. Power, however, rested with the head of the government. Even more meaningless, when read collectively, were the clauses relating to the stipulation that no laws could be enacted by the legislature which were 'repugnant to the injunctions of Islam'. Clause two of the constitution expressly denied judicial intervention in case the National Assembly did enact a law which violated Islamic prescription.[51] However, the fact that such features had been made a part of the constitution at the insistence of the *'ulamā* was certainly a moral, if not a political, victory for the orthodox. It could be said that even as the orthodox remained weak, orthodoxy gained ground.

In 1956 a report of the Commission on Marriage and Family Laws recommended that 'the laws of divorce be changed to make it impossible for a man to divorce his wife by saying rapidly "I divorce thee, I divorce thee, I divorce thee" '. This practice of divorce had been regarded as valid by the four *imams* and was, therefore, strongly defended by the traditionalist member of the Commission. However, 'in this instance the majority were able to adduce strong Qur'ānic support'.[52] After the inception of Pakistan this appears to have been the first serious effort to extend the liberal Islamic framework of men like Syed Ahmed Khan and Mohammad Iqbal. The initiative in this case was provided by Khalifa Abdul Hakim, who headed the government-sponsored Institute of Islamic Culture in Lahore and combined a liberal orientation with an extensive knowledge of Islam. It is unfortunate that his philosophical style prevented him from gaining a wide popular audience and that his views, by and large, received limited exposure. As the Commission's secretary, however, he proved a valuable asset because it went on to recommend monogamy. Abbot has explained this method:

Citing Iqbal as their authority they insisted that *ijtihād* — independent judgement in legal matters exercised by learned scholars — was necessary for jurists and judges, for 'life can improve only by freedom of judgement'.[53]

The emphasis on being learned scholars in Islam by a liberal group was a step in a new direction. By now, being learned in Islam had come to mean, almost by definition, being orthodox. Once again, however, the limitations of an elite style were obvious. They had woken to the need for asserting their right to *ijtihād* but were unwilling (or unable) to posit the issue of *ijmah* or popular consensus. However, if the recommendations of the Commission on Marriage had to await the approval and good will of an unelected army dictator before these could take the form of law as the Family Laws Ordinance of 1961, then something was drastically wrong.

One indication of how fragile this kind of a process could be came soon after the ordinance was enacted when, during the 1965 elections, Ayub Khan decided to put Islam in the service of his own election campaign and got more than a hundred *'ulamā* to give *fatwas* declaring that the election of Fatima Jinnah would be un-Islamic because a woman could not become the head of an Islamic state. Of course, the supreme irony was that the *Jamā'at-i-Islāmî*, reversing its previous stand on the issue of a woman becoming head of state, came out in support of Fatima Jinnah. The orthodox remained weak because of the differences within their ranks, which were based on everything from theological hair-splitting to personality clashes, so that many orthodox groups ended up supporting the 'secular' Ayub Khan while the *Jamā'at* supported Fatima Jinnah. It could be said that the bureaucracy, which ruled as an almost equal partner with the army under Ayub Khan, had as much to do with ensuring Ayub's success in the election as the *'ulamā*. And, of course, the army and the bureaucracy, with their pre-independence ethos more or less intact (particularly at the higher levels), remained firmly committed to the only liberal tradition they knew and felt strongly about (though at a somewhat superficial level).

Ayub Khan's resort to the *'ulamā* had sown the seeds of a mutually beneficial, although unequal, relationship between the institution of the military and the establishment of the orthodox. It was in 1971 that these bonds were qualitatively further strengthened. But this time the orthodox establishment was not represented by an amorphous group of *'ulamā* but by the well organised *Jamā'at-i-Islāmî*. Not only were its leaders vociferous in providing justification for the army action in East Pakistan, but also the *Jamā'at* rank and file 'took an active part in the "Peace Committees" which were organised by the army to help it suppress the revolt'.[54] At the ideological level, too, the *Jamā'at*'s support must have come as a welcome relief to the beleaguered army:

> It was said that un-Islamic ideas pervaded Bengali literature instead of Islamic, because Tagore and his followers played a leading role in the creation of this literature.[55]

That the inherent ideology of a Bengali Muslim included Tagore's poetry was of course unthinkable for the *Jamā'at*, let alone acceptable. That a large proportion of the West Pakistani elite held similar views was at least in part a result of the *Jamā'at*'s efforts. The creation of Bangladesh made no difference to the basic premise of the *Jamā'at*, for it could now be claimed that precisely those influences against which the *Jamā'at* had repeatedly warned (Hindus, Bengali nationalists, etc.) had succeeded in splitting the country in two. National elections had already been held in the December of the previous year, and the *Jamā'at* had been all but demolished at the polls. It would not be far-fetched to assume that as a consequence it had given up the strategy of achieving power through popular consensus and that the events of East Pakistan gave it just the opportunity it needed to cement its ties to those who could 'get it in through the back door'. However, the army, completely shattered (more psychologically than in any structural or institutional sense), was for the moment exclusively concerned with its own rehabilitation.

The party which swept the polls in West Pakistan was the Pakistan People's Party (PPP) of Zulfiqar Ali Bhutto and in East Pakistan the Awami League of Sheikh Mujibur Rehman. Neither party made Islam its central plank. Each emphasised a 'nationalist' position and focussed on the deeply felt issue of economic exploitation. Mujib's 'nationalism' simply assumed Islam as a given factor, not least because the average Bengali had never felt his Muslim identity as being under any kind of a threat from West Pakistan. It was, however, that part of his identity which he derived from his soil — his language, music and literature — along with his political and economic rights that seemed to be constantly denied by West Pakistan. And this is what Mujib made use of, with telling effect. Bhutto, in his effort, was helped by Pakistan's 1965 war with India in two ways. First, it put a severe strain on Pakistan's financial resources and thereby compounded the misery of the common man. Second, he used the Pakistan-India agreement at Tashkent (after which he resigned) to acquire the image of a hard-driving nationalist. Denouncing the agreement as a sell-out, he would often declare in his public meetings that 'we will fight India for a thousand years'. Thus, while Bhutto made much of the slogan 'bread, clothing and shelter', nationalism also figured prominently in his framework. Why, then, did we see the rout of the *Jamā'at* at the polls and, on the other hand, the success of two parties, neither of which used Islam as a central political plank?

Apart from factors like leadership and charisma, a major cause of their success was the motivating components central to the inherent ideology of the people in both wings — in the case of East Pakistan, a Bengali nationalism at odds with an exploitative foreigner and in the case of West Pakistan, an anti-Indian nationalism combined with an emphasis on social justice. The *Jamā'at*, for its part, focussing much more on Islam, also tried to take up some of the economic issues, e.g., a ceiling on land holdings. It, however, lacked credibility as a party that was concerned with anything other than religion, and that in the popular perception was not an issue — it was a comprehensive presence informing everyday life. To classify the *Jamā'at* and other orthodox parties like the *Jamā'at-i-Islāmī* as pro-Islam and by implication the PPP and the Awami League as anti-Islam is erroneous, particularly if one goes on to infer on the basis of this classification a vote *against* Islam in the 1970 elections and *for* more secular and progressive ideas. To do so is to introduce a false dichotomy between Islam and secularism. By far the great majority of those who voted for the two winning parties never doubted for a moment either the validity of their faith or their own credentials as at least believing, if not 'good' or practising, Muslims. The identification of these parties with nationalism, socialism or democracy was not seen as a commitment that was contrary to, or outside the framework of, Islam.

Having assumed power in a postcrisis situation after defeating the religious orthodox parties much as the Muslim League had done in 1947, the PPP went on to repeat the error of the Muslim League. Instead of elaborating an ideology from the principles to which people had responded so enthusiastically and providing it with an institutionalised underpinning, it threw itself into what the PPP thought were the more critical and immediate tasks: to administer and to rule. Meanwhile the widespread enthusiasm and fervour that had been created by the PPP's message slowly degenerated into popular cynicism and indifference. The inability (or unwillingness) to fulfil commitments of economic progress and uplift, the dismissal of popularly elected provincial governments and the army action in Baluchistan undermined the popularity of the regime. The nature of the failure had nothing to do with Islam, but once again opposition to it developed around the religious orthodox parties and their slogan of a utopia located in idealised Islamic (as distinguished from Muslim) history: *Nizam-i-Mustafa*, which roughly translates into 'Mohammad's system' or the 'golden age of Mohammad's rule'. And as in the case of the Muslim League, this development was directly the result of the PPP's failure to elaborate an ideology which was not vulnerable to an orthodox attack on the grounds that it was less Islamic merely because it sought democracy and greater social justice. If anything, on this score, Bhutto yielded ground to the orthodox. He passed a law approving minority status for the *Qadianis*, allowed the *Jamā'at* a relatively free hand in educational institutions to keep radical groups from becoming irritants to the government and, in a final effort to appease, declared Friday as the weekly holiday, banned horse racing, etc., all to no avail, of course.

Institutionalisation of the Orthodox Framework

Since its assumption of power in 1977 the military regime has applied itself quite consistently to the task of elaborating a positive ideology appropriate to its needs. Its use of Islam seeks not to mobilise but to disarm the greatest number. This up to a point it has succeeded in doing, much as, on the ideological plane, the *Jamā'at* and other orthodox parties managed to immobilise the overwhelming majority on the *Qadiani* issue in 1953 (the year in which the Muslim League was soundly defeated in the East Pakistan provincial elections). The blueprint for the institutional underpinnings with which this ideology is being secured appears to have been borrowed from the *Jamā'at*'s scheme. The *Majlis-i-Shoora*, the *qazi* courts, and the mosque schools are all highly recommended in various expositions of the *Jamā'at*'s position and programme. The profit and loss sharing (PLS) scheme, the emphasis on *zakāt* and *ushr* and Zia ul Haq's own carefully publicised reputation as a practising Muslim are all geared to draw attention to the 'Islamic' nature of the regime and to defuse, therefore, popular opposition to it. For, by definition (in a Muslim country), such a regime calls for tolerance, if not support. So far this ideological edifice has served its purpose and, if anything appears to be in the process of becoming more firmly grounded as new laws are passed and new institutions take shape, supposedly bringing in a greater degree of Islamisation. The *Jamā'at* has emerged as a very junior partner to the military regime and is sometimes reminded quite unambiguously by the latter of its real place in the scheme of things as in the case of the government's decision in February 1983 to ban student unions, which were largely controlled by the *Jamā'at* and were considered to be its most active arm. Again, therefore, the political philosophy of the *Jamā'at* seems to have gained more political ground than the party itself. Increasingly, however, as the *qazi* courts and *madrassah* (mosque school) and *zakāt* and *salat* (prayer) committees are manned, the *Jamā'at*'s role may become more crucial and its hold on civil society more immediate. Even though for the moment the regime appears to be keeping the initiative in its own hands within the politico-religious realm, other alternatives have sprung up in the course of Zia ul Haq's rule.[56] However, the efficiency of the *Jamā'at*'s organisation will be difficult to match, in the short run at least. In tasks as varied as keeping the universities 'under control' and in work among the Afghan refugees, the *Jamā'at* has shown itself, with the regime's help, capable of a degree of organisation unmatched by most other political parties, orthodox or liberal, which have been rendered 'defunct' for the last five years.

The *Jamā'at*'s formulation being implemented by the army (which remains the dominant political actor in the Pakistani state) has benefitted greatly from the collapse of Bhutto's 'socialist' experiment. It is not that the people disillusioned with 'socialism' have moved to Islam, but it is that a utopion formulation came apart for reasons that are not entirely clear to many. During the Bhutto years, energetic and inspired individuals in the middle and lower middle classes were mainly influenced by two kinds of goals. One involved working with the PPP and striving to bring about institutional change with its promised rewards for the many.

The other involved a passage to the Middle East and the promise of material improvement on a virtually phenomenal scale. Those who stayed are still unable to offer, after all these years, a convincing explanation of where it all went wrong. Those who went out can afford to let their bank accounts and their VCRs do the talking. They stand, in sharp contrast to the so far confused and defeated mass that confronts them, reaffirmed in the correctness and validity of their choice. The *Jamā'at*'s formulation not only offers them a justification for their material development but will also be seen to guarantee their hold over what they have gained. After all, they have seen a similar system do as much for the privileged classes in Saudi Arabia and the Gulf states. Their experience in these countries will have provided them with a less democratic and more traditional orientation. And this is the class which in the crucial urban sector will, on the basis of its strengthened material foundations coupled with a desire for greater 'security', play a pivotal role in the socio-political framework envisaged by Zia ul Haq's regime. Also, they are likely to emerge as dominant within their class, unless those who remain ideologically adrift in the post-Bhutto era are somehow able to revitalise themselves.

Another important feature of the regime's ideological offensive has been its mode of dealing with that aspect of Islam which through the centuries has articulated the more universalist and essentially humanist values that it embodies. On the one hand, the cultural space occupied by the *Sufi* tradition is being progressively and systematically reduced. The festivities accompanying the annual '*urs*' of various *Sufi* saints are carefully monitored for 'un-Islamic' practices like dancing and drumming. Folk singers are discouraged from presenting *Sufi* poetry sharply critical of organised and ritualistic aspects of religion. Devotional attendance at the tombs of *Sufi* saints is frowned upon, in Friday sermons, for instance, as a slight upon the sanctity of *touhid* (unqualified faith in one God). On the other hand, a relatively soulless representation of this aspect of Islam has also been assiduously incorporated in the regime's ideology. Important government functionaries give long-winded speeches to commemorate the birth of this or that *Sufi* saint, repairs and extension of their tombs are frequently seen in progress and care is taken, generally, to ensure that no antagonism, or lack of preference, on the part of this regime towards the *Sufi* tradition is discernible at the popular level. In substance, however, the Islamic humanist tradition is being restricted from acting as a countervailing force to the advance of institutionalised orthodoxy, albeit through methods and institutions which in themselves may be quite modern — e.g. institutes which conduct public opinion polls and a military establishment which uses state of the art F-16s.

Undoubtedly, the overall ideological framework is one that guarantees stability, in the short run. Over a longer period, however, the very nature of such a framework can create its own problems. Today, two of Pakistan's major aid-givers (Saudi Arabia and the USA, though for somewhat different reasons) lend it their support. On the other hand, Pakistan's neighbour, Iran, being predominantly *Shi'a*, regards it with considerable antagonism and distrust. The situation acquires greater complexity due to the existence of a small but well organised *Shi'a* minority in Pakistan, who are not entirely unconcerned with Iranian religious sentiments. In any case, *Shi'a* practice forbids the paying of *zakat*, for instance, to the state, and already *Shi'a* protest has led to their being exempted from it being deducted compulsorily (from saving deposits, etc.). Even within the *Sunnis*, differences of interpretation exist depending on which school of *fiqh* one adheres to. Even within one school, one *'ālim* has been known to declare the other non-Muslim. For instance, Maulana Hussain Ahmed Madani, one of the most prominent *'ulamā* of Deoband, declared in a *fatwa* that ' . . . both the *Jamā'at-i-Islāmī* and its founder Maudoodi are not Muslims'.[57] Both of them belonged to the *Hanafi fiqh*, the school with most adherents in Pakistan.

The other difficulty that such a rigid doctrinaire formulation is likely to run into is that it does not incorporate within it the desires and aspirations of the people for a just system and better life, which are profoundly felt and implicitly recognised as valid and right. As the history of Pakistan has shown, in such a situation, a subnational group can proceed to delink itself from the Muslim *nation-state* while at the same time remaining firmly secured to the Muslim *'umma*.

Islam, therefore, must inform the nature of the choices made in pursuit of higher productivity, democracy and distributive justice. It cannot serve as a substitute for these choices. It must be elaborated as an ideology to encompass the advances that have been made in the various fields of human knowledge and activity so that it is not merely a shell without content but for the people an ideal that remains eternally valid.

References and Notes

1. C. Geertz, *Islam Observed* (Chicago: University of Chicago Press, 1968), p. 91.

2. J. Galtung, *A Structural Theory of Revolutions* (Rotterdam: Rotterdam University Press, 1974), p. 51.

3. D. S. McLellan, W. C. Olson, and F. A. Sondermann, *The Theory and Practice of International Relations* (Englewood Cliffs, N. J.: Prentice Hall, 1974), p. 32.

4. G. Rude, *Ideology and Popular Protest* (London: Lawrence and Wishart, 1980), p. 28.

5. Ibid

6. A. Gramsci, *Prison Notebooks*, ed. & trans. Q. Hoare and G. Smith (London: Lawrence and Wishart, 1971), p. 377.

7. G. Rude, *Ideology*, p. 23.

8. A. M. Zaidi, ed., *Evolution of Muslim Political Thought in India*, vol. 1

(New Delhi: Michiko and Panjathan, n.d.), p. 51.

9. Ibid., p. 38.

10. Ibid., p. 45. The following passage from Syed Ahmed's speech at Lucknow underscores this aspect: 'The time is, however, coming when my brothers, Pathans, Syeds, Hashmi and Koreishi, whose blood smells of the blood of Abraham, will appear in glittering uniforms as Colonels and Majors in the army.'

11. A. Ahmed, *Studies in Islamic Culture in the Indian Environment* (Karachi: Oxford University Press, 1970), p. 255.

12. K.B. Sayeed, *Pakistan: The Formative Phase* (Karachi: Oxford University Press, 1978), p. 25.

13. A. Seal, *The Emergence of Indian Nationalism* (Cambridge: Cambridge University Press, 1971), p. 303.

14. Sayeed, *Pakistan*, p. 33.

15. Ibid., P. 43.

16. G. Minault, *The Khilāfat Movement* (New York: Columbia University Press, 1982), p. 126. The following passage provides a good illustration of 'localisation': 'The effort to spread political activity into the countryside produced almost as many variations on the theme of non-cooperation as there were local organizations. In areas of agrarian unrest like UP peasant grievances were tacked onto the non-co-operation programme by emphasizing that the government was really the friend of the landlord. In Bengal and Assam labour disputes were brought under the rubric of non-co-operation. In predominantly Muslim area, *'ulamā* and *Sufis* were the chief messengers of the movement, armed with *fatwa* and religious rhetoric. For Hindu audiences, religious symbolism was also employed: the promised *swaraj* became *Ram Raj* or *Gandhiraj*, the rule of virtue versus the present *Ravanraj*, the rule of evil.'

17. Sayeed, *Pakistan*, pp. 57-8.

18. G. Minault, *The Khilāfat Movement*, p. 203.

19. Ibid.

20. A. Ahmad, *Studies in Islamic Culture*, p. 268.

21. Sayeed, *Pakistan*, p. 97.

22. Minault, *The Khilāfat Movement*, p. 66.

23. Zaidi, *Evolution*, vol. 4, p. 67.

24. Ibid.

25. Ibid.

26. Ibid.

27. Ibid.

28. E. Mortimer, *Faith and Power* (London: Faber & Faber, 1982), p. 200.

29. K. B. Sayeed, *The Political System of Pakistan* (Boston: Houghton Mifflin Co., 1967), p. 59.

30. Ibid., p. 54.

31. Ibid., p. 58.

32. M. Munir, *From Jinnah to Zia* (Lahore: Vanguard Books Ltd., 1980), p. 20.

33. Zaidi, *Evolution*, vol. 4, p. 66.

34. Sayeed, *The Political System of Pakistan*, p. 53.

35. Government of Pakistan, *Report of the Court of Enquiry Constituted under Punjab Act 11 of 1954 to Enquire into the Punjab Disturbances of 1953* Lahore: Government of Pakistan.), p. 255. This is popularly

referred to as the *Munir Report* (after the court's president Justice M. Munir).

36. Sayeed, *Political System of Pakistan*, p. 53.

37. Mortimer, *Faith and Power*, p. 208.

38. Note the contrasting tenor of Jinnah's and Iskander Mirza's views on the subject respectively. See A. Syed, *Pakistan: Islam, Politics and National Solidarity* (New York: Praeger, 1983), p. 56: 'What we want is not to talk about Bengali, Punjabi, Sindhi, Baluchi, Pathan and so on. They are, of course units . . . No we are Muslims.' Also see S. Venkataramani, *The American Role in Pakistan* (Lahore: Vanguard Books Ltd., 1984), p. 287. Referring to the proposal to amalgamate the provinces of West Pakistan into a single administrative unit for essentially political purposes, he states that 'one unit is a steam roller. Have you seen a steam roller being stopped by small pebbles on a road? . . . '

39. W. C. Smith, *Islam in Modern History* (Princeton: Princeton University Press, 1957), p. 231.

40. Ibid., p. 222.

41. K. Bahadur, *The Jamā'at-i-Islāmî of Pakistan* (Lahore: Progressive Books, 1978), p. 50.

42. Ibid., p. 51.

43. Smith, *Islam*, p. 208.

44. Ibid., p. 234.

45. *Munir Report*, p. 251.

46. Ibid., p. 386.

47. Ibid., p. 13.

48. Ibid., p. 14.

49. Mortimer, *Faith and Power*, p. 210.

50. Syed, *Pakistan: Islam, Politics, and National Solidarity*, p. 78.

51. Ibid., p. 82.

52. F. Abbot, *Islam and Pakistan* (Ithaca: Cornell University Press, 1968), p. 199.

53. Ibid., p. 200.

54. Bahadur, *Jamā'at-i-Islāmî*, p. 134.

55. Ibid., p. 132.

56. For instance, the Quran Academy founded by Dr. Israr Ahmad.

57. Bahadur, *Jamā'at-i-Islāmî*, p. 171.

4. Maudoodi's Islamic State

by Zafaryab Ahmed

Nature of the State

The historical, cultural and religious factors that urged the Muslims of the Indian subcontinent to seek a separate homeland have been dealt with elsewhere in this book. It was in response to this urge and the struggle of various sections of Indian Muslims that the British government accepted the Muslim League's demand for a separate Muslim homeland. The Indian Independence Act of 18 July 1947 declared that 'as from the fifteenth day of August, nineteen hundred and forty-seven, two independent dominions shall be set up in India, to be known respectively as India and Pakistan'. Hence, direct British rule in India came to an end on 14 August 1947, and Pakistan appeared on the map of the world as a new state under the leadership of Quaid-i-Azam Mohammad Ali Jinnah. The tasks ahead were no less gigantic in nature than the achievement of Pakistan and required immediate resolution. One of the foremost tasks faced by the new state was to frame a constitution, and until such time that a new constitution was framed, the new state was to be governed by the Government of India Act of 1935.

With the convening of the Constituent Assembly, a debate ensued on the nature of the constitution and its Islamic content.[1] During this debate the demands of the constituent units were rejected by interpreting Islam as favouring a unitary form of government. Outside the Constituent Assembly, the *'ulamā*, a large majority of whom had opposed the Pakistan Movement and were facing a crisis of credibility, were arguing that the *Sharī'ah*, as they interpreted it, be made the basis of the future constitution, which would have secured for them a position of preeminence in the future polity.

Whereas there was a need to understand the nature of the new social formation as well as to appreciate the aspirations of the peoples of the various regions that constituted Pakistan, the democratic demands of the people from the constituent units were declared parochial and against the 'national interest'.[2] It was argued by the ruling hierarchy that such demands were inconsistent with the aspirations and the interests of the people of Pakistan and should not be considered while framing the new

95

constitution. However, not much had been said during the Pakistan Movement about the future structure of the state, except for the application of the democratic and egalitarian principles of Islam. These lofty ideals could be achieved only by restructuring the socio-economic set-up established by British colonialism, which had created strong vested interests. Ironically, all those demands that aimed, directly or indirectly, at the restructuring of society were treated in the fashion of the colonial rulers and were brushed aside by Pakistan's new ruling hierarchy.

With the passage of time, however, the socio-economic aspirations of the people of Pakistan began to crystallise, and new dimensions were added to the debate about the nature of the constitution. Though general democratic demands were made in and outside the Constituent Assembly, the mass movement of the late 1960s brought out at the popular level the contradictions between the democratic aspirations of the people and the existing socio-economic structure.[3] The movement, which had begun with certain democratic demands, culminated with demands that could not be met without drastically restructuring the neocolonial socio-economic framework. The mass movement of 1968-69 was a watershed in the political history of Pakistan. Henceforth, institutionalised politics had to be premised on socio-economic issues confronting the common people. The mandate of the people in the general elections of 1970 therefore went to those parties which included in their programmes the alleviation of socio-economic problems. The parties that failed to appreciate these problems faced disastrous defeat. Those political parties which had displayed an antipeople attitude during the mass movement of the late 1960s, by their opposition to the Movement for the Restoration of Democracy in the 1980s again showed a lack of appreciation of the problem. They repeated their attitude of the late 1960s by characterising all popular democratic aspirations of the people as a 'threat to Islam'. In the forefront of these political forces was the right-wing *Jamā'at-i-Islāmī*, which has always tried to interpret Pakistani politics with reference to the Islamic character of the state.[4] In an attempt to thwart the rising consciousness of the people, it has time and again campaigned against progressive tendencies in Pakistani politics.

In order to oppose popular movements launched for the achievement of socio-political rights, the *Jamā'at-i-Islāmī* has always raised the slogan of 'Islam in danger' in order to establish itself as the sole custodian of Islam. Such a position has helped the ruling hierarchy to take advantage of the situation by suppressing popular aspirations in the name of Islam. The *Jamā'at-i-Islāmī*'s leader and ideologue, Sayyid Abul Ala Maudoodi, has over the years produced theoretical arguments for different political situations in Pakistan.[5] Translating the situation to suit his political objectives, this corpus of literature presents Maudoodi and the *Jamā'at-i-Islāmī* as distinct from all *'ulamā* and political parties and has succeeded in gaining for Maulana Maudoodi the status of a scholar versed not only in

Islamic theology but in the modern social sciences as well. It is significant that the present ruling hierarchy in Pakistan draws its ethos from Maudoodi's theory of the Islamic state and is experimenting with his model. To understand the situation in Pakistan, it is necessary therefore to study the concept of Maulana Maudoodi's Islamic state.

Sovereignty and Political Power

The pivotal point in Maudoodi's theory of an Islamic state is the sovereignty of God over the universe. This he presents in contradistinction to other notions of sovereignty. He asserts that 'sovereignty belongs only to God. He is the lawgiver. Any person, even a prophet, is not entitled to issue orders or withdraw the orders [of God]'.[6]

Anyone with an understanding of the concept of sovereignty in its literal sense, i.e. as the highest unlimited power, would find any kind of sovereignty in a state to be in conflict with the 'sovereignty of God'. For if a person or an institution is sovereign, it implies that the word of that person or institution would be law, and the sovereign would have unlimited power to impose his will. The same would be the case if the people are declared sovereign, because then the people would have the right to make or change laws. Interestingly, however, Maudoodi does not treat sovereignty in its literal sense. He claims that his understanding is in accordance with the understanding of jurists and lawyers. It appears that, from the writings of the advocates of absolute sovereignty in 16th- and 17th-century Europe, Maulana Maudoodi has constructed a definition of sovereignty to suit his political objectives. He has constructed it carefully to make it appear similar to the attributes of God:

> In the vocabulary of political science the concept is used for the highest absolute authority. If a person, a group of persons or an institution holds this authority, it implies that the orders issued by the one who is sovereign constitute law. He has unlimited powers to issue orders. People are bound to obey his orders unconditionally, willingly or unwillingly; except for his own will there is no check on his authority. People have no right against him, *all rights are granted by him*, if he withdraws any right it automatically becomes extinct. *A legal right comes into existence because the lawgiver desires*, and if the lawgiver withdraws it there is no provision to demand it back. Law comes into existence by the will of the sovereign and binds people to obey him, but there is no law to bind the sovereign. He in himself is absolute authority. There is no question of good or evil, right or wrong, concerning his orders. Whatever he does is good. None of his subjects has the right to reject it as evil; whatever he does is correct. None of his subjects can declare it wrong. Hence, he must be accepted as over and above weakness and without any fault. This is the concept of *legal sovereignty* presented by lawyers and jurists. *Nothing short of this can be called sovereignty* (emphasis added).[7]

Maulana Maudoodi makes a further assertion:

> It has been finally decided that legal sovereignty should be accepted of the one who has sovereignty over the entire universe and indivisible sovereignty over people.[8]

By limiting the sovereignty of God to the 'Islamic state', Maudoodi divides the indivisible sovereignty of God over the entire universe and all people among different states. He also limits God's sovereignty over the entire universe to a small part of the universe, the 'Islamic state' of Pakistan. Moreover, Maudoodi appears to ignore the fact that the God of the Qur'ān is not an exclusive God: 'He is the lord of worlds, the lord of all persons of whatever faith. He is your God as well as mine' (Qur'ān, 19: 36).

However, the above paragraph is not a complete presentation of Maulana Maudoodi's theoretical construct of sovereignty. He draws a further distinction between legal and political sovereignty and argues that legal sovereignty 'remains hypothetical, unless it is supported by real sovereignty. In the vocabulary of political science, this is called "political sovereignty" — the owner of political power to implement the legal sovereignty'.[9] He then poses the question, 'who has political sovereignty in an Islamic state?'[10] His answer is:

> That too belongs to God, because any agency with political power created to enforce the legal sovereignty of God cannot be characterised as sovereign according to the concepts of jurists and political scientists. The agency whose powers have been limited and curtailed by a supreme law, and which does not have the power to alter it, cannot be sovereign. Now which word should be chosen to define this position? This question has been solved by the Qur'ān. The Qur'ān interprets it as *khilāfat*. The *khalifa* himself is not the sovereign but the deputy of the sovereign.[11]

It should be noted that the word *khalifa* or *khilāfat* in the Qur'ān is not used in Maudoodi's sense. In the Qur'ān, *khalifa* designates the owner of political power who enforces the laws of God. Nor is there any distinction in political theory between legal and political sovereignty, as Maulana Maudoodi argues, except for the distinction between *de facto* and *de jure* sovereignty. These too have different connotations than Maudoodi gives them. However, the concept of sovereignty can be appreciated properly only when it is placed in its historical context. The origin of the concept is rooted in the search for stability in the political situation of 16th-century France. At the time there was an attempt to find a locus of authority that could defend the realm externally and maintain law and order internally. Even at that time, when the concept was being presented in absolute terms, it did not have the same connotations that Maulana Maudoodi attributes to it. This can be seen from what it meant to Jean Bodin, the first exponent of the concept.

Bodin's treatise entitled *The Republic* was published in 1576, a period of civil war and strife in France between the claims of the Church and the monarch:

> Published only four years after the massacre of Saint Bartholomew, *The Republic* formed the main intellectual production of an already growing body of moderate thinkers, known as *politiques*, who saw in royal power the mainstay of peace and order and who therefore sought to raise the king, as a centre of national unity, above all religious sects and political parties.[12]

This crisis of stability, which started in Europe in the beginning of the 16th century, was a crisis of the feudal social order that had outlived its usefulness. Bodin responded to this by presenting a theory of a strong government, which, however, did not preclude the king's responsibility to God. Modern state apparatuses and the concept of popular sovereignty were alien to that age. The state for Bodin was 'a lawful government of several households and their common possessions, with a sovereign power'.[13] In such a state, sovereignty was defined as 'supreme power over the citizens and subjects unrestrained by law', but Bodin did not doubt that 'the sovereign was answerable to God and subject to the natural law'.[14]

It appears that Maudoodi, in an attempt to preserve the status quo and eliminate all possibilities of popular participation in affairs of state, has borrowed categories of political thought from feudal monarchical Europe. Maudoodi's understanding of human nature also appears to be limited to that of the Middle Ages, when people had not emerged as the motive force of history — a force that can lead the process of social change. No account of the evolution of popular rights would substantiate the statement that laws are simply the 'desires' of the 'will' of the sovereign which can be bestowed or withdrawn at will. The nature of the Indian nationalist movement, the *Khilāfat* Movement, the agitation against the Rowlatt Act and the Pakistan Movement all indicate the role of the people in shaping history and their refusal to accept the will and desire of the sovereign.

'Islamic Democracy'

Maudoodi's peculiar interpretation of 'Islamic democracy' is a manifestation of his aversion to democracy, which he finds contrary to the principles of Islam:

> Philosophically, democracy is a form of government in which the common people of a country are sovereign. Laws are made with their opinions and can be amended only with their opinion. Only that law can be implemented that they want, and the law which they do not want would be removed from the statutes.[15]

But an Islamic state, according to Maulana Maudoodi, is bound by the laws of God and hence, 'the best name for it would be *Ilahi hukoomat* or 'theocracy'. But Islamic theocracy is different from Western theocracy.'[16] He further states:

> Islamic theocracy is not controlled by a special religious group of people but by ordinary Muslims. They run it according to the Qur'ān and *Sunnah*. And if I am allowed to coin a new word, I would call it 'theo-democracy'. It would grant limited popular sovereignty to Muslims under the paramount sovereignty of God. In this [state], the executive and the legislature would be formed in consultation with the Muslims. Only Muslims would have the right[17] to remove them. Administrative and other issues, regarding which there are no clear orders in the *Shari'ah*, would be settled only with the consensus of Muslims. If the law of God needs interpretation no special group or a race but all those Muslims would be entitled to interpret (*ijtihād*) who have achieved the capability of interpretation.[18]

One should not think that all the Muslims would have these rights in Maudoodi's 'Islamic state' or that his notion of 'limited popular sovereignty' does not put any limits on the popular sovereignty of Muslims; nor should one believe his contention that he is not aiming at establishing a theocratic state. Indeed, he is arguing for the role of a limited minority with the knowledge of *Shari'ah* who would interpret and implement the laws of God. Moreover, according to Maudoodi's calculations, among those who claim to be Muslims, the percentage with any knowledge of Islam is not more than .001%.[19] With his exclusive claim over knowledge of the *Shari'ah*, Maudoodi throws all those outside the pale of Islam who do not accept his interpretation of the *Shari'ah*. If one looks into the practical side of this suggestion, it amounts to nothing but limiting suffrage, as the military regime of Pakistan has attempted to do.

Politically, the sovereignty of the people, in its broadest sense, is the right of the people to elect their own representatives to run the affairs of state. But Maudoodi considers the people to be incapable of electing their representatives and therefore denies them this right. Even in the West those people get elected, he asserts,

> who can fool the people on the basis of their knowledge, wealth and shrewdness. If we analyse this so-called Western democracy which claims that the people are sovereign, we would find that all the people who constitute a state do not make or implement the laws.[20]

Maulana Maudoodi goes on to state that when

> laws are made with the will of the people, experience has shown that the common people themselves cannot understand their interests. It is a natural weakness of human beings that in most matters relating to their life they

consider some aspects of the matter and overlook others; generally their judgement is one-sided.[21]

Thus according to the Maulana, the majority of humans are incapable of understanding their interests, and their judgement is mostly one-sided, which he asserts is a natural and God-given state of affairs. If this is true, then who has this capacity? How does one gain it? Is this capacity genetically determined? Can some overcome this weakness, or is it eternal? The answer that history puts forward is that people learn from their own mistakes and the mistakes of others, and experience is the only school in which they learn to overcome their weakness. Maulana Maudoodi, however, seems to consider this weakness as eternal. If he accepts that this weakness can be overcome, then there would be no justification for establishing the hegemony of those whom he considers to be capable of thinking.

Maulana Maudoodi has also defined the position of those who are chosen to implement the laws of God in his 'Islamic state'. He quotes verse fifty-five from *Sura Al Noor*: 'God has promised to those of you who believe and do righteous deeds that he will make them succeed (*khalifa*) on earth as he made those before them.' Maulana Maudoodi then states that this verse elaborates two fundamental points for the theory of the state in Islam: 1) that Islam advocates *khilāfat* (this he translates as 'vice-gerency') instead of 'sovereignty'; 2) that the promise of *khilāfat* is for all the *maumins* and is a vice-gerency.[22] It is important to bear in mind that there is no mention of the word 'state' in the *sura* from which the Maulana quotes. Succession or vice-gerency is promised on earth, not in a state. Even if the verse is taken in its political sense, as Maulana Maudoodi does, then the promise of God is for those who do righteous deeds, and the people as the keepers of the promise would choose those as their representatives and rulers whom they find doing righteous deeds. Deeds of righteousness in Islam mean doing good to other human beings, not concern for one's own personal salvation, and not simply knowledge of Islamic history and the *Sharī'ah*. The concept of doing good or righteous deeds is necessarily social; honesty and justice are the best virtues according to Islam, because they involve the good of others. Thus the community organised in Medina enjoyed compulsory charity for orphans widows, elderly, travellers and the poor. However, in the present social order, the concept of righteousness cannot be practised as long as the existing socio-economic system based on the exploitation of the majority by a minority exists. Charity could have been a social good in the days when the weak and poor lived at the expense of the rich, but this is not possible in a system where the rich live at the expense of the poor, where the system is such that a vast majority must remain poor so that a tiny minority can remain rich.

After equating an authoritarian state based on limited suffrage with *khilāfat*, Maulana Maudoodi has tried to establish the authority of the state, referring to verse fifty-nine in *Sura Al Nisa*, which lays out general principles of submission to authority:

> O you who believe, obey Allah and his Prophet and those among you who have authority; and then if you differ on anything among yourselves, refer to Allah and his Messenger. If you really believe in the last day, this is the best and fairest way of settlement.

Contrary to Maulana Maudoodi's interpretation, there is no suggestion in this verse of a coercive apparatus of the state for implementing the laws of God. Submission is required to 'authority' (by implication, lawful authority) and not to the coercive power of the state.

For Maulana Maudoodi, the verse from *Sura Al Nisa* 'is the first clause of the manifesto of the Islamic state and the basis of Islam's religious, civic and political set-up'.[23] In this interpretation of submission to those in authority, he reduces the religious, civic and political life of the Muslims to submission and obedience. However, instead of asking Muslims to obey the state directly, Maulana Maudoodi states that

> the concept of *ul ul amr* [the word used in the Qur'ān for those who hold authority] is for all those who are responsible for the collective affairs of the Muslims: they may be the intellectual and theoretical leaders of the Muslims, the *'ulamā*;[24] or the ones who provide political guidance, the leaders; or the ones who manage the affairs of the country, the admistrators; or the ones who make decisions in the court, the judges; or the ones who guide in *muhallas* and *bastis* and tribes in civic and social affairs, the sheikhs and sardars. In short, who has authority in whatever capacity among Muslims deserves obedience. It is not correct to dispute with them and disturb the life of the community.[25]

In contrast to the Maulana's concept, the Qur'ān stipulates that authority should be based on the prestige that one wins through good deeds and is not premised on coercion. Moreover, the authority of *ul ul amr* cannot be identified with political power, because power and authority are not synonymous. Authority is social power that a person or a group believes to be legitimate, proper and justified. The only test of the effectiveness of authority is its voluntary acceptance by the people, whereas power relies on coercive means to realise its effectiveness in case of non-compliance.

Organs of the State

Having stated that authority is based on coercion and power, Maulana Maudoodi proceeds to deal with the nature of the three main organs of the state — the legislature, the judiciary and the executive. He equates the modern legislature with the body that formed the consultative body during the time of the Prophet and the *rightly guided* caliphs called the *shoora*.[26] Maulana Maudoodi uses the term *ahl al hal wa al aqd* (capable of resolving issues and prescribing solutions) and ascribes the *shoora* the following four tasks: 1) to make rules and regulations for the implementation of the Qur'ān and *Sunnah*; 2) to select one interpretation where the injunctions of the Qur'ān and *Sunnah* can have more than one interpretation; 3) to look into the books of *fiqh* for laws on issues for which there are no injunctions in the Qur'ān and *Sunnah*; and 4) to make laws on matters on which there is no provision in the Qur'ān, *Sunnah* or *fiqh*.[27] The modern judiciary for Maulana Maudoodi is similar to the institution of *qazis*, which existed in the days of the caliphs: '*Qazis* were appointed by the *khalifa*. After the appointment of the *qazi*, even the *khalifa* could not influence his decisions.'[28] The institution of the executive in a present-day Islamic state, Maulana Maudoodi states, 'is the same thing which the Qur'ān calls *ul ul amr*'.[29]

While discussing the relationship between the three organs of the state in Islam, Maulana Maudoodi states, 'there are no instructions for this'.[30] This is precisely because these institutions did not exist then, and society did not need such elaborate institutions to manage its affairs. But Maulana Maudoodi appears determined to establish a relationship between the state in Islamic history and a modern authoritarian state:

> We get complete guidance from the practice of the Prophet and the caliphs that . . . the president is the head of all the three organs of the state. This was the position of the Prophet and the caliphs.[31]

Maulana Maudoodi's understanding of the three institutions of the modern state seems to be inadequate, and in an attempt to justify an authoritarian state, he gives unlimited powers to the chief executive. In Maulana Maudoodi's opinion the chief executive can overrule the decisions of the legislature (*ahl al hal wa al aqd*). The actual responsibility for organising the affairs of the state falls on the president, who is bound to consult *ahl al hal wa al aqd* but is not bound to act in accordance with their majority or unanimous decisions. 'In other words, he has the right to veto.'[32] The will or personal judgement of the president is made final and absolute, and there is no check on his authority. The head of state is indeed the 'paramount' authority.

Dealing with the formation of the government Maulana Maudoodi says that 'the most important issue is the appointment of the head of state, in Islam given different names — *imam*, *amir* and *khalifa*'.[33] Regarding the method of his appointment, he suggests, 'we would have to have recourse to the early history of Islam'. The Maulana admits, however, that

> there is no fixed method for this in Islam. Different methods can be adopted according to the needs and requirements of the situation, provided that such a method can reasonably tell who enjoys the confidence of the people.[34]

The president, as we have seen, is the linchpin of Maulana Maudoodi's theory of the Islamic state. Referring to the period of the caliphs, Maudoodi makes the following assertion:

> He was not just the president of the state but the prime minister as well. He attended the parliament himself, presided over its meeting and fully participated in its debates. He was responsible for the affairs of his government and accounted for his personal affairs as well. He had neither an official party nor an opposition party; the entire parliament acted as his party as long as he followed the right path, and the whole parliament acted as the opposition party if he followed the wrong path. Each member was free to oppose or support his decisions; even his own ministers used to oppose him in the parliament. Nevertheless, the president and his cabinet got along very well; no one ever resigned from his office. The *khalifa* was answerable not only to the parliament, but to the entire *qaum* [nation] for all his activities, even concerning his private life.[35] He faced the public five times a day in the mosque and addressed them at Friday prayers. People could find him in the streets and *muhallas*, and anybody could stop him to ask for his rights. Not only could the members of parliament question him on prior notice but anyone could ask him questions at public places.[36]

No account of Islamic history gives an interpretation of the *khilāfat* like that of Maulana Maudoodi. Except for his account of the relationship prior to the expansion of the caliphate, when direct contact with the community was possible due to the small size of the society, the rest of the Maulana's account appears to be motivated by his political philosophy. In contrast to the Maulana's interpretation, the principle that can be derived from the practices of the caliphs is that they held the *'umma* more important than the ruler.

To analyse the nature and formation of the legislative assembly, Maulana Maudoodi again has recourse to the history of the early years of Islam and shows how the *majlis-i-shoora* of the Prophet was formed:

> The message of Islam started in Mecca in the form of a movement, and it is characteristic of all movements that those who take initiative to join the movement first become the companions, friends and advisers of the leader. In Islam as well, those who joined the movement first naturally became the companions and advisers of the Prophet, whom he consulted on matters for which there was no clear commandment from God. Gradually, more people entered the fold of Islam, and the struggle with hostile forces intensified. During the course of this struggle, those persons came to the forefront who showed wisdom and rendered extraordinary services and made sacrifices. Their selection was not made through elections but through test and experience — a natural method and better than election. Hence, two categories of people entered the Prophet's *majlis-i-shoora* before his

migration to Medina and enjoyed the confidence of Muslims, similar to that the Prophet himself enjoyed.[37]

In Medina, Maulana Maudoodi continues,

the movement of Islam took the shape of a political system and a state. Now it was natural that the people who played a central role in the spread of Islam in Medina should have assumed positions of leadership in the new society. The *ansārs*, a third category, also entered the Prophet's *majlis-i-shoora*. These people were also selected through the natural method, but they were such respected leaders of the Muslim tribes that even under the modern system of elections they would have been elected. Later, in the society of Medina, two new categories of people rose to prominence: (1) those who performed extraordinarily in the military and missionary campaigns of the previous eight or ten years, to whom people looked for advice on all important matters; (2) those who gained a reputation on the basis of their knowledge of the Qur'ān, as the *fuqahā* of *dīn*. They were considered authorities on *dīn*, and the Prophet himself sanctioned their authority by asking people to consult them on matters relating to the Qur'ān and *dīn*. These two categories also entered the *majlis-i-shoora* by the natural method.[38]

Maulana Maudoodi's view of the role of the consultative assembly contradicts his theory that the chief executive has the power to veto even their unanimous decisions:

Ahl al hal wa al aqd were, during the period of the rightly guided caliphs, appointed and were entitled to make decisions on all important matters concerning the *millat*. Therefore, there is no reason to assume that the *khalifa* could call for consultation anybody whom he liked.[39]

The principle that the Maulana himself infers for the selection of members of the *majlis-i-shoora* contradicts his previous contention about the inability of the common people to choose their representatives. He goes on to remark:

From the practice of the caliphs and even from the traditions of the Prophet, the principle that can be inferred is that the *amir* does not consult all the people, nor does he consult the people of his own choice, but those who enjoy the confidence of the Muslim masses, whose sincerity and ability people trust, whose participation in government decisions would ensure that the implementation of these decisions enjoys the wholehearted support of the people.[40]

Then Maulana Maudoodi tries to find the method of forming a *majlis-i-shoora* today:

. . . the specific conditions that existed in the early days of Islam do not exist today. Even the obstacles that existed then do not exist today. Hence we can use all established and possible methods to find out who enjoys the confidence of the people, in accordance with our present needs and situations. The present system of elections is also one of the 'just' methods.[41]

These contradictory assertions of Maulana Maudoodi are rooted in his erroneous method of constructing a model of an Islamic state by looking for parallels to modern institutions and concepts in the history of early Islam. Here he offers the following comment about the state he would like to establish:

This system of government, to which none of the modern concepts can be applied, is in consonance with the temperament of Islam and is our ideal. It can only become practicable when society has been fully prepared in accordance with the revolutionary principles of Islam.[42]

The Authoritarian State

Maulana Maudoodi's method of organising society in accordance with the revolutionary principles of Islam is to use the coercive power of the state. Granting religious sanction for the use of force, he says 'Allah prevents all those things using the power of the state, which the Qur'ān does not prevent'.[43] He further says, 'reforms that Islam wants to introduce cannot be introduced just by preaching. To implement them, political power is needed.'[44] Maulana Maudoodi thus prepares the ground for an authoritarian state based on coercion. This justification for authoritarianism to implement Islam is not in keeping with the spirit of Islam. The traces of an authoritarian state cannot be found in the society of Medina at the time of the Prophet.

The modern state apparatus and its repressive character are results of the subordination of all forces to its own interests, including those which helped the bourgeoisie gain political power. The objective was not to organise society on the basis of equity and justice but to make individuals conform to the conditions of a new kind of exploitation. To organise a society in the present situation on the basis of equity and justice, it is necessary to understand the mechanics of the existing socio-economic system in its national and international context. Maulana Maudoodi's thesis that organising society in accordance with the revolutionary principles of Islam in the prevailing socio-economic conditions requires coercion is an attempt to legitimise repression in the interest of those who hold economic and political power. The basis of their power is not any Islamic principle but their self-interest in the prevailing socio-economic conditions.

Maulana Maudoodi's justification for an authoritarian state is based on his own understanding of human nature, according to which coercion is essential for organising civic life:

> It is obvious that to organise collective life, in all circumstances there is a need for a coercive power, which is called the state. No one has ever denied this need except for the anarchists, or communist theory, which contemplates a stage when humanity would not need a collective state. All these are idealistic contemplations which cannot be supported by observation and experience . . . Human history and the knowledge of human nature show that the establishment of civic life is essentially dependent on a coercive power.[45]

His account of the development of civic life in Medina, where the first city-state of the Muslims developed under the guidance of the Prophet, however, contradicts his rhetoric of coercion. To judge the validity of Maulana Maudoodi's understanding of human nature, one need only go through an account of primitive times. It would show that there was a time when there was no state. What existed then was a patriarchal family or clan family; people lived according to kinship and tribal relationships. It would show the predominance of custom and respect for the authority of clan elders. Hence, there was a time when a state with special apparatuses for systematic repression to subjugate the people did not exist.

However, in Maulana Maudoodi's concept, the coercive role of the state is self-justifying, and he sees the success of coercion in absolute terms:

> Not just the collective but the personal life of the people, willingly or unwillingly, is moulded by the state with coercion and domination. Those who live in a state and yet do not agree with its basic philosophy and plan of action and are not willing to accept it — they too have to give up 90 percent of their faith and belief in favour of the beliefs and philosophy of the state. On the remaining 10 percent they gradually lose their grip.[46]

Except for the fascist and Nazi states, such a state has never existed, and no historical account validates this experience. Nor did those states succeed in the absolute conversion of the people to Nazi and fascist points of view. In other bourgeois democratic states, the existence of differences of opinion is considered to be essential for a healthy civic life. Moreover, the attempt to establish tyranny is quite contrary to the injunctions of the Qur'ān, where there is a strong disapproval of compulsion in matters of faith:

> There is no compulsion in religion (*Sura al Baqr*, verse 256).

> If it had been God's will all the people on earth would have believed. Will you then compel people until they become believers against their will? (*Sura Yunus*, verse 99)

> And do not dispute with the possessors of the Book, but argue in the most argumentative manner, except for those who are unjust and tyrants (*Sura Ankboot*, verse 46).

Despite the prohibition of compulsion in matters of religion Maulana Maudoodi appears bent upon implementing Islam with the coercive power of the state and goes to the extent of equating the state with *dīn*:

> In fact, the word '*dīn*' has the same meaning as 'state' at present. Acceptance and submission by the people to a paramount authority are required in the state. This is the meaning of *dīn* as well.[47]

Hence, since *dīn* is all-pervasive, the state would also be all-pervasive, its scope extending to all walks of human life:

> The sphere of activity of this kind of state (Islamic state) cannot be limited. It is an all-encompassing state. Its sphere of activity includes all walks of human life. It intends to mould all the departments of civic and social life in accordance with its own ethical philosophy and reformatory programme. No one can avoid its intervention in any matter by saying that the matter is related to his personal life.[48]

According to this concept, there is no sphere of human activity, including human thought, where the state cannot step in. Yet, the Maulana asserts that 'despite its all-pervasiveness it is not like a present-day totalitarian or authoritarian state. In this state, personal freedom is not withdrawn.'[49] Anyone acquainted with history or politics would say that this is an argument for a totalitarian and authoritarian state. In the present socio-economic context, Maulana Maudoodi's theory of the Islamic state serves only the interests of the exploiting classes.

In the Islamic state, Maulana Maudoodi asserts, there is no place for differences of opinion or for political parties:

> If you wish to organise your political and economic life in accordance with the teachings of Islam, then you need not divide yourself into different parties. Only one party, the *Hizb-i-Allah* (the party of God) is sufficient for all these tasks. Why? Because in an Islamic society there is no conflict between capitalists and workers, landlords and peasants, rulers and the ruled.[50]

The Maulana is unable to recognise the fact that the modern capitalist society which has come to dominate most of the Muslim World is not organised on the egalitarian principles of Islam, but on an exploitative social order. Hence he does not acknowledge or accept differences and inequalities in society. This refusal has led him and the *Jamā'at-i-Islāmī* to lend support to the repressive measures of various regimes in Pakistan. Within the past decade, the *Jamā'at* rejected the national aspirations of the Bengali Muslims and supported military action in East Pakistan (now Bangladesh). It welcomed the present military government and joined its ministries. It strongly opposed trade union activities until it felt the need to organise its own labour bureau. In the early years of Bhutto's regime, when the labour movement was gaining momentum, it unleashed a campaign against the *Qadianis*, and the struggle of the working class was defused by giving a religious colour to the political climate.

The Muslim Community — Monolithic or Diverse?

To establish his version of an Islamic state, Maulana Maudoodi presents a monolithic concept of the Muslim community. This cannot be justified by any account of the development of the Muslim community, whether in the Middle East, Africa or the Indo-Pakistan subcontinent. In the spread of Islam in the subcontinent, the Indian Muslim community was homogeneous neither in its origin nor in its formation.[51] Maulana Maudoodi, however, is not willing to accept the diverse nature of the community and says that Islam came to eliminate national, ethnic and racial differences:

> Besides the ignorance of *kufr* and *shirk*, if there was any enemy of Islam it was the satan of *watan* and race . . . If you pick up the books of *Ahadīth* you would find how the Prophet fought against distinction based on blood, soil, colour, language and social status.[52]

No one denies the Prophet's struggle against these distinctions and differences. But present society is not the continuation of the society established by the Prophet. The tradition of the Prophet's struggle against inequalities and distinctions cannot be kept alive by refusing to accept the existence of these differences. To eliminate these differences from present-day society, the socio-economic set-up that gives rise to these differences and inequalities would have to be eliminated. More-over, Islam's message of the unity of the *'umma* does not preclude particular distinctive features and aspirations of different people constituting the *'umma*. Nor does it allow the stronger sections of the *'umma* to exploit and live at the expense of the weaker sections of society. Simply denying the existence of these differences amounts to nothing but supporting the oppression and exploitation of the weak at the hands of the strong. It serves as a justification for the existence of social privileges and inequalities and for the continuation of exploitation. In short, it is a justification for all kinds of injustice.

To strengthen his argument, Maulana Maudoodi declares that Muslims are neither a community nor a nation but a party in the modern sense of the word. For this purpose, he extracts words from the Qur'ān and tries to show them to be in consonance with the word 'party'. 'The word that the

Qur'ān has used for the community of Muslims', the Maulana states, 'is *hizb*, which means party.' He then compares it with the word 'nation': 'the basis of a nation is race and descent, and the basis of a party is its programme and principles . . . therefore, Muslims in reality are not a nation but a party.'[53] This rather primitive definition of the word 'nation' relates to times when only race and descent were the basis of distinction among various peoples and the basis for the formation of communities. Modern nation-states are not formed on the basis of race or descent alone. For example, the American nation or the Russian nation today is not constituted into a nation on the basis of common race or common descent alone.

Another word that is used in the Qur'ān for Muslims in the sense of 'party', according to the Maulana, is *'umma*:

> '*Umma* is that *jamā'at* which has been formed by some unifying factor. The people who have something in common are called *'umma*; people belonging to a historical period can form an *'umma*, and those people belonging to one race or a country are also called *'umma*. But the common factor that makes Muslims an *'umma* is not racial, regional or economic — it is the mission of their life and principles and the programme of their party.[54]

This cannot provide a basis for declaring Muslims a party, because parties exist in Muslim countries today which are organised on regional and economic grounds, with well-defined programmes and principles. To work for the implementation of a party programme is the mission of the members of a political party. None of the modern concepts can be applied to the society of the time of the Prophet and the caliphs, as Maulana Maudoodi tries to do. The same is true of the modern concept of a party. It seems that what Maulana Maudoodi had in mind was a political party, but even then the equation is not valid. Historically, the political party emerged with the development of representative institutions and the expansion of suffrage in the 19th century. The institution of the political party has undergone changes in its structure and functions with the advance in political processes and the increase of political consciousness among the people.

We have seen that Maulana Maudoodi's theory of the Islamic state is a justification for an authoritarian state. If the sovereign is accepted as the vice-gerent of God, entitled to intervene in all spheres of human activity including thought and conscience, it would provide a justification for coercion in the name of religion. The head of the state, whatever the means by which he assumed his office, is the paramount authority for organising and deciding the affairs of the community. The legislature would, according to Maulana Maudoodi, simply be a consultative body. It would be a one-party state because, according to Maudoodi, Muslims are themselves a party without any economic, political, social or regional differences. One may therefore conclude that Maudoodi's 'Islamic state' is a device to give religious cover to what may otherwise appear to be the arbitrary and tyrannical acts of the ruling hierarchy.

References and Notes

1. The Constituent Assembly of Pakistan consisted of deputies who were elected in 1946 to the Constituent Assembly of united India by the provincial legislatures on the basis of one seat for one million inhabitants.

2. The Chief Minister of East Pakistan presented a list of demands on 1 March 1948, in the Constituent Assembly, concerning centre-province relations. The foremost demand was for a fair and proper share in the armed forces. The Prime Minister in his reply refused to accept any differences between the central and provincial governments and suggested 'we must kill this provincialism'. On another occasion, in response to the demand to use Bengali in the Constituent Assembly along with Urdu, the Prime Minister replied as follows:

> Pakistan is a Muslim state, and it must have its lingua franca, the language of the Muslim nation . . . Pakistan has been created because of the demand of one hundred million Muslims, and the language of one hundred million Muslims is Urdu . . .

See Keith Callard, *Pakistan: A Political Study* (Oxford University Press, 1968), pp. 174 and 182.

3. For details see Zafaryab Ahmed. 'The Mass Movement — 1968-69' (Master's thesis, Department of Political Science, University of the Punjab, 1976).

4. The *Jamā'at-i-Islāmī* was formed on 26 August 1941, fifteen months after the passing of the Lahore Resolution. It opposed the struggle of the Muslims for a national state. However, Maulana Maudoodi came to settle in Pakistan and started a campaign for an Islamic state.

5. Maulana Maudoodi died in September 1979.

6. Abul Ala Maudoodi, *Islamī Riyasat* (Lahore: Islamic Publications Ltd., 1969), p. 127. All quotations from Maulana Maudoodi's works referred to in this chapter are translations by the author from Urdu.

7. Ibid., pp. 313-4.

8. Ibid., p. 317

9. Ibid., p. 314.

10. Ibid., p. 319.

11. Ibid.

12. G. H. Sabine, *A History of Political Theory* (London: George G. Harrap and Co. Ltd., 1963), p. 399.

13. Ibid., p. 406.

14. Ibid., p. 408.

15. Maudoodi, *Islamī Riyasat*, p. 129.

16. Ibid.

17. It should be pointed out here that the emphasis on 'only Muslims' does not exclude only non-Muslims, but Muslim women as well. In Maulana Maudoodi's Islamic state, the domain of a woman in her home, and

women should not mix with men because males can be 'lured' away by women from vital tasks. The Maulana's work entitled *Purdah* deals with the position of women in society. See for details Sayyed Abdul Ala Maudoodi, *Purdah* (Lahore: Islamic Publications Ltd., 22 Muharam 1359 A. H.).

18. Maudoodi, *Islamī Riyasat*, p. 130.

19. Abul Ala Maudoodi, *Tehrik-i-Azadī-i-Hind-aur Mussalman*, part II (Lahore: Islamic Publications Ltd., 1983), p. 140.

20. Maudoodi, *Islamī Riyasat*, 131.

21. Ibid., p. 132.

22. Ibid., pp. 139-40.

23. Ibid., p. 185.

24. It should be noted that Maulana Maudoodi separates religious from political authority, whereas he is strongly opposed to the division between religion and politics.

25. Maudoodi, *Islamī Riyasat*, p. 186.

26. The term *rightly-guided* caliphs used here means those who are generally accepted as having followed in the footsteps of the Prophet.

27. Maudoodi, *Islamī Riyasat*, pp. 323/4.

28. Ibid., p. 328.

29. Ibid., p. 325.

30. Ibid., p. 328.

31. Ibid.

32. Ibid., p. 331.

33. Ibid., p. 336.

34. Ibid., p. 340.

35. It appears that Maulana Maudoodi is averse to using the word *qaum* for the Muslim community.

36. Maudoodi, *Islamī Riyasat*, p. 345.

37. The choice of candidates in the modern electoral system is also made on the basis of the services that the candidate and his party have rendered to the community in the constituency and the country at large. It is difficult to understand the fine distinction Maudoodi is trying to make.

38. Maudoodi, *Islamī Riyasat*, pp. 341-2.

39. Ibid., p. 343.

40. Ibid., p. 344.

41. Ibid.

42. Ibid., p. 346.

43. Ibid., p. 57.

44. Ibid.

45. Ibid., p. 67.

46. Ibid., p. 68.

47. Maudoodi, *Tehrik-i-Azadī-i-Hind*, p. 123.

48. Maudoodi, *Islamī Riyasat*, p. 136.

49. Ibid.

50. Ibid., p. 47.

51. Almost all accounts of the Indian Muslim community highlight this fact. See Ishtiaq Hussain Qureshi, *The Muslim Community of Indo-Pakistan* (Karachi: Ma'aref Limited, 1977); Mohammad Yasin. *A Social History of Islamic Indian* Lucknow: The Upper India Publishing House, 1958); M. Mujeeb, *The Indian Muslims* (London: Allen and Unwin), 1967); Peter Hardy *The*

Muslims of British India (Cambridge: Cambridge University Press, 1972).
    52. Maudoodi, *Islamī Riyasat*, p. 222.
    53. Ibid., p. 246.
    54. Ibid., p. 249.

5. Islamisation of Society in Pakistan

by Ziaul Haque

Introduction

The recent history of Pakistan, which has been characterised by political instability, is a classic case of a comprador regime based on a weak national bourgeoisie, a degenerate semifeudal structure and an over-developed bureaucracy. In such a situation foreign interference, while bolstering authoritarian regimes, has played an important role in perpetuating feudalistic-comprador capitalism. The problems of economic retardation, general poverty and political instability in Pakistan are exacerbated by the blatant manipulation of Islamic/religious ideology. This ideology is based on vague notions and mediaevalistic categories of thought and is articulated in servile subservience to foreign capital. The basic aim of the 'Islamisation' process, as will be substantiated in the course of the following discussion, is to justify the existing economic relationships and the status quo by obfuscating the immediate socio-economic problems of the masses.

As this chapter is an appraisal of the process of 'Islamisation' of society and economy, it would be appropriate to define clearly what is meant by Islam. The term has been grossly misunderstood and misused — sometimes tendentiously — by scholars, statesmen, politicians, and apologists of capitalism (and even Islamic socialism). As every ruling class needs an ideology to perpetuate its rule, Islam has been variously interpreted throughout the centuries in the Muslim World by different classes, political groups, autocratic rulers, fundamentalists, modernists and religious fanatics. Unless the concept of Islam is clearly defined, emotive and confusing terms like 'militant Islam', 'upsurge of Islam', 'renaissance of Islam', 'Islamic democracy', 'Islamic economics', 'Islamic science', etc. cannot be correctly understood. For simplicity's sake, all such interpretations in this chapter have been categorised into 1) original or revolutionary Islam of the Qur'ānic conception; 2) feudal or mediaeval Islam; and 3) capitalist or bourgeois Islam — the forms of interpretation which actually pertain to different historical periods, socio-economic formations and conditions of mediaeval and modern times.

The Phenomenon of Underdevelopment

The economies of developing societies are in the main dependent on the advanced capitalist countries and form a part of the international capitalist system. They are bound to the metropolitan centres of the rich countries. The political independence of these former colonies and semicolonies did not lead to economic independence because the colonial social and economic structures remained more or less intact. Hence, the larger economic decisions of what to produce, how to produce and for whom to produce in these economies remained in the hands of indigenous ruling elites and foreign colonialists. As the modern world has come to be divided into two polarised economic systems of capitalism and socialism, with antagonistic models and world-views, the social and economic problems of Third World countries have been aggravated for lack of a coherent plan, purpose, direction and identity. They vacillate between the two poles. Economic chaos, social anarchy and intellectual confusion are the natural outcome of their general aimlessness.

The economy of the modern world is thus divided into a small number of advanced and rich countries and a large number of poor and developing countries. The poor countries of the Third World are internally divided into a tiny minority of rich people, who own the basic means of production, and a vast majority of working people, who sell their labour power to the former in order to live. Pakistan, as a part of this amorphous conglomerate of developing societies, shares many traits of a retarded social and economic development on the one hand and political instability on the other. Such a situation is due to 1) the weakness of the ruling elite in relation to international monopoly capitalism; 2) the lack of homogeneity among the ruling classes and the resultant contradictions among them; and 3) the deep dissatisfaction and discontent of the lower social classes of the working proletariat, who are deprived by the rulers of the basic necessities of life and of cultural amenities. That foreign capital can cause instability in these developing countries, where native ruling classes are weak, is a well-known fact of modern history.[1]

After 37 years of political independence, Pakistan is still a semicolonial and semifeudal country inexorably tied to international monopoly capitalism through economic processes and 'planning' in which economic surplus is generated and concentrated in the hands of the capitalists at the cost of the working classes. These processes and planning for capitalism, have ultimately resulted in the strengthening of the feudal lords in the countryside and the rise of a comprador bourgeoisie in the urban areas, with other parasitic elements connected with the exploiting classes. In spite of efforts aimed at industrialisation (of the import-substitution type), Pakistan in the mid-1980s is still characterised by three overlapping and interpenetrating socio-economic formations: pastoral-tribal, as in the north-western tribal belts of NWFP and Baluchistan; semifeudal, as in the interior of Punjab and Sind; and 'capitalist', as in the urban industrial enclaves where modern industrial and finance capital has concentrated and ensconced itself, confortably spreading its tentacles all over the country.

These pastoral-tribal, feudal and capitalist systems and subsystems are marked by specific and exclusive socio-economic relationships such as those between tribal chiefs and their illiterate *raiyyat* (subjects), feudal lords and their 'serfs', and capitalists and their wage-labourers. All these social formations and economic systems in various unevenly developed regions are bound in a subservient relationship to the powerful international monopoly capitalism of powerful multinational corporations through thousands of threads: economic, financial, political, cultural and intellectual. The capitalist mode of production is thus predominant.

This confluence of various and simultaneous social formations and their concomitant systems also corresponds to different and conflicting intellectual perceptions embedded in traditional religion and modern science. In Europe, one formation succeeded the other in history; capitalism replaced feudalism, and the rising class of the modern bourgeoisie wrested power from the effete feudal classes. But in Pakistan, the weak ruling classes, instead of propagating science and reason, are seeking desperately through religious dogma and superstitution to try to abridge a frightening gap of several centuries. This approach cannot succeed, for Muslim society in modern times has witnessed no industrial, social and intellectual revolutions, no renaissance of the sciences and no reformation of traditional religious attitudes.

Revolutionary Islam

The original or Qur'ānic concept of Islam is essentially revolutionary. This statement needs explanation and qualification. The Qur'ān is a holy book of revealed truths. It is a niche, a receptacle of truths both natural and social, and the discovery of knowledge was condensed in a religious framework which was readily understood by the Arabs of a prefeudal pastoral tribal society, since the Qur'ān was revealed in the Arabic idiom. It comprises 114 *sūras* or chapters. It was divinely revealed to the holy Prophet Mohammad Ibn 'Abd Allah Ibn 'Abd al-Muttalib in Mecca and Medina in the years 610-632 — a period of almost 23 years. The verses of the Qur'ān (90 Meccan and 24 Medinan) relate in general to the social, political, economic, religious, spiritual and intellectual conditions of a community of revolutionaries headed by this great Prophet-revolutionary (570-632), who was born in Mecca in the tribe of Hāsham of the merchant clan of Quraysh. He was a poor orphan and grew up as an extremely honest young man, whom even his enemies called *sādiq* (truthful) and *amīn* (trustworthy).[2] He grew up in a society which was riven with moral corruption, deep social inequality and religious and social decadence. It was a tribal society surrounded by feudalist regimes of Byzantium (at that time part of the Eastern Roman empire), Persia and Ethiopia.

After his call to Prophethood in 610, the Prophet preached the divine message of the unity of God, unity of mankind (in place of the anarchic atomism of the tribal system) and human equality to the people of Mecca. The early converts were the people of lowly social origins — slaves, artisans, blacksmiths, carpenters, masons, tribal outcastes, women and orphans — the pariah people who had no rights and no privileges.[3]

This community of early revolutionaries arose in Mecca gradually, and so also grew the opposition of the oligarchy of rich merchants of the Quraysh, the tribal chiefs and the privileged priestly class, whose social and economic power was now threatened. The new converts were ridiculed, humiliated and persecuted. They were called *sābi'un*, the godless heretics, sorcerers and foreign agents. Their leader, the Prophet-revolutionary, was labelled a madman (*majnūn*), a sorcerer-magician (*sāhir*) a poet (*shāir*) and a soothsayer (*kāhin*), because the new movement had ripped apart society — alienating father from son, brother from brother, mother from child and husband from wife, thus tearing the social fabric apart and uprooting the tribal structures and the vested interests attached to them.[4] The decadent social order was overthrown, privileges challenged, and autocrats and the mercantile oligarchy threatened. The entire structure of this unjust tribal society was thus menaced. The priests, the usurers, the merchants, the landlords of agricultural settlements and the exploiters of the weak saw in the new movement their ultimate ruin.[5] They formed a formidable alliance to kill the Prophet and crush the rising slaves and workers. The Prophet and his followers left their hearths and homes, their wealth and families, in search of a new world and a new order of equality and justice which the Qur'ān had promised them. This was the famous *Hijra*, or migration for their cause (622), when they left for Yathrib (afterwards Medina).

The Qur'ān has termed this movement 'Islam' (literally, *aslama* means to surrender or submit to the will, cause or way of God).[6] This Qur'ānic term actually means a prophet's submission or surrender to the way and laws of God to seek His countenance, His will, i.e. the divine cause, His unity etc.[7] Translated from the religious to the social plane, the term means the establishment of a regime of social and economic equality and the abolition of all injustices and inequalities of privileges and wealth which impede the fullest development of natural faculties and potentialities of all human beings. Religious rites such as prayers and fasting are a means to achieve these social ends. The Qur'ān also uses the term 'Islam' in opposition to *kufr*. A *kafir* is a person who denies the truth of Islam, who, according to the Qur'ān, may believe in God, as a Christian or a Jew does, if he does not believe in the unity of God and the unity of mankind and its corollary, the social and economic equality of human beings, he is not a Muslim. *Kufr* and *batil* (falsehood) both denote falsehood, and Islam and *haqq* are both truth.[8] Islam is therefore the establishment of truth in society, and as the Qur'ān implies, the concept of this truth may vary from time to time. Under the specific pastoral conditions of biblical times, under the tribal milieu of *Hijāz* and under the industrial conditions of modern times, truth acquires different shapes. Consequently, conceptions of truth and falsehood change under different conditions. But ideally, says the Qur'ān, Islam stands for truth (*haqq*) against the forces of *kufr* and *batil*. Islam is the way of life — *dīn* — based on social equality and justice (*adl*); *kufr* is the way of life based on inequality and *zulm* (exploitation, transgression). According to the Qur'ān, there are in general three broad social classes: *al-mustakbarūn*, the rich who deny the truth of divine unity and social equality of mankind; *al-mustad'afūn*, the poor who believe in this truth; and *al-munāfiqūn*, the hypocrites who vacillate between these two classes. They belong neither to this nor to that but waver between *haqq* and *batil* in the quagmire of opportunism.

'Feudal Islam'

The ideal of one God and one community exemplified in the perfect social equality of all the believers/revolutionaries in the classless egalitarian society was termed Islam by the Qur'ān. Social equality was the *grundnorm*, the ideal and the cornerstone of early Muslim society. The subsequent abolition of ground-rent, usury/interest (*ribā*), *muzāra'a* and all speculative/exploitative economic practices and the emancipation of the lower social classes, slaves, women and orphans initiated by the Prophet were the beginnings of this revolution. But this social revolution was short-lived. It could not be consolidated. The Prophet died before he could finally abolish all the centuries-old exploitative institutions. The civil wars after the death of 'Umar Ibn al-Khattāb, 13-23 AH' (633-44 AD), the second caliph, gave the death blow to this Islamic regime of egalitarianism. The counter-revolution of the Umayyads starting under the third caliph 'Uthman Ibn 'Affān was the finale of this revolutionary ethos of Islam.

The emergence of the Umayyad autocratic regime was really the transformation of revolutionary Islam into a feudal dispensation. How this transformation took place and how the new interpretations of Islam in a feudal society were formulated are other topics, which are beyond the scope of this chapter. Suffice it here to note that the social relationships of kings and subjects, landlords and serfs, masters and slaves were rationalised by the Muslim scholars, mainly the jurists (*fuqahā*), for the social stability of the feudal system. This feudal character is discernible in the social, legal and economic literature produced throughout mediaeval times. The pre-Qur'ānic institutions of ground-rent, interest, usury, landlordism, slavery and hundreds of other exploitative practices were justified by the majority of Muslim jurists through a legal and administrative apparatus erected by the autocrats and ruling classes on the foundations of the pre-Islamic regimes. The legal instruments and concepts elaborated by the jurists, like *qiyās* (analogical reasoning) and *ijmāh* (consensus), gave sanctity to these institutions with a view to consolidating the Muslim community against its formidable enemies.

Let us see how pre-Qur'ānic institutions and concepts were reinterpreted in the feudal/mediaeval period. It is an established fact that the Prophet, in addition to the Qur'ānic ban on usury and interest, had abolished leasing of lands by declaring that lands belonged to those who cultivated them. This negates landlordism in all its forms. But the *fuqahā* rationalised the age-old institution of ground-rent for the reason that the entire political superstructure of their times, the incomes of the ruling classes, were derived mainly from the revenues paid by the peasantry in the form of *kharāj* — taxes.[9]

As there were no financial institutions, like banks, joint-stock companies, industries and stock exchanges etc., mediaeval jurists justified the ancient institution of *mudāraba*, a primitive form of business organisation suitable for distant journeys. It was a pre-Islamic commercial institution (called '*commenda*' in Southern Europe) in which a capital owner entrusted his capital to a worker for some business. They both shared the profit thus earned in pre-agreed proportions, as one-third, two-thirds etc. All loss was borne by the capital owner. Such commercial transactions were carried on in mediaeval times under mediaeval economic conditions when capital could be mobilised only as a usurer's or as a merchant's capital. This has no basis in the Qur'ān or *Hadīth* of the Prophet.[10]

The *fiqhī* Islam, as interpreted by the *fuqahā* of the early and late mediaeval times, reflects the feudalist mode of production and its related social, economic and political relationships based on autocratic monarchies, feudal estates and the existence of serfs and slaves perpetually bound to the soil they tilled from generation to generation. The Qur'ānic terms of *zakāt*, *sadaqā* (alms) and others were also reinterpreted under feudalism. Private property had not developed under early Islam because of the clear abolition of landlordism and because the objective pastoral and tribal conditions of the Arabian peninsula did not encourage it. Therefore early Islam had enunciated that basic needs (*al-'afw*) must be given to the poor in order to level all inequalities.[11] The early evidence shows that orchards and wells — the sources of scarce water and staple food (dates) of the common people — were given as common *waqfs*, mortmains or trusts by Muslims for the use of all whenever the Prophet urged them to do so.[12] Even the Prophet (and his family) subsisted on water and dates throughout his life. Dates were the staple food of the poor.[13]

It has also been reported that no other community of any Prophet faced so large a number of orphans, abandoned women, widows and poor as that of Mohammad Ibn 'Abd Allah.[14] So private property in land was discouraged. *Zakāt* was generally levied on cattle, agricultural produce, money (gold and silver), etc.[15] It appears that the jurists in their literal interpretation of *zakāt* tended to confine its meaning to personal property. Land therefore came to be exempted. But conscientious people voluntarily continued to pay *zakāt* on their land possessions.[16] Under the feudal conditions of society *zakāt* lost its real meaning and content. It was originally a concept which meant transfer of surplus wealth from the rich to the poor in order to level inequalities.

On the face of it, feudal Islam is a negation of Qur'ānic Islam, which stands for social and economic equality. It does not, however, mean that all the great saints and scholars who were also great jurists, like Mohammad ibn Idris al-Shāfi'i (d.204 AH/819-20AD), Abū Hanīfa (d.150 AH/767-8AD), Malik ibn Anas (d.179 AH/795-6AD), Ahmed ibn Hanbal (d.241 AH/855-6AD) and others who justified a number of pre-Islamic social and economic institutions, did not understand the real message and ideal of Qur'ānic Islam. With their intellects and knowledge of the sources of Islam, they made genuine efforts to apply the teachings of Islam to solving contemporary problems, but their efforts were circumscribed and limited by the social formations in which they lived. In their personal lives early scholars like Ahmed ibn Hanbal, Mālik and Abu Hanīfa did not compromise with oppressive and exploitative regimes. But they could not go beyond the contemporary systems and their structures. Their remarkable and ingenious development of Islamic legal principles and sciences to understand and apply the original revolutionary principles of the Qur'ān and the Prophetic *Ahadīth* must be evaluated and appreciated in this context.

'Bourgeois Islam'

In modern times, in particular after the 16th century when European colonialism conquered Muslim societies, capitalism as a modern mode of production began to penetrate them. Its modern phase, imperialism or monopoly capitalism, has succeeded in reducing Muslim societies to dependent economies — mere appendages of more powerful advanced capitalist countries. These developing economies and societies of Muslim lands are ruled by the native upper classes of capitalists, businessmen, landlords, and bureaucrats — both civil and military. These classes are generally in league with the foreign bourgeoisie, who supply them in aid and trade capital goods and the related advanced technology. The economies of Muslim lands have thus become a part of the international capitalist system, and the ruling elite forms a part of imperialist culture and civilisation.

Capitalism is based on the principles of private ownership of the basic means of production by a tiny minority of capitalists, free enterprise, profit motive and exploitation of the working classes. Whereas the original Qur'ānic Islam had abolished interest, usury, ground-rent and all speculative economic transactions, modern capitalism promotes private ownership of the means of production, like land and capital. It develops finance capital, joint-stock companies, stock exchanges and banks. It thrives on the earnings of profits, interest, ground-rent and exploitation of the labour of the working classes. These are clearly antagonistic to the basic teachings of the Qur'ān and the *Ahadīth* of the holy Prophet, which consider all these earnings, incomes and profits *harām* (illicit).

In the wake of the European movements of Renaissance and Reformation after the decline of feudalism, the capitalist mode of production gradually emerged as the dominant mode of production from the 16th century onwards. Subsequently, religion came to be separated not only from the natural and social sciences but also from the state structures. This new social order, liberated by the rising bourgeoisie, was based on reason, science and a democratic/pluralistic political dispensation. In advanced capitalist societies, with the progress of science and industry, religion receded from many areas of thought and action because man now began to control nature. Natural and social phenomena, so avers the modern scientific method, are ruled by laws which the human mind tries to discover. Modern capitalist (and socialist) societies are industrial societies, which have been competing with each other in the discovery of modern scientific knowledge, its application and conquest of nature and the universe. The religious sensibilities of the static feudal ages have therefore given place to rational and scientific perceptions. This means that science and religion, as far as their concepts and historical developments are concerned, belong to two different epochs and milieux. Therefore to term any science 'Islamic', 'Christian' or 'Hindu' would be meaningless because modern science has become universal, and modern society has become international in the sense that all societies share the heritage of science, knowledge and technologies.

Islamic Ideology and the Process of 'Islamisation'

The ruling classes of Pakistan after the 1977 military coup have gradually turned the country into a feudal-comprador regime which has become more servile and subservient than ever before to international monopoly capitalism. Pakistan's ruling elites have ingeniously devised an 'Islamic' ideology to conserve and justify social and economic relationships based on a decadent status quo of feudalism and comprador-capitalism. Knowing that all Muslims have great love for the holy Prophet and Qur'ānic Islam, the ruling classes are exploiting the fair name of Islam and have turned Qur'ānic concepts into institutions which are the citadels of vested interests.

Various 'ideological' institutions have been working in order to help the government (central and provincial) to 'reconstruct society on truly Islamic lines'. The Council of 'Islamic' Ideology, 'Islamic' Research Institute, 'Islamic' University and scores of other 'Islamic' institutions are aiding the ruling classes in their efforts to 'Islamise' the present social and economic structures of moribund feudalism and capitalism. By 'Islamisation', the present rulers mean transformation of society according to the basic teachings of Qur'ānic Islam. In actual practice, as has been discussed elsewhere, the ruling elites are appealing to the historical categories of feudalist Islam, that is, pre-Qur'ānic mediaeval forms of *ribā*, *mudāraba*, *muzāra'a*, *zakāt*, *ushr*, etc., which originated and developed within different social contexts and which have not lost their original meaning and significance.[17] *Mudāraba* (profit-sharing), for example, is being reinterpreted and projected as a sacred religious principle to justify the maximisation of profits under capitalism, both industrial and comprador. A new 'Islamic' enterprise, Islamic or interest-free banking, is being developed on the basis of the mediaeval concept of *mudāraba*.[18] The mediaeval concept of *muzāra'a*, or share-cropping, is interpreted to justify the present semifeudal system of absentee landlordism.[19] *Zakāt* has become an instrument to tax the personal savings of the lower middle classes and agricultural produce (*ushr*). Landed estates and capital gains have been exempted. *Ribā* is interpreted sometimes as interest on loanable capital and sometimes as usury or unearned income in a broad sense, as was done under the early revolutionary Islam.[20]

This means that the real purpose of this political process of 'Islamisation' is to develop a capitalist or bourgeois Islam in line with the principles of international monopoly capitalism. This process deliberately aims through plans and strategies at consolidation of the propertied classes, encouragement of private ownership of the basic means of production and the opening up of all sectors (by the compradors and feudal lords) to the powerful multinational corporations, at the cost of genuine industrialisation. The absence of capital goods industries and the retarded growth of the economy have arrested the further development of genuine industry and scientific and democratic culture because the national bourgeoisie, in the face of powerful foreign capital, has remained feeble. All scientific processes have been subverted, and such terms as 'Islamic economics', 'Islamic education', 'Islamic science', 'Islamic banking', and 'Islamic democracy', have been coined in a purely tendentious way to serve the interests of international capitalism by interpreting Islam in feudalist and bourgeois terms.[21] Some political parties and economic institutions which promote the interests of capitalists both native and foreign impudently exploit the fair name of Qur'ānic Islam.

Real Qur'ānic Islam has been discarded by the ruling elite of Pakistan for the reason that its application would do away with the institutions of feudalism and capitalism. The feudal/mediaeval form of *fiqhī* Islam suits the interests of the ruling elite, because feudal Islam is in the main reactionary, mediaevalistic and dogmatic. It promotes the interests of feudal lords and compradors. However, the feudal and retrogressive superstructure of legal, political, social and intellectual ideas and notions scaffolded by the ruling elite does not accord with the capitalist mode of production, which is based on industry, a national attitude of mind and modern technology. To illustrate this point, let us examine the nature of 'Islamic economics', a discipline developed by some 'Islamic economists' at the International School of Islamic Economics. This has been established in the Islamic University, Islamabad, Pakistan on the lines of the International Centre for Research on Islamic Economics (Jeddah, Saudi Arabia) to undertake study and research in 'Islamic economics.' But 'Islamic economics' has not been clearly defined by 'Islamic economists'.[22] The syllabi and courses of 'Islamic economics' comprise a smattering of old *fiqhī* treatises of the 9th century such as the *Kitāb al-Kharāj* of Abu Yusuf, knowledge of the Arabic language and modern econometrics and a selected collection of commentaries on Qur'ānic verses and Prophetic traditions, whereas in the advanced universities of the world, economics is taught as a modern social science as related to the economic and industrial phenomena of modern societies. It was the first social science which came to embrace scientific methods of enquiry and reasoning. In its latest development, it is closely concerned with the empirical measurement of relationships and testing of hypotheses on a large scale. 'Islamic economists', on the other hand, are trying to develop a 'non-secular' religious economics loaded with metaphysical axioms and postulates which do not relate to living human beings but rather deal with dead fossils, abstract dogmas, mediaeval categories and institutions and vague notions leading to confusion and complexities. To tie the modern science of economics to traditional religion and theology is to suppress the spirit of enquiry, investigation and scientific reasoning. Such institutions of mediaeval conception tend to become islands and monasteries cut off from the international mainstream of science, scholarship and knowledge which ultimately decay and die like plants which wither away without light and water.

Conclusion

The political use of religion and the suppression of scientific and democratic processes have generated acute tensions, aggravated social and economic disparities and led to general disequilibrium in Pakistani society. This has strengthened the feudal reactionary and comprador elements and has resulted in a rigid and fossilised class structure. The contradictions between the capitalist mode of production of the urban sectors, the tribal-feudal mode of production and social relationships of underdeveloped areas and the related official process of 'Islamisation' under the aegis of international monopoly capitalism have resulted in a sharp and dangerous polarisation of society. It has also unleashed an accelerating proliferation of graft, greed, selfish profit motive, corruption, shallow religiosity, hypocrisy, moral decadence and degeneration of almost all the civil institutions — economic, political, cultural, educational and religious.

The recent history of Europe, Russia, China and Latin America reveals that if societies do not bring radical changes in their social structures, they are bound to explode through violence and revolutions. The effete upper classes cannot suppress the lower classes in the limbo of a decadent status quo, whether through authoritarianism or religious dogma. The short-sighted policies of the ruling oligarchy of capitalists, landlords, civil and military bureaucrats are leading Pakistan to the brink of disaster and to virtual economic serfdom because, as has happened with other developing countries, Pakistan's retarded economic and social development will reduce it to a subservient, subordinate and insignificant existence dependent on the developed imperialist countries. Societies which fail to develop their economies end up as adjuncts of international monopoly capitalism. Without economic independence there cannot be any political, social, cultural and intellectual freedom. Without bringing revolutionary changes in the social and economic structures, the problems of the broad masses of Pakistan cannot be solved. This means that liberation from the slavery of monopoly capitalism is a *sine qua non* of real and genuine independence and honourable existence for Third World developing countries like Pakistan. The only way to ameliorate the worsening socio-economic conditions of Pakistan, in the words of A.K. Bagchi, is 'to change the social structure and eliminate private profit-making at the cost of society, as a whole'. Without transforming the pastoral-tribal and feudal social structures into higher industrial formations and without bringing corresponding revolutions in political, cultural and intellectual perceptions commensurate with the requirements of a modern, scientific, democratic and popular culture, no society can be viable in present times. The feudalistic capitalist system of present-day Pakistan has not only maimed, enfeebled and exploited the working classes but has also weakened the ruling elite, who lack the will and imagination and in utter desperation and defeat take refuge in religious dogma.

Talking about the manipulation of religion by the ruling classes in the Third World, Paul A. Baran offers the following comment:

> . . . the ruling classes in the underdeveloped countries spare no energy and receive a great deal of American support for their effort to strengthen the sway of religious superstitions over the minds of their starving subjects. What do they or the imperialists care that these superstitions represent a major roadblock on the way to progress? What do they and their Western accomplices care that the cost of maintaining religious obfuscation is increased starvation, multiplied death![23]

Since capitalism cannot develop Third World societies as progressive and viable economies, its apologists are forced to rely on ideological 'claptrap rather than on reason'. Even the transition from precapitalist relations to capitalist relations of production cannot be facilitated by manipulating traditional religious concepts and notions of tribal epochs. It is possible only by identifying the emerging categories in the present economic structures, which fundamentally relate to the precarious existence of the working classes. Otherwise the comprador and colonial regimes and their bourgeois economists and ideologues will continue justifying the loot of indigenous resources by the monopoly capitalists.

References and Notes

1. See for details a recent study of the causes and factors of the Third World's retardation and underdevelopment by A.K. Bagchi, *The Political Economy of Underdevelopment* (London: Cambridge University Press, 1982), p. 197. Another important work is Paul A. Baran, *The Political Economy of Growth* (New York: Monthly Review Press, 1957; paperback ed., 1968), chapters V-VIII.

2. Ibn Hishām *Sīrat al Nabī* (Cairo: al-maktaba al-tijāriyya), I, p. 197.

3. See for details the following: Qur'ān, chapter 6, verses 52-63; Al-Wāhidi, *Asbāb al-Nuzūl* (Cairo: Matba's Hindiyya, 1315 AH), pp. 162-3; Ibn Hishām, *Sirat al Nabi*, I, p. 420; Tabarī, *Tafsīr al Qur'ān* (Cairo), XI, pp. 374-5.

4. See early Meccan *sūras*: 51, 54, 68, 69, 74, 81 etc. See also Ahmed Ibn Hanbal, *Musnad* (Beirut: Dār Sādir, n.d.) IV, pp. 341-44.

5. Qur'ān, 2: 275-81; 9: 34.

6. Qur'ān, 3: 19-20, 83-5; 5: 111; 10: 90.

7. The socio-religious missions and ways of life of the prophets like Ibrāhīm, Ya'qūb, Ishāq, Mūsā (Moses), and Christ (Isā) are also called Islam. See Qur'ān, 3: 64-7.

8. Qur'ān, *sūras* 43, 98, 109 etc.

9. See the work of the present writer: *Landlord and Peasant in Early Islam* (Islamabad: Islamic Research Institute, 1977), chapters I, II, VII and III.

10. See for details on the origin and development of the concept of *mudāraba* (profit-sharing) in mediaeval times the forthcoming work of the present writer: *Islam and Feudalism* (Lahore: Vanguard Books, 1984).

11. Qur'ān, 2: 219.

12. There is abundant evidence in the compilations of *Hādīth* (by Bukhārī, Muslim, Mālik, Nasaī, Tirmidhī, Ahmed Ibn Hanbal) under the chapters of *zakāt* and *sadaqa*, which suggests that the Prophet used to persuade his companions to give their wells, orchards and other forms of wealth for common use by all the people. See for example Ahmed ibn Hanbal, *Musnad*, III, p. 115; VI, p. 7.

13. Ahmed ibn Hanbal, *Musnad*, VI, pp. 71, 128.

14. Ahmed ibn Hanbal, *Musnad* (Cairo edition), I, 185.

15. Mālik ibn Anas, *Kitāb al-Muwatta'* (Cairo: Dār Ihyā' al-Kutab al-'Arabiyya, 1351/1370), II, 244-45.

16. Hāfiz Abū al-Faraj 'Abd al Rahmān ibn al-jawzī, *Manāqib al-Imām Ahmad ibn Hanbal* (Cairo: Matba'a al-Sa'ādah, n.d.), pp. 223-4.

17. Hasan Gardezi et al. (ed.), *Pakistan: Unstable State* (Lahore: Vanguard Books, 1983); see the chapter entitled 'Pakistan and Islamic Ideology'.

18. A type of literature on *mudāraba*, profit-sharing, and interest-free

'Islamic' banking has recently appeared. See for example Muazzan Ali (ed.), *Islamic Banks and Strategies of Economic Cooperation* (London: New Century Publishers, 1982); Zia ud Din Ahmad et al., *Money and Banking in Islam* (Islamabad: Institute of Policy Studies, 1983); Khurshid Ahmad (ed.), *Studies in Islamic Economics* (Leicester: The Islamic Foundation, 1981).

19. See Government of Pakistan, Council of Islamic Ideology, *The Consolidated Recommendations on the Islamic Economic System* (Islamabad: Government of Pakistan, December 1983).

20. See for details the article of the present writer: '*Ribā*, Interest and Profit', in *Pakistan Economist*, 24 and 31 May 1980.

21. See for details on the concept of Islamic education S.N. Al-Attas, *Aims and Objectives of Islamic Education* (Jedda: King Abdul Aziz University, 1979). The book develops the idea that the modern system of education (in unversities and colleges) is secular in approach as basic assumptions behind natural, applied and social sciences are not drawn from religious sources.

22. See the present writer's review of Khurshid Ahmad (ed.), *Studies in Islamic Economics*, in *Hamdard Islamicus*, V, No.1 (Spring 1981), pp. 93-108.

23. Paul A. Baran, *Political Economy*, p. 253.

6. Political and Economic Aspects of Islamisation

by Omar Asghar Khan

Introduction

In its short but eventful history, Pakistan has seen three spells of military rule. But neither of the earlier two military regimes, of Ayub Khan in the 1960s or of Yahya Khan in the early 1970s, had emphasised Islam in the way the regime of General Zia ul Haq has done. Although Islam has been manipulated by sections of the ruling classes to eliminate popular participation in the affairs of the state, never before has a regime arrogated to itself the task of Islamising the country's institutions in their entirety.

Devoid of a popular mandate and dependent for its survival on the support of reactionary and opportunistic sections of the population, Pakistan's military regime's so-called Islamisation policies are a means for preserving an exploitative and oppressive social order. Aware of the attachment of the masses to Islam, the ruling classes hope to secure a future for themselves by establishing an authoritarian and exploitative system, which they claim to be Islamic. It is with this aim in view that the so-called Islamisation of state and society has been undertaken in Pakistan. Paradoxically, however, this is where problems arise — problems that could threaten the very existence of the state. There are many whose concept of Islam differs from that of the persons in power. Opposition to the regime's Islamisation policies by those with a more enlightened interpretation of Islam is creating strains in Pakistan.

Islam means different things to different people. There is no consensus of opinion among the people on the interpretation of Islamic injunctions or Muslim history, both of which are made the basis for erecting an Islamic system. As will be discussed in this chapter, it is from the 'dark ages' of Muslim history, when a tolerant and egalitarian social order had given way to an oppressive system, that concepts have been borrowed to resurrect in Pakistan a mediaeval political and economic system with a sprinkling of modern institutions. Thus the Islamisation of Pakistan's political and economic institutions, besides being governed by dictates of expediency, bears an imprint of a reactionary socio-economic system where both feudal and capitalist institutions coexist.

Islam and the State

When viewed in the context of its appeal to various social classes and communities, Islam is essentially a religion of the downtrodden. Be it the socially dispossessed or economically and culturally alienated communities or groups, Islam has a strong attraction for the underprivileged. But the vitality of this great religion as a living social force depends on whether it is made a closed, dogmatic and politically expedient code in the hands of the ruling elite or is given a dynamic and progressive interpretation and made the basis for the social and cultural uplift of the oppressed masses. The following Qur'ānic verse, while capturing the essence of Islam, shows a clear bias in favour of the poorer sections of society: 'And we desired to show favour unto those who were oppressed on earth, and to make them examples and make them inheritors, and to establish them on earth' (Qur'ān 28: 56).

Despite the unambiguous egalitarian spirit of the Qur'ān, sections of the *'ulamā*, in adopting a conciliatory approach towards the ruling elite, have invoked Islamic injunctions to confer legitimacy on the status quo and authoritarian rule. Historically speaking, whereas Islamic injunctions have been invoked to legitimise authority and repression, Qur'ānic verses and Prophetic traditions have also been cited to call upon the people to struggle against authoritarian rule. Contrary to the conservative view, which describes the political tradition of Islam as submissive towards authority, Muslims throughout the ages have challenged the illegitimate authority of the state and have often stood up against oppression.[1]

Whenever rulers have tried to impose a particular religious creed or a doctrine on the people without their participation or consent, there has been popular opposition to it. The submissiveness of the orthodox *'ulamā* stands out in sharp contrast to the activist role of the unorthodox and popular sections of Muslim society. Imam Hussain's revolt against Yazid and his martyrdom are the ultimate symbols of the refusal to accept the illegitimate authority of a usurper and represent the extent to which a Muslim should be prepared to go in the struggle against tyrannical and undemocratic rule. That *Imam* Abu Hanīfa, the great Muslim jurist, refused to accept the position of an official judge under the Abbasids and was flogged for criticising the corrupt practices of government officials points towards the presence of dissenting view-points among the *'ulamā*. Similarly, Ahmed ibn Hanbal chose to be flogged and imprisoned rather than accept a particular doctrine enforced by some Abbasid rulers.

The popularity of the great Muslim saints of the Indian subcontinent like Khawaja Muin-ud-Din Chishti, Nizam-ud-Din Aulīa, and Mahr Jan-i-Jana or that of the *Sufi* poets such as Baba Farīd, Shah Abdul Latīf, Sachal Sarmast and Bulleh Shah has been caused by the socially symbolic contrast their austere life-styles offered to the extravagant and corrupt living of the ruling classes. When viewed in a societal context, it is this progressive tradition with its selflessness and enlightened interpretation of Islam, elaborated by 'ulamā such as Shah Waliullah and Shah Abdul Azīz that has deeper roots among the masses than the doctrinaire interpretation of the officially sponsored 'ulamā. However, the great *Sufis* were essentially 'introvert rebels', who instead of 'waging war' against the oppressors withdrew to their popular centres. They nevertheless, in their own way, defied the oppressors and stood for the social equality and true egalitarianism characteristic of early Islam of the Prophet's time.

In contrast to the progressive spirit of Islam, there is no dearth of so-called 'Islamic scholars' who are only too willing to oblige the rulers of the day with their flattery and unconditional support. These so-called scholars, while following in the footsteps of their predecessors, take great pains to emphasise that the people must obey their rulers unquestioningly. They, however, conveniently remain silent on the fundamental questions concerning the inalienable rights of the people to hire and fire their rulers. To justify the perpetuation of undemocratic regimes, Islam is misinterpreted to sanction the establishment of a coercive state with a mediaeval political and legal code. By interpreting Islam narrowly, reactionary elements have been presenting an intolerant and inflexible image of Islam, which is a far cry from the Islam whose purpose has been to permit rather than arrest the growth of humanitarian values.

Islam is much more than just a political system, which by its very nature is limited to a particular social structure and period. Nor is there any provision in Islam for a particular class to interpret Islamic injunctions. Dr. Ishtaiq Hussain Qureshi in his book *'Ulamā in Politics* has made the following observations:

> It is essential to understand a characteristic of Islam which is not found in other religions. Islam does not distinguish between religious and profane . . . In a sense Islam is a secular religion . . . With this philosophy of a religious life, there arises no need for the spiritual guardianship of the people by a priesthood. Therefore, Islam did not create one.[2]

This class is in fact a creation of the monarchical period in Muslim history and has no sanction and place in Islam. In an attempt to thwart the development of an enlightened social consciousness and a truly democratic ethos among the people, the term 'secular' has been misinterpreted as 'irreligious' by reactionary elements in society. The correct interpretation of the term 'secular' is 'worldly', implying that Islam, besides being concerned with the affairs of the hereafter, is concerned with man's conditions of existence in this world. In Islam there is no place for an ecclesiastical authority invested with special powers to decide religious matters.

That the people themselves are considered to be the best judges in any age concerning both religious and temporal affairs is what is meant by the statement that 'Islam does not distinguish between religious and profane'. There is no place in Islam for a class of intermediaries between the Almighty and man. Dr. Ali Shariati, the great Iranian revolutionary philosopher, has pointed out that

> Islam is the first school of thought that recognises the masses as the basis, the fundamental and conscious factor in determining history and society — not the elect as Nietzsche thought, not the aristocracy and nobility as Plato claimed, not those of pure blood as Alexis Carrel believed, not the priests or the intellectuals, but the masses . . . We see throughout the Qur'ān addresses being made to *al-nās*, i.e. the people. The Prophet is sent to *al-nās*, he addresses himself to *al'nās*, it is *al-nās* who are accountable for their deeds; *al-nās*, are the basic factor in decline — in short, the whole responsibility for society and history is borne by *al-nās*.[3]

It is on the question of the nature of the state that a controversy has raged between protagonists of an 'Islamic' and 'secular' state. Conservative sections of the *'ulamā*, in the name of 'Islamising' the state, have tried to establish their hegemony over the state apparatus. Much of this controversy, however, appears to be misplaced as there can be little doubt that the state by its very nature is an institution that is neither eternally given nor divinely ordained. Since its inception, the state has basically been a social organisation with a material base rooted in the economic and political structures prevalent at a particular time and place.[4] The state thus cannot be termed 'Islamic'. Its inhabitants can, however, be Muslims with a distinct culture and national identity. It is precisely for these reasons that the Qur'ān contains no reference to the establishment of an Islamic state with a particular kind of structure or ideology. Moreover, it was not necessary for there to be an 'Islamic state' for the Prophet to begin his mission of spreading Islam in Mecca. The state predates Islam, and Islam preceded the evolution of a state in the Hijaz.

The city state of Medina, with the Prophet as its spiritual and temporal head, was neither a state in the modern sense of the word nor was it anywhere close to the 'Islamic state' that is being built up in Pakistan today. When the Prophet migrated from Mecca to Medina and gathered round him those who had come to believe in the message of Islam, Medina had developed into a community of believers governed by the values of justice, equality, tolerance and solidarity. Gradually, in response to social and economic necessities, the political structure of Medina developed into a more sophisticated entity, with central authority vested in the Prophet. As there was no other authority which enjoyed the support of a large number of tribes in other parts of the Hijaz at that time, the establishment of the city-state of Medina was the beginning of the evolution of a central authority in the Hijaz. The establishment of the city-state of Medina was therefore not part of the Prophetic mission. Nor did he have any blueprint or plan for a particular kind of state structure. With conflict and differences between the tribes assuming antagonistic proportions as a result of social, economic and political tensions, the need for a central authority with a 'national' and universal perspective rather than narrow tribal and parochial values arose. It was at such a stage that the Prophet's call to Islam was heeded by the inhabitants of Yathrab (Medina) and surrounding areas.

The Charter of Medina, a document of great historic significance, highlights the contrast between the conservative view of a coercive state with its emphasis on punitive measures for maintenance of the status quo and the democratic and essentially secular view of the state that the Prophet strove to create by bringing together the various tribes. One of the generally accepted *Ahadīth* clearly indicates the secular nature of his philosophy regarding the state:

> I am no more than a man, but when I enjoin anything respecting religion receive it, and when I order anything about the affairs of the world then I am nothing more than a man.[5]

The Charter of Medina, which was basically a code of conduct drawn up by the Prophet to regulate the lives of the inhabitants of Medina, was essentially an agreement between the different tribes to live in peace and tolerance. According to the spirit of the agreement, even the Jews of Medina were to observe the Charter, and their rights were to be respected by the Muslims. The Jews of Banu Awf were free to practise their religion.

The period of 'tribal democracy' starting with the Prophet was, however, short-lived. The conquests brought with them riches and threw up new classes who demanded a share in political power. After the brief transitional period of 'tribal democracy', socio-economic and political pressures soon began to be felt, and the structure of the state, in order to accommodate the conflicting demands of the different classes, began to change. With the incorporation of large territories of the Byzantine and Sassanid empires, dominated by feudal agrarian structures, the feudal classes gradually came to control the reins of government. It was under monarchical forms of government dominated by the feudal classes that most of the *fiqh* (Islamic code of life, legal systems in Islam) were codified, and sections of the *'ulamā* conferred legitimacy on the monarchical-feudal form of government.

Neither does the Qur'ān nor do the *Ahadīth* lay down a framework for a political system because concepts such as forms of government and political institutions, which are social categories, are continuously in a state of flux, evolving with the times and the changing socio-economic milieu. Principles regarding the nature of the state are therefore not static but change with the time. To have restricted Muslims to a particular political system would have been against the natural laws of evolution, which the Qur'ān and enlightened Muslim philosophers uphold. The Qur'ān, besides being concerned with fulfilling man's spiritual needs, has elaborated certain universal and eternal values for the individual and society. In the absence of a definition of the nature of the state in either the Qur'ān or the *Ahadîth*, it is not only possible but essential for Muslims to evolve appropriate forms of government, keeping in view the social, economic and political imperatives of the time.

As in the past, in these days also we find Qur'ānic verses being misinterpreted to justify concepts and institutions that have nothing to do with either the Qur'ān or the spirit of Islam. By invoking the concept of an Islamic state and defining it in accordance with their own predilections, certain classes aim at establishing their political hegemony. They argue that since a modern parliamentary form of government with political parties has nothing in common with Islam, Pakistan, which was founded on the basis of Islam, cannot have a modern parliamentary form of government. It is inappropriate to judge Islam in terms of its being a political system approaching either democracy or dictatorship. This, however, does not mean that Islam has no relationship with democracy or that its achievements in the multifarious fields of science, statecraft and philosophy have not influenced the evolution of progressive thought. Islam, with its emphasis on the spirit of enquiry, justice and tolerance, on entering Spain and Sicily at a time when Europe was passing through an era of darkness, influenced the minds of the torchbearers of the Renaissance in Europe.

In upholding the principle of sovereignty not being vested in the people in an 'Islamic state', the ruling classes attribute to themselves the right to exercise sovereignty on behalf of God. To justify their privileged position in the decision-making hierarchy, it is said that, as these decisions are 'sacred', they are to be executed in the name of the Almighty by the 'chosen' ones. Muslim history is full of instances where the ruling classes, while attributing sovereignty to God, have retained the right to interpret and administer what are termed 'divine' laws. This they have done to perpetuate themselves in power as well as to defend their class interests. It is precisely such forms of government, where the ruling classes have claimed divine sanction for their actions, that have been the most dictatorial and divisive in Muslim history.

In contrast to the progressive spirit of Islam, the structure of the monarchical and mediaeval Islamic state is being made out by certain sections to be the ideal form of democracy, euphemistically termed 'Islamic democracy'. Such an anachronistic interpretation of Islam, with all its implications of increasing the power and privileges of the vested interests vis-a-vis the popular sections, is neither in keeping with the spirit of Islam nor acceptable to the people at large. It may not be out of place to mention that it is only in a modern democracy, established through the struggle of the people against vested interests, that the people are recognised as sovereign in a legal sense and, with the establishment of necessary institutions, are for all practical purposes the centre of political power.

Democratic or Ideological State?

In contrast to the political culture of a modern democratic state, the ideology of the Pakistani state, which has been dominated by feudal-military-bureaucratic interests, has been elaborated by members of the ruling classes to suit their own material interests. While Islam is interpreted by them to justify the status quo, the pressing social and economic problems faced by the masses are given little importance. This process of building an emotional-ideological smoke-screen in the name of Islam between the people and their conditions of existence in Pakistan has its origin in the role played by feudal elements in the leadership of the Muslim League during and immediately after the Pakistan Movement.

The main concern of the Quaid-i-Azam and the League in the period immediately preceding the establishment of Pakistan was the creation of an independent homeland for the Muslims of India, free of both sectarian persecution and exploitation. Obsessed and preoccupied with this goal, the Quaid, who had to struggle relentlessly and almost single-handedly, could therefore not give the necessary attention to a detailed elaboration of the nature of the state and polity to be. Even though the League was heavily burdened by the weight of a feudal leadership, the Quaid nevertheless indicated his preference for a democratic Pakistan with an egalitarian socio-economic structure:

> Who are the people present here? They are not rich; the League constitution is a democratic constitution, and if there are rich and selfish people in the League, it is because of your weakness . . . The leaders draw their strength from the masses, the poor people . . . I have no sympathy with the capitalists . . . Why would I turn my blood into water, run about and take so much trouble? Not for the capitalists surely, but for you, the poor people . . . In Pakistan, we will do all in our power to see that everybody can get a decent living . . . My power is derived from you, the masses. Leaders are made by you. If they do not act honestly, do not make them the leaders. You can do that to me as well.[6]

While Mohammad Ali Jinnah and the Muslims masses were struggling for the creation of a democratic Pakistan in which sovereign authority would be exercised by the representatives of the people, the feudal elements, who found common cause with sections of the *'ulamā*, were bent upon preventing the establishment of a democratic state. Having seen the popular response that the demand for a democratic Pakistan based on the principles of social justice evoked in the masses in the Muslim majority areas, the feudal elements did not fancy the idea of a people's democracy coming into existence. They knew that by its very nature such a form of government would encroach upon their 'divinely ordained' privileges. In the Punjab a large section of Muslim feudalists opposed Jinnah and the League by supporting the Unionist Party. It was not until the League had generated substantial popular support that members of the feudal aristocracy started joining the League and making an indelible mark upon it. The same class has wielded political power to a lesser or greater extent in today's Pakistan. They have done this either indirectly through their links with the military-bureaucratic oligarchy or directly, in the 1970s, through their representatives in the People's Party government. Bhutto's role during the East Pakistan debacle symbolised the attitude of the feudal class, which was not prepared to accept the Awami League as the majority party. Had the Awami League been able to form the government at the centre along with other democratic forces in West Pakistan, the power of the Sindhi and Punjabi feudals would probably have been curtailed and a more progressive and democratic social and political system developed.

Given the pattern of rural society prevailing in East Pakistan as well as the presence of a larger religious minority, the Awami League's outlook, while reflecting Bengali political culture, was more democratic and tolerant than that of its West Pakistani counterparts. Whereas tribal sardars, landlords and religious personalities had a sizeable representation in the assembly from West Pakistan in the 1970 elections, the members of the assembly from East Pakistan were largely of middle- and lower-class origin with a more developed political consciousness. Besides the social structure inherited at the time of Partition by the respective wings of the country, political developments also played a part in influencing the differences in socio-economic structures between the two wings of the country. Since in East Pakistan, prior to Partition, large land-holdings were under the control of Hindus, most of whom had at the time of Partition migrated to India, ownership rights over these lands after Partition were assumed by Muslim tenants and landless peasants. The abolition of the much weaker *jagirdari* system did not therefore have to face the same opposition in East Pakistan as it did, and still has to, in what remains of the country. It is the prevalence of the feudal social structure that perpetuates unscientific, backward and reactionary modes of thought and attitudes.

Unfortunately, the Quaid died before the necessary social and political institutions could be established to realise his goal of an egalitarian and democratic Pakistan. Soon after the Quaid's death, Islam began to be interpreted in such a manner as to justify an autocratic and undemocratic political system. It was in this context that parts of the Objectives Resolution of 1949 were formulated in a vague manner, making it amenable to the machinations and ulterior designs of the ruling elite. Particular parts of this resolution have provided reactionary elements with an opportunity to interpret Islam in a manner that increases their power at the expense of the people along with the attendant confusion and controversies regarding the political structure, rights of minorities and sovereignty of the people.

To perpetuate themselves in power, the feudal-military-bureaucratic elite have portrayed themselves as the defenders of the ideology of Pakistan. As opposed to the utterances of the ruling elite regarding Pakistan as an ideological state based on a reactionary and narrow interpretation of Islam, none of the speeches of the Quaid refer to Pakistan as an ideological state. According to the Quaid, Pakistan was to be a democratic state where Muslims of the subcontinent would be able to condition their lives in accordance with Islamic social and cultural values as they understood them. The Quaid-i-Azam understood very well that a democratic state cannot at the same time be an ideological state, for the latter involves an element of compulsion, which is the negation of democratic principles. It was not until 1962, when a member of the *Jamā'at-i-Islāmī* in the National Assembly, during a discussion of the political parties bill, demanded that Pakistan be termed an ideological state.[7] This, however, was not clearly defined then, nor has it been to this day.

The lack of a continuous political process and the weak roots of intellectuals with a progressive interpretation of Islam among the masses have provided the ruling classes the opportunity to impose a repressive state with the orthodox *'ulamā* providing the ideological cover. Most people, due to their emotional attachment to Islam, are easily susceptible to rhetoric such as *Pakistan ka matlab kiya- La Illaha Illallah* [What does Pakistan mean — there is no other God but Him]. While conveniently avoiding addressing themselves to the basic socio-economic problems, the ruling elite has manipulated such slogans to suit their own interests.

By imposing limitations on legislation, denying sovereignty to the people and not granting equal rights to minorities, the ruling classes, in collaboration with the obscurantist *'ulamā*, have in the name of Islam denied the people the opportunity of living within a democratic and tolerant social milieu. In their version of an Islamic state, all laws must conform to Islam as they interpret it. They, along with others whom they consider 'competent', would like to pronounce judgment on the validity of laws framed by a parliament whose members must pass the litmus test of being 'good' Muslims. If Pakistan were to become an Islamic state of the type that the obscurantist *'ulamā* and their patrons, the ruling classes, are attempting to build, democratic institutions, rationality and tolerance would never take root.

The manner in which Islam has been manipulated for political ends and used to label political opponents as anti-Islamic has created divisions in society. That discord, intolerance and undemocratic practices, along with corruption and exploitation, should become the order of the day is indeed a sad reflection on a society that takes great pride in calling itself Islamic. If citizens are compelled to adhere to a state ideology as defined and interpreted by those who have usurped political power, if freedom of expression and opinion is not allowed, and if a group of so-called experts, calling themselves the 'Islamic Ideology Council' can sit in judgment over laws passed by parliament, such a state is a far cry from what is understood to be a democratic state.

There is a fundamental difference between a modern nation-state with democratic institutions and an ideological state of the kind that the ruling classes are trying to establish in Pakistan. In the 'ideological' state of Pakistan, citizens who do not adhere to the official ideology do not enjoy the same rights as those who claim to adhere to the state ideology. To deny equal rights to religious minorities on the basis of religion, as is presently done in Pakistan, not only militates against the democratic principle of equal opportunities for all but also does not conform to the Quaid's vision of Pakistan:

> If you change your past and work together in the spirit that everyone of you, no matter to what community he belongs . . . is first, second and last a citizen of this state with equal rights, privileges and obligations, there will be no end to the progress you will make . . . You are free to go to your mosques or to any other place, belong to any religion or caste or creed — that has nothing to do with the business of the state. We are starting in the days when there is no discrimination, no distinction between one community and another, no discrimination between one caste or creed and another. We are starting with this fundamental principle that we are all citizens and equal citizens of one state . . . I think we should keep that in front of us as our ideal and you will find that in course of time Hindus would cease to be Hindus and Muslims would cease to be Muslims, not in the religious sense because that is the personal faith of each individual but in the political sense as citizens of the state.[8]

In modern nation-states, where democratic institutions have been established after a protracted struggle against feudal structures and ecclesiastical authority, there is in legal terms no discrimination on grounds of ideology or religious beliefs. In such states, individuals or different social classes are free to adhere to different religious beliefs or world-views (ideologies) without being relegated to the status of second-class citizens. In order to translate their ideas into action, they may form political organisations. In a multi-class and diverse society like Pakistan's there cannot be a consensus of opinion on the question of ideology. This is because the ideology of an individual or a class tends to be based not only on religious beliefs but on ideas that are derived from some economic or political system. Ideology cannot therefore be equated with religion. Ideology is an ensemble of ideas, drawing upon both religious and secular aspects of life concerning man, his relationship with other men and the world around him.

As opposed to scientific thought, which only observes and does not judge phenomena, insofar as ideology is the manner of thinking of an individual or a class, it is normative in content in that it deals with how things and social relations ought to be arranged. When in the hands of the ruling classes, ideology is a means to justify the status quo and subjugate oppressed classes. In the hands of the oppressed it can act as a means to mobilise the oppressed classes against exploitation and injustice. But if an ideology is to emancipate the people from deprivation and exploitation it would have to have as its basis an economic and political system that does not necessitate exploitation or coercion. Such a system should allow human potential to be fully realised. Such an 'ideology' then tends to take on a scientific character.

Historical and Theoretical Roots of Islamisation

Taking advantage of the absence of a clearly defined political and economic framework, the feudal-military-bureaucratic elite have found, in the orthodox interpretation of Islam as elaborated by the *Jamā'at-i-Islāmī*, a defence of the status quo. There was no other political organisation at the time of independence representing these classes, other than the *Jamā'at*, that presented a well articulated so-called 'Islamic' solution to the political and economic problems facing the Pakistani nation. Their 'solution', formulated and popularised by Maulana Maudoodi, founder of the *Jamā'at-i-Islāmī*, has been directed at the petite bourgeoisie and the relatively better-off sections of rural society in the Punjab. Sections of these classes see in the *Jamā'at*'s pro-status quo philosophy a defence against the social, economic and cultural consequences of industrialisation and commercialisation.

While analysing the nature of a political organisation, its history must be kept in mind. Not only has the *Jamā'at-i-Islāmī*'s political history shown that it opposed the Pakistan Movement, but since independence, as an extension of its past role, it has consistently counterposed Islam to the democratic aspirations of the people. This has been done to make it appear that the one excludes the other at a time when the democratic movement was gaining strength. Starting from the Pakistan Movement to the Movement for the Restoration of Democracy in the 1980s, the *Jamā'at* has time and again opposed the popular and democratic demands of the people. In the mass movement of 1968-69, instead of concentrating on democratic demands, the *Jamā'at* chose to articulate a crusade against progressive tendencies in the movement. Then in 1971, in opposition to the democratic aspirations of the East Pakistanis, it supported the military government of General Yahya Khan. Instead of supporting a political solution to the problem, Yahya Khan, with the active support of the *Jamā'at*, unleashed a reign of terror against the Bengalis. This was all done in the name of Islam, for the greater glory of Islam, for the greatness of a Pakistan that was later dismembered precisely because of the shortsightedness and the political ambitions of self-styled defenders of the so-called ideology of Pakistan.

Later, in 1977, at the time of the movement launched by the Pakistan National Alliance (PNA), the *Jamā'at*, by raising the demand for Islamisation, prepared the ground for the democratic demands of the people to be put aside. It is significant that when martial law was imposed on 5 July 1977, all the prominent politicians except the *amir* of the *Jamā'at*, Main Tufail Mohammad, were arrested. The *Jamā'at-i-Islāmī* later joined the martial law government when a number of its leaders accepted federal ministries in 1979. The civilianisation of the cabinet was, however, short-lived.

The *Jamā'at-i-Islāmī's* Islamic Model

The very timing of the genesis of the *Jamā'at-i-Islāmī* — the early 1940s — just after the Pakistan Resolution had been adopted by the Muslim League and the demand for a separate homeland for the Muslims of India was gaining momentum, was portentous of the practice that the *Jamā'at* was to adopt in relation to popular movements in the future. At a time when there was an urgent need for Muslims to unite and struggle against the oppression and domination of the British colonialists on the one hand and a caste-ridden social structure on the other, Maulana Maudoodi opposed the creation of an independent state for Muslims. In fact, the Maulana attacked the Quaid and the Muslim leadership on the grounds that they were not good Muslims:

> Alas, not a single one of the greatest leaders of the lowliest followers of the League is such as has the Islamic mentality and Islamic way of thought, and looks at problems from the Islamic view-point. These people do not know anything of the meaning of Mussalman and his special position.[9]

Thus, the Quaid-i-Azam had to contend with three opposing forces — the British colonialists, the Indian National Congress and the *Jamā'at-i-Islāmī*, which claimed to represent the Muslims of India. Instead of attacking the British, the *Jamā'at* launched its offensive against Jinnah and the Muslims supporting the Quaid and the nationalist movement. In an attempt to discredit the nationalist movement of the Indian Muslims, Islam, the most emotional of all slogans for Muslims, was articulated by the *Jamā'at*. The nationalist movement led by Jinnah was termed un-Islamic by Maulana Maudoodi. While attacking the demand of the Muslims for a separate homeland by invoking the universal creed of Islam, the *Jamā'at-i-Islāmī* attempted to justify its opposition to the creation of Pakistan.

It must be remembered that the demand for Pakistan had its roots precisely in all that the *Jamā'at-i-Islāmī* refused to acknowledge, i.e. a common historical experience of struggle against British imperialism as well as a desire among the people of the north-western and north-eastern parts of the subcontinent to come together on an equal basis within a federal structure and in the process free themselves from an exploitative socio-economic order. Furthermore, in contrast to the monolithic view of Muslim society elaborated by Maulana Maudoodi, the spread of Islam in the subcontinent is attributed to the recognition of and respect for the diverse cultural and social values of the people. The very origin of this great religion had to do with the Holy Prophet's recognition of the ethnic, cultural and religious diversity of the tribal society in which he lived and at whom his call was directed. Moreover, the Qur'ānic injunctions and the *Ahādīth* were aimed at transforming society, keeping in view the diverse social and cultural conditions prevailing at that time. Later, as the area under the caliphate expanded and various social and cultural practices were assimilated, so the more diverse did Muslim society and culture become. Thus the Muslim World, as it has come to be known, today encompasses many diverse cultural, social, ethnic and linguistic groups, some similar, others diverse, but having a common faith. It is for these reasons that there is nothing contradictory between nationalism and Islam, as Maulana Maudoodi would have liked the Muslims of the subcontinent to believe at the time of the Pakistan Movement.

The inconsistencies in the *Jamā'at*'s political philosophy and its practice are highlighted in the volte-face of the *Jamā'at* since 1947. Under the leadership of Maulana Maudoodi the *Jamā'at* after 1947 accepted all such concepts as 'Muslim nationalism', 'Pakistani nation', and 'national interest' as articles of faith, against which its entire energy and political activity had revolved in pre-Partition India. Since it could not continue its opposition to Pakistan once Pakistan had become a living reality, the *Jamā'at* chose to adopt a contradictory role. Publicly it declared its allegiance to the fledgling state, but in practice it opposed the democratic aspirations of the people.

The *Jamā'at-i-Islāmī*, starting with its opposition to the right of self-determination for the Muslims of the subcontinent in pre-Partition India, has been averse to democratic principles. While Maulana Maudoodi's opposition to nationalism was based on the religious argument of not recognising geographical or ethnic limits to Islam, his arguments against democracy appear to have been based on his interpretation of the so-called Islamic political system. While opposing the Pakistan Movement, Maulana Maudoodi's argument against a state being created on the basis of democratic principles was that such a state would not be a truly Islamic state since the masses and the leaders were *nasli* (racial), as opposed to *asli* (real), Muslims. It was on the basis of the distinction between the 'apparent' and the 'real' that Maulana Maudoodi opposed the Pakistan Movement, which essentially was a democratic movement supported by the Muslim masses. Maulana Maudoodi contended that since the majority of Muslims were not *asli* (real) Muslims, they could not be entrusted with the responsibility of electing their representatives, who, according to him, must be 'real' Muslims.

According to Maulana Maudoodi's criteria, the majority of Muslims, '999 out of 1000', are not real Muslims and should therefore be excluded from the pale of Islam as well as deprived of the right to vote in elections. The Maulana has stated his position thus:

> This huge crowd, which is called the Mussalman nation, is such that 999 out of 1000 have got neither any knowledge of Islam, nor are they aware of the distinction between truth and falsehood. From the father to the son, and from the son to the grandson they have just been acquiring the name of Mussalman. Therefore they are neither Muslims, nor have they accepted the truth by recognising it as truth, nor again rejected falsehood by recognising it as falsehood. If by handing over the reins of guidance into the hands of their majority vote somebody believes that the carriage will move along the path of Islam, his misconception is indeed praiseworthy.[10]

Until and unless the people are converted to the kind of Islam the *Jamā'at* stands for, elections, according to its view, should be replaced by a process of selection in which such persons should wield power who are 'good' Muslims. According to the *Jamā'at*, the purpose of the creation of Pakistan was to create an 'Islamic state', the political structure of which would ensure that only 'good' and 'real' Muslims wield power.

As mentioned earlier, at the time the Pakistan Movement was gaining momentum under the leadership of the Quaid, it was Maulana Maudoodi and his party that attacked the nationalist movement on the grounds that it was secular in nature. Having failed to prevent the success of the Pakistan Movement, which culminated in the creation of Pakistan, Maulana Maudoodi and the *Jamā'at*, on coming to Pakistan, changed their strategy. The Pakistan Movement, which they had previously termed as un-Islamic since it was based on the concept of nationalism, was eulogised and supported by reinterpreting it in terms of being a religious movement aimed at the creation of an Islamic state.

Blueprint for Authoritarianism

Consistent with this philosophy, the *Jamā'at* has used Islam to build an ideological smoke-screen between the masses and the harsh socio-economic realities that they have to face. The 'Islam' that the *Jamā'at* and the ruling classes have been propagating is undemocratic and unconcerned with human rights or the emancipation of the poorer classes. Coercion is the hallmark of such an Islamic system. Attaining state power is eulogised and once captured is meant to be used by the *Jamā'at* to realise its political ends. To justify the seizure of political power at any cost, Maulana Maudoodi has interpreted the *Ahadīth* and Qur'ānic verses to suit the *Jamā'at*'s political aims and philosophy. For instance, he has interpreted one *Hadīth* thus: 'Either give me power or make some government support me so that I can use its power to put in order the chaos in the world.'[11]

In another place, Maulana Maudoodi' while interpreting *sura Alhadid*, has used the Qur'ānic verses to reinforce his political views in support of a powerful and coercive state apparatus: 'And we send down iron (power and coercion of the state) in which is great power, as well as many benefits for mankind.'[12] In translating and interpreting Qur'ānic verses, Maulana Maudoodi has tried to show that the attainment of state power, coupled with the creation of a powerful and coercive government structure, are the objectives towards which they must strive. This is how he justifies the *Jamā'at*'s role as a political organisation concerned with seizing state power with a view to establishing a coercive state where a minority — only those who adhere to his view — would rule. That in such a state dissent will not be tolerated is obvious. It would be a one-party state. Once in power, only the party of God, *Hizb-i-Islāmī*, to use the Maulana's terminology, 'would be allowed to function'.[13]

Maulana Maudoodi's interpretation of the reference to 'iron' in the Qur'ān as implying divine sanction for the establishment of a coercive state is a distortion and appears to be an attempt to manipulate Qur'ānic verses to justify his own political philosophy. It was precisely regarding such an attitude towards religion that Allama Iqbal said, *khud badaltay nahin Qur'ān ko badaltay hain* (they do not change themselves but distort the Qur'ān).

In contrast to Maulana Maudoodi, Yusuf Ali, in his authoritative translation of and commentary on the Qur'ān, interprets the use of 'iron' in *sura Alhadid* thus:

> Iron is the type and emblem of strength and reliability, on which depends the real virtue expounded in this *Sura* such as real humility, large-heartedness and charity, as opposed to monasticism and niggardliness.[14]

As for the translation of that part of the Qur'an in which Maulana Maudoodi has interpreted 'iron' to mean a strong and coercive state, Yusuf Ali has in contrast translated it thus: 'And we send down Iron in which is material for Mighty War, as well as many benefits for mankind.'[15] In Yusuf Ali's version the emphasis is on the reform of the individual and society though persuasion and exemplary conduct, whereas in Maulana Maudoodi's interpretation emphasis is on coercion and seizure of political power. He appears to use the Qur'ān to justify, as divinely ordained, a strong and coercive state. He has also interpreted the *Ahadīth* to prove that if Islamic values as defined by him are not adopted by Muslims through persuasion, the coercive power of the state should be used to force them to do so. Without going into the controversy over the authenticity or interpretation of the *Ahādīth*, suffice it to say that compulsion in matters concerning religious beliefs and practices is contrary to the spirit of Islam.

Through its penetration of educational institutions, the media, and the administrative and coercive organs of the state, the *Jamā'at* has increased its control over vital organs of state power. An organisation like the *Jamā'at-i-Islāmī* depends for its strength on the infiltration it can achieve and control it can exercise over the coercive apparatus of the state of which the army, the police and the intelligence services are important parts. In order to put its opponents on the defensive, any criticism of it is termed 'un-Islamic'. While religion is used to evoke an emotional response in support of its political programme, it is also considered to be a convenient cover for the realisation of the *Jamā'at*'s political aims.

It is argued by some that since the *Jamā'at-i-Islāmī* does not enjoy mass support, it is not a formidable political force. Those who hold this view believe that if the establishment withdraws its support from it, or when a democratic government comes to power, the *Jamā'at-i-Islāmī* will cease to be politically relevant. It should be remembered that the *Jamā'at* is not a mass party and does not rely for its strength on mass public support. It relies for its strength on its organisational structure and the degree to which it can control the government machinery by vertical and lateral penetration in the key departments of state. Working on this strategy, it has over the years managed to penetrate various organs of the state with the result that the present structure of the state reflects to a large extent the ideology of the *Jamā'at*. The line dividing the *Jamā'at* from the government has thus become very thin.

It is the *Jamā'at* that has provided the military regime with not only political allies but the ideological framework to perpetuate itself in power. The so-called 'Islamisation' of legal, political and economic institutions that has been undertaken by the regime reflects the *Jamā'at*'s blueprint as formulated by their chief theoretician, Maulana Maudoodi. If this process is not checked by popular political organisations by presenting a democratic and progressive world-view rooted in the traditions and cultural experience of the people, the *Jamā'at* will continue to rule and oppress the people through its control over the ideological and coercive apparatuses of the state.

Having witnessed the apparent success of Bhutto's populist rhetoric in the 1970s, the *Jamā'at* in order to broaden its social base has on occasions adopted a somewhat populist style. This it has done through the utterances of some of its leaders who, while stressing the egalitarian precepts of Islam, have at times gone so far as to attack capitalists as well as feudalists. These attacks are, however, directed more at their immoral life-styles and their neglect of social obligations than at the exploitative socio-economic structure that these classes represent and perpetuate. Notwithstanding such criticism, due to its highly selective organisational structure, idealistic political philosophy and hypocritical political practice, the *Jamā'at* has been unable to win the confidence and support of the masses. The people to a large extent have been able to see through the contradictions between some of its populist rhetoric on the one hand and its conformist, pro-establishment reactionary political practice on the other. On the whole, therefore, the *Jamā'at*'s socio-economic framework may be termed anachronistic and reactionary.

In the name of establishing its version of an Islamic state and society, the *Jamā'at* aims at creating a coercive and bureaucratic state apparatus that perpetuates an exploitative status quo. It is not the democratic and egalitarian structure that existed at the Prophet's time that they take as their model. On the contrary, Maulana Maudoodi and the *Jamā'at* have elaborated a socio-economic framework that has borrowed certain elements from the feudal-monarchical tradition that prevailed in the Muslim World after the early Muslim conquests. On such a socio-economic structure, Maulana Maudoodi has superimposed certain capitalist institutions so that both semi-feudal and capitalist relations may coexist.

It is the state that assumes a 'relatively autonomous' role in the *Jamā'at*'s framework, in that while being all-powerful it is neither under the control of the weak industrial bourgeoisie nor under the influence of the feudal classes. The *Jamā'at* can be regarded as representing the interests of sections of the merchant classes as well as of sections of the feudal classes. It is the aim of these classes to maintain a status quo in which they are able to check the economic and political power of the national bourgeoisie and working classes.

It appears that in Pakistan today the industrial bourgeoisie, small, weak and devoid of a nationalistic and progressive outlook, has come to accept a situation where they are junior partners in an alliance where the upper echelons of power are occupied by the feudal-merchant-military-bureaucratic elite. They have come to accept such a situation because for them to effectively challenge the hegemony of the feudal-bureaucratic-military elite would mean developing class alliances with sections of the middle classes, working class and peasantry. This they are shy of doing because of the feudal or mercantile background of sections of the industrial elite, who after having entered industry have developed neither a dynamic entrepreneurial spirit nor an enlightened political culture. An enlightened and progressive political culture takes root only when a prolonged and systematic struggle is launched at the political, social, intellectual and cultural levels against feudalism and the values it represents.

Politics of Islamisation

The people of Pakistan during the military regime of General Zia ul Haq have been subjected to the regime's Islamisation policies as if members of the junta and those close to them were the only Muslims in the country.

Those who may have threatened the regime by way of political opposition have been deprived either of their freedom or opportunity to reach the people through recognised political processes. In the name of Islam and with the support of sections of the *'ulamā*, the regime has tried to establish something very close to a theocratic state. This it has done not only to perpetuate itself in power but also to pave the way for vested interests to exploit the masses in the name of Islam. Rulers in such a state generally arrogate to themselves the right to formulate and interpret the law, which they claim has divine sanction. In other words, in the system of government that the military regime has established neither is sovereignty exercised by the people nor is authority entrusted to the people's representatives. Such a system of government invariably results in the abuse of political power by the ruling classes on the one hand and the subservience of religion to the machinations of the persons in power on the other. It was precisely for these reasons that the founder of the nation, Mohammad Ali Jinnah, made the following statement:

> What are we fighting for? What are we aiming at? It is not a theocracy nor a theocratic state. Religion is there and religion is dear to us. All the worldly goods are nothing to us when we talk of religion; but there are other things which are very vital — our social, our economic life.[16]

Pakistan under the Islamisation policies of the military regime has certainly come a long way from the state that the Quaid and the millions of Indian Muslims, who had struggled for Pakistan, had envisaged at the time of independence.

The obsession that the military regime has shown with the Islamisation of the country's institutions appears to be born out of its political motives. Islamisation is seen by the regime as an instrument that provides it with legitimacy on the one hand and political allies on the other. The justification provided by General Zia ul Haq for his continuation in power is the 'divine mission' undertaken by him to Islamise Pakistan before power can be transferred to 'Islamic-minded' people.

Having seen the powerful mass movement led by the PNA, in which besides the fundamental demand for re-elections, the religious parties talked of implementing an Islamic system, the junta, on assuming power, considered it expedient to start harping on the tune of Islamisation. Such a policy did no doubt find some ready support among some of the PNA component parties. However, the *raison d'être* of the PNA movement was the massive rigging of the March 1977 elections and not *Nizam-i-Islam* (an Islamic system) articulated by the religious parties within the PNA. The PNA did not comprise only fundamentalist religious parties. It also had in its fold and enjoyed the support of certain progressive and democratic elements opposed to the autocratic tendencies of the Bhutto regime. The PNA's demands were twice formally formulated by the PNA Council. In March 1977 the PNA decided to launch a mass movement if its sole demand of annulling the rigged 7 March elections were not met.[17] Later, on 29 April 1977, the PNA Council again reiterated its demand for re-elections and added a number of additional demands relating to freedom of the press, independence of the judiciary, etc.[18] The demand for re-elections with no mention of *Nizam-i-Islam* was maintained by the PNA Council till General Zia ul Haq staged a coup d'état on 5 July 1977, which put an end to the negotiations between the PNA and the Bhutto regime. That the PNA's charter of demands focussed on re-elections was largely due to the presence in the PNA of democratic elements.

It was at the height of the mass movement, when the Bhutto regime was resorting to violent and repressive methods to try to crush the movement, that Islamic slogans were raised, not so much as a demand for the implementation of an Islamic system but to give sustenance and courage to the demonstrators in their confrontation with the police, the Federal Security Force and later the army. To appease the democratic elements that had taken part in and had supported the PNA movement, the junta, on assuming power, promised to hold elections in 90 days. To perpetuate itself in power the military regime, however, soon went back on its promise to hold elections. In October 1979, having banned all forms of political activity and having postponed elections for the second time, General Zia ul Haq and the ruling junta gave up all pretence of returning the country to democracy. Instead, 'Islamisation', a euphemism for authoritarian rule, became the most important declared objective of the junta. The perpetuation of military rule necessitated a crack-down on the political opposition on the one hand and a greater emphasis on the 'Islamisation' for the purpose of gaining some sort of legitimacy on the other. The state's ideological and coercive apparatuses were thus brought into full play.

The junta's sectarian interpretation of Islam, while representing the interests of the privileged classes to the exclusion of the interests of the people at large, has failed to conceal the exploitation, corruption and chicanery that have become rampant. Consequently, the state's repressive apparatuses have been brought into play to check those struggling to establish a just and truly democratic social order. Islamic history is replete with instances when rulers have done the same and justified their actions in the name of Islam. Even the Qur'ān has not been spared by self-proclaimed messiahs. By misinterpreting Qur'ānic verses and the *Ahadīth* in complete disregard of the historical context, many a Muslim ruler has distorted Islamic injuctions in a crude attempt to legitimise his rule. In keeping with these traditions, the military regime of Pakistan has used the cover of Islam to thwart the aspirations of the people for a change in the social order and the establishment of a democratic system of government.

Social Costs of Islamisation

The military regime's emphasis on Islamisation, ranging from the so-called *isalah-i-muashra* (social reform) drive to the introduction of profit and loss counters in banks, has its theoretical roots in the *Jamā'at-i-Islāmī*'s interpretation of an Islamic system as propounded by Maulana Maudoodi. Maulana Maudoodi in his various writings, adopting an idealistic approach, considers the solution of man's socio-economic problems to be primarily in transforming moral values through religious indoctrination. Although he does not deny the importance of socio-economic problems, these for him appear to be the result of moral degeneration. The 'Islamic' solution to man's economic problems, according to Maulana Maudoodi, would involve first and foremost becoming 'good Muslims' in spirit as well as in letter. In the name of enforcing an Islamic moral code, the *Jamā'at-i-Islāmī* aims at increasing its grip on society through increasing its own as well as the state's repressive powers. This is done by forming vigilante squads on the one hand and infiltrating and exercising control over the coercive and ideological apparatuses of the state on the other.

The emphasis of the military regime through the media and other channels on a highly reactionary interpretation of Islam has been instrumental in whipping up religious hysteria verging on insanity. The perverted sense of morality being propagated by self-styled defenders of the faith has in recent years resulted in a number of social tragedies. In one such case a young student slaughtered his mother and sister in the name of Islam. From the statement of the accused, an ex-student of the Engineering University, Lahore, one can gather that the only 'crime' of his mother and sister was that, despite his repeated warnings, they did not wear what he termed 'Islamic' dress. In another unfortunate incident a crowd instigated by a local *maulvi* stoned to death, outside a mosque in Karachi, a newborn for no other reason than that it was left there by its mother, giving rise to the suspicion that it was illegitimate. That the incident took place very close to a police station is all the more deplorable. In yet another incident, a person, after having dreamt that he was ordered in the biblical tradition of Abraham to sacrifice his son, slaughtered his baby son while reciting verses from the Qur'ān. But the tragic consequences of religious fanaticism were most vividly brought out by an incident in which more than 20 persons, including women and children, drowned in the sea near Karachi, when, in response to what was termed a divine call, they decided to 'sail' in steel trunks to the Holy Kaaba in Saudi Arabia.

It is in the sphere of its policy towards women that the record of the military regime has been the most dismal. In the name of Islamisation, the regime has followed a conscious policy of discrimination against women. It is for this reason that women have been vocal and determined in their opposition to the regime's particular brand of Islamisation. For a number of women, this has meant being incarcerated and subjected to police brutality. In order to win the support of sections of the orthodox *'ulamā* and in complete disregard of parental responsibility, directives were issued to educational institutions that females must wear *chadars*. As a result, young girls are harassed and victimised on the slightest pretext by those who take advantage of a situation where there is official sanction for discrimination against the fair sex. In February 1983, when a group of women assembled close to the Lahore High Court to petition the Chief Justice of the Lahore High Court against the proposed Law of Evidence, which aimed at making the evidence of two women equal to that of one man, they were brutally beaten and manhandled by both male and female police. In the ensuing furor, sections of the *'ulamā'* went so far as to demand the death penalty for these women, who according to them had committed apostasy by demonstrating against Qur'ānic injunctions. A careful reading of the Qur'ān and the considered opinion of Muslim scholars is that neither the Qur'ān nor Islam supports the view that the evidence of two women is equal to that of one man.

Contrary to the officially sponsored view, equality between the sexes is clearly established in the following Qur'ānic verses:

> For Muslim men and women
> For believing men and women
> For devout men and women
> For true men and women
> For men and women who are patient and constant
> For men and women who humble themselves
> For men and women who give in charity
> For men and women who fast (and deny themselves)
> For men and women who guard their chastity, and
> For men and women who engage much in God's praise
> For them has God prepared forgiveness and great reward
> (Qur'ān 33:35).

From the above it is clear that the Qur'ān lays down equal duties and obligations on both men and women. There is no distinction between men and women in what is expected of them. The Prophet also was very clear about the status of women when he made the following statement:

> They [Muslims] are equal as the teeth on a comb. There is no claim of an Arab over a non-Arab, or of a white over a black person, or of a male over a female. Only God-fearing people merit preference with God.[19]

Nowhere in the Qur'ān is it mentioned that a single woman is disqualified from giving evidence. There is, however, a particular verse in *Sura al-Baqra* of the Qur'ān which mentions the evidence of one man and two women. It is this verse that is generally cited by reactionary elements to equate the evidence of two women with that of one man. It is important, however, to remember that this verse relates to business transactions only. Even here men and women are seen as equal witnesses.

The role of the second female witness is not as a primary witness. She is there only to accompany and to remind. Today, as a result of her knowledge and experience, a woman is capable of giving evidence in all matters. Any law which by discriminating against a particular section of society creates discontent and frustration cannot be in keeping with the spirit of Islam whose message is peace, equality and tolerance.

In the absence of healthy entertainment, as well as the dearth of meaningful cultural activities, the youth in particular and the masses in general have over the past few years been denied exposure to the rich cultural heritage of this region. As a result, the pent-up energy of the youth is finding an outlet in socially undesirable activities such as drug addiction, crime etc.

In the name of Islamising the legal system, the power of the judiciary has been so curtailed as to make a mockery of the once respected judicial system of the country. *Sharîat* benches (Islamic courts) have been set up, but their jurisdiction has been restricted. They can neither interfere in fundamental constitutional matters nor hear appeals against martial law orders or judgments of military courts. Ironically, in the 'Islamic Republic of Pakistan,' the *sharîat* courts, which are supposed to interpret divine laws, are subservient to the military courts which pronounce judgment in accordance with the edicts of the military regime. By arrogating to himself a position in law superior to that of God, the Chief Martial Law Administrator has made a mockery of his much-trumpeted process of Islamisation. It is not surprising that the obscurantist *'ulamā* have learnt to live with this absurdity and are supporting the regime. The Islamisation of the legal system has therefore been a selective process. Political expediency has been the basis of the Islamisation drive. While *sharîat* benches have been set up and *qazi* (judge) courts are to come into operation, care has been taken to restrict their powers, lest at some stage they threaten the regime.

In complete disregard of the dynamic and humanitarian nature of Islam, and to further strengthen the coercive powers of the state, various ordinances and laws have been promulgated. Contrary to the spirit that prevailed at the time when Muslim culture was at its peak, these laws and ordinances do not reflect a consensus of opinion among the people. Nor do they meet the requirements of a society that needs to keep pace with the multifarious developments taking place in the world. By introducing amendments in the legal system and by introducing so-called Islamic punishments of a most inhuman kind, the self-styled defenders of the faith have done a great disservice to Islam, whose primary message is justice, benevolence and tolerance. In Pakistan's so-called Islamic state, where justice has become a purchasable commodity, it is a common occurrence for the rich to get away with almost anything, while the poor are made answerable to the 'law'. Claiming to be moral reformers, the persons at the helm of affairs are imposing on society a moral code that aims at distracting the people's attention from the real issues confronting society.

Islamisation within a Feudal-Capitalist Framework

In the economic sphere the military regime, with the support of feudal and big business interests, claims to have embarked upon Islamising the economy by introducing profit and loss counters in banks on one hand and imposing *zakāt* (poor tax) and *ushr* (tax on agricultural produce) on the other. If the objective of Islamisation is to abolish an exploitative socio-economic system, then neither has the introduction of profit and loss counters achieved this, nor has the imposition of *zakāt* reduced the level of poverty in the country. In fact, over the last few years, the system has become more exploitative and oppressive. According to a recent study, while 35% of the rural population were living in abject poverty in 1977, the percentage of poor people in the rural areas had increased to 37% in 1979.[20]

While the introduction of profit and loss counters in banks was acclaimed by government circles as a 'great leap forward' towards the elimination of *ribā* (increase in capital on loans or sales) from the economy, the entire socio-economic system has become more exploitative.[21] The introduction of interest-free banking in an essentially capitalistic economy, where a fairly large proportion of deposits belongs to the lower middle class, discriminates against the poorer depositors. These depositors, theoretically speaking, will be paid no profit in the event of a loss. In such a system the investor can receive loans from banks at zero interest with a nominal service charge and thus make a large profit. While the profit to be paid to depositors is determined by the banks' operations, in fact investors borrowing from banks may well be earning much larger profits than the depositors receive under the PLS system. The depositor may thus receive only a nominal profit. Thus, within a capitalist economy, the replacement of the principle of limited liability by a system of sharing profit and loss would tend to result in the exploitation of the depositor, who has limited information regarding the inner functionings of a corporation.

In a country like Pakistan, where in order to avoid taxes businessmen can get away with maintaining 'multiple account books', the profit and loss system, if generalised, is likely to result in fraud on a large scale. As happened in the case of the large number of financial houses that sprang up in the country a few years ago, large amounts of money were embezzled and could not be retrieved by ignorant depositors. However, so long as the profit and loss system is confined to the nationalised banks and a couple of *mudāraba* (profit-sharing) companies as at present, there is little danger of the depositors suffering a major loss. If this were to happen, the acquisitive spirit that has come to permeate a large section of society would compel people to think twice before entrusting their

149

savings to the banks. It is probably because of the government's awareness of the possibility of widespread fraud, as well as the structural constraints imposed by the present structure of a dependent economy, that it has adopted a rather cautious approach to the introduction of the profit and loss system of banking. It is evident that the profit and loss system has been introduced more as an eye-wash rather than as an overall system aimed at the abolition of exploitation and speculation.

Although the government in June 1984 announced that all interest-bearing financial instruments will be replaced by the profit and loss sharing system, a substantial proportion of the banking sector will continue to operate under the interest-based system. The federal Finance Minister, while asserting that the interest-free system would supplant the existing system was, however, quick to state that 'all the pledges made under the existing system would be honoured, and dealings with foreign governments and international finance institutions will continue un-changed'.[22] The interest-based system would thus continue to be opera-tive in the case of large amounts of foreign exchange being lent to the industrial sector by state-controlled financial institutions, such as the Pakistan Industrial Credit and Investment Corporation (PICIC), the Industrial Development Bank of Pakistan (IDBP) and the National Development Finance Corporation (NDFC). These are, in turn, financed by foreign countries and international finance institutions. As a senior development banker remarked, 'these institutions are not willing to experiment with the Islamic system. Interest is equally a "theologi-cal" issue with them.'[23]

The profit and loss sharing system of banking can be expected to be used by the bureaucracy within the present socio-economic framework to further its own interests at the expense of others. Such fears have been expressed by sections of the business community. They are of the view that the public sector-controlled nationalised banks would tend to keep a close watch on them after advancing credit on a profit and loss sharing basis. They would tend to interfere in the management of projects since the nationalised banks would, under the profit and loss sharing system, be partners in loss as well as gain. These fears of the private sector have been confirmed by public sector bank officials when one of them remarked 'banks would be justified in keeping an eye on the projects and advise the borrowers because the banks will be partners in loss as well'.[24] While such a system of lending would increase the already ubiquitous control of the bureaucracy over the economy, it would make a mockery of the much publicised 'liberalisation' of the economy, to which the government claims to be committed. It is not by introducing profit and loss accounts in the organised financial sector that exploitation and extortion can be checked. Interest is functional to the capitalist economic system, a system in which the decisions to save and invest are taken by independent parties in response to signals given by the market. Exploitation in such a system takes place at the level of profit-making. Therefore, to make the elimination of interest the focus of attention alone is to adopt a superficial view of capitalist exploitation. Interest paid by the corporation to the banks is merely the sharing of profit among various capitalist interests.

From the Islamisation policies followed by the military regime, as well as the recommendations of the Islamic Ideology Council, it appears that the purpose of the government is not so much to abolish the institution of interest as to make it appear to the public that interest has been eliminated from financial transactions. The Islamic Ideology Council in its report on the elimination of interest has suggested ways of getting round the theoretical prohibition of *ribā* while retaining the essential characteristics of a capitalist economy.[25] The report rather ingeniously suggests that the nomenclature of the price of and return on capital, which has come to be known as interest, be altered to profit in the case of *mudāraba* companies and service charges in the case of banks.

It may be relevant to point out that the concept of profit-sharing is not a system confined to Islamic theological opinion. The principle of investing on a profit and loss sharing basis was also prevalent in pre-industrial Europe, a period noted for the severest forms of exploitation. The concept of investment on a profit and loss sharing basis was elaborated at a time when financial institutions, banks and large industrial concerns had not yet developed:

> *Mudāraba* was an ancient type of commercial capital; it existed before Islam in Arabia and southern Europe. It was a sort of primitive commercial organisation in which the capital-owner entrusted his capital to an agent/ worker on the basis of profit sharing in a prearranged proportion . . . All risk was borne by the owner . . . This institution is not based on any explicit text (*nass*) of the Qur'ān or the *Hadīth*.[26]

Later, with the expansion of markets, as the prospects of making a profit either through trade or manufacturing became more widespread, it became difficult for share-holders to monitor the profits of companies whose size had increased. As a result, profit and loss sharing as an investment technique was gradually supplanted in Europe by a fixed predetermined rate of return called interest.

In Pakistan there have been a large number of cases where the interest-free system has been exploited by feudal and capitalist interests to their own advantage. A large number of interest-free or low interest loans earmarked for small farmers have been advanced to large and influential farmers with contacts with the ruling hierarchy. Moreover, in a capital-scarce economy like Pakistan's, with a highly inequitable pattern of income distribution, the availability of zero-interest loans would, by making the use of capital profitable, further displace labour. In such a situation, since demand for credit would be greater than its supply, credit would have to be rationed. This, in turn, would tend to increase the possibility of a select few with contacts with the regime pre-empting credit facilities.

Landlordism and *Ribā*

If the purpose of the abolition of *ribā* is to eliminate all forms of extortion in financial transactions as well as unearned income, the measures taken by the military regime have been most unsatisfactory. Even if the abolition of *ribā* is taken in the narrow sense to mean elimination of extortion from financial transactions, the regime has not taken any concrete measures to prohibit the extortionate interest rates charged from small farmers and landless peasants by money-lender landlords in the rural area. This however, would only have been possible if far-reaching land reforms had been carried out and alternative political institutions created. Given the reliance of the military regime for political support on rich landlords it cannot implement a meaningful land reform. It should also be noted that those political parties whose leadership is predominantly feudal cannot be expected either to redistribute land in favour of the landless and small farmers or to set up the necessary institutions to give them a share in political power. There is a fundamental difference between reforms introduced from above and those brought about by the active participation of the oppressed whom the reforms are meant to benefit.

It is within the rural social structure that *ribā* and the institution of *muzāra'a* (share-cropping, ground rent) need to be eliminated in their various forms, whether in the form of extortionate interest rates or the feudal system of share-cropping. Due to the prevailing system of share-cropping practised on tenant-operated farms, a large number of tenants have to give to the landlord half the produce.[27] The elimination of *ribā* in rural areas would put an end to the exploitation of the millions of poor peasants at the hands of feudal lords who thrive on extortion and unearned income.

As in the case of Europe, where in the Middle Ages sections of the clergy invoked religious injunctions to justify an iniquitous status quo, in Pakistan today the ruling classes and sections of the *'ulamā*, devoid of a popular mandate, interpret Islam so as to uphold an exploitative social order. The exploitative nature of the Pakistani social formation is brought out by an examination of the structure of rural society and economy. Here the government's so-called Islamisation policies have done nothing to alter the exploitative social and economic structure in which a small elite, by virtue of its loyalty to successive governments, owns and controls a large proportion of land. According to the agricultural census of 1980, large farmers (50 acres and above), whose holdings made up only 2 per cent of total farm area, controlled 24 per cent of farm land. On the other hand, small farms (25 acres and less), which constituted 92 per cent of total holdings, had only 60 per cent of the total farm land.[28] A comparison of the 1980 and 1972 censuses shows that the distribution of land between small and large farmers has become more unequal.[29]

To justify the highly inequitable system of land ownership, sections of the *'ulamā* do not hesitate to refer to parts of *fiqh* on the one hand and to the prevalence of a system of share-cropping and absentee landlordism during Islamic history on the other. Conversely, there are those who in building up a case against the feudal order refer to the egalitarianism of the Prophet's practice.[30] These contrasting interpretations of Islamic history and injunctions relating to the question of landlordism are understandable, for the social structure of Muslim society underwent major changes between the early period of the Prophet and that of the conquests when new lands and a feudal agrarian system were incorporated into the caliphate. It was during the later period, after the conquests, that the codification of *fiqh* took place. Notwithstanding the condemnation of *muzāra'a* by *fuqahā* (Islamic jurists) like Abu Hanīfa (d. 767-8), Ahmed ibn Hanbal (d. 891-2), and Mohammad ibn Idris al-Shāfi'i (d. 795-6), *fiqh*, as codified, did not prohibit share-cropping or landlordism. The practice of share-cropping was thus legalised on the basis of actual practice and expediency. This was in spite of the fact that the Prophet disapproved of the institution of share-cropping, as has been pointed out by an Islamic scholar:

> According to evidence which remains unimpeached the Prophet expressly disapproved of the landowner sharing with the actual worker the products of agriculture, though some thought it was only in the nature of an informal rebuke rather than a formal ban.[31]

After the Prophet's death, successful attempts were made in the reign of the Caliph 'Umar to prevent the institution of share-cropping from establishing itself. But later, with the expansion of the caliphate and the incorporation of new lands with strongly entrenched feudal structures, the social structure of the Muslim community underwent a transformation. From one based on collectivism with a strong egalitarian spirit, the agrarian social order began to rest upon power being derived from control over land. Even *fiqh*, which was codified within a feudal milieu, did not place any restriction on the transfer of land from self-cultivating farmers to non-cultivating owners.[32] Thus the widespread transfers of land resulted in the gradual dispossession of the peasantry and the emergence of a landowning class with strong links to the ruling hierarchy. It was in the post-Prophetic period that the democratic spirit of Islam was replaced by the dynastic rule of Umayyads, and a feudal-monarchical structure came to dominate most of the Muslim World.

Why is it that discussion of the Islamisation of the economy in Pakistan has concentrated on the elimination of interest from only the organised financial sector and has not focussed attention on the widespread prevalence of *ribā* and *muzāra'a* in the economy? There are a number of reasons for this. First, the main theoreticians of the concept of an 'Islamic economy' have elaborated it to be based principally on an interest-free system and *zakāt*. Second, popular discussion and elaboration of the concept of an Islamic economy have been restricted mainly to the propertied classes. It is not in their interest to elaborate the true meaning and significance of the elimination of *ribā* and *muzāra'a* as it would threaten their interests. Thus a static and politically expedient interpretation has been given to Islamic injunctions, including the elimination of *ribā*.

Throughout Muslim history ways and means have been found to avoid the prohibition of *ribā* and *muzāra'a*. *Hiyal* (ruses avoiding prohibitions) has been a common device whereby in the face of Islamic injunctions prohibiting *ribā* and *muzāra'a* these practices have been permitted in various forms in different times and places in the Muslim World. Scholars of various legal schools have found ways of getting round theoretical prohibitions of *ribā*. Out of the four *Sunni* schools of Islamic jurisprudence, the *Hanafi* school applies the principle of 'practical necessity' to overcome the theoretical prohibition of *ribā*. Similarly, the *Māliki* and the *Shafi'i* schools of Islamic jurisprudence, to get round the injunctions prohibiting *ribā*, have permitted *hiyal* in a limited number of cases. Various books were devoted by Muslim scholars of law, such as Abu Bakr Ahmad al Khassaf (d. 874) and Abu Hatim Mahmud al Qazwini (d. 1050), mainly of the *Hanafi* school, to expounding the forms in which interest was permitted. Similarly, certain *fuqahā* of the *Māliki* and *Shāfi'i* schools have justified the institution of *muzāra'a* on the basis of actual practice.

Development of Capitalism in Muslim Societies

By the time of the Abbasid revolution in 750, vast areas had been brought under the control of central authority. Meanwhile, the Arabisation of the caliphate, which had been initiated by the Umayyad ruler Abdul Malik (685-705) helped to create the conditions for widespread commercial activity.[33] Arabic came to replace Greek and Persian as the state language, and Arabs took over the civil administration. The caliphate expanded rapidly following the classical pattern of conquests and conversions on the one hand and commercialisation of production and expansion of trade on the other. With the centralisation of authority and the development of communication networks the opportunities for production for the market increased greatly.[34] The growth of industries producing for export was rapid in areas such as Khazistan (south-eastern Iraq), Syria, Bokhara and Baghdad. As a result of the increased demand for goods, the need for finance both for investment and trade increased. The Muslims, however, preferred to retain the more prestigious positions in the bureaucracy and military, while allowing other religious groups, especially Jews, to indulge in finance and trade.[35] However, in areas where other religious groups were not significant, Muslims themselves undertook commercial and financial activity. Where there were possibilities of making a profit through trade, credit was made available, and interest was charged by both Muslims and non-Muslims so that capital could fructify. The observant eye of ibn Khaldun, probably the greatest of Muslim historians, was able to grasp the nature of commercial practices of an important section of Muslim society in the Middle Ages, notwithstanding the injunctions prohibiting *ribā*:

> Commerce means increasing one's capital by buying merchandise and attempting to sell it for a price higher than its purchase price, either by waiting for market fluctuations or by transporting the merchandise to a country where that particular merchandise is more in demand and brings higher prices, or by selling it for a high price to be paid at a future date . . . Now traders are few. It is unavoidable that there should be cheating, tampering with the merchandise.[36]

Regarding financial practices which were based on interest, Ibn-Khaldun was of the view that delay in repayment of debt is harmful to the creditor as it does not allow his capital to fructify.[37] Besides the observations of Ibn Khaldun, historical records covering different periods and regions of the Muslim World, for instance trade and commercial manuals, indicate that lending and borrowing at interest practised in different forms had been fairly widespread, despite Islamic injunctions to the contrary.[38] Wherever the Muslims themselves indulged in the financial practice of money-lending or borrowing from other communities or religious groups, they depended on the institution of *ribā* for the accumulation of capital.

It seems therefore that the economic imperatives of commercialism and profit took precedence over the textual rendering of Qur'ānic injunctions prohibiting interest. With the expansion of the Muslim community, the socio-economic structure of the areas that came to make up the Muslim World bore little resemblance to the tribal society and economy that characterised the city-state of Medina at the time of the Prophet. As new lands were incorporated into the caliphate following the conquests, the socio-economic structure of the Muslim community underwent profound changes. In order to accommodate the well-to-do communities and classes of the new lands, religious injunctions were not always strictly followed. As these communities and classes started developing close ties with the ruling hierarchy on the one hand and sections of the *'ulamā* on the other, they were able to get round Islamic injunctions which threatened their material interests. Not only were they able to prevent the application of Qur'ānic injunctions prohibiting *ribā*, but they were also successful in influencing the thinking of certain legal schools of thought.

Changes in theological opinion, represented by the emergence of different schools of thought, which in turn reflected structural changes at the social, economic and political levels, have not been confined to Muslim society alone. They were a feature of mediaeval European society as well. In the case of Europe, religious thinking and popular opinion, which had hitherto been hostile to the practice of lending and borrowing on interest, which was termed usury, were gradually reconciled to the rising tide of capitalist practices and institutions. The popular thinking in Europe that led to the acceptance of interest towards the end of the Middle Ages may be summed up as follows: 'why should a creditor, who may himself be poor, make a loan gratis, in order to put money into the pockets of a wealthy capitalist who uses the advance to corner the wool crop or to speculate on exchange?'[39]

Changes at the institutional level have therefore been accompanied by changes in popular and theological opinion. At the theological level, the reconciliation of secular and religious opinion was undertaken in Europe by John Calvin towards the end of the 16th century. It was not only Calvin's condonation of lending and borrowing on interest but also his overall world-view that broke through the stagnant intellectual milieu of feudal-dominated mediaeval Europe:

> It is not wholly fanciful to say that on a narrower stage, but with not less formidable weapons, Calvin did for the bourgeoisie of the sixteenth century what Marx did for the proletariat of the nineteenth, or that the doctrine of predestination satisfied the same hunger for an assurance that the forces of the universe are on the side of the elect as was to be assuaged in a different age by the theory of historical materialism.[40]

At a general level, be it Buddhism, Christianity or Islam, usury in particular and the exploitation of man by man in general have been denounced on moral grounds and because of their adverse economic consequences. The excessive concentration of wealth in the hands of the few is considered to breed arrogance and selfishness on the one hand and poverty and deprivation on the other. A society with a large number of poor and underfed persons, it is argued, can neither be economically healthy nor socially stable. One reason for the general consensus of opinion regarding the prohibition of usury among the various religious and early philosophical schools of thought has been the exploitative nature of most borrowing and lending in largely subsistence economies.

In societies where production is largely for subsistence, it is only in times of dire need that borrowing is resorted to. Taking advantage of the weak bargaining position of the persons in need, the well-to-do classes with a surplus advance on credit commodities or money. Such advances are made on the condition that within a specified period the borrower return not only the amount advanced but a certain percentage of the principle as interest. The rate of interest on the loan advanced depends on a number of factors, such as the degree of competition between the lenders and borrowers, the accessibility to credit markets and the bargaining position of the borrower.

Lending and borrowing in various forms have been practised ever since society was divided into the two main classes of surplus producers and appropriators. The propertied classes, who have traditionally controlled the surplus, have permitted the direct producers to exist barely at a subsistence level. When due to an increase in the rate of exploitation or to unpredictable natural factors, the level of existence of the direct producers falls below the subsistence level, they are forced to borrow to keep themselves alive. It is such borrowing, which is still prevalent in large parts of the rural areas of Pakistan, that is highly exploitative.

Usury of *ribā* has derived its exploitative nature in the popular mind from the highly unequal relationship between the money-lenders, who in a large number of cases have been owners of large estates, and weak and poor borrowers. This was the case in Western Europe prior to the development of modern capitalism and still is the case in the Indo-Pakistan subcontinent and many other Third World countries. It is the reaction among the poorer sections, who in times of need are forced to seek subsistence loans, that has been articulated by sections of religious opinion as a vehement attack on the institution of money-lending. When we find reference to the prohibition of *ribā* in Islamic thought or usury in Christian religious opinion of the Middle Ages, we must bear in mind that

> like the modern profiteer, the usurer was a character so unpopular that most unpopular characters could be called usurers, and by the average practical man almost any form of bargain which he thought oppressive would be classed as usurious.[41]

Although the above observations of Professor Tawney, describing the popular perception of usury, relate to feudal Europe during the Middle Ages, the same kind of description of both usurers and usurious loans could very easily be applied to Muslim societies past and present. Complaints about usurers that appear in Islamic literature of the mediaeval period point towards not only the prevalence of the institution of money-lending but the contempt in which the usurer was held. In a poem attributed to the 11th-century Ismaili propagandist Nasir-i-Khosraw, usurers are defined as 'contemptible creatures who drink the blood of the poor and are destined to end up in eternal fire'.[42] Notwithstanding the aversion to money-lending at the popular level, the position of the money-lender, who in a number of cases was also the owner of large estates, was protected in the case of mediaeval Europe by sections of the clergy and in Muslim societies by sections of the *'ulamā*.

In countries like Pakistan, where feudalism still persists alongside a modern capitalist sector, the concept of *ribā* should encompass the whole gambit of oppressive and exploitative relations between the exploiter and the exploited: the feudal lord and the landless tenants, the capitalist owner and the worker, the extortionate merchant and the consumer. All these exploitative relations stem from a social structure that gives rise to

157

the division of society into the exploiter and the exploited and the oppressor and the oppressed. The concentration of economic wealth and power in the hands of a privileged few implies the denial of economic opportunities and well-being to the majority of the populations. Unless the social, economic and political structures that perpetuate the exploitation of the many by the few are changed by the organised strength of the oppressed classes, mere moral exhortations in the name of Islam will not put an end to the pressing problems of poverty, deprivation and socioeconomic backwardness. Instead of making the elimination of interest and the institution of *zakāt* and *ushr* the cornerstones of a so-called Islamic economy, the propagators of a so-called Islamic economy should concentrate on the establishment of a society where true egalitarianism exists. This, however, they will not do. Paradoxically, whereas the exploiting classes see in the feudal and oppressive practices of the Muslim ruling classes a justification for the status quo, the oppressed classes see in Islam a panacea for their sufferings.

So-called Islamic governments may claim that *ribā* has been prohibited, but in fact exploitative socio-economic structures are still prevalent. This is because the socio-economic structures of most countries which claim to be Islamic are actually distorted extensions of those in developed capitalist countries. Parts of these societies are backward, with semifeudal or tribal structures interacting with the more developed centres of finance, commerce and industry. Since capitalism is the more developed mode of production, capitalist relations tend to dominate those social formations where capitalist and semifeudal relations coexist. The so-called Islamic policies adopted by a state representing both capitalist and feudal interests are aimed generally at appeasing conservative and well-to-do sections of society rather than at achieving objectives such as the elimination of *ribā*. It is not possible to eliminate *ribā* without first demolishing the exploitative socio-economic edifice on which society and economy are based. Whereas Pakistan's rural society is yet to free itself from the stranglehold of feudal interests and values, the urban areas have a long way to go before they experience meaningful industrialisation from which workers and ordinary people can benefit.

Historical and Structural Roots of Underdevelopment in Pakistan

Pakistan's economy has been conditioned by the socio-economic structure inherited at the time of Partition on the one hand and the influence that sections of the ruling classes have exercised on the government on the other. At the time of Partition there was hardly any industry in Pakistan, and most manufactured commodities were imported. Thus Pakistan, at the time of independence, inherited a feudal-dominated agrarian economy with hardly any industry. With the demand for manufactured goods being fairly high and diversified, there was considerable scope for investment in industry. Given the government's commitment to a laissez-faire policy, its restrictive import policy, and the liberal inflows of United States' aid, a favourable climate for private investment was created. Taking advantage of such a situation, a number of Muslim trading families who had moved to Pakistan from India or belonged to areas within the territories that made up Pakistan started investing in industry.

The transformation of merchant capital into industrial capital did not follow the classic laissez-faire model of Western Europe, where there had been a protracted struggle at the economic, political, social and cultural levels between the feudal lords and the emerging industrial bourgeoisie. Whereas in the case of Western Europe at the time of the genesis of the modern nation-state feudal power and influence had waned, in the case of Pakistan this was not so. The Pakistan Movement did not incorporate in it an antifeudal programme, nor did the policies of successive governments after independence provide for a meaningful land reform.

After Partition, the commercial classes were not in the same socially and politically dominant position as the feudalists, who wielded greater influence in their respective areas. The migrant trading classes, with their distinct ethnic and cultural identity, did not really integrate into the sociocultural milieu of the regions where they settled. Instead of checking the power of the feudals by developing alliances with the middle classes, the working classes and the peasantry, the trading classes, in their haste to transform themselves into industrialists, developed links with the bureaucracy with whose patronage and support they developed. Since the industrialists could influence the government's policies through links with the bureaucracy, they did not find it necessary to develop an independent political base by challenging the hegemony of the feudalists. As a result, large areas of feudal domination existed alongside the centres of capitalist activity. On the other hand the feudalists either directly controlled state power or, through their links with the military-bureaucratic oligarchy, wielded influence over government policies. On the economic level such a structural relationship based on the coexistence of semifeudal and capitalist relations has given rise to an uneven pattern of development.

The concentrated structure of land ownership which characterises Pakistan's agrarian structure and the accompanying consumption pattern of the rural elite leave few resources for productive investment. A large amount of resources are transferred from the rural to the urban areas in the form of luxury consumption by the feudal classes. A significant proportion of the luxury consumption of the rural elite is in the form of expensive imported items. Such wasteful consumption does not encourage the growth of domestic industry but rather diverts a significant proportion of foreign exchange resources from essential imports such as raw materials and capital goods. Besides the wasteful expenditure of the feudal and capitalist class, the maintenance of a large bureaucratic-military machine, which has historically proved its role as a protector of the status quo, consumes a large amount of resources. This leaves little for investment in productive and socially desirable programmes. In 1984-85 the federal government's non-development budget (Rs. 70,736 million) was double that of the development budget (Rs. 33,290 million).[43] The largest share of the resources was taken up by the defence services, for which Rs. 29,191 million were budgeted.[44] Adding to the defence budget, the expenditure on administration, law and order and internal security raised the government's expenditure on itself to Rs. 32,929 million or close to 50 per cent of the total current expenditure.[45] Given the wasteful and non-productive expenditure incurred by an exploitative economic structure, foreign resource inflows have been needed to meet investment requirements. In 1982-83 gross aid inflows were $1,122 million, which was close to 40 per cent of the fixed investment in the public sector. By December 1983 the country had accumulated an outstanding foreign debt of ten billion dollars, which was over 35 per cent of the country's current income.[46]

Besides the financial costs of aid, which the country has had to bear in terms of higher prices of commodities and interest charges, there have also been other costs of a political and economic nature. The political cost of aid depends upon the nature of the regime in power on the one hand and the degree of dependence and diversification of sources of aid achieved by the recipient on the other. Due to the heavy dependence on foreign aid contracted from traditional sources such as the USA, the World Bank and the IMF, aid-giving agencies have in recent years come to play an important role in influencing the formulation of economic policies in Pakistan. It is common knowledge that 'aid' is generally advanced with a *quid pro quo*, which for the recipient besides restricting its sovereignty involves granting concessions to commercial interests in donor countries. In the case of the $1.7 billion three-year Extended Fund Facility advanced to Pakistan by the IMF in 1980, the country was required to restructure its economic policies in deference to the IMF's wishes contained in what were euphemistically termed 'stabilisation' policies. In the IMF's parlance 'stabilisation' inevitably involves import liberalisation, devaluation, withdrawal of subsidies, a harsh labour policy and cutting down public sector investment programmes. While having a salutary effect on investment in donor countries, such policies have affected adversely the poorer sections in the country and have made a mockery of so-called national economic planning. The terms and conditions under which foreign aid has been advanced to Pakistan have not permitted the economy to develop in a balanced and self-reliant manner.

Conclusion

Why is it that the Muslim World, which some ten centuries ago was one of the leading civilisations in the world, is today underdeveloped and dependent economically, militarily and technologically on foreign powers? It has become convenient to invoke modern theories of imperialism to explain the cultural and economic backwardness of the Third World, of which most Muslim countries are a part. In emphasising the effects on the colonies of developments in the centres of Western imperialism, such explanations, however, do not give sufficient weight to indigenous social and cultural factors. While interacting with external factors, indigenous factors have given rise to underdevelopment in its various dimensions.

Broadly speaking, the intellectual reaction to imperialist domination in the Muslim World has taken two forms — doctrinaire and institutionalised Marxism on the one hand and Islamic fundamentalism on the other. Both of these responses have, however, not been able to strike deep enough roots among the masses to be able to create the conditions for the social transformation of Muslim communities in the present stage of social evolution. Whatever the official ideology adopted by the ruling classes, the basic structure of most Muslim countries remains exploitative and authoritarian, and feudal and capitalist modes of production coexist in varying degrees. Even if, under pressure from the oppressed classes, the egalitarian message of Islam is emphasised in official ideology, the ruling elites try to prevent the participation of the masses in political power by not allowing the establishment of effective political, economic and social institutions.

In the case of Pakistan we have seen the manner in which the ruling elites have, while accepting Islam as the official ideology, given it a reactionary interpretation. Those institutions have not been allowed to develop which could revolutionise the lives of the downtrodden and oppressed classes, for whose uplift Islam was popularised by the Prophet. On the other hand, fundamentalist Islamic groups such as the *Jamā'at-i-Islāmī*, which enjoys the support of the establishment, present an authoritarian and reactionary interpretation of Islam. The objective of the ruling hierarchy and the *Jamā'at* appears to be to retard social progress by not allowing the emancipation of the masses. Their interpretation of Islam regards the social order as something static and unalterable. Their concern with economic issues is not caused by anxiety for reform but by concern with the maintenance of an idealistic moral code, of which economic conduct forms an essential part. Their idealistic moral code, based on the appealing universal values of brotherhood, egalitarianism and justice, is essentially bound up with economic and social structures of the past, canonised during a period of history when society and economy were not as complex as today. Such concepts of morality in the present era of modern capitalism are alone incapable of eliminating exploitation and oppression.

References and Notes

1. For a discussion of the contrasting trends in the politics of Islam see Eqbal Ahmed, 'Islam and Politics', in this book.

2. I. H. Qureshi, *'Ulemā in Politics* (Karachi: Ma'aref, 1972), pp. 3-4.

3. Ali Shariati, *On the Sociology of Islam* (Berkeley: Mizan Press, 1979), p. 49.

4. For a discussion of the city-state of Medina see Sibt-i-Hasan, *Naveed-i-Fikr* (Karachi: Maktab-i-Danial, 1982), pp. 39-77.

5. *Mishkat*, book 1, chapter 4, quoted in M. Munir, *From Jinnah to Zia* (Lahore: Vanguard Books, 1979), pp. 145-6.

6. From a talk to Muslim League workers by Quaid-i-Azam on 1 March 1946, quoted in Fatehyab Ali Khan, 'Objective of the Pakistan Movement', *Islamabad Daily Muslim*, 12 May 1984, Friday Magazine.

7. M. Munir, *From Jinnah to Zia*, pp. 25-6.

8. Extracts from Quaid-i-Azam's presidential address to the Pakistan Constituent Assembly 11 August 1947, quoted in Sharif-al Mujahid, *Quaid-i-Azam Jinnah — Studies in Interpretation* (Karachi: Quaid-i-Azam Academy, 1981), p. 248.

9. Abul Ala Maudoodi, *Tehrik-i-Azadi-i-Hind Aur Mussalman*, vol. II (Lahore: Islamic Publications, 1983), p. 42, quoted in 'Zeno', 'Maudoodi and Colonialism', *Pakistan Times*, 28 September 1968.

10. Abul Ala Maudoodi, *Tehrik-i-Azadi*, pp. 139-40, quoted in 'Zeno', 'Maudoodi — the Past', *Pakistan Times*, 12 July 1968.

11. Abul Ala Maudoodi, *Tafhim-ul-Qur'ān* vol. II, 5th ed. (Lahore: Maktab-i-Tamir-i-Insaniat, 1973), p. 638.

12. Abul Ala Maudoodi, *Islami Riyasat* (Lahore: Islamic Publishers, 1967), p. 20.

13. Ibid., p. 47.

14. *The Holy Quran*, ed. and trans. by Yusuf Ali (Lahore: Sh. Mohammad Ashraf), p. 1497.

15. Ibid., p. 1505.

16. Quaid-i-Azam's address to the Delhi convention of the All-India Muslim League, 1946, quoted in *Viewpoint*, September 1983.

17. *Lahore Nawa-i-Waqt*, 13 March 1977.

18. Ibid., 30 April 1977.

19. A. Rauf, *Islamic View of Women and the Family* (Washington: Islamic Centre), quoted in Women's Action Forum, 'Position Paper on Proposed Law of Evidence', Lahore, February 1983 (typewritten).

20. 'Poverty in Rural and Urban Pakistan', in Asian Regional Team for Employment Promotion (ILO-ARTEP), *Employment and Structural Change — Issues for the Eighties* (Bangkok, January 1983), p. 239.

21. Broadly defined, *ribā* is an increase in income earned without expending labour. It therefore covers the capitalists' income as well as that of landlords, earned through renting out land to share-croppers.

22. *Karachi Dawn*, 15 June 1984.

23. Babar Ayaz, 'Islamic Banking: Island in Capitalist Ocean', *Karachi Dawn*, Economic and Business Review, 17 June 1984.

24. bid.

25. Council of Islamic Ideology, *The Elimination of Interest from the Economic* (Karachi: Government of Pakistan, 1980), passim.

26. Ziaul Haque, 'Book Review: *Studies In Islamic Economics*, ed. by Khurshid Ahmad', *Hamdard Islamicus*, 5, No. 1 (Spring 1982), p. 105.

27. According to the 1980 agricultural census of Pakistan, close to 36% of the total farm area in Pakistan was tenant-operated. See Agricultural Census Organisation, *Pakistan Census of Agriculture — 1980* (Islamabad: Government of Pakistan, 1983), p. 5.

28. Ibid., p. 3.

29. M. Mahmood, 'Changes in the Agrarian Structure of Pakistan', *Islamabad Daily Muslim*, 6 July 1984, Friday Magazine.

30. See Ziaul Haque, *Landlord and Peasant in Early Islam* (Islamabad: Islamic Research Institute, 1977).

31. S. M. Yusuf, *Studies in Islamic History and Culture* (Karachi: Islamic Book Service, 1970), pp. 198-9.

32. Ibid., p. 26.

33. For a discussion of the Arabisation of the caliphate under Abdul Malik (685-705), see S. F. Mahmud, *A Short History of Islam* (Karachi: Oxford University Press, 1960), pp. 74 and 77.

34. For a discussion of expansion in trade and growth of production for the market in the early Abbasid period see Mahmud, *History of Islam*, pp. 130-2 and M. Rodinson, *Islam and Capitalism* (Harmondsworth: Penguin, 1974), pp. 28-75.

35. See Rodinson, *Islam and Capitalism*, pp. 37-8.

36. Ibn Khaldun, *An Introduction to History — The Muqaddimah* trans. F. Rosenthal, abridged and edited N. J. Dawood (London: Routledge and Kegal Paul, 1967), p. 312.

37. Ibid.

38. See Rodinson, *Islam and Capitalism*, p. 31.

39. R. H. Tawney, *Religion and the Rise of Capitalism* (Harmondsworth: Penguin Books, 1977), p. 185.

40. Ibid., p. 120.

41. Ibid., p. 157.

42. Rodinson, *Islam and Capitalism*, p. 40.

43. Government of Pakistan, Finance Division, *Annual Budget Statement, 1984-85* (Islamabad: Government of Pakistan, 1984), pp. 11-13.

44. Ibid.

45. Ibid.

46. Government of Pakistan, Finance Division, *Pakistan Economic Survey, 1983-84* (Islamabad: Government of Pakistan, 1984), p. 84 and Statistical Annexure.

47. Ibid., p. 82 and Statistical Annexure.

7. Rewriting the History of Pakistan

by Pervez Amirali Hoodbhoy
and Abdul Hameed Nayyar

From indoctrination's foul rope
Suspend all reason, all hope
Until with swollen tongue
Morality herself is hung.

Introduction

Education in Pakistan, from schools to universities, is being fundamentally redefined. This development is expected to have profound implications for the future of the country's society and politics. Most changes are traceable to factors related to the stability of the present government, but there are also others which cannot be analysed as a mere response to immediate threats. A new concept of education now prevails, the full impact of which will probably be felt by the turn of the century, when the present generation of school children attains maturity.

Having pledged to divorce education from liberal and secular ideals, Pakistani rulers view education as an important means of creating an Islamised society and as an instrument for forging a new national identity based on the 'Ideology of Pakistan'. Important steps have already been taken in this direction: enforcement of *chadar* in educational institutions; organisation of congregational *zuhr* (afternoon) prayers during school hours; compulsory teaching of Arabic as a second language from sixth class onwards; introduction of *nazara* Qur'ān (reading of Qur'ān) as a matriculation requirement; alteration of the definition of literacy to include religious knowledge; elevation of *maktab* schools to the status of regular schools and the recognition of *maktab* certificates as being equivalent to master's degrees; creation of an Islamic university in Islamabad; introduction of religious knowledge as a criterion for selecting teachers of all categories and all levels; and the revision of conventional subjects to emphasise Islamic values.

It is not the intent of this chapter to analyse in its totality the restructuring of education under the present martial law regime. We

164

focus, instead, on a relatively narrow area — the revised history of Pakistan as currently taught to college students at the intermediate and degree levels. To this end, all officially prescribed Pakistan studies textbooks have been examined, together with books recommended at different institutions. In addition, material has also been included from a number of other books dealing with the history of Pakistan which were written after 1977 and which have discernible official approval. We have discovered that, apart from relatively minor variations in emphasis and style, all present-day textbooks are essentially identical in content. Thus this chapter accurately represents the currently taught version of Pakistani history.

The task of rewriting history books started in earnest in 1981, when General Zia ul Haq declared compulsory the teaching of Pakistan studies to all degree students, including those at engineering and medical colleges. Shortly thereafter, the University Grants Commission issued a directive to prospective textbook authors specifying that the objective of the new course is to 'induce pride for the nation's past, enthusiasm for the present, and unshakeable faith in the stability and longevity of Pakistan'.[1] To eliminate possible ambiguities of approach, authors were given the following directives:

> To demonstrate that the basis of Pakistan is not to be founded in racial, linguistic, or geographical factors, but, rather, in the shared experience of a common religion. To get students to know and appreciate the Ideology of Pakistan, and to popularize it with slogans. To guide students towards the ultimate goal of Pakistan — the creation of a completely Islamised State.[2]

In fulfillment of this directive, modern texts of Pakistani history are centred around the following themes:

1. The 'Ideology of Pakistan', both as a historical force which motivated the movement for Pakistan as well as its *raison d'être*
2. The depiction of Jinnah as a man of orthodox religious views who sought the creation of a theocratic state
3. A move to establish the *'ulamā* as genuine heroes of the Pakistan Movement
4. An emphasis on ritualistic Islam, together with a rejection of liberal interpretations of the religion and generation of communal antagonism

In the remainder of this chapter, each of the above has been examined in turn.

Genesis of the 'Ideology of Pakistan'

The 'Ideology of Pakistan' occupies a position of central importance in all post-1977 Pakistani history textbooks. This ubiquitous phrase permeates all discussion, serves as the reference point for all debate, and makes its appearance at the very outset in all textbooks: 'As citizens of an ideological state . . . it is necessary to first know the basis upon which Pakistan was founded, the ideology of Pakistan.'[3] A virtually identical beginning is found in another book: 'Pakistan is an ideological state . . . the Ideology of Pakistan was the inspiration and the basis of the Movement for Pakistan.'[4] General Zia ul Haq considers the 'Ideology of Pakistan' to be of crucial importance. In one of his speeches he stressed that 'the armed forces bear the sacred responsibility for safeguarding Pakistan's ideological frontiers'.[5]

The 'Ideology of Pakistan' is defined in a number of ways. For example, one source states that 'the Ideology of Pakistan is Islam'.[6] In another textbook, the 'Ideology of Pakistan' is more explicitly defined as:

> . . . that guiding principle which has been accepted by the Muslims of the majority regions of the South Asian subcontinent and which allows them to lead their lives individually and collectively, according to the principles of Islam.[7]

The above definitions do not limit the 'Ideology of Pakistan' to the boundaries of Pakistan. All Muslim majority areas of the subcontinent, including Bangladesh, are covered. Moreover, the manner in which Muslims ought to lead their collective lives in the modern world is assumed to be well defined and beyond controversy. The underlying belief is that there exists a unique definition of an Islamic state.

In stark contrast to modern textbooks, no textbook written prior to 1977 contains mention of the 'Ideology of Pakistan'. Indeed, this phrase was not a part of the political parlance then. Although its precise genealogy is hard to ascertain, ex-Chief Justice Mohammad Munir claims that it has relatively recent origins. In his monograph *From Jinnah to Zia* he writes:

> The Quaid-i-Azam never used the words 'Ideology of Pakistan' . . . For fifteen years after the establishment of Pakistan, the Ideology of Pakistan was not known to anybody until in 1962 a solitary member of the *Jamā'at-i-Islāmī* used these words for the first time when the Political Parties Bill was being discussed. On this, Chaudhry Fazal Elahi, who has recently retired as President of Pakistan, rose from his seat and objected that the 'Ideology of Pakistan' shall have to be defined. The member who had proposed the original amendment replied that the 'Ideology of Pakistan was Islam', but nobody asked him the further question 'What is Islam?' The amendment to the bill was therefore passed.[8]

While this event may or may not be the first significant use of the term 'Ideology of Pakistan', it does hint at the involvement of the politico-religious party, the *Jamā'at-i-Islāmī*, in the propagation — and perhaps creation — of the phrase in question. Therefore, with the aim of arriving at a better understanding of this important phrase, we turn to a brief discussion of the *Jamā'at* and its political programme.

Founded by the late Maulana Abul Ala Maudoodi, the *Jamā'at-i-Islāmī* is a fundamentalist party which categorically asserts the superiority of the Islamic *Sharī'ah* over all other principles and forms of political and social organisation. Much of the *Jamā'at's* appeal derives from rhetorical denunciation of Western civilisation and Western democracy. It has also evolved a version of an Islamic state — the same view currently being popularised by modern textbooks in Pakistan.

The *Jamā'at's* view of an Islamic state is that of an Islamic theocratic state — a state governed according to divinely revealed principles wherein the head of state, elected or otherwise, interpets such principles and translates them into practical matters of the state. Although Maudoodi, in his *Islamic Law and Constitution*, states that 'Islam vests all the Muslim citizens of an Islamic state with popular vice-gerency', he is quick to point out that all vice-gerents need not be of equal consequence. He demands that constitution makers

> evolve such a system of elections as would ensure the appointment of only those who are trustworthy and pious. . . . They should also devise effective measures to defeat the designs and machinations of those who scramble for posts of trust and are consequently hated and cursed by the people in spite of their so-called 'victories' in the elections.[9]

In this 'state without borders' any Muslim anywhere can be a citizen. It will be the best governed not only because its leaders are pious but also because only those will vote who are themselves pious.

With characteristic sternness, the *Manifesto of the Jamā'at-i-Islāmī* (formulated in January 1951, reapproved by its *Majlis-i-Shoora* in December 1969) requires all political activity in Pakistan to obey the following code of ethics (note occurrence of 'Ideology of Pakistan' below):

> Nobody should indulge in anything repugnant to the *Ideology of Pakistan* [emphasis added] . . . Any effort directed towards turning this country into a secular state or implanting herein any foreign ideology amounts to an attack on the very existence of Pakistan.

Notwithstanding occasional sparring, there exists a confluence of basic interests and perceptions of the *Jamā'at* and Pakistani rulers. It is highly significant that, with no essential change in meaning, the phrase 'Ideology of Pakistan' has been elevated from the relative obscurity of the

Manifesto of the Jamā'at-i-Islāmī into legally unchallengable national dogma.

Religious Ideology and the Movement for Pakistan

Independent of precisely when and where the phrase 'Ideology of Pakistan' was first used, it is incontrovertibly true that its common use, both by national leaders and in textbooks, is a post-1977 development. In contrast, the 'Two-Nation Theory' — the basis of Pakistan — has genuine historical roots almost a century old. It was Mohammad Ali Jinnah who, for the first time, proclaimed that India was inhabited by two distinct nations — Hindus and Muslims — who could not live together in one state. In his presidential address to the Muslim League session at Lahore in 1940, he argued that 'Hindus and Muslims belong to two different religions, philosophies, social customs, literatures'.[10] Jinnah expounded his views with such eloquence and force that most Muslims, and even some Hindus, came to believe in them. The Muslim League demand for Pakistan was rooted in this theory, and India was eventually partitioned on the premise that Muslims constitute a distinct entity. Modern textbooks state that this Two-Nation Theory was the predecessor of the 'Ideology of Pakistan':

> This righteous demand (for a separate homeland) was given the temporary name of 'Two-Nation Theory'. Now that right has been achieved, the same theory in this land is called the Ideology of Pakistan.[11]

In post-1977 Pakistan, the 'Ideology of Pakistan' is invariably equated to the 'Two-Nation Theory'. This raises the following questions: prior to 1947, what was the new state envisaged to be? In what sense, and to what extent, was the demand for a theocratic Islamic state the driving force behind the movement for Pakistan? We now turn to a consideration of these questions.

From all historical accounts it appears that in the heat of the struggle for Pakistan the structure of the new state — theocratic, democratic, or whatever — received no serious thought. Although they made their case on the assumption of a distinct Islamic identity, the Muslim League leadership was generally liberal in religious matters, and there had been no sudden revival of faith among them. For Jinnah the matter was particularly clear: he wanted a homeland for the Muslims, not an Islamic state. But there was a definite conflict between this secular constitutional way of thinking and that of the more religious young Muslim Leaguers, who had responded wholeheartedly to the League's call. There was, in fact, a long difference of opinion between Jinnah and the Raja of Mahmudabad, the youngest member of the League's working committee.

Because it throws into sharp focus the issues of the times, it is extremely instructive to study the Raja's memoirs, particularly with reference to the difference in opinion between Jinnah and himself on the nature of the future state:

> I was one of the founder members of the Islamic *Jamā'at*. We advocated that Pakistan should be an Islamic state. I must confess that I was very enthusiastic about it and in my speeches I constantly propagated my ideas. My advocacy of an Islamic state brought me into conflict with Jinnah. He thoroughly disapproved of my ideas and dissuaded me from expressing them publicly from the League platform lest the people might be led to believe that Jinnah shared my view and that he was asking me to convey such ideas to the public. As I was convinced that I was right and did not want to compromise Jinnah's position, I decided to cut myself away and for nearly two years kept my distance from him, apart from seeing him during working committee meetings and other formal occasions. It was not easy to take this decision as my associations with Jinnah had been very close in the past. Now that I look back I realize how wrong I had been.[12]

According to the Raja — and this is also a view shared by many scholars — three principle factors, in descending order of priority, transformed the Muslim League from the position of a feeble political minority in 1937 into a great mass movement less than a decade later:

> One was the Congress attitude of indifference and, at times, hostility. Another was the leadership which, under Jinnah, broke new ground and fashioned new political strategy. Still another was the part played by religious appeal in the heightening of this consciousness. The leadership at the top was generally secular-minded and trained in modern political methods, but on the lower levels and especially among the field workers propaganda on religious lines was the general practice.[13]

To understand correctly Jinnah's concept of Pakistan, it is necessary to examine his position to greater detail.

Jinnah's Mind: Secular or Communal?

It is frequently said that without Jinnah there would have been no Pakistan, and Jinnah is himself known to have remarked that it was he, with the help of his secretary and typewriter, who won Pakistan for the Muslims.[14] Irrespective of the extent to which this is true, it is certainly the case that Jinnah is revered in Pakistan to an extent which no other political personality approaches even remotely. His speeches and writings, therefore, often serve as a reference point for debates on the nature of the Pakistani state and its future.

Modern textbooks invariably portray Jinnah as the architect of an Islamic ideological state:

> The All-India Muslim League, and even the Quaid-i-Azam himself, said in the clearest possible terms that Pakistan would be an ideological state, the basis of whose laws would be the Qur'ān and *Sunnah*, and whose ultimate destiny would be to provide a society in which Muslims could individually and collectively live according to the laws of Islam.[15]

Paradoxically, Jinnah began his political career as an exponent of Hindu-Muslim unity and as the leader of the liberal left wing of the Congress. His efforts culminated in the Lucknow Pack of 1916 between the Congress and the League. But when he again led the League almost twenty years later, the call was no longer for unity but for Hindu-Muslim separation. Khalid bin Sayeed, one of his more respected biographers, gives convincing evidence that in the period 1929-1935 the Congress' intransigence was a major factor that changed him from an 'idealist' into a 'realist' who saw no future for Muslims in a united India.[16]

In his personal life, Jinnah was liberal and Westernised. Overcoming the taboos of cross-communal relations, he married a Parsi lady in the face of her parent's opposition — a marriage destined to end in tragic separation and the premature death of his wife. Jinnah maintained his inner secularism even in the seething cauldron of communal hatred following Partition, as is evident from the fact that he appointed Joginder Nath Mandal, a Hindu, to serve in Pakistan's first cabinet. His famous 11 August 1947 speech before the nation is the clearest possible exposition of a secular state in which religion and state are separate from each other:

> We are starting with the fundamental principle that we are all citizens and equal citizens of one State . . . Now I think that we should keep that in front of us as our ideal, and you will find that in due course of time Hindus would cease to be Hindus and Muslims would cease to be Muslims, not in the religious sense, because that is the personal faith of each individual but in the political sense as citizens of the state. . . . You may belong to any religion or caste or creed — that has nothing to do with the business of the State.[17]

In an interview to Doon Campbell, Reuter's correspondent in New Delhi in 1946, Jinnah made it perfectly clear that it was Western-style democracy that he wanted for Pakistan:

> The new state would be a modern democratic state with sovereignty resting in the people and the members of the new nation having equal rights of citizenship regardless of their religion, caste or creed.[18]

Note the highly significant phrase 'sovereignty resting in the people'. In contrast, in Maulana Maudoodi's Islamic state, 'sovereignty rests with Allah'. Thus, Jinnah rejects the basis for a theocratic state. This is stated even more explicitly in his 1946 speech before the Muslim League convention in Delhi: 'What are we fighting for? What are we aiming at? It is not theocracy, nor a theocratic state.'[19] The historian K.K. Aziz has remarked that 'on the record of their writings and speeches, Jinnah comes out to be far more liberal and secular than Gandhi'.[20]

All of Jinnah's speeches were not so unequivocal about the nature of the future state. In the 1945 elections, the Muslim League was aided by a number of influential *'ulamā*. It is in this period that we find in Jinnah's speeches the greatest number of references to Islam and society. For example, in November 1945 he said that 'Muslims are demanding Pakistan so that they may live according to their code of life and traditions, and so that they may govern themselves according to the rules of Islam'.[21] How does one interpret this speech of Jinnah's, together with others of essentially similar nature, with the outright secular declarations quoted earlier? At least two interesting possibilities suggest themselves. Jinnah may have made a compromise with the *'ulamā* in the interest of achieving unity on the primary goal — the attainment of a homeland for the Muslims. On the other hand, it is possible that he saw Islam in such liberal terms that he saw no essential conflict between it and his desire for a modern, democratic state along Western lines. Here one might add that Maulana Abul Kalam Azad, a venerated religious authority whose understanding of the Qur'ān was no less deep than that of his contemporary, Maulana Abul Ala Maudoodi, nevertheless interpreted the political message of Islam in a totally different way from the latter. It is evident that Jinnah also did not accept the fundamentalist interpretation of Islam and the Islamic state.

The Role of the Religious Parties

All history bears evidence that religion has been a powerful nexus between individuals and groups, a potent instrument which has often welded a heterogeneous group into a distinct nationality. Through appeal to supernatural authority, religion promotes national unity as a divine command. When coupled with appropriate social and economic forces, it can forge a powerful and irresistible nationalism. Contemporary history is replete with examples: the Greek church as a source for Greek nationalism, the Catholic church as a factor in Irish separatism, Judaism and the state of Israel, Islam and Pakistan.

Since the movement for Pakistan was rooted in the social, cultural, and religious distinctions between Muslims and Hindus, one might logically expect that Muslim religious parties would have played a major, if not a leading, role in mobilising the Muslim masses. Paradoxically, aside from exceptions of no great importance, these parties had bitterly opposed Jinnah and the demand for Pakistan. Indeed, the exponents of Muslim nationalism were forced to battle on three formidable fronts. First, they had to persuade the British of their separate identity. Second, it was necessary to convince Congress of their determination to live as two separate nations. And third, the efforts of the *'ulamā*, who opposed Pakistan on grounds that nationalism was antithetical to Islam, had to be nullified.

The pre-Partition position of the politico-religious parties on the Pakistan question contrasts oddly with their present enthusiasm for religious nationalism. Maulana Maudoodi and the *Jamā'at-i-Islāmī* had rejected nationalism because it 'led to selfishness, prejudice, and pride'. Till 1947 Maudoodi maintained that he would not fight for Pakistan, that he did not believe in Pakistan, and that the demand for it was un-Islamic. Some ten years before Partition he had maintained that 'Muslim nationalism is as contradictory a term as "chaste prostitute" '.[22] *Jamā'at* literature would sometimes use the derogatory word *Na-Pakistan* for the proposed state. There were frequent indictments of Jinnah as lacking 'an Islamic mentality or Islamic habits of thoughts'.[23]

The *Jamā'at-i-Islāmī* was not alone in its opposition to Pakistan. The *Majlis-i-Ahrar*, another politico-religious party, took a similar position. However, unlike the *Jamā'at*, it was aligned with the Congress. *Ahrar* leaders termed Jinnah the *Kafir-i-Azam* (the great infidel) as a rebuttal to the title *Quaid-i-Azam* (the great leader) conferred upon him by the Muslim League. Alamma Mashriqi's *Khaksar* party went a step further and once sought to assasinate Jinnah, albeit unsuccessfully. Significantly, *Jamā'at-i-Islāmī*, *Jamiat-ul-'ulamā-i-Hind*, *Majlis-i-Ahrar*, and *Khaksar* were absent at Jinnah's funeral. A rather curious situation arose after Pakistan became a reality in 1947 since most political-religious parties were confronted with the dilemma of being in a country whose creation they had opposed. Political expediency caused many leaders to abruptly volte-face. For example, Mian Tufail Mohammad, now *amir* of the *Jamā'at-i-Islāmī*, who had once denounced as 'sinners' all those who supported or joined Jinnah's government, stated on television recently that, in fact, there had existed an understanding between Jinnah and the *Jamā'at* that both would work separately towards the same goal. It has also become usual for many modern textbooks to refer to Maudoodi as one of the intellectual founders of the Pakistani Movement. This startling fact suggests that the influence of the *Jamā'at-i-Islāmī* on national education may be deeper than is normally assumed.

Those politico-religious parties which had resisted the creation of Pakistan may well have made good the political damage. Their allegiance to an Islamic state now entitles them to rewards which go beyond mere forgiveness: 'the services rendered by the *'ulamā* and *mashaikh* to the cause of the Pakistan Movement are worthy of writing in golden letters'.[24] One textbook devotes an entire chapter to their role, claiming that 'when Allama Iqbal and the *Quaid-i-Azam* presented their programme for an Islamic state, it met with the enthusiastic support of the *'ulamā* and *mashaikh*'.[25]

1947-77: The Gulf of Silence

Nations which can rationally analyse their past, and particularly their defeats and periods of collective suffering, are far more likely to survive and prosper than those in which absence of free expression forbids truthful self-examination. Japan and Germany after World War II, Argentina after the Falklands War — historical examples abound in which positive shifts in national policy, domestic and foreign, occurred as a result of decisive defeat. Indeed, there were expectations of a critical assessment of the role of elites and readjustment of regional policies within Pakistan following the 1971 civil war and the subsequent Indian invasion. In this war, tens of thousands died, millions were displaced, and the country was rent asunder. Thirteen years later, this optimism has proven to be unfounded.

From the year 1947, the establishment of Pakistan, through the year 1977, the start of the *Nizam-i-Mustafa* Movement, all recent Pakistan studies texts maintain total, or almost total, silence on political events of this period. The most detailed account of history until 1968 to be found in any of these books is reproduced in full here: 'In October 1958, General Ayub Khan imposed martial law and thus saved the country from chaos.'[26] Of the few books which mention the Bangladesh episode, one has the following to say:

> As a result of the 1970 elections, the political differences between East and West Pakistan grew and led to their separation. The cause of Islamic unity received a setback, but one should not interpret this as a rejection of Islamic Ideology by the people. Indeed, unless Islam is presented as a whole, and not as just worship and prayers, it remains incomplete. The forces of atheism and worldliness, in this case, can influence the minds of people through modern education and public media.[27]

This strict economy of words is in striking contrast to the extensive coverage given to Islamisation after 1977. Nevertheless, this small paragraph invites more than just cursory reading.

There is little doubt that the painful separation of Bangladesh from Pakistan strikes at the very roots of Pan-Islamism — the belief that Muslims all over the world belong to one nation and that differences among them are insignificant. Modern textbooks, therefore, are reluctant to discuss the issue in any detail. It should also be observed that the above quoted paragraph attributes the separation of East and West squarely to the fact that elections were held in Pakistan. This serves to create the fear that if elections and democracy broke up Pakistan in 1971, then Pakistan may again be mortally endangered if elections and democracy are restored at some point in the future. Finally, note that the last lines of the paragraph implicitly acknowledge the lack of success of the Islamic parties in the 1970 elections. However, students are instructed

173

to disregard this because 'modern education' encouraged 'atheism and worldliness' and was the reason for defeat.

The 1947-77 gap in textbooks makes it difficult to develop an adequate background for the *Nizam-i-Mustafa* Movement, which culminated in General Zia ul Haq's government's accession to power. Restrictions, whether self-imposed or otherwise, do not allow explicit mention of the names of key national figures. This constraint occasionally leads to awkward situations. For example, all textbooks give 'rigging of elections' as a motivation for the *Nizam-i-Mustafa* Movement, but none can explicitly state that these were rigged by Bhutto. Curiously, we were unable to discover any mention of the PNA (Pakistan National Alliance), which spearheaded the movement against Bhutto.

Subtle propaganda is not a sin of which our textbook writers are guilty.

Islamisation in Textbooks

Islamisation is the central concern of all modern Pakistan studies textbooks. After Partition, only three subsequent events are discussed in detail. First, they treat the Objectives Resolution of 1949, which gave the sovereignty over the state of Pakistan to Allah and which separated Muslims from non-Muslims as having different rights of citizenship. Secondly, they harp on the presentation to the government of a twenty-two point programme framed by thirty-one prominent *'ulamā* in 1951. This programme later became part of the *Manifesto of the Jamā'at-i-Islāmî*, acknowledged on the front cover of this document. The third event, which forms the bulk of post-Partition history, is the implementation of Islamic principles by General Zia ul Haq.

Modern textbooks heavily stress the formal and ritualistic aspects of Islam, as against those which emphasise social justice. Science and secular knowledge are held in deep suspicion. Modern education, according to one book, should be shunned because it leads to atheism and worldliness. Another book describes an utopian society, one which supposedly existed at the time of Hazrat Nizam-ud-Din, as one in which ritual was meticulously adhered to:

> Young and old, small and great, everyone had become regular at prayers. Apart from the five prayers, people enthusiastically said supplementary prayers of *ishraq*, *chasht*, *zawal*, and *awabin*. People used to ask each other of the verses to be read, or how many times to recite *drud-sharif* after prayers . . . they kept supplementary fasts even after the month of Ramazan.[28]

The emphasis on ritualistic Islam in modern textbooks is accompanied by a conscious promotion of sentiment against certain non-Muslim communities, particularly Hindus and Qadianis. This is not something new, one may legitimately argue, nor is the exacerbation of communal antagonism limited to Pakistan alone. India, which claims to be secular rather than Hindu, is nevertheless regularly ravaged by communal riots with the majority of victims being Muslims. Hindu chauvinism is a powerful factor in Indian politics and expresses itself through a variety of newspapers and magazines, even though propaganda through school texts is officially forbidden. However, in Pakistan, because of the adoption of an exclusivist national ideology, there are no constraints on the free expression of communal hatred. Thus, the Hindu is portrayed as monolithically cunning and treacherous, obsessively seeking to settle old scores with his erstwhile masters. This Hindu is responsible for the break-up of Pakistan:

> The same Bengali Hindu was responsible for the backwardness of East Pakistan. But, hiding the story of his two-century old sins, atrocities, and pillage, he used 'Bengali nationalism' to punish innocent West Pakistanis for sins they had not committed.[29]

Justice Shameem Hussain Kadri, ex-chief justice of the Lahore High Court, writes of the 'diabolical Hindus' and 'Hindu conspiracies' in his officially circulated book.[30] There are countless similar examples.

In part, the existence of anti-Hindu sentiment is a consequence of the wholesale communal massacres during Partition, which left around half a million dead on each side. Even under the best conditions the scars would need many decades to heal. But the explanation for the revival of communalist sentiment is not to be found wholly in the tragedies of 1947. An examination of history texts written soon after Partition — a time when the grief of shattered families was at its peak — shows them to be incomparably more liberal. The history of the subcontinent was taken to start with the ancient Indus valley civilisations rather than with the conquest of India by the first Muslim invader, Mohammad bin Qasim, in 712. In contrast to present-day books, these books contained discussions of the empires of Ashoka and the Mauryas. The movement for Pakistan was presented as a defence against Hindu domination, not as a movement for religious revival.

The deliberate revival of communal antagonism over 30 years after Partition suggests that political expediency, rather than religious factors, has asserted a dominant influence in this matter. The permanent militarisation of society requires a permanent enemy. For many reasons, Pakistan's other neighbours are unsuitable for this purpose. On the other hand, rulers in both India and Pakistan have long found mutual hostility and tension indispensable political tools.

Conclusion

The change in character of Pakistan education, and the rewriting of

175

Pakistan history, coincide with the change in nature of the ruling elites and altered needs. The Westernised liberal elite, which had inherited political power from the British, had given to education a basically secular and modern character which might have eventually created a modern, secular-minded citizenry. But the self-seeking and opportunistic nature of this elite forced it progressively to abandon liberal values in the face of exigencies, political and economic. Discriminatory laws against non-Muslim minorities were passed, the feudal structure of rural society was left intact, and quality education was limited to a tiny minority. The ambient corruption in society gradually diffused into institutions which could have transformed and modernized Pakistani society. By the time of the 1977 army coup, liberalism was already moribund.

The recasting of Pakistani history is an attempt to fundamentally redefine Pakistan and Pakistani society and to endow the nation with a historic destiny. Islam is the integrative ideology, its enforcement a divine duty. Viewed from this angle, it becomes essential to project the movement for Pakistan as the movement for an Islamic state, the creation of which became a historic inevitability with the first Muslim invasion of the subcontinent. The revised history of Pakistan uses much the same idiom, and the same concepts of Islamic state and of politics in Islam, as the *Jamā'at-i-Islāmī*. Its wholesale dissemination through educational institutions demonstrates both the influence of the *Jamā'at* on education as well as the confluence of interests and philosophy of military rulers and the *Jamā'at*.

References and Notes

1. University Grants Commission directive, quoted in Azhar Hamid, et al. *Mutalliyah-i-Pakistan* (Islamabad: Allama Iqbal Open University, 1983), p. xi.

2. Ibid., pp. xii-xiii.

3. Government of Pakistan, Federal Ministry of Education, *Pakistan Studies (Compulsory) For Intermediate Classes* by Safdar Mahmood, et al. (Islamabad: Government of Pakistan). Approved for the Departments of Education of the Punjab, Sind, NWFP, Baluchistan, Federal Areas, and liberated Kashmir vide notification number F.11-16/81-HST, dated 2 November 1981, as the sole text book for intermediate classes.

4. S. Husain and M. A. Hasan, *Mukhzum Mutalliyah-i-Pakistan* (Lahore: Kitab Khana Danishwuran, 1981), p. 1.

5. *Nawa-i-Waqt* (Karachi), 14 August 1984.

6. S. Husain and M. A. Hasan, *Mukhzum Mutalliyah*, p. 2.

7. M. D. Zafar, *Pakistan Studies for Medical Students* (Lahore: Aziz Publishers, 1982), p. 20.

8. Mohammad Munir, *From Jinnah to Zia* (Lahore: Vanguard Books Ltd., 1980), p. 26.

9. Abul Ala Maudoodi, *Islamic Law and Constitution*, ed. Khurshid

Ahmed (Karachi: *Jamā'at-i-Islāmī* Publications, 1955).

10. Jamiluddin Ahmed, *Recent Writings and Speeches of Mr. Jinnah* (Lahore: Sheikh Mohammad Ashraf, 1947), p. 176.

11. Azhar Hamid, et al., *Mutalliyah-i-Pakistan*, p. 27.

12. Raja of Mahmudabad, 'Some Memories', in *Partition of India — Policies and Perspectives 1937-1947*, eds. C. H. Philips and M. D. Wainwright (Cambridge, Mass.: MIT Press, 1970), pp. 388-9.

13. Ibid., p. 389.

14. C. H. Philips and M. D. Wainwright, *Partition of India*, p. 32.

15. Azhar Hamid, et al., *Mutalliyah-i-Pakistan*, p. 221.

16. Khalid bin Sayeed, 'Personality of Jinnah and his Political Strategy', in C. H. Philips and M. D. Wainwright, *Partition of India*, pp. 276-93.

17. M. Munir, *From Jinnah to Zia*, p. 30.

18. Ibid., p. 29.

19. Jamiluddin Ahmed, *Recent Writings and Speeches*, p. 248.

20. K. K. Aziz, *The Making of Pakistan* (Islamabad: National Book Foundation, 1976).

21. Quoted in Sarwat Sawlat, *Pakistan Ke Baray Log* (Lahore, 1982), pp. 295-6.

22. Abul Ala Maudoodi, *Mussalman Aur Maujooda Syasi Kashmakash*, quoted in K. K. Aziz, *The Making of Pakistan*, p. 148.

23. Maulana Kausar Niazi, *Maudoodiat Awam Ki Adalat Men* (Lahore, n.d.).

24. Zia-ul-Haq, quoted in M. D. Zafar, *Pakistan Studies*, p. 147.

25. S   M   Rafeeq, *Tehrik-i-Pakistan* (Lahore: Standard Book House, 1983), p. 271.

26. Azhar Hamid, et al., *Mutalliyah-i-Pakistan, p. 233*.

27. Ibid., p. 235.

28. Ibid., p. 41.

29. Ibid., p. 32.

30. Justice Shameem Hussain Kadri, *The Creation of Pakistan* (Lahore: Army Book Club, 1983).

8. Ideological Problems for Science in Pakistan

by Pervez Amirali Hoodbhoy

Introduction

The year 1984 finds science in Pakistan in a state of dismal collapse. The situation appears far from temporary, and explanations based on paucity of resources appear implausible.

The scenario on the academic front is grim. Mathematics, as a research discipline, has ceased to exist.[1] Physics, once a promising field, has now fewer than a total of twenty genuine, but wearied, practioners scattered over dozens of its subfields.[2] Relative to mathematics and physics, chemistry and the biological sciences are in a better position and can boast of a few hundred Ph.Ds. However, research activity in these fields is localised to one or two centres only.[3] It is rare to find seminars, lectures, or discussions in Pakistani universities and still more rare to find a teacher who adequately understands his subject. As a producer of scientific literature, Pakistan ranks below the 100th position in the list of nations. By comparison, neighbouring India ranks seventh.

At the level of applied research, the situation is scarcely better. The Pakistan Atomic Energy Commission, the largest science organisation within the country, is, for all its shrouds of secrecy, nevertheless widely known to be wasteful and unproductive in practically every field of endeavour. The director of another huge organisation, the PCSIR (Pakistan Council for Scientific and Industrial Research), in a recent television interview euphemistically referred to the 'limited impact' of his organisation. As a matter of fact PCSIR annual science exhibitions contain fewer innovations and achievements than in a good high school or college science fair. Smaller R&D (Research and Development) institutes, organisations, and associations have steadily increased in number over the years to the present figure of 120. Functioning as bureaucracies along the lines of the Islamabad Secretariat with identical grades, pay scales, and promotion rules, these institutions are visibly the creation of vested bureaucratic interests. Since no reasonable system of accountability exists, funds are not cut off even if productivity is nil unless, possibly, some clash of bureaucratic interests occurs.

More worrisome yet is the state of science education in Pakistani schools, colleges, and universities. It is widely felt that educational standards have dropped to a calamitously low point over the past several years. The limited amount of quantitative evidence available supports this view.[4] Even the Minister of Education admits that Pakistan's education system has been 'crippled'.[5] There is every indication that for science education, as well as for education in general, the worst is yet to come.

Within the country, there exist several analyses of the present state of science and recommendations for its rehabilitation. There are those who consider inadequate financial resources the cause and advocate a sixfold increase in expenditure from the present 0.17% of the GNP to 1% of the GNP. Not only do important bureaucratic interests support this, but the pride of Pakistani science, Professor Abdus Salam, also sees it as essential. Dr. Mahbub ul Haq, federal minister for planning and development, has expressed strong enthusiasm for the creation of a gigantic University of Science and Technology in Islamabad at an estimated cost of $150 million, to be patterned on MIT, Harvard, and the Indian IITs. Another suggestion, currently in the process of implementation, is to change the medium of instruction from English to Urdu and thereby make science subjects more readily comprehensible.

There is no need to comment on, or attempt to evaluate, any of the above recommendations. Useful or otherwise, their impact is bound to be superficial, and the hope offered by them is illusory. The failure to develop science is more than a mere failure of policy, and a meaningful analysis requires nothing less than an examination of fundamental social values and attitudes. The enthusiasm of the present government for science, as expressed by top officials on numerous occasions, is, unfortunately, unlikely to be of much help given the ideological constraints it has set for itself and the nation. As with Mrs. Squeers, who opened an abscess on her pupil's head with an inky penknife, the goal is entirely laudable even though the means are of questionable efficacy.

Defining Science

Having used the word 'science' in a rather cavalier fashion, it is necessary first to clarify the sense in which it is to be used. In the common Pakistani conception 'science' is perceived in either one of two ways. First, it is thought to be a horrific bundle of irrelevant facts, diagrams, and equations which must be crammed quickly prior to examinations and forgotten just as quickly. By efficiently promoting this view, the national education system produces a totally justified hatred of science subjects. On the other hand, computers, jet aircraft, lasers, chemicals, medicines and what-not are thought to be an embodiment of science. But, in fact, these trinkets of modern technology do not constitute science, and acquisition of fancy gadgetry alone advances the cause of science by not an inch. Science lives not in machines, but in the minds of men and women.

Modern science is, above and beyond all else, a commitment to reasoning as a means of understanding the physical universe, which combines the power of logic with the necessity of experimental observation. Blind commitment to a theory is not an intellectual virtue; it is an intellectual crime. Even the best scientific theories are only conditionally accepted and critically re-examined in the light of new experiments and observations. Indeed, according to Sir Karl Popper, a theory can be 'scientific' only if one is prepared to specify in advance a crucial experiment (or observation) which can falsify it, and it is pseudo-scientific if one refuses to specify such a 'potential falsifier'.

A necessary requirement that any scientific theory must fulfil is the need to predict novel facts, facts which have been either undreamt of or which have been earlier rejected as false. On the other hand, it is totally irrelevant that a theory may be understood by only a handful of people, or even just one person, and is rejected by everyone else. Let us look at the historical example which illuminates these points:

In 1686, when Newton published his theory of gravitation, there were two current theories concerning comets. The overwhelmingly more popular one regarded comets as a signal from an angry God warning that he would strike and bring disaster. On the other hand, a little known theory of Kepler's held that comets were celestial bodies moving along straight lines. Now, according to Newtonian theory, some of them moved on hyperbolas and parabolas never to return; others moved in ellipses. Halley, working on Newtonian lines, observed a brief path of one 'dangerous' comet and thereafter predicted that it would return in seventy-six years. He calculated to the minute when it would be seen again at a well-defined point in the sky. This was incredible. But seventy-six years later, when both Halley and Newton were long dead, Halley's comet returned exactly as Halley had predicted.

The Birth of Modern Science

It is indisputably true that not all social and political circumstances provide an environment suitable for the growth of science and its application, technology. Hence a crucial question arises: what societal factors contribute to, and sustain, scientific growth? No answer can be complete without an examination of the history of modern science.

Historians of science are divided on this question.[6] There are those who view science as a collective expression of natural human curiosity and the urge to know and create. On the other hand, Marxist historians place at least an equal amount of stress on science arising as a consequence of productive needs and social formations. Thus, for example, scientific underdevelopment in the Third World is often attributed by Marxists to imperialist penetration of national economies or the lack of an independent capitalist national order. At the present level of analysis we shall not examine these issues in detail: both schools of historians agree that acceptance of rationality is a crucial ingredient.

The birth of modern science took place in Europe some 350 years ago. The 17th and 18th centuries were times of intense social and political tumult, as well as of liberalism and enlightenment. Descartes, Voltaire, Rousseau, Diderot, and Kant revolutionised social thought and redefined social values. For a thousand years prior to the Renaissance, the Church had ruled Europe with an iron hand. Intolerance, prejudice, suspicion, and superstition made scholarly learning an impossibility. Suspicious of every attempt at independent thinking, the Church violently suppressed all teaching that was not in direct conformity with its preachings. Religious tribunals sentenced tens of thousands of suspected witches and heretics to death by torture. Convicts were tied between horses and torn to pieces, disembowelled, hung or burnt at the stake. Even the dead were not forgiven: the famous Archbishop Ussher had concluded from his study of the Bible that the world began at 9 am, Sunday 23 October 4004 BC. However, a long dead scientist, Wycliffe, had suggested that the earth was at least some hundred thousand years old and recited supporting geological evidence. Unable to tolerate such an affront to his authority, Ussher ordered that Wycliffe's bones be dug out, broken to pieces, and thrown into the sea so that the germs of dissent and doubt would no longer contaminate the earth.

The rigidity of the Church's dogmas made scientific progress in Europe a virtual impossibility for centuries. Thus the brilliant achievements of contemporary Islamic civilisation and science would make little impact. Nevertheless, the age of experimental science began in Europe after the translation of Arabic texts into Latin. In the early 13th century, an enterprising scientist, Roger Bacon, started experiments based on Ibn Haitham's theory of optics — a dangerous thing to do. The Church administered his sentence of imprisonment with a stern admonition:

> Your writings bespeak strange thoughts. Let thee not forget that learning and devotion to books hath often led men away from the Tree of Life and unto the fiery Depths of Hell and Torture.

Why was the Church so adamant in its position and so bitterly opposed to men like Bacon, Wycliffe, Bruno, Galileo and hundreds of others? Bernard Shaw had an interesting and unconventional analysis:

> Galileo is a favoured subject with our scientists; but they miss the point because they think that the question at issue at his trial was whether the earth went round the sun or was the stationary centre round which the sun circled. Now, that was not the issue. Taken by itself, it was a mere question of physical fact without any moral significance, and therefore of no consequence to the Church. But what the authorities had to consider was whether the Christian religion, on which to the best of their belief not only the

civilization of the world but its salvation depended, and which had accepted the Hebrew scriptures and the Greek testament as inspired relevations, could stand the shock of the discovery that many of its tales, from the tactics of Joshua in the battle of Gideon to the Ascension, must have been written by somebody who did not know what the physical universe was really like.[7]

In 1982, three centuries later, the Vatican formally acknowledged as unjust the punishment of Galileo. No apology was proffered.

The Rise and Fall of Science in the Muslim World

At a time when Europe was lost in the gloom of the Dark Ages, Islamic civilisation was at its peak of brilliance and scientific attainment. A recent issue of the scientific journal *Nature* contains the following paragraph:

> At its peak about one thousand years ago, the Muslim world made a remarkable contribution to science, notably mathematics and medicine. Baghdad in its heyday and southern Spain built universities to which thousands flocked. Rulers surrounded themselves with scientists and artists. A spirit of freedom allowed Jews, Christians and Muslims to work side by side. Today all this is but a memory.[8]

Muslim contributions to premodern science are acknowledged by most Western scholars of repute. In his monumental treatise on the history of science, George Sarton divides scientific progress into ages with each age associated with one towering thinker and lasting for half a century.[9] From 750 to 1100, the Muslims dominate completely. It is only after this period that the first European names appear — Gerard of Cremona and Roger Bacon. The tribute to Muslim science is obvious.

To what may one ascribe the flowering of science in Islamic civilisation? We recall that in this era Islam was in a period of vigorous expansion, and Islamic society was vibrant and dynamic. Prosperity from trade and conquest created a leisure class at home, allowing indulgence in the finer things of life such as science and the arts. The court of the caliph, and the homes of the nobility, received sages and scholars as dignitaries. In part the motivation was intellectual curiosity and in part achievement of a status symbol. Many centuries later the French aristocracy similarly entertained men of learning in their palaces and chateaux. Islamic science grew from strength to strength in this environment of liberalism and tolerance.

The support of enlightened caliphs and the wealthy, while it made scholars dependent on the mood and fortunes of their providers, nevertheless offered crucially important protection from the wrath of religious fanatics who perceived science as a threat to Islam. Fundamentalists were dogmatically opposed to the application of reason, in the form of Greek dialectics, to religious questions. In part, anger also arose from jealousy because the *mulla*s observed that a man of inferior status — the scholar — had much greater access to the halls of power, and even to the caliph himself. Al-Mamun (813-833), for example, was much influenced by the *Mu'tazila* doctrine which sought to establish Islam on rational and scientific principles. This patronisation generated an antirationalist backlash, the *Ash'arite* movement, which maintains an explicit presence even today. Another difficulty faced by Islamic science was its elite nature, preventing its dissemination in society at large. Unlike in post-Renaissance Europe, Islamic science did not spawn a technology used by merchants and armies. Hence it could not penetrate beyond the upper crust of society.

By the 13th century Islamic science had virtually ceased to exist. The Mongol invasions were one cause, but internal decay is thought to be no less important. Tolerance and enlightenment retreated as religious fanatics went on the rampage. Many prominent Muslim scientists and scholars were forced to flee their lands, Ibn Sina and Ibn Khaldun being among these. Thus ended the glorious period of Muslim science.

Efforts Towards a Muslim Renaissance

Inspired by the past, Muslim thinkers of the Indian subcontinent have long sought to understand the reasons for the decay of Muslim science and civilisation and dreamt of a rebirth. Syed Ahmed Khan (1817-98) is the most important and influential among them.[10] His efforts towards a Muslim renaissance can be traced to the failure of the 1857 uprising against the British, a traumatic experience for Indians and for Indian Muslims in particular.

Born in an aristocratic family of Mughal ancestry, Syed Ahmed was convinced that desperate remedies were needed if the Muslims of India were ever to become anything other than 'stableboys, cooks, servants, and cutters of grass'. As he saw it, this backwardness was a result of superstitious beliefs and rejection of *maaqulat* (rationality) in favour of blind obedience to *manqulat* (doctrine). In his opinion, the power of the *mulla*s was a principal cause of degeneration. As a replacement for traditional orthodoxy, he worked out a liberal interpretation of Islam compatible with the 19th-century West, closely similar to it in outlook, in harmony with its science, and sharing its humanitarianism.[11]

For Muslims of the Indian subcontinent, the period after the end of Akbar's reign had been one of unbroken conservatism. Some two hundred years before Syed Ahmed the influential Sheikh Ahmed Sirhindi and other religious figures had issued *fatwa*s against mathematics and the sciences, demanding that the education of Muslims be exclusively along religious lines. Rebelling against this view, Syed Ahmed wrote as follows:

> Now with great humbleness I ask: of the different religious books which exist today and are used for teaching, which of them discusses Western philosophy or modern scientific matters using principles of religion? From where should I seek confirmation or rejection of the motion of the Earth, or about its nearness to the sun? Thus, it is a thousand times better not to read these books than to read them. Yes, if the Mussulman be a true warrior and thinks his religion right, then let him come fearlessly to the battleground and do unto Western knowledge and modern research what his forbearers did to Greek philosophy. Then only shall religious books become useful — mere parroting will not do.[12]

For Syed Ahmed as a religious scholar, one of the foremost tasks was to free the genuine message of the Qur'ān from its entanglement with outdated elements of Greek astronomy, such as the ptolemaic concept of seven heavens. In a startling break with tradition, he proposed that the Qur'ān be reinterpreted so as to remove all apparent contradictions with physical reality. Since the Qur'ān was the word of God, he argued, and since scientific truths were manifestly correct, a real contradiction was impossible. Syed Ahmed consequently proposed the following mode of interpretation.[13] First, a close enquiry should be made into the use and meaning of Qur'ānic language so as to yield the true meaning of the word and passage in question. Secondly, the criterion employed to decide whether a given passage needed metaphorical interpretation, and which of several interpretations ought to be selected, is the truth established by science. Such truth is arrived at by *aqli dalil* (rational proof) and demands firm belief. Thirdly, Syed Ahmed follows Ibn Rushd in his problem of reconciling *maaqul* (demonstrative truth) with *manqul* (scriptural truth) by stating that if the apparent meaning of the Scripture conflicts with demonstrable conclusions, it must be interpreted metaphorically. Yet, Sir Syed makes it clear that such metaphorical and allegorical interpretation is precisely what the Author of Scripture intended.

This radical reinterpretation of theology led Syed Ahmed to some rather unconventional positions. He accepted the Darwinian theory by interpreting the fall of Adam and Eve as actually the cause for man to distinguish between good and evil and to become *mukallaf* (under obligation) in distinction from other living beings. He also proposed allegorical interpretations for the Great Flood, miracles of Jesus, the Ascension, and other phenomena which he felt conflicted with nature.

In the conservative climate of his times, Syed Ahmed's interpretations were not well received. Aligarh Muslim University, Syed Ahmed's creation, was boycotted. From the *'ulamā*, *fatwa*s of *ilhād* (apostasy) and *kufr* (grievous disbelief) were issued. The *mutawalli* (keeper) of the Holy Kaaba declared Syed Ahmed to be an enemy of Islam and *wajib-i-qatl* (deserver of death).

Although Syed Ahmed is revered in Pakistan as the first exponent of Muslim nationalism, his views on science and religion have found few takers. His almost cringing tributes to the imperial British, and his exhortations to remain faithful to India's masters, do not endear him to many present-day nationalists. Nevertheless, he was far ahead of his contemporaries in his efforts to comprehend the world rationally within an Islamic framework.

Science and the *Maulvi*

We now turn to a consideration of the ideological positions on science held by important contemporary religious figures. There is, in Pakistan, a new and growing movement which rejects modern science as a form of *maghreb zadgi* (affliction of the West) and calls for its immediate replacement with 'Islamic science'. It is stated with great vehemence that science is an ideological discipline and that Islamic science is a distinct and superior entity from 'Christian science' and 'communist science'. The goals and means of Islamic science are completely different, it is argued, and derive inspiration from the Holy Qur'ān. At the lavishly organised 'Islamic Science Conference' of November 1983 held in Islamabad, attended by hundreds of delegates from Islamic countries, it was clear that this view was widely shared.

A leading proponent of the Islamic science philosophy is the *Jamā'at-i-Islāmī*, a fundamentalist politico-religious party commanding substantial support among college and university students as well as workers at scientific research organisations. *Jamā'at* literature is characterised by a rhetorical condemnation of Western science and civilisation. One of its most articulate spokespersons, Maryam Jameelah, writes:

> Modern Science is guided by no moral values, but naked materialism and arrogance. The whole branch of knowledge and its applications is con-teminated by the same evil. Science and technology are totally dependent upon the set of ideals and values cherished by its members. If the roots of the tree are rotten, then the tree is rotten; therefore all its fruits are rotten.[14]

She decries the emphasis that modern science puts on constant progress and change.

> (In Islamic society) originality, innovation and change were never upheld as intrinsic values. The ideal of Islamic culture was not mechanical, evolu-tionary progress but the permanent, immutable, transcendental, divinely revealed moral, theological, and spiritual values of the Qur'ān and *Sunnah*.[15]

In Maryam Jameelah's view, it is neither necessary nor desirable for

Muslim science to 'catch up with the West'. Repelled by the narrowness of technical education, she pleads for the return of the *'ālim* (sage) as a replacement for the modern scientist.

Maulana Abul Ala Maudoodi, founder of the *Jamā'at-i-Islāmī*, also levies bitter criticism against Western science. In a lecture on Islamic education, he states that geography, physics, chemistry, biology, zoology, geology, and economics are taught without any mention of Allah and his Messenger and are hence a source of *gumrahi* (straying from the truth).

> Reflection on the nature of modern education and customs immediately reveals their contradiction with the nature of Islamic education and customs. You teach young minds philosophy, which seeks to explain the universe without Allah. You teach them science which is devoid of reason and a slave of the senses. You teach them economics, law, and sociology which, in spirit and in substance, differ from the teachings of Islam. And you still expect them to have an Islamic point of view?[16]

As a solution to this evil, the Maulana presents the following proposal:

> The entire blame for this sorry state of affairs rests on the separation of *dīnī* (spiritual) from *dunyawī* (worldly) education. As I have just pleaded, this separation is totally un-Islamic. In the new system of education a new course on *dīnyāt* is not needed. Instead, all courses should be changed into courses of *dīnyāt*.[17]

The *Jamā'at-i-Islāmī* does not stand alone in its condemnation of Western science. Among many others, an influential Iranian scholar makes the following statement:

> The fact that science and technology in its present form did not develop in Islam's bosom is not a sign of decadence, as is claimed, but the refusal of Islam to consider any form of knowledge as purely secular.[18]

In this way of thinking, Islam rejects all forms of knowledge which are not derived from religion.

The attitudes of the Saudis are also worthy of note. In late 1983, a high-level conference was convened in Kuwait to discuss problems facing the promotion of science and technology in Muslim countries. Seventeen Arab university rectors, including eleven from Saudi Arabia, were present. Reportedly, the discussion turned to a single topic: was science in harmony with Islam or not? While the Saudis were enthusiastic in their support for technology, they unanimously voiced their opposition to laying stress on pure science since, in their opinion, this was potentially subversive of belief.

Attitudes of this kind have had some curious manifestations in scientific and technical matters. For example, an Islamic journal, published from London with Saudi subsidy, decries as false Abdus Salam's Nobel Prize-winning theory which unifies the weak and electro-magnetic forces of nature.[19] It claims that Salam is a victim of the *Wahdat-ul-wajud Sufi* philosophy, which seeks unity among the many manifesta-tions of God, and has thus been led astray.

The fervent rejection of Western science by the religious right wing is accompanied by equally fervent assertions about the superiority of Islamic science. But this approach is not free of contradiction. On the one hand, it is stated that Western science is a mere continuation of a discipline whose foundations were laid by the Muslims. But almost in the same breath, Islamic science is held to be infinitely more noble. Rejection of one is not viewed as a rejection of both in spite of the common ground on which they stand — reason and experiment. Again, these authors are not uncomfortable in claiming that Islamic science is exclusively Islamic, ignoring the fact that Muslim scientists had borrowed heavily from, and improved upon, the knowledge of the ancient Greeks. In much right-wing literature there is only cursory mention, and sometimes total ommission, of the Greek contribution to science. But science is a collective human venture which has borrowed from all great civilisations and which has grown from one to the next. To claim that it was developed by any one civilisation is extreme folly.

Returning to Mediaevalism

Over the past few years, there has emerged a new interpretation of 'Islamic science'. This science is not just the science of early Muslims, but, rather, it is that which seeks to explain all scientific theories and all natural facts from interpretation of appropriate Qur'ānic verses. The Qur'ān is a complete code of life, it is argued, and hence contains all possible science in it. Armed with such philosophy, 'Islamic scientists' have announced some startling discoveries as a consequence of their endeavours. In the following, we discuss some of their achievements.

The first example concerns a Pakistani professor with a Ph.D. in physics from a British university. A former chairman of the national research organisations PCSIR and ATDO (Appropriate Technology Development Organisation), this gentleman is also a *muballigh* for a large religious organisation. In addition to being a prominent science educationist, he plays an important role as a science planner. According to a recent newspaper report, he currently represents Pakistan at the U.N. Commission for Science and Technology. This gentleman is well-known for his exotic theories. One of his discoveries, presented at the Islamic Science Conference in 1979, established that heaven is literally running away from us at a speed of only one centimetre per second less than the speed of light. The professor interprets a particular Qur'ānic verse — stating that worship on the night of *lailat al qadar* is better than a thousand nights of ordinary worship — as an instance of Einsteinian time dilation. Inserting the factor of 1000 into a formula from the theory of relativity, he arrives at his conclusion! Another theory concerns the seven heavens: the professor says that these are like quantum levels of an atom. Just as an atom changes levels by absorbing or emitting energy, so also does one go between heavens by earning *sawab* or committing *gunah* (sin).

Another Islamic scientist, who shall be referred to simply as Dr. B. M. is highly placed in the Pakistan Atomic Energy Commission. Dr. B. M. appears to be not only deeply religious, but also thoroughly committed to the application of 'Islamic science' as a panacea for social problems. In one of his papers, he argues that Qur'ānic evidence supports the existence of *jinn*s as fiery beings possessing unlimited energy. Therefore, proposes Dr. B. M. this energy can and should be used as fuel. The oil crisis will be of no concern after that, he optimistically concludes. Another theory claims the existence of 'eight fundamental types of cattle' in analogy to the 'eightfold symmetry' in particle physics. Yet another momentous discovery reveals the true nature of heaven: heaven is a black hole, according to Dr. B. M.[20]

Bookstores and libraries in Pakistan contain an increasing number of books written along similar lines. The latest addition has been a thick, glossy, well-printed book put out by publishers for the Army Book Club. We need not comment extensively on it since it has already received flattering reviews in the national press. Engineer Fateh Mohammad, the author, shows in detail how everything from quantum mechanics through gene splicing can be understood in the light of the Qur'ān. Incidentally, he proves that hell — and not heaven — is a black hole. This fact must undoubtedly relieve some readers.

Another new book, entitled *God, Universe, and Life*, is also worthy of remark. Armed with the formidable weapon of atomic physics laced with sex, the author makes a devastating assault on godless materialists who think that the force between a proton and electron is purely mechanical:

> We must take these atomic charges as carved out of spiritual attractions and not simply the blind electromagnetic forces that the materialists would make us believe. It is strange that while people indulge in loving and chasing each other in their capacity as men and women they have never appreciated the scientific reality in their own division in sexes.[21]

Using his somewhat unusual form of logic, the author concludes that the earth is no less a living being than birds or animals.

A German delegate to the November 1983 'Islamic Science Conference' threw a theological bombshell when he proposed a new interpretation of God. Using the language of mathematical topology, he calculated the 'Angle of God'.

> God cannot be one highest monad, a source where all souls rest: a crosspoint
> of high multiplicity N-1 is overstrained by congestion/stagnation/deflection
> under the angle pi/N. God can be identified with the substance free and
> immovable rotation axis of time in the universal carousel of space.[22]

Readers unable to comprehend the above passage need not be discouraged — ordinary professional mathematicians are likewise be-
fuddled by it.

Islamic scientists have been quick at recognising the potential of the
miracle micro-chip and high-speed computer. A widely circulated book
says that 'with the findings of the computer in our possession, no Moslem
need talk about it in excited whispers' because 'a giant computer has now
finally proven the Authorship of the Holy Book' using 'the exact science
of numbers, namely Mathematics'.[23] The work is based on the researches
of Dr. Rashad Khalifa, who claims that certain words occur in the Qur'ān
in exact multiples of the number 19, a fact which establishes it as the work
of divine intelligence. Presumably, any person who accepts Dr. Khalifa's
research ought also to be prepared to reject the final conclusion of divine
authorship if, at any stage, an error is discovered in the computer
programme or its general logic.

Although much of 'Islamic science' is mere opportunistic quackery
designed to suit the present ideological climate in Pakistan, other efforts
in this field have been genuinely motivated by considerations closely
similar to those expressed by Maulana Maudoodi.

> Taking guidance from the Qur'ān, one should take not only a survey of
> existing scientific knowledge, but also make new observations and discover-
> ies of physical laws along lines specified by the Qur'ān.[24]

The concerns of 'Islamic science' are remarkably similar to those which
prevailed during the Dark Ages of Europe. Identification of witches,
exorcism of evil spirits, determining the qualities of fire and brimstone in
the labyrinthine depths of hell, proofs of the flatness of the earth: these
goals had engaged European minds for a thousand years. Other problems
were of a logical nature: could God make a stone so heavy that He could
not lift it? How many angels, weightless and occupying no space, could
dance on the tip of a pin? Fierce controversy had raged on these questions
for hundreds of years. Those who dared to differ with the Church met a
terrible death.

There are many scientists in Pakistan who believe that the mediaevalism of 'Islamic science' is an affront to Islam, in addition to being
opportunistic quackery. Nevertheless, exponents of this science are
deeply entrenched in positions of power and privilege within educational
institutions and R&D organisations. Obscurantism has been elevated to a

position of dignity, while permanent intrigue and institutional politics make the environment in these places unattractive for working professionals.

Promoting Illogic through Education

With an illiteracy level exceeding 70%, much of Pakistani society is steeped in centuries-old superstitions and ignorance. Superstitious beliefs pervade every aspect of life: the rearing of children, matrimonial and sexual affairs, matters of food and drink, health and hygiene, and much else. Exceptionally tragic consequences occasionally make it to the newspapers. For example, there is the famous Hawkes Bay incident, in which some hundreds of villagers from northern Pakistan, inspired by a village maiden's dream, jumped into the stormy waters of the Arabian sea on a Karachi beach hoping to reach the Holy Kaaba. Over thirty corpses were recovered. Another recent story involved a man who saw a divine command asking for his son's blood sacrifice. When booked for murder, he calmly recited Abraham's example. Then there is the story of a childless woman who was advised of a cure for infertility by the local *pir*. She promptly slaughtered her neighbour's child and bathed herself in its blood.

There are a thousand other such tragic incidents every year, mostly unreported, which appear to be the acts of madmen but which, in fact, are indicators of a deep and growing social malaise. Were this limited to the illiterate, it would be more understandable, though no less horrific. But superstition and dangerous irrationality pervade all strata of society through a variety of means: Urdu newspapers carry widely read 'spiritual columns' with prescriptions for every sort of physical and spiritual illness, the most popular book in Pakistan explores life in the hereafter, and captive audiences are regularly subjected to the crude outpourings of semiliterate *mulla*s.

In such circumstances, the teaching of science — the ultimate manifestation of human rationality — ought to, with the precision of a surgeon's knife, separate truth from superstition and fact from dogma. But science education in Pakistan seeks to achieve no such goal. Students are coerced into memorising a bundle of worthless, unrelated facts of no use or consequence. Physics and chemistry are taught no differently from, say, Pakistan studies or *Islamiat*. Authority is infinitely remote and unchallengeable: this or that is true because it's in the text. Deliberately and systematically, schools rob a child of natural creative powers.

The statements of the preceding paragraph, however, need to be qualified: these are true only for the overwhelming majority of schools and not for the few high quality English medium schools reserved for the future elite. The latter are, in educational philosophy and technique, not different or inferior to their American and British counterparts. Indeed, students in these institutions sit for 'O' and 'A' level examinations in a manner no different from students in Britain. Some such institutions have even begun to make use of the computer as a leaning tool. Students from these schools generally aim for lucrative professions such as management, medicine, banking, etc. Few opt for engineering or the academic professions, and still fewer return to Pakistan after studying abroad. Thus, their contribution to the intellectual milieu in Pakistan is insubstantial.

To see how non-science coexists with science in ordinary Pakistani educational institutions, it is instructive to look at a magazine named *Fikr-i-No* put out by the science club of a Karachi degree-level college. The pages of this magazine are a revealing indication of what students, as well as teachers, make of their subject. The first, and most prominent article, is written by a science teacher who pours withering scorn onto Darwin's theory of evolution. Another essay speaks of miracles, challenging scientists to explain how the Prophet restored the sight of one Muslim warrior whose eye had been torn clean outside its socket, and how some magic inscription outside a Mughul emperor's tomb was kept shining over the years. Yet another article covers great events in science: specific gravity was discovered when Archimedes slipped in his bathtub, the steam engine was born when George Stephenson saw a kettle boiling, the theory of gravity is owed to an apple falling on Newton's head, and so on. One is led to the conclusion that the edifice of science would have crumbled had these events not taken place.

If there is concern among Islamabad planners over the collapse of science education, and education in general, then that concern is certainly a well-kept secret. Like Tennyson's 'Gods on a hill, careless of Mankind', bureaucrats of the Education Ministry and University Grants Commission have maintained a calm serenity, together with totalitarian control over educational matters, indifferent to meaningful suggestions for a way out. Education appears not to be a priority issue, or even a serious issue at all.

Conclusion

A massive technological transformation, uncontrolled and irreversible, is changing the face of Pakistan and, inevitably, the character and values of Pakistani society. Changes may be slow in some areas, fast in others. But unquestionably, much of the traditional society is on the way out. The bullock cart is seen with increasing rarity; tractors rule the fields and farms. Suzuki vans have replaced the tonga, car pollution and traffic jams are proudly acknowledged as problems, high-rise buildings stand in place of graceful colonial structures, supermarkets and shopping plazas are replacing traditional bazaars, modern telecommunications link cities, and VCRs are the principal urban entertainment. Hundreds of watts of audio power pour out from high efficiency loudspeakers in mosques, summoning the faithful to prayer. The computer has made its debut; the 'revolution' will inevitably follow.

The metamorphosis into a society relying more and more on modern technology has not, however, been accompanied by an acceptance of rational principles for social organisation or behaviour. Indeed, the reaction against science as an instrument of reason, whether applied to social matters or even natural phenomena, appears to intensify with increasing technological dependence on the West. The degree to which this phenomenon is sustainable is a matter of speculation. However, one clear consequence has been the tremendous elevation in importance of the transnational corporation, the most important purveyor of modern technology. The import of technology makes possible the simultaneous coexistence of mediaevalism with the space age.

One single issue, the ideological obstructions to science in Pakistan, has been stressed in this chapter. It is sometimes claimed that this is a mere reflection of the economic and class structure of Pakistani society. This is a vulgarly mechanistic view which sacrifices truth to convenience and dogma. But this is not to deny that other factors are perhaps of equal importance.

Technology, while preserving the feudal character of Pakistani society, has not led to the creation of a powerful capitalist class. Industrial capitalism — the force which had transformed European society — is weak and dependent on international markets and suppliers. Transnational capitalism is, as has been suggested, powerful and exploitative. Its local beneficiaries — managers, engineers, and professionals — are a sizeable, Westernised, outward-looking, cynical, and ruthless elite who privately look at present trends in education and politics with disdain, but who are shrewd enough to recognise that their prosperity depends upon maintaining the status quo. The army, the dominant force in Pakistan, is inherently pro-technology, but its political role forces it to abandon progressive values. Thus, class factors also militate against a wider dissemination of science and scientific thought in Pakistan. However, it would be wrong to attribute ideological attitudes entirely to class structure.

What is the way out, if any? In the climate of the times, this appears to be a moot question. However, assuming circumstances arise so that science and rationality become desirable ends, this will become a question requiring serious thought. Scientific education in schools and colleges should certainly be reformed to reflect genuine scientific knowledge. However, conventional education alone may not be adequate. In a recent article a Pakistani professor of physics argues that the Kerala People's Science Movement (KSSP) in India has demonstrated an efficient strategy for bringing science to the masses.[25] The KSSP was started about 22 years ago by a group of intellectuals, growing to a large organisation of some 8000 members. Activities of the group are grouped as follows: 1) publication; 2) non-formal education; 3) activities connected with formal education; 4) rural science forum; 5) environment and ecology; 6) health; 7) art and science; 8) women and children's group. Six monthly science magazines are produced catering to a whole range of people from children to grown-ups. The circulation of their children's magazine is 30,000. Quiz competitions, popular lectures in the local languages, a science centre, afforestation campaigns, a KSSP health brigade — these have contributed significantly towards making science accessible and understandable to common people.

The battle for science and rationality has yet to seriously begin in Pakistan. It cannot be lost, because the alternative is perpetual ignorance and despair.

References and Notes

1. The Salam Mathematics Prize Committee, in its search for mathematicians among talented mathematicians in Pakistan under 35 years of age, was unable to discover a single applicant with a record of original publications.

2. The Department of Physics at Quaid-i-Azam University was the foremost institution in this field in the late 1960s and early 1970s and achieved world renown for achievements in theoretical physics. It rapidly degenerated when, disillusioned with university policies and practices, the department's founder as well as several other scientists resigned from the university or were dismissed.

3. The HEJ Institute of Chemistry in Karachi is a unique example of a successfully operating scientific institution in the country.

4. A test for admission into graduate studies in physics at MIT attracted great interest and was attempted by 120 first division students of M.Sc.,M.Phil., and Ph.D. from all over Pakistan. Candidates were required to answer 200 B.Sc. level questions from multiple choice answers, consultation of any number of books being permitted during the four-hour exam. The pass marks were 160. The highest marks attained were 113, and the average marks were 70. Statistically, a person totally ignorant on the subject would have achieved 67 marks had he guessed the answers randomly. Even allowing for the unfamiliarity of students with this mode of examination and difference of syllabi, the fact that not even one Pakistani student came even close to qualifying is telling. A decade ago, several students would make it to the top-quality US institutions.

5. Dr. Mohammad Afzal, in an interview given to the daily *Jang*, 6 February 1984.

6. J. D. Bernal, *Science in History* (Cambridge: MIT Press, 1981) and A. E. Mckenzie, *The Major Achievements of Science*, Vol. I (Cambridge: Cambridge University Press, 1960).

7. *The Complete Prefaces of Bernard Shaw*, (London: Paul Hamlyn, 1965), p. 369.

8. Francis Ghiles. 'What is Wrong with Muslim Science?' *Nature*, 24 March 1983.

9. George Sarton. *Introduction to the History of Science*, Vol. I (Baltimore, 1927), passim.

10. A good discussion of Syed Ahmed's views on science can be found in Sibt-i-Hasan, *Naveed-i-Fikr* (Karachi: Maktab-i-Danial, 1982).

11. C. W. Troll, *Sayyed Ahmed Khan — A Reinterpretation of Muslim Theology* (Karachi: Oxford University Press, 1978), passim.

12. Maulana Mohammad Ismail Panipati, *Maaqulat-i-Sir Syed*, Vol. I (Lahore: Majlis-i-Tarraqi-i-Adam, 1962), pp. 97-8.

13. Troll, *Sayyed Ahmed Khan,* pp. 168-70.

14. Maryam Jameelah, *Modern Technology and the Dehumanization of Man* (Lahore: El-Matbaat-ul-Arabia, 1983), p.8.

15. Ibid.

16. Abul Ala Maudoodi, *Taalimat* (Lahore: Islamic Publishers, n.d.), p. 20.

17. Ibid., p. 86.

18. Sayyed Hossein Nasr, *The Encounter of Man with Nature* (London: George Allen and Unwin Ltd., 1968), p. 94.

19. Abdus Salam, 'Science and Technology in Islamic Countries — Past, Present, and Future', lecture delivered at the University of Kuwait, November 1983.

20. A black hole is a burnt-out star so dense that even light cannot escape its gravitational field.

21. Mohammad Munir, *God, Universe and Life* (Islamabad: M. A. Idrees, 1983), p. 45.

22. Abstracts of paper presented at the International Conference on Science in Islamic Polity — Its Past, Present, and Future, Islamabad, 1983, p. 82.

23. Mohammad F. Khan, *Al-Qur'ān — The Ultimate Challenge* (Bangalore: Educational Press, 1980), p. 6.

24. Maudoodi, *Taalimat*, p. 93.

25. Q. I. Daudpota, letter to the editor in *Viewpoint*, 24 May 1984, Lahore.

9. Pakistan: The Crisis of the State

by Akmal Hussain

Introduction

Pakistan is in the grip of perhaps the most acute and wide-ranging crisis in its history. The political, legal, and social institutions through which the aspirations of the people are articulated and which constitute the basis of the creative development of the people are on the verge of collapse. At the same time, the state apparatus, bereft of a legitimising ideology, stands today in stark confrontation with the people. At such a moment, a serious analysis of the crisis is a pre-requisite for its creative resolution. Such a resolution of the crisis is necessary if the people and the state they embody are to survive and remain independent.

To understand the principal elements of the present crisis in terms of the interplay of political and economic forces, it is necessary to examine the nature and genesis of the Pakistan Movement. It is also necessary to analyse the dominance of the state apparatus over the political process in Pakistan — a dominance whose trajectory brings the power of the state into confrontation with the power of the people. An analysis of the nature of the development of the military-bureaucratic oligarchy is also relevant to an understanding of the situation in Pakistan, as is also an examination of the relationship between the process of economic growth, the political environment, and the crisis of the state.

In considering the nature and origins of the Pakistan Movement, one comes across two kinds of equally simplistic views at opposite ends of the ideological spectrum. At one end, there is the metaphysical view of Muslim communal 'historians', who confine the concepts of culture and nation strictly within the bounds of religion. In this view Pakistan is seen as a historical inevitability rooted in the doctrinal differences between Hinduism and Islam. At the other end of the spectrum, there is the view that conceives history in terms of the political manipulations of individuals or governments. This view regards Pakistan as the result simply of a British conspiracy to divide and rule. Such approaches, however, cannot explain why religious differences between Hindus and Muslims acquired the importance they did in the first half of the 20th century in India or why the British policy of sowing discord fell on such fertile ground. These questions can be answered only by examining the nature of the political and economic forces at play during the twilight of the raj.

The origin of the demand for Pakistan can be located in the dynamic interaction of three political forces within India during the period from 1857 to 1940:

> 1. The British imperial government, which it can be argued was interested in undermining the gathering momentum of the national liberation movement by accentuating its internal contradictions.
> 2. The Congress, representing the interests of an Indian national bourgeoisie, which was essentially underdeveloped and therefore lacked genuine secularism in its political choices and political language. Consequently, the Congress was susceptible to Hindu communalist pressures, thereby increasingly alienating the Muslim fraction of the Indian bourgeoisie.
> 3. The nascent Muslim fraction of the Indian bourgeoisie, which was even less mature than its Hindu counterpart. Due to acute weakness in its rivalry with the more powerful Hindu fraction, the Muslim bourgeoisie was induced to seek support from Muslim landlords and the colonial state on the one hand and reliance on an explicitly religious ideology on the other.

The Emerging Muslim Bourgeoisie, the British and the Congress: 1857–1905

One of the earliest attempts at articulating the political and economic interests of propertied Muslims in British India can be traced to the Muslim education movement of Syed Ahmed Khan. His political ideas during the 1850s expressed the interests of the rising Muslim bourgeoisie and the smaller landlords, who resented the feudal system in India and wished to receive economic concessions from the British authorities. Thus, Syed Ahmed Khan opposed the 1857 War of Independence as an attempt to restore the old feudal nobility and supported the British on this issue. While being a staunch loyalist of the British raj he urged industrial and commercial development and argued for administrative reforms whereby Indians could be given a place in the country's administration.[1] He called upon Muslims to educate themselves and to be receptive to modern scientific ideas. In the pursuit of this objective he founded a scientific society in 1864. In 1877, helped by the British, Syed Ahmed Khan founded the Muslim College at Aligarh. This institution sought to inculcate loyalty to the raj in Muslims and at the same time became an influential political and ideological centre of Muslim propertied classes. Aligarh College made an important contribution in producing a corpus of literature and a Muslim separatist political party in India.

The correspondence between the interests of the British raj and the political efforts of Syed Ahmed Khan can be judged from his complete change in posture in the period before and after the formation of the Indian National Congress in 1885. Until 1885, he was a champion of

Hindu-Muslim unity and conceived of Hindus and Muslims as part of the same nation:

> Do not forget that Hindu and Muslim are names referring to the religious denomination, *but whether Hindu, Muslim or Christian, so long as these people live in our country, they form one nation regardless of their faith* [emphasis added].[2]

The formation of the Indian National Congress in 1885 was an attempt by Indian nationalists to challenge the political status quo and pressurise the British authorities for reforms and self-rule. Even though in the early phase of the Congress this struggle was conducted strictly within the structure of the colonial state, Syed Ahmed Khan and the Muslim propertied interests whom he represented strongly opposed the Congress struggle. Syed Ahmed Khan, who only a few years earlier had championed Hindu-Muslim unity within a single nation, now made an equally passionate attack on the notion of composite Indian nationalism. In a speech at Lucknow on 28 December 1887, he remarked as follows:

> Now supposed that all the English were to leave India — then who would be the rulers of India? Is it possible that under these cirucmstances *two nations, Mohammedan and Hindu, could sit on the same throne and remain equal in power? Most certainly not.* It is necessary that one of them should conquer the other and thrust it down. To hope that both could remain equal is to desire the impossible and inconceivable [emphasis added].[3]

The sharp change in Syed Ahmed Khan's position on the relationship between religion and nationhood expressed the imperatives operating upon the infant Muslim bourgeoisie. The bourgeoisie of north-west India historically emerged much later than the bourgeoisie operating in Bengal and Bombay. In the latter regions, because of their proximity to the sea, the pattern of expansion of the colonial economy brought it to commercial and industrial activity much earlier than in northern India, where the production of cash crops remained the predominant function of the colonial economy. Consequently, the Muslim bourgeoisie which originated in north-west India was much weaker than the Hindu bourgeoisie, and in its competitive struggle against the latter, it had to rely on the support of Muslim landlords and British authorities. Accordingly, as the Congress emerged to threaten the interests of British metropolitan capital, the weak Muslim fraction of the Indian bourgeoisie saw that in opposing the Congress it could win concessions from the British.

Soon after the founding of the Congress, Syed Ahmed Khan organised the first anti-Congress organisation of Muslim landlords and bourgeois intellectuals, called the United Friends of India society. As Syed Ahmed said in a letter to his English friend, Graham, the purpose of this society was to combat the politics of the Congress.[4]

As the Congress organisation was formed, the newly appointed Governor-General of India, Lord Dufferin, assisted by the British politician Allen Hume, discussed with British officials the chances of provoking anti-Congress disorders, in an attempt to undermine the nationalist movement.[5]

Soon after the formation of the Congress, a Hindu movement against cow-slaughter, which provoked Hindu-Muslim riots, arose as part of a movement for the purity of Hinduism. The Congress then declared that it was an all-India organisation representing both Hindus and Muslims. However, the Indian national bourgeoisie was not fully developed, since it had emerged within the highly restrictive structure of the dependent colonial economy. Its growth had not occurred in the context of an economic and cultural conflict with feudalism, as in the European case. Accordingly, the Indian national bourgeoisie had not transcended the religious elements in its culture to achieve a secular political language. It was therefore not in a position to oppose effectively the anti-cow-slaughter movement. This failure led Syed Ahmed to brand the Congress a Hindu organisation and to argue that the Congress' notion of self-rule would result in Hindu dominance of India.[6]

As the Congress gained organisational strength and enlarged its social base, its demand for a system of democratic representation of the Indian people began to press the British authorities. It was at this stage that Aligarh College began to play an active role against the Congress by posing the fact of different religious communities in India as an argument against a simple democratic representation, in which the Hindus would have been in the majority.

The Nationalist Movement and the Communal Question: 1905-28

The Indian national bourgeoisie, because of its low level of development, had not been able to achieve genuine secularism in its consciousness. It was therefore susceptible to Hindu religious influence in both its political language as well as occasionally its political choices. This was an important factor in fostering a sense of insecurity about Congress intentions among the Muslim fraction of the Indian bourgeoisie. The nascent Muslim bourgeoisie was relatively so much weaker than its Hindu counterpart that it felt obliged to conduct its rivalry by aligning itself with the British authorities and Muslim landlords and by using an explicitly Muslim communal ideology in its anti-Congress rhetoric. This pushed the Congress even further towards a Hindu communalist direction. Thus, the veiled communalism of the Congress and the open communalism of the Muslim bourgeoisie fed off each other due to the underdeveloped nature of both the Hindu and Muslim fractions of Indian bourgeoisie. Whenever the nationalist movement led by the Congress intensified, the doubts and misgivings between the Hindu and Muslim communities were also accentuated. This sociological and psychological characteristic of the relations between the Hindu and Muslim fractions of the Indian bourgeoisie was reinforced by the political imperatives operating on the British colonial regime, which aimed at intensifying communal conflict as a device to weaken the nationalist movement. It is this particular interplay of forces that explains the fact that at the high tide of the nationalist movement, in 1905, we see the emergence of the Muslim League as a separate political party of the Muslims.

As the national liberation movement in India gathered momentum and mobilized the masses, three important developments took place: 1) the partition of Bengal in 1905; 2) British support for the establishment of the Muslim League in 1906, which at that stage explicitly called upon its members for loyalty to the British; [7] and 3) the introduction of separate electorates in 1909.

The real causes of the partition of Bengal were rooted in Hindu-Muslim communalism rather than in a desire to emancipate the poor of East Bengal. This was made clear during Lord Curzon's tour of East Bengal, where he addressed an assemblage of Muslim landlords in Dacca and argued that the partition of Bengal would bring untold benefits to the Muslims of Bengal. The partition of Bengal did indeed liberate many of the Muslim small landholders and poor peasants in East Bengal from the oppression of Hindu landlords and money-lenders. However, the Muslim landlords in this region remained untouched. In fact, in order to quell fears of Muslim landlords of increased taxes in East Bengal, the British authorities announced hastily that land taxation after partition would remain unchanged.[8]

The growing communalism in India during the first decade of the 20th century was not merely the result of British intrigue. The particular form of political mobilisation conducted by the Congress also accentuated the existing distrust between the Hindu and Muslim communities. While the Congress was formally a secular organisation, in practice, its campaigns and political language were characterised by Hindu symbolism. During the 1905-11 campaign against the partition of Bengal, the Congress could have won the support of most Muslim landlords because few Muslims supported the division of Bengal. Yet the Congress leaders alienated their Muslim supporters by using Hindu anthems and Hindu symbols in their mass campaigns. Many Muslim nationalists were outraged by this imagery and left the movement.

The Muslim middle classes in the competition for jobs felt at a disadvantage vis-à-vis their Hindu counterparts. The Aligarh group, with the support of the British authorities, directed this tendency towards the demand for separate electorates and an intensification of the communal issues. The English principal of Aligarh College, Archibald, undertook to arrange for a Muslim delegation to see the Viceroy. In 1906 Archibald went to Simla to meet the Viceroy's secretary (Colonel Dunlop Smith) and discussed the address which the deputation was to hand to the

Viceroy.

Archibald proposed that the deputation should reject the principle of election to legislative councils on the grounds that it would be detrimental to the Muslim minority's interests. He suggested that nomination, or representation on the basis of religion, should be demanded instead. Although the Muslim delegation that went to see the Viceroy did not carry Archibald's idea of nomination as against representation, nevertheless the key proposal of Archibald for representation on a religious basis was the central issue that the delegation discussed with the Viceroy. Further evidence of the British attempt at formenting Hindu-Muslim communal tension is proved by a private conversation between Mohsin ul Mulk, and the Viceroy, Lord Minto. The Viceroy emphasised that Muslim political activities should aim at achieving community representation for Muslims in order to combat the political power of the Hindus; the Viceroy further pointed out that the British had high hopes for the loyalty of the Aligarh group.[9]

The British policy of opposing the Hindu and Muslim communities finally found a formal expression in the Indian Councils Act of 1909, which brought about separate electorates for Hindus and Muslims.

The Emergence of the Muslim League

The efforts of the Muslim landlords and Muslim commercial interests to form a separate Muslim political party intensified in an environment characterised by the Congress' mass campaign for self-rule. This was increasingly couched in Hindu mythological images, thereby generating a growing concern among the bourgeoisie, landlords and middle class elements of the Muslim community.

The first specific proposal for a Muslim political association was made by Nawab Salimullah of Dacca. He argued that such an association should support the British administration, combat the mounting influence of the Congress and protect Muslim communal interests.[10] The essentials of Salimullah's proposals were accepted at a subsequent Dacca Conference of Muslim leaders, chaired by the well-known Aligarh figure, Viqar ul Mulk. This conference named the new organisation the All-India Muslim League.

The first conference of the All-India Muslim League opened in Karachi on 29 December 1907. The founding fathers of the Muslim League belonged to the Muslim groups of landlords and intellectuals from the Central and the United Provinces, Bengal and the Punjab. The most influential group among these founding fathers was the Aligarh group. These were intellectual nawabs from established families who had begun their careers in the ICS (Indian Civil Service) in the UP, later supported Syed Ahmed's Education Movement and finally devoted themselves to the Aligarh College. Included in the founders of the Muslim League were a few Muslim manufacturers, the most notable being Adamjee Pirbhai. The Aga Khan (elected the first president of the league), apart from being head of the Ismaili community, was closely connected to the Muslim manufacturers of Bombay.

The resolution in the Dacca Conference where the Muslim League was born defined the following goals:

1) To promote among the *Mussalmans* of India feelings of loyalty to the British Government and to remove any misconception that may arise as to the intention of the government with regard to its measures.

2) To project and advance the political rights and interests of the *Mussalmans* of India and to respectfully represent their needs and aspirations to the government.

3) To prevent the rise among the *Mussalmans* of India of any feeling of hostility towards other communities without prejudice to the other afore-mentioned objects of the League.[11]

Those few industrialists who had joined the Muslim League, while wanting to use the pressure of the League to win concessions from the British, also wanted the freedom to conduct business with the Hindu and Parsi communities. These Muslim industrialists put pressure on the predominantly landlord leadership of the League to adopt a less antagonistic attitude towards the Congress. It was this influence of the industrialists that resulted in the League adopting the third point of non-hostility towards other communities.

In 1908-10 the Muslim League established its main provincial bodies. These were headed by big landlords and conservative Muslim intellectuals closely associated with the landed elite. Thus, for example, the Punjab League was led by Shah Din and Mian Mohammad Shafi; the East Bengal branch was headed by Nazimuddin and Nawab Salimullah. The Muslim League leader from the United Provinces was Rajah Naushad Ali Khan (the biggest landlord of the region), and in south India the Nizam of of Hyderabad and other princes and landlords headed the League. Only in Bombay, Bihar and Madras was League leadership in the hands of members of the bourgeoisie.

By the eve of the First World War, big Muslim merchants had begun to invest in industry. This generated a new dialectic of unity and rivalry between the Hindu and Muslim fractions of the Indian bourgeoisie: on the one hand, the developing Muslim industrial bourgeoisie had an interest in strengthening and uniting the struggle of the Indian bourgeoisie against the colonial regime, and, on the other, as the Muslim commercial interests entered the domain of industry, their contention with the established Hindu industrialists intensified.

Jinnah grasped this dialectic before any of the other League leaders and called for a united action by the Congress and the League for a constitutional struggle for self-rule. Mohammad Ali Jinnah was a well-known Bombay lawyer. Gifted with an incisive intellect and fierce personal integrity, he was to emerge later as the Quaid-i-Azam — the charismatic leader of the Muslim community. With his vigorous constitutionalist approach to issues and liberal ideas, Jinnah was in his early political career ideally suited as the champion of Hindu-Muslim unity. During the period of the First World War, Jinnah, while still a member of the Congress, rose to become an influential leader of the Muslim League. Both the League and the Congress accepted his idea for a joint session of the two parties in Bombay in December 1915. During this session, while urging rapprochement with the Congress, Jinnah also proposed that the agreement provide for the principle of special Muslim representation in the legislative bodies. The latter device was used to incorporate within the agreement the tendency of rivalry with the Hindus that prevailed among the Muslim bourgeoisie and rising middle class.

These efforts bore fruit in the Lucknow Pact of 1916, which was endorsed by the League and the Congress at their respective sessions. The pact envisaged that the two parties would jointly struggle to establish self-government bodies by direct elections on the territorial principle, while retaining the system of separate representation for about ten years.

Between 1916 and 1920 there was a limited degree of co-operation between the Congress and the Muslim League. However, strains began to appear when during 1918-20 anti-British Muslim *'ulamā* mobilised Muslim masses for the *Khilāfat* Movement and Congress declared support for it. Jinnah and his group in the League disapproved of the *Khilāfat* Movement on constitutional grounds. Matters came to a head when at the end of 1920 the Congress launched a mass civil disobedience movement, and Jinnah attacked the decision on tactical grounds. He stated in a letter to Mahatma Gandhi that he would not support it, because the movement put the masses in motion and thus would lead to chaos: 'What the consequences of this may be, I shudder to contemplate.'[12] At the 1921 session of the Muslim League in Calcutta, Jinnah argued that Gandhi's way was the wrong way. 'Mine is the right way', he declared. 'The constitutional way is the right way.' The opposing positions adopted by Gandhi and Jinnah on the issue of the civil disobedience movement partly reflected the opposing political styles of the two leaders: Gandhi's flamboyant politics of the street as opposed to Jinnah's constitutional style of the legislative assembly. In any case, following disagreement on the civil disobedience movement, Jinnah resigned from the Congress in 1921, and the lukewarm Congress-League cooperation begun with the Lucknow Pact in 1916 suffered a serious setback.

While the civil disobedience movement was in progress, the Moplah revolt broke out in 1921. This was essentially an uprising by the poor peasantry of Malabar against the landlords. However, since the peasants were mainly Muslims and the landlords mostly Hindus, the British press publicised it as a communal Hindu-Muslim war. The British interpretation was questionable, since in many places poor Hindus joined the revolt. Kunna Ahmed Haji, a peasant chief, wrote to the Madras daily *The Hindu* rebutting charges of communalism and accusing the government of attacking Hindu temples to induce discord between the communities. The rebellion was crushed by the army, resulting in the killing of over 2,000 peasants.[13] Neither the Congress nor the League raised a voice in support of the peasants when they were being massacred by the British.

During the period 1923-27 the frequency of communal riots between Hindus and Muslims increased alarmingly, resulting in 450 dead and thousands injured. To reduce the mounting communal tension, Gandhi and Muslim nationalists like Abul Kalam Azad initiated a move for a new 'national pact' between the Congress and the Muslim League. Jinnah and the League responded favourably.

In March 1927 at Delhi, there was a meeting of Muslim intellectuals who favoured a united movement for home rule by the Congress and Muslim League. During this meeting a press statement was issued by the Muslim intellectuals declaring that the principle of general elections to central and provincial legislative bodies (as advocated by the Congress) was acceptable on the following conditions: 1) the establishment of Sind as a separate province; 2) provincial self-government for NWFP and Baluchistan on an equal footing with other provinces; 3) seats for Muslims in the Punjab and Bengal provincial legislative bodies in proportion to the Muslim population of these provinces; and 4) not less than one-third of the seats for Muslims in the central legislatures.

This document, which became famous as the Delhi Manifesto, was drawn up by Jinnah and Maulana Mohammad Ali and was the basis of a new, albeit transient, understanding between the Muslim League and the Congress. The League declared that it was prepared to disown the separate representation system on the terms set out in the manifesto, a position it was to maintain until 1937. This was an important concession. The Congress in its Madras session the same year also declared approval of the Delhi Manifesto and called for an all-parties conference to devise a new constitution.

These events appeared to indicate that a favourable situation for Hindu-Muslim unity had arisen. Yet communal conflicts soon expressed themselves in the relations between the Congress and the League, as indicated earlier. The Congress, in spite of its secular ideology, was susceptible to Hindu communal influence in its political language and its choices. The political position adopted by the Congress at the All-Parties Conference was an important illustration of this fact. Under pressure from the right-wing Hindu religious party called the *Hindu Mahasabha*, the Congress leadership in violation of its earlier stand rejected the basic points of the Delhi Manifesto. Jinnah urged that the basic demands of the Delhi Manifesto be worked into the constitution being devised at the All-Parties Conference. However, his appeals were turned down by the All-

Parties Conference in both Lucknow (June 1928) and Calcutta (December 1928). Thoroughly disillusioned by the Congress, Jinnah declared after the abortive Calcutta conference: 'This is the parting of the ways.'[14] History proved him right.

After the failure of the attempts at League-Congress cooperation in 1928, and with the onset of the world economic crisis (1929-33), the prospects of growth of the Muslim bourgeoisie in alliance with the Indian national bourgeoisie were severely constricted. There was a growing awareness among the leaders of the Muslim League that its political future lay across classes with all Muslims. This required an ambitious political programme with a broad-based appeal. The first step towards this objective was the formulation of Jinnah's fourteen points, after the All-Parties Muslim Conference in Delhi in January 1929. The crucial feature of these fourteen points (later submitted to the Round Table Conference in 1930) was the recognitition of the regional diversity of India and the need for provincial autonomy. Jinnah demanded a federal constitution with residuary powers vested in the provinces and a uniform measure of autonomy for all provinces. Jinnah also demanded guarantees for the free development of the various national languages and the freedom of religion. The most important of the points affecting the interests of Muslims were as follows:

1) The reservation of not less than one-third of the seats in the central and provincial cabinets for Muslims;
2) Granting Muslims an adequate share along with other Indians in all the services of the state and local self-governing bodies;
3) Solution of communal questions to be subject to an affirmative vote of three-fourths of the community concerned;
4) Establishment of Sind province, which was to be separated from the Bombay presidency;
5) Legislative bodies for NWFP and Baluchistan.

Jinnah's fourteen points won the support of almost all the Muslim political groups, including those which had taken part in the civil disobedience campaign. This constituted the first step in enlarging the support of the Muslim League among all Muslims.

When the British government announced the Communal Award and the fundamentals of the new constitution, the Muslim League initially supported it. However, by the time the Government of India Act was published in 1935 the campaign of the Congress against the new constitution had gained wide popularity among the masses, including many Muslim peasants. Jinnah had the sagacity to recognise that continued support for the constitution would preclude the possibility of the Muslim League gaining a mass following among the Muslims. Accordingly, in its April 1936 session at Bombay, the Muslim League reversed its earlier position and refused to approve the constitution of

1935. This was a turning point in the history of the Muslim League, for it represented a recognition by the Muslim League leadership of the need to gain the support of broad sections of the Muslims of India.

The results of the 1937 elections showed that the Indian National Congress had emerged as an all-India organisation, capturing 716 out of 1585 seats and qualifying to form ministries in six provinces.[15] At the same time the Congress claim that as a secular party it represented all communities was not borne out by the election results. For the Congress failed to get a significant percentage of the Muslim vote — having won only 26 out of a total 482 seats reserved for Muslims (i.e. 5.4%). While the Muslim League made a stronger showing compared to the Congress in the Muslim reserved seats — winning 109 seats out of 482 (i.e. 23%) — it could not claim on the basis of 23% of the Muslim reserved seats to be the representative of Indian Muslims.[16] What was perhaps even more worrying for the Muslim League was that it was weakest in the Muslim majority provinces. For example, the League won only two seats in the Punjab (compared to the Unionists, who won 101 out of 167 provincial assembly seats); in Sind and NWFP the Muslim League could not win even a single seat.

The results of the 1937 elections brought home an important lesson to the Muslim elite which led the League: if the Muslim League were to negotiate with the British as a representative of Indian Muslims, then an effective party organisation in at least the Muslim majority areas was of crucial importance. Equally important was the need to articulate a new political programme and new slogans which could mobilise the emotional charge of broad sections of the Muslim masses.

Soon after the elections the Muslim League, in its October 1937 session at Lucknow, adopted a new constitution. The basis of this new constitution was the 'Two-Nation' Theory and the demand for autonomy of Muslim majority provinces within a fully independent Indian federation. The new constitution catered to poorer sections of Indian Muslims by opening its membership to all Muslims regardless of class, reducing its membership fee to a nominal two annas per month and envisaging a reduction in rent, relief from usury and a guaranteed minimum wage for workers.

The demand for the autonomy of the 'Muslim nation' was accompanied by campaigning for specifically Muslim chambers of commerce, industry and similar organisations in the agriculture sector. The Muslim League campaign of focussing politics along the communal principle found expression in the first session of the Sind branch of the Muslim League. At this session (presided over by Jinnah) there was a demand for the division of India into a federation of Hindu and Muslim states.

The new constitution contributed to the increased influence of the Muslim League among the Muslims of India. Another factor enhancing support for the League among Muslims was the deterioration of Hindu-Muslim relations as the result of the mode of operation of the Congress

provincial ministries. The Congress ministries, while ignoring the demands of Muslims, claimed to represent the interests of Muslims as well
as Hindus. It therefore recognised only Muslim members of Congress as
representative of the Muslims. What outraged the religious feelings of the
Muslims was that whereas legislation passed in provinces where Congress
governments were in power permitted songs and dances in front of
mosques, killing cows, which was against the religious beliefs of Hindus,
was made a criminal offence. The suspicion among Muslims that the
Congress had a Hindu communal orientation was given further weight by
the fact that *Bande Matram*, a patriotic hymn expressed in Hindu images,
was declared the national anthem. The Congress stand on the language
issue also incensed many Muslim intellectuals. Hindi was made compulsory in schools while the Congress refused to introduce the Urdu
language and Arabic and Persian literature even in regions where the
traditional Muslim community regarded these as the basis of Muslim
education.

This susceptibility of the Congress to Hindu communal influence,
together with the appeal to Muslim communalist sentiment by the
political campaign of the League, intensified the polarisation between the
Hindu and Muslim communities. By the time of the Second World War,
the earlier demand of Muslim leaders for autonomy of Muslim majority
provinces within an Indian federation began to be replaced by the
demand for secession of these provinces. The Working Committee of the
Muslim League, in the session of 17-18 September 1938, rejected the
federal objective on grounds that such a federation would 'necessarily
result in a majority community rule' and argued that this was totally
unacceptable in a country 'which is composed of various nationalities and
does not constitute a national state'.[17]

In December 1939 with the resignation of Congress ministries in
NWFP, Sind and Assam, followed by anti-Congress riots in many
provinces, communal passions rose to a new pitch. As the momentum of
communal conflict built up, the Muslim League at its Lahore session on
20-23 March 1940 made a historic declaration. It was proclaimed that the
Indian Muslims sought the division of India on religious principles and
the establishment of a Muslim state called Pakistan.[18] Subsequently,
between 1940 and 1946, the Muslim League in its negotiations with the
Congress and the British authorities kept open the option of a number of
solutions short of the outright partition of India. However, by 1946 all
other options were closed, and Pakistan came into being as an independent state on 14 August 1947.

As Imran Ali in a well-documented paper on the decade 1937-47 has
argued, the growth of mass popularity of the League in this period was
associated with the growth of tension between the Hindu and Muslim
communities. However, on the regional level, ' . . . the role of non-
communal factors such as class, the existing power structure . . . and
internecine rivalries can by no means be discounted'.[19] In the Punjab, the

emergence of the League as a major political force involved not only an exercise in the use of popular politics, but also an accommodation with the Punjab National Unionist Party — the party of the big feudal landlords of the Punjab. An important factor in the victory of the Muslim League in the 1946 election was that by then, through a combination of intimidation and conciliation, the Muslim League had won over from the Unionist Party the most powerful of the Muslim feudal landlords of the Punjab.[20] In the vital months that followed the 1946 election up to August 1947, the Muslim League and the Pakistan Movement were controlled mainly by the Punjabi feudal elite.[21] This phenomenon led to the dominance of Pakistan's power structure by the landlords of the Punjab during the post-Partition era.

It has been seen that the vicissitudes of Jinnah's attempts at achieving Hindu-Muslim unity (1909-28) expressed the contradictions of an emerging Muslim bourgeoisie, which was competing for a market against an established Hindu bourgeoisie. These contradictions became antagonistic because they occurred in a situation where the economic space for both was severely restricted by the economic structure of a colonial regime and the predominance of metropolitan capital. What gave these economic contradictions between two fractions of an embryonic class an explosive political potential was a deep-rooted tension between the Hindu and Muslim communities, which had ebbed and flowed with the rise and fall of the Mughul empire. The process of the development of state structures and ruling ideologies in India had not succeeded in creating the institutions within which diverse communities of the subcontinent could evolve a fundamentally unified identity.

The Military-Bureaucratic Oligarchy

The predominant position of the bureaucracy and the army in the structure of state power in the newly formed country was due to the *form* of the freedom struggle on the one hand and the *nature* of the Muslim League on the other. Since the freedom struggle was essentially a constitutional one, the state apparatus of the colonial regime remained largely intact at the time of independence. The bureaucracy and the army, which constituted the 'steel frame' of the raj, continued after the emergence of Pakistan to determine the parameters within which political and economic changes were to occur. The predominance of the bureaucracy and military in the exercise of state power in Pakistan was also due to the fact that, unlike the Indian National Congress, the Muslim League was more a movement than a political party. During the Pakistan Movement, it had not been able to institutionalise its popular support in terms of a stable party structure, a manifesto based on mass support for the solution of Pakistan's economic and political problems and a political culture which could ensure the primacy of representative political governments in the stucture of state power. The dominance of the

Muslim League by retrogressive landlords had further undermined the ability to create, in the new country, a political framework within which popular aspirations could be realised.[22]

At the time of independence, the principle protagonists in the exercise of state power were the bureaucracy, the military, the big landlords and the nascent bourgeoisie. Hamza Alavi in a seminal paper has argued that because of colonial development the institutions of the army and the bureaucracy are 'overdeveloped' relative to the ruling classes (the landlords and the bourgeoisie),[23] Accordingly, the military-bureaucratic oligarchy has 'relative autonomy' within the state and is able to intervene and mediate whenever the rivalry between the ruling classes becomes so intense that it threatens the framework within which rivalry is conducted. Having restored the framework within which the ruling classes pursue their interests, Alavi suggests that the military-bureaucratic oligarchy withdraws from the conduct of political affairs.

Alavi's characterisation of the function of the military-bureaucratic oligarchy may have been relevant during the 1950s and 1960s, but it would need to be modified in order to explain the contemporary crisis of the state. The reason is that important changes have occurred since the 1960s *within* the military-bureaucratic oligarchy and in its *relationship* with civil society.

The military-bureaucratic oligarchy in Pakistan was never a static monolith but an institution whose internal social composition and relationship to society were subject to change in the process of economic and social development. Thus in the immediate post-independence period the officers were predominantly from the landowning class with an ideology derived essentially from the British military traditions. Attitudes of professionalism and the need to insulate the armed forces from the daily conduct of civil affairs prevailed. However, during the mid-1960s and 1970s the social origin of the officer corps shifted towards the petite bourgeoisie in the urban areas and in the countryside. This shift in the class origins of the officer corps was accompanied by increasing ideological factionalism in terms of a fundamentalist religious ethos on the one hand and a liberal left-wing ethos on the other.[24] The tendency towards the emergence of opposing political perspectives within the officer corps was reinforced by two important developments. First, the right-wing *Jamā'at-i-Islāmī* systematically sent its sympathisers and many of its cadres to seek commissions in the armed forces; second, the radical nationalist rhetoric of former Prime Minister Z.A. Bhutto and the rapid promotion of officers who appeared committed to his regime also influenced the officer corps.

The most important consequence of the opposing ideological trends within the military was its politicisation as an institution and thus the erosion of its 'relative autonomy'. To the extent that the military was politicised by opposing political forces operating outside it, the ability of the 'military-bureaucratic oligarchy' to 'mediate' between these opposing political forces was undermined. Moreover the task of mediation was also made increasingly difficult as the regional question gained importance of Pakistan, and the military began to be seen as the representative of the interests of the ruling elite of the Punjab by the people of the other provinces of Pakistan. It is in the context of the change in the social composition of the armed forces and its increasing penetration by political forces operating in the country that Alavi's theory of the 'relative autonomy of the military-bureaucratic oligarchy' needs to be modified. In any case, the issue of whether this institution was ever 'relatively autonomous' also merits re-examination. Even if the military-bureaucratic oligarchy was 'relatively autonomous' during the 1950s vis-à-vis the indigenous ruling classes, it could be argued that it was never autonomous (even relatively) vis-à-vis the interests of metropolitan capital.

In Pakistan, the military and the bureaucracy assumed control of state power soon after independence. Such dominance of the military-bureaucratic oligarchy was derived from the structure of state power itself; moreover, political institutions and the forms of mobilising political power were not developed enough to ensure the dominance of the popular will. In contrast to the political institutions, the military-bureaucratic oligarchy which Pakistan inherited from the colonial state was highly developed, and after independence it began to reign supreme.

Mohammad Ali Jinnah, the first Governor-General of Pakistan, was a man with a towering personality and a democratic vision. However, at the dawn of independence he was too ill to wield effective control over the state. He was therefore unable to establish an institutional framework through which the military and the bureaucracy could be subordinated to the political process. He was a sick man during most of the first year of Pakistan and died in September 1948.

Prime Minister Liaqat Ali Khan, Jinnah's trusted assistant, lacked the initiative and imagination to control the affairs of state effectively after Jinnah's death. The provincial assemblies were elected on the basis of a limited franchise extended to only 15% of the populace. Consequently, members of these assemblies and the cabinets which they elected were aware of their isolation from the masses. They therefore willingly became instruments of the military-bureaucratic oligarchy. This comes out clearly in the events of 1953. In April 1953, the Governor-General, Ghulam Mohammad, who was an old bureaucrat, dismissed the Nazimuddin government even though the Constituent Assembly had given it a vote of confidence. Soon after the dismissal of the Nazimuddin government by the Governor-General, the Constituent Assembly met again and passed another vote of confidence — this time in favour of the new prime minister, Mohammad Ali Bogra, who had been nominated to that office by the Governor-General. Not only did the Governor-General appoint a new prime minister, but he also nominated ministers and assigned them their respective portfolois. Thus, state power effectively passed into the hands of the Governor-General. The function of the Constituent

Assembly was reduced merely to rubber-stamping the actions of the Governor-General and the military-bureaucratic oligarchy whom he represented. Over the years there have been some shifts in the relative power exercised by each partner, but what has remained is the complementarity between these partners in the military-bureaucratic oligarchy.[25]

The Sociology of the Officer Corps

Indian officers in the British Indian Army were recruited from the landowning class, though not necessarily from the aristocracy. As MacMunn suggests, 'the staunch old Indian yeoman who came into the Indian commissioned ranks via the rank and file of the Indian landowner of lesser class made the Indian officer as we know him'.[26]

In the post-Partition period in Pakistan, two factors have further integrated the officer corps into the propertied class: 1) since the Ayub era, the policy of giving land grants to senior army officers has created a landed elite among even those officers who did not come from large landowning families. This phenomenon has continued to this date, with the addition that now many officers are being granted land in urban estates; and 2) Many army officers have been provided with opportunities of joining the trading or industrial elite. A number of officers were given prestigious places on boards of companies after retirement, while for others contracts and credits were arranged to help set up prosperous firms. Since 1977, this tendency has appreciably intensified. The appointment of army officers as chairmen of many public corporations in the nationalised sector as well as WAPDA (Water and Power Development Authority) and the NLC (National Logistics Cell) has increased the military's ability to grant lucrative contracts to officers operating private firms in trade and industry. Thus, an influential section of the army establishment is now closely integrated with the landed and business classes of Pakistan.

According to Stephen Phillips Cohen, there have been three distinct generations in the Pakistan officer corps:[27] 1) the 'British' generation: pre-1947; 2) the 'American' generation: 1953-65; and 3) the Pakistani generation: 1965 to date. It must be emphasised that each generation absorbed some of the characteristics it inherited from the earlier generation, through the culture embodied in the process of training, promotion and daily social life of the officer.

The British-trained officers who entered the Pakistan Army at the time of Partition consisted of three distinct groups, but all three had served during the 1939-45 war. Two of these groups had entered the British Indian Army during peace time and received their training either at Sandhurst (e.g. Ayub Khan) or at the Indian Military Academy at Dehra Dun (e.g. Mohammad Musa). The third group of officers (the Indian

Emergency Commissioned Officers) joined the British Indian Army during the Second World War (e.g. Mohammad Zia ul Haq). All the prewar officers have now retired, and only a few who entered during the Second World War remain in the Pakistan Army today. However, the older officers left a permanent impact on the culture and attitude of the officer corps, for they had organised the main training and educational establishments after Partition and served as a model for the younger officers.

Officers who joined the British Indian Army on regular commissions before World War II were carefully selected from prestigious or upper-class families. A few were included from the ranks and were generally the sons of JCOs (Junior Commissioned Officers) who had distinguished themselves in service. However, the same rigorous criteria of selection did not apply to officers who had joined during the war through the Emergency Commissioned Officers' scheme. The official British analysis regarding such officers was that they were on the whole inferior to both regular Indian Commissioned Officers and their British Emergency Commissioned Officer equivalents.[28]

Apart from the differing professional and attitudinal characteristics of the officers who originated in the British Indian Army, there was another important sociological characteristic. About 12% of the Muslim officers in the British Indian Army were not from areas that later constituted Pakistan. Many Muslim officers from Delhi, UP (United Provinces), Eastern Punjab and Central Provinces constituted an important section of the senior ranks of the Pakistan army until recently. The sons of these officers constitute an important fraction of the current officer corps. These officers exercised the option of migrating from their home towns in India and are especially charged with a sense of communal feeling against the Hindus and a sense of mission about living in an Islamic state. For example, one of the most senior officers of the Pakistan Army stated in an interview with Cohen:

> I am a pure Rajput; my family has been Muslim for only two or three generations. But I felt that India had to be divided, and told Messervey (the first Commander of the Pakistan Army) that I would rather live in a small country as a free man than as a sweeper in a large country . . . I did not want to see my children serve under Hindus.[29]

Another senior officer who was a lieutenant colonel in 1946, and who also chose to leave his home for Pakistan, saw the new state as an opportunity to build a society according to Islamic values:

> I basically belong to India, Lucknow; all the people who belong to this part of the world (Pakistan), they came here automatically. We had the choice or option: but I think more than anything else it was a desire to have a homeland of your own where you could model it according to your own ideology, your own genius.[30]

211

With the establishment of Pakistan's military relationship with the US in 1953, extensive changes took place in the Pakistan military establishment at the level of organisation and training. But perhaps even more important was the Americanisation of the ethos of the officer corps. This occurred essentially as the result of two aspects of the American military aid programme. 1) Hundreds of Pakistan Army officers were sent to the US for specialised training; the mental attitudes that were inculcated during this period and the ideological perspective adopted were then diffused within the officer corps on their return. 2) An extensive motivation programme was mounted by US Army personnel in Pakistan; this was done by creating a separate cell in the Inter-Services Directorate and involved systematic indoctrination of the Pakistan officer corps.

Evidence of the extensive organisational changes and of the Americanisation of the Pakistan Army's ethos is provided by a close associate of former President Ayub Khan:

> The changes brought about in this army — few other armies went through such extensive tremendous changes. The field formations, the schools, the centres and even GHQ — everything was changed. The Americans affected everything — the scales were completely different, hundreds of our officers went to America, and we had new standards of comparison.[31]

The profound effect which the training of Pakistan army officers of the US had on their minds can be judged by the views of a young Pakistani colonel who was trained with the US Special Forces:

> . . . We were friends. I made many friends in the U.S. Didn't you know we were the best friends and allies you had in the area, the only dependable one? Why don't you realize that? *Our two countries are so much alike, we think alike, we like the same things* . . . there could be a new alliance to hold back the Russians.[32]

Perhaps the most effective penetration by US Army personnel at the ideological level was done by means of the motivation programme conducted by a special cell in the Inter-Services Public Relations Directorate:

> The USIS extended its operations in Pakistan under the so called Motivation (later Troop Information) Program. A separate cell was created in the (Pakistan) Inter-Services P.R. Directorate to handle the collection and distribution of American journals, books and films throughout the Pakistan Army, Navy and Air Force. The so-called Motivation Program was an elevation of normal P.R. to a higher sphere of intellectual education and indoctrination. It formed an integral part of the entire military aid program.[33]

This infiltration of the ideological and institutional structure of the

Pakistan military establishment by US military personnel reached a stage where the very national image of the armed forces was affected:

> The American military presence somewhat compromised the purely national image of the armed forces . . . It seemed as if there were two military establishments in one country: one national, the other foreign.[34]

The foregoing analysis has indicated that close organisational and ideological links between the Pakistan and US military establishments developed during the period 1953-65. Thus, in the very period in which the military-bureaucratic oligarchy could be regarded as being 'relatively autonomous' from the domestic ruling classes, we find that it had close structural connections with the institutions of metropolitan capital.

The important characteristics of officers who have joined the Pakistan Army in the last fifteen years are as follows: 1) they are drawn much more from the middle classes than the landowning classes as in earlier years; and 2) they have been subjected the least to direct foreign professional influence and are the products of the purely domestic educational system.

Many such officers who joined in about 1971 are now majors or colonels. As Eqbal Ahmed has suggested, this generation of officers with petit bourgeois social origins and a purely indigenous specialisation is highly susceptible to the fascist ideology of the *Jamā'at-i-Islāmî*.[35] This tendency may be further reinforced by two factors: 1) the active attempt made by the *Jamā'at-i-Islāmî* to penetrate the officer corps with its own trained cadres on the one hand and to distribute its literature in the military establishment on the other; and 2) the new programme of sending combat officers to universities in Pakistan has subjected many officers to more systematic indoctrination by the *Jamā'at*, which dominates some of the important universities of the country.

Politicisation of the Military

During the period after 1971 not only was the officer corps subjected to the indoctrination of the *Jamā'at-i-Islāmî* but officers were also exposed to the populist rhetoric of the Pakistan People's Party. Many young officers with a social conscience who were worried about the economic deprivation of the masses and the crisis of the state saw in Bhutto the harbinger of a strong new Pakistan. The nationalisation of some big industries, the melodramatic handcuffing of some of the biggest industrialists, and the radical rhetoric against feudalism had an impact on not only the middle peasants and urban professional classes but also the new generation of army officers who originated from these classes. That the army top brass itself is aware and concerned about the influence of the Bhutto phenomenon of the minds of army officers is indicated by a 'prayer' issued to all units by General Headquarters, Military Intelligence

213

Directorate, Rawalpindi in 1978-9: 'God will provide men to the army who have strong minds, great hearts, true faith, and ready hands . . .' There is an implicit reference to the just-executed Prime Minister Bhutto: 'men who can stand before a demagogue and damn his treacherous flatteries without winking.'

It appears that perhaps the fundamental feature of the 'Pakistani generation' of officers is that they were politicised from both the left and the right wing of the political forces in civil society. This suggests that underlying the strict discipline there may be potential or actual factionalism among the officers, which may manifest itself if the armed forces as an institution are used to crush a popular political movement in Pakistan.

To the extent that politicisation of the officer corps has occurred, the military may have lost the 'relative autonomy' which Alavi regards as the basis of its ability to mediate between opposing political forces. In fact it can be argued that the politicisation of the army and the erosion of its ability to mediate between opposing political forces are apparent from the nature of Pakistan's military regime. It has three characteristics which provide evidence for our argument: 1) the fact that the military regime is not using a politically neutral ideology (as was the Ayub regime) but is using a particular form of religious ideology that is explicitly linked with the political position of a particular political party (the *Jamā'at-i-Islāmī*); 2) the thinly veiled support of the regime for the *Jamā'at-i-Islāmī* and, more importantly, the provision of access to the political apparatus of the *Jamā'at* into various institutions of the government; and 3) the failure of the military regime to constitute a convincing civilian facade behind which it can retreat, as in the case of the Ayub regime.

These three characteristics of the regime suggest that this military regime is organically linked with particular political forces. Therefore the military cannot now be regarded as having political 'neutrality' and relative autonomy on the basis of which it is supposed to mediate between opposing political forces to re-establish civilian rule.

Apart from the current erosion of its 'relative autonomy', it is important to consider its nature even in the 1950s, when the military-bureaucratic oligarchy was much less politicised. It was precisely in that period that the military-bureaucratic oligarchy in Pakistan developed close organisational and ideological links with the US military establishment. Therefore, in dealing with the issue of 'relative autonomy', a distinction should be made between the domestic ruling classes and the metropolitan ruling classes. Even in the period when the Pakistan military-bureaucratic oligarchy could be said to be 'relatively autonomous' with respect to the domestic ruling classes, it was nevertheless integrally connected with the institution of metropolitan capital. Such a formulation would enable us to grasp that the framework within which the military-bureaucratic oligarchy mediated the conflicts between the domestic ruling classes, was conditioned by the long-term interests of metropolitan capital.

Contradictions and the Nature of Economic Growth

The ruling classes at the dawn of independence consisted of an alliance between the landlords and nascent industrial bourgeoisie backed by the military-bureaucratic oligarchy. The nature of the ruling elite conditioned the form of the economic growth process. However, the latter process itself generated powerful contradictions that in turn influenced the form in which state power was exercised. To comprehend the factors that have led to the recent crisis of the state in Pakistan, it is necessary to examine the principal elements of the growth strategy that was devised by the capitalist-landlord elite. It will also be necessary to analyse the consequences of the growth process in terms of the major contradictions it generated and the conditions for the emergence of the Pakistan People's Party. The changing class composition of the PPP after it came to power as well as the economic and social conditions underlying the anti-PPP movement also require close examination.

The basic objective of the planning strategy during the decade of the 1960s was to achieve a high growth rate of gross national product (GNP) within the framework of private enterprise. The investment targets were to be achieved on the basis of the doctrine of 'functional inequality'. This meant deliberately transferring income from the poorer sections of society, who were thought to have a low marginal rate of savings, to the high income groups, who were expected to have a high marginal rate of savings.[36] It was thought that by thus concentrating income in the hands of the rich, the total domestic savings, and hence the level of investment, could be raised.[37] It was argued that in the initial period, when domestic savings would be low, the gap between the target level of investment and actual domestic savings would be filled by a large inflow of foreign aid. It was thought that as growth proceeded and income was transferred from the poor to the rich, domestic savings would rise, until by the end of the Perspective Plan in 1985, the country would become independent of foreign aid.[38]

During the decade of the 1960s, the above strategy was put into practice, and at a superficial level at least, in terms of its growth targets, it was successful. For example, the growth rate of GNP was 5.5% per annum; manufacturing output increased by an average annual rate of about 8%, with large-scale manufacturing increasing at over 10% per annum. The elite farmer strategy of concentrating new agricultural inputs in the hands of rich farmers also bore fruit by generating a growth rate in agricultural output of 3.2% per annum (compared to less than 1.5% in the previous decade). However, this impressive performance in terms of aggregate growth rates was accompanied by an economy which became structurally and financially so dependent on the advanced capitalist countries that the very sovereignty of the state began to be undermined. Apart from this, the nature of the growth process generated such acute inequalities between regions that the internal cohesion of society began to be seriously eroded.

The particular growth process in Pakistan generated four fundamental contradictions: 1) a dependent economic structure and the resultant high degree of dependence on foreign aid; 2) an acute concentration of economic power in the hands of 43 families and the resultant gulf between the rich and the poor in urban areas; 3) a growing economic disparity between regions; and 4) a polarisation of classes in the rural sector and a rapid increase in landlessness.

Underlying the apparently impressive figures of the growth of manufactured output (10% per annum in the large-scale manufacturing sector) was an inefficient and lop-sided industrial structure. Growth was concentrated not in heavy industries which could import self-reliance to the economy but rather in consumer goods produced with imported machines. Thus, by 1970-71, cotton textiles alone accounted for as much as 48% of value-added in industry, while basic industries such as basic metals and electrical and transport equipment accounted for only 21% of the value-added in manufacturing in Pakistan. Not only was growth concentrated in consumer goods industries, but also the efficiency of these industries was very low. This was due to the high degree of protection and support given by the government in the form of high import tariffs, an overvalued exchange rate, tax holidays and provision of cheap credit.[39] Industrialists could thus earn annual profits of 50% to 100% or more and were under no pressure to increase efficiency. Apart from this, export subsidies enabled manufacturers to export goods at an extremely high rupee cost per doller earned. In some cases, goods were profitably exported at dollar prices which were less than the dollar value of the raw materials embodied in the goods.[40]

Given the failure to develop a heavy industrial base and the emphasis on import-dependent consumer goods industries, the structure of Pakistan's industry induced increasing dependence on imported inputs. At the same time the failure to increase domestic savings pushed the economy further into dependence on foreign aid. The policy of distributing income in favour of the industrialists succeeded, but the assumption that this would raise domestic savings over time failed to materialise. Griffin points out, for example, that 15% of the resources annually generated in the rural sector were transferred to the urban industrialists, and 63% to 85% of these transferred resources went into increased urban consumption.[41] Far from raising the domestic savings rate to the target level of 25% of GNP, the actual savings rate never rose above 12% of GNP and in some years was as low as 3% to 4%.[42]

The low domestic savings caused by the failure of capitalists to save out of their increased income resulted during the decade of the 1960s in growing dependence on foreign aid. According to Government of Pakistan figures, foreign aid inflow increased from $373 million in 1950-55 to $2701 million in 1965-70.[43] This sevenfold increase in the volume of aid was accompanied by a continuing change in the composition of aid from grants to loans so that whereas 'grant and grant-type' assistance constituted 73% of total aid received during 1950-55, this type of assistance declined to 9% by 1965-70. Thus not only had the volume of aid increased dramatically but also the terms on which it was received had become increasingly harder. The result was that debt servicing alone by the end of the 1960s constituted a crippling burden. While debt servicing as a proportion of export earnings was 4.2% in 1960-61, by 1971-72 it had become 34.5%. Clearly, such a magnitude of export earnings could not be spent on debt servicing if vital food and industrial inputs were to be maintained. Thus, by the end of the 1960s, economic survival began to depend on getting more aid to pay back past debts. This pattern of aid dependence continues to this day. In 1981, for example, 66% of gross aid received was returned as payment for debt servicing charges on past debt; foreign aid financed 37% of gross domestic investment in 1981. What is perhaps even more significant is that the conditionality clauses of 'foreign aid' specify in great detail the economic policy that the government of Pakistan is required to follow.[44] Aid-giving agencies, for example, specify policies from the price of gas and fertiliser to the import policy, from the method of administering the railways to the allocations to be made by the government in each sector of the economy. These increasingly comprehensive macro-economic policy packages accompanying foreign aid seriously erode the sovereignty of Pakistan's economic decision-making.

The process of economic growth upon which Pakistan embarked during the 1960s was designed to concentrate incomes in the hands of the industrial elite on the one hand and the big landowners on the other. It is not surprising therefore that by the end of the 1960s a small group of families with interlocking directorates dominated industry, banking and insurance in Pakistan. Thus 43 families represented 76.8% of all manufacturing assets (including foreign and government assets). In terms of value added, 46% of the value added in all large-scale manufacturing originated in firms controlled by 43 families.[45]

In banking the degree of concentration was even greater than in industry. For example, seven family banks constituted 91.6% of private domestic deposits and 84.4% of earning assets. Furthermore, there is evidence to show that the family banks tended to favour industrial companies controlled by the same families in the provision of loans. State Bank compilation of balance sheets of listed companies indicates which banks these companies dealt with. In virtually all cases, banks controlled by industrial families were one of the two to four banks that were dealt with by the industries controlled by the same industrial families.[46]

The insurance industry, although smaller in size than banking, also had a high degree of concentration of ownership. The 43 industrial families controlled 75.6% of assets in Pakistani insurance firms. The portfolios of these industrial family-controlled insurance companies tended to favour industrial companies owned by the same group. The insurance company investments were used for providing a ready market for the shares of the families' industrial companies whenever they wished to sell shares without depressing the share price.[47]

The major industrial families and entrepreneurs were a fairly close-knit group. Not only did many of them have caste and kinship relations, but members of the families tended to sit on each other's boards of directors. About one-third of the seats on the boards of directors of companies controlled by the 43 families were occupied by members of other families within the 43.[48]

Not only were the 43 families dominating industry, insurance and banking, but they also had considerable power over government agencies sanctioning industrial projects. For example PICIC (Pakistan Industrial Credit and Investment Corporation) was the agency responsible for sanctioning large-scale industrial projects. Out of the 21 directors of PICIC, seven were from the 43 industrial families. It is not surprising then that the 43 leading industrial families were actively involved and influential in the administrative institutions that directly affected their economic interests.

During the process of rapid economic growth of the 1960s while an exclusive and highly monopolistic class was amassing wealth, the majority of Pakistan's population was suffering an absolute decline in its living standards. For example, the per capita consumption of foodgrain of the poorest 60% of Pakistan's urban population declined from an index of 100 in 1963-64 to 96.1 in 1969-70. The decline was even greater over the same period in the case of the poorest 60% of the rural population. In their case, per capita consumption of foodgrain declined from an index of 100 in 1963-64 to only 91 in 1969-70.[49] There was an even larger decline in real wages in industry. For example, Griffin suggests that in the decade and a half ending in 1967, real wages in industry declined by 25%.[50] S. M. Naseem, in a more recent study for the ILO, has estimated that in 1971-72 poverty in the rural sector was so acute that 82% of rural households could not afford to provide even 2100 calories per day per family member. (2300 calories a day per head are regarded as the minumum for a healthy active life.)

In an economy where investment takes place on the basis of private profitability alone, there would be a cumulative tendency for investment to be concentrated in the relatively developed regions. Consequently, regional economic disparities would tend to widen over time. This is in fact what happened in the case of Pakistan. The Punjab and Sind provinces, which had relatively more developed infrastructures, attracted a larger proportion of industrial investment than the other provinces. In Sind, however, the growth in income was mainly in Karachi and Hyderabad. Thus economic disparities widened not only between East and West Pakistan, but also between the provinces within West Pakistan. During the 1960s the factor which accelerated the growth of regional income disparities within what is today Pakistan was the differential impact of agricultural growth associated with the so-called 'Green

Revolution'. Since the yield increase associated with the adoption of high-yield varieties of foodgrain required irrigation, and since the Punjab and Sind had a relatively larger proportion of their area under irrigation, they experienced much faster growth in their incomes, compared to Baluchistan and NWFP.[51]

In a situation where each of the provinces of Pakistan had a distinct culture and language, the systematic growth of regional disparities within the framework of the market mechanism created acute political tensions. Defusing these tensions required a genuinely federal democratic structure with decentralisation of political power at the provincial level. Only such a polity and large federal expenditures for the development of underdeveloped regions could ensure the unity of the country. In the absence of such a polity, the growing economic disparities between provinces created explosive political tensions.

The failure to conduct an effective land reform in Pakistan has resulted in a continued concentration of landownership in the hands of a few big landlords.[52] Thus, in 1972, 30% of total farm area was owned by large landowners (owning 150 acres and above).[53] The overall picture of Pakistan's agrarian structure has been that these large landowners have rented out most of their land to small and medium-sized tenants (i.e. tenants operating below 25 acres).[54] In such a situation, when 'Green Revolution' technology became available in the late 1960s, the large landowners found it profitable to resume some of their rented-out land for self-cultivation on large farms using hired labour and capital investment. It is this process of the development of capitalist farming which has generated new and potentially explosive contradictions in Pakistan's rural society. These contradictions have resulted from the highly unequal distribution of landownership.

During the period when high-yield varieties of foodgrain were being adopted, there was a rapid introduction of tractors. The number of tractors increased from 2000 in 1959 to 18,909 in 1968.[55] By 1975 there were 35,714 tractors with an additional 76,000 tractors being imported between 1976 to 1981.[56] What is significant is that most of these tractors were large-sized in a country where 60% of the farms are below 25 acres.

An important reason why large tractors were introduced was that large landowners, responding to the new profit opportunities, began to resume rented-out land for self-cultivation on large farms. Given the difficulty of mobilising a large number of labourers during the peak season in an imperfect labour market and supervising labourers to ensure satisfactory performance, the large farmers found it convenient to mechanise even though there is no labour shortage in an absolute sense.

Polarisation has occurred in the size distribution of farms, especially in the Punjab; i.e., the percentage share of large and small farms is increasing, while the percentage share of medium-sized farms (eight to 25 acres) is declining.[57] This polarisation is essentially the result of large landowners resuming their rented-out land for self-cultivation on large farms. The land resumption has had the greatest impact on medium-sized tenants.

Along with polarisation in the rural class structure, landlessness has increased as many tenants are evicted following land resumption by big landowners. It has been estimated that during the decade of the 1960s, 794,042 peasants became landless labourers; i.e. 43% of the total agricultural labourers had entered this category following proletarianisation of the poor peasantry.[58] Unlike in Europe, where the growth of capitalism in agriculture was associated with the emancipation of the peasantry, in Pakistan the development of capitalist farming has intensified the dependence of the poor peasantry. The reason is that in Pakistan capitalist farming has occurred in a situation where the political and economic power of the landlords is still intact. Consequently, the big landlord is able to control local institutions for the distribution of credit and other inputs. The result is that the poor peasant, in order to buy tubewell water, seeds, fertiliser and pesticides and to market his output, has to depend on the good offices of the landlord. Thus, as the inputs for agricultural production become monetized and insofar as access to the market is via the landlord, the poor peasant's dependence has intensified.

As money costs of inputs increase without a proportionate increase in yield per acre of the poor peasant (due to poor timing and inadequate inputs) his real income is being reduced. Evidence shows that both the quantity and quality of diet of poor peasants have deteriorated.[59]

The *particular form* that capitalist farming in Pakistan has taken is increasing landlessness, unemployment, class polarisation and poverty. Each of these features has arisen because capitalist farming is occurring in a situation where landownership is highly unequal, and where the feudal power of the landlords is intact and, because of the nature of the prevailing political system, is being further consolidated.

Class Composition of the Pakistan People's Party and the State Apparatus.

The PPP was originally composed of radical elements of the petite bourgeoisie of the Punjab and Sind on the one hand and substantial elements of capitalist farmers on the other. The radical elements of the petite bourgeoisie were dominant in the PPP until 1972. This was evident from the manifesto, which was anti-imperialist, antifeudal, and against monopoly capitalism. The same stratum also played a key role in devising a propaganda machine suited to the manifesto and presenting it as a 'revolutionary' programme, thereby getting the support of the urban workers and poor peasantry.

This radical stratum was, however, drawn from diverse social origins and had differing political objectives, and its members therefore connected themselves to Bhutto in separate groups or fractions. The inability of different factions of the radical petite bourgeoisie to constitute them-selves into a single bloc within the PPP facilitated the purges that came after 1972.

By 1972 Bhutto had consolidated his power and began to shift the balance of class forces within the PPP in favour of the landlord group. This shift was not accidental, not was it a personal betrayal of the radicals on Bhutto's part as it was subjectively experienced by the party cadres. Changes in the internal class composition of the PPP were objectively determined by the changed position of the PPP in relation to the state. In the pre-election period the dominance of the radical petite bourgeoisie and its radical rhetoric were necessary if the PPP was to get a mass base for an election victory.

After the elections, Bhutto realised that if the socialist rhetoric of the left wing of the PPP was to be implemented, it could not be done through the existing state apparatus. It would involve institutionalising party links with the working class and the peasantry by building grass-roots organisations. This would soon generate a working-class leadership which would not only threaten his own position within the party but would also unleash a momentum of class conflict that would place the PPP on a collision course with the military and the bureaucracy. Given Bhutto's own commitment to seek social democratic reforms within the framework of the state as constituted at the time, he was unwilling to take a path that would lead to a confrontation with the state apparatus. Consequently the socialist rhetoric of the PPP had to be toned down, its radical petty bourgeois elements quietened or purged from the party, the rudimentary organisational links with the working class and poor peasants broken and the landlord elements of the PPP firmly established as the dominant element within the party.

The decision to purge the radical elements within the PPP and to separate it structurally from its worker-peasant base meant that Bhutto had to rely on the bourgeois state apparatus to respond to the political challenges emanating from three directions: first, the intensification of the nationalist struggle in Baluchistan; second, the growing militancy of the working class in the Punjab and Sind; and finally, those parties representing the industrial bourgeoisie.

The strategy of selective repression of the political opposition neces-sitated changes in the state apparatus so as to make it more effective as a coercive instrument. Bhutto brought about three types of changes. 1) He streamlined and strengthened the internal security services and formed a new para-military organisation called the Federal Security Force, consisting initially of 10,000 men. This was essentially a political police force responsible directly to the Prime Minister. 2) An attempt was made to reduce the power and autonomy of the elite CSP (Central Services of Pakistan) cadre of the bureaucracy. This was done first by purging 1300 officers on grounds of misuse of power and filling their vacancies by pro-PPP men. Second, a new system of lateral entry was instituted. Through this, direct appointments at all levels of the administrative services were made on recommendation from the PPP leadership. By thus short-circuiting the hierarchy of the CSP and penetrating it with officers who were loyal to the PPP, large sections of the bureaucracy were politicised and made more amenable for use by the PPP. 3) In the armed forces, Bhutto conducted two purges in quick succession. He first discarded the five top generals who had dominated the government before and during the Bangladesh crisis, and second, he ousted those commanders like Lieutenant-General Gul Hassan Khan and Air Marshal Rahim Khan who had been instrumental in the transfer of power to Bhutto himself. Thus enemies and benefactors alike were removed on grounds that they had Bonapartist tendencies. The new chief of the army staff was Tikka Khan, who was succeeded by Zia ul Haq, whom Bhutto promoted by super-seding four other generals in the hope that he would be obliged to be loyal. However, as was realised later, a coup d'état cannot be prevented by simply placing loyal generals in command. What is necessary is to change the very structure of the armed forces and its relationship to the political system. What he had to do to prevent a coup was to subordinate the armed forces as an *institution* to the *political system*. This change in the structural position of the armed forces within the state, from a position of dominance to a position of subordination to the political system, could only have been achieved by organisationally linking the PPP to its mass base. This was something that Bhutto was not prepared to do.

While Bhutto in his attempt to use the state apparatus to quell political opposition was internalising some sections of the state apparatus into his political apparatus, a parallel process of infiltration was being covertly conducted by another political party — the *Jamā'at-i-Islāmī.*

The *Jamā'at-i-Islāmī* is an extreme right-wing religious party composed of the most retrograde section of the urban petite bourgeoisie. It had suffered a humiliating electoral defeat in 1970, having obtained only 5% of the vote and three National Assembly seats. After this defeat it started concentrating on preparing for a coup by increasing its infiltration of the army and bureaucracy.[60] The *Jamā'at* from its very inception was a semisecret, extreme right-wing organisation of disciplined cadres, some of whom are given combat training. After 1970 it was able to expand its influence over strategic sections of the state apparatus for a number of reasons. 1) The earlier generation of generals in the high command were British-trained, liberal officers, drawn largely from the affluent land-owning class. However, in the 1960s a new generation of officers began to occupy command positions. These were less literate and more religious, drawn largely from the economically depressed migrants from East Punjab (like General Zia ul Haq) and the unirrigated Potwar region of West Punjab. This new generation of officers was socially more conservative than the earlier generation, was brought up in a religious culture and was highly susceptible to the puritanical ideology of the *Jamā'at.*[61] 2)

Similarly, patterns of general recruitment in the army had changed, whereby many of the rank and file as well as the junior officers tended to come not from the prosperous central Punjab, but from the relatively impoverished northern districts of the province, where a fundamentalist religious ethos still prevails.[62] 3) The demoralisation of the armed forces following the defeat in Bangladesh had opened the way for an obscurantist ideology. In the absence of ideological work among the ranks by the left, the average soldier turned to the Islamism of the *Jamā'at* for an explanation both of his failure as well as his future purpose.[63] 4) The *Jamā'at*'s propaganda among troops was officially sanctioned by commanding offers at the battalion level and above. General Zia ul Haq, a close relation to Mian Tufail (the chief of the *Jamā'at*), provided ample protection for secret cells of the *Jamā'at* inside the armed forces[64]

It appears that the relative autonomy and internal coherence of the state apparatus has been considerably undermined due to its infiltration by PPP sympathisers on the one hand and by *Jamā'at* cadres on the other. The consequent factionalising process within the armed forces and the bureaucracy is an important factor in the nature of the July 1977 coup as well as an explosive element in the present crisis of the state.

Socio-Economic Causes of the Anti-Bhutto Movement

The essential political aspect of the nationalisation of nine basic industries, banks and insurance companies was that it enabled the PPP to buy the political support of a section of the urban petite bourgeoisie through provision of credit and contracts for consultancy, construction projects and production of components. The nationalisation of banks particularly enabled the PPP to strengthen its support among the kulaks by providing them with low-interest loans. For example, in 1975 alone, Rs. 1,650 million were provided to kulaks. In the period 1971-72 to 1975-76, loans from nationalised commercial banks for tractors and tubewells increased by 400%, and loans for other farm needs (so-called *taccavi* loans) increased by 600%. Similarly, government subsidies for chemical fertilisers rose from $2.5 million to $60 million during the period 1971 to 1976. The same rapid expansion of rural credit is indicated by loans given by the Agricultural Development Bank:

	1971-72	1975-76
Tractors	Rs. 370.41 million	Rs. 2,200 million
Tubewells	Rs. 180.41 million	Rs. 860.67 million

The nationalisation of banks and the subsequent credit expansion for financing loans to industries and capitalist farming led to heavy deficit financing and an increase in the money supply. Thus, notes in circulation increased from Rs. 23,000 million in 1971-72 to Rs. 57,000 million in

1976-77. There was a sharp slowing in the growth rate of both agriculture and industry. Thus, industrial growth fell from an average of 13% per year during the 1960s to only 3% per year during the Bhutto period from 1972 to 1977. Similarly, the agricultural growth rate declined from an average of 5.65% in the 1960s to a mere 0.45% in the period 1970-75.

The sharp increase in the money supply during a period of virtual stagnation in agriculture and industry was reflected in a very sharp rise in the rate of inflation. The wholesale price index at 1959-60 prices rose from 150.3 in 1971-72 to 288.8 by 1974-5, with the sharpest increases being recorded in foodgrain prices, which rose by 200% over the three-year period. It appears then that, although nationalisation of industry and credit expansion enabled the PPP to buy the support of a section of the urban petite bourgeoisie through the provision of jobs, contracts, licences and loans, the available funds and contracts were not large enough to enrich the *entire* petite bourgeoisie. In fact a section of the lower middle class that did not gain from the PPP, especially salaried lower-level employees in the government and the private sector, suffered an absolute decline in their real incomes due to the high inflation rate. It was the frustrated section of the urban petite bourgeoisie and the large lumpen-proletariat which had been stricken by inflation that responded to the call for a street agitation in March 1977. The agitation was of course fuelled by the fact that the PPP had blatantly rigged election results in a number of constituencies.

Conclusion

The current crisis of the state in Pakistan has arisen out of a state structure in which the dominance of the military-bureaucratic oligarchy systematically constrained the development of the political process. The oligarchy devised a political framework which, while allowing rivalry between the landlords and the industrial bourgeoisie for the division of the economic surplus, maintained the mode of appropriation of the surplus through which the existence of these elites could be perpetuated.

The predominance of the army and bureaucracy in the structure of state power in Pakistan was due to the *form* of the freedom struggle in the pre-Partition period on the one hand and the *nature* of the Muslim League on the other. At the time of independence, the state apparatus of the colonial regime was largely intact, and it articulated the framework within which politics were to occur. The second factor in the failure to subordinate the army and bureaucracy to the political system lay in the two basic characteristics of both the Muslim League before Partition and the Pakistan People's Party during the 1970s.

Both the Muslim League in the pre-Partition period as well as the Pakistan People's Party during the 1970s were *movements* rather than parties. They were therefore unable to establish an organisational structure on the basis of which the power of the people could be institutionalised and used to subordinate the army and the bureaucracy to the political system. The Muslim League in the decade before Partition, and the PPP during the early 1970s, were taken over by landlords whose political interest lay in constraining the process of political development within the confines specified by the military-bureaucratic oligarchy.

The nature of economic growth which occurred in an economy dominated by the landlords and the industrial bourgeoisie generated acute economic inequality between rich and poor on the one hand and between regions on the other. These economic contradictions manifested themselves in growing political tensions between classes and regions — tensions which could have been mitigated (although not necessarily resolved) only within a democratic political system that was responsive to the aspirations of the dispossessed classes and poor regions. As it was, in a state structure within which the political system was severely constrained by the military-bureaucratic oligarchy, these tensions merely built up pressure on the state structure. The growing political tensions between social groups and regions developed at a time when the internal cohesion of the military-bureaucratic oligarchy was being eroded as the result of its politicisation. Thus, while the task of mediating the conflicting political forces became increasingly difficult, the ability of the military-bureaucratic oligarchy to do so became weaker. It is in this perspective that the following major elements of the contemporary crisis of the state in Pakistan can be understood:

1) The repressive apparatus of the state has itself become the political apparatus. Mediation between the propertied classes and the propertyless is sought not by a populist party but by the *Jamā'at-i-Islāmî*, which has a narrow social base. This has therefore accentuated class tension.

2) The state dominated by the repressive apparatus is highly centralised and does not recognise, let alone grant, the rights of the various nationalities. This will enhance separatist tendencies since the army is drawn predominantly from the dominant province of the Punjab.

3) The state's interpretation of religion is seen by the people as sanctifying particular class interests and justifying repression against those who dare to question it. The state is therefore bereft of a legitimising ideology. For this reason the army, unlike in the past, cannot withdraw behind a civilian facade. Its explicit presence in running the government has become necessary in a situation where the ruling class cannot justify its rule except by the threat of force.

4) The prolonged military rule and the demise of the 1973 constitution have eroded the balance between the various institutions of the state, i.e. the armed forces, the bureaucracy, the judiciary etc. There is therefore an institutional crisis of state authority.

References and Notes

1. Syed Ahmed Khan, *Asbab-i-Baghavat-i-Hind*, cited in Y. V. Gankovsky and L. R. Gordon Polonskaya, *A History of Pakistan 1947-1948* (Lahore: People's Publishing House, n.d.), p. 14.

2. A. Akhtar, ed., *Muzamin-i-Sir Syed* cited in Gankovsky and Polonskaya, *History*, p. 16.

3. Speech by Syed Ahmed Khan, *Times* (London), 16 January 1888.

4. A. B. Rajput, *Muslim League Yesterday and Today*, cited in Gankovsky and Polonskaya, *History*, p. 19.

5. Ibid., p. 18.

6. The Lucknow Speech was reported in *Times* (London), 16 January 1888.

7. *Aligarh Institute Gazette*, 9 January, 1907, cited in Gankovsky and Polonskaya, *History*, p. 34.

8. Ibid., p. 27.

9. Ibid., p. 30.

10. Ibid., p. 32.

11. Ibid., p. 34.

12. H. Bolitho, *Jinnah: Creator of Pakistan* (London, 1954), p. 84.

13. Tariq Ali, *Can Pakistan Survive?* (Harmondsworth: Penguin Books, 1983), pp. 24-5.

14. H. Bolitho, *Jinnah*, p. 95.

15. Z. H. Zaidi, 'Aspects of the Development of Muslim League Policy 1937 47', in C.H. Phillips and M.D. Wainwright, eds., *The Partition of India* (London: George Allen and Unwin, 1970), p. 253.

16. Imran Ali, *Punjab Politics in the Decade Before Partition*, Research Monograph Series No. 8, South Asian Institute (Lahore: University of the Punjab, 1975), p. 1.

17. *Speeches and Documents on the Indian Constitution, 1921-1947*, 2 vols. (London, 1957), pp. 488-90, quoted in Gankovsky and Polonskaya, *History*, p. 71.

18. Chaudhri Mohammad Ali, *The Emergence of Pakistan* (New York: Columbia University Press, 1967), pp. 38-9.

19. Imran Ali, *Punjab Politics*, p. 5.

20. Ibid., p. 48.

21. *Punjab Legislative Debates 1936* and *1946*, cited in Imran Ali, *Punjab Politics*, p. 48.

22. For a more detailed analysis and documentation of this proposition see Imran Ali, *Punjab Politics*, pp. 7-54.

23. Hamza Alavi, 'The State in Post-Colonial Societies: Pakistan and Bangladesh', *New Left Review*, July-August 1974.

24. These ideological factions do not normally manifest themselves due to the rigid chain of command in the military hierarchy and the stake of all officers in the integrity of the armed forces as an institution. Nevertheless, the successful attempt at a coup d'état in 1977 by what later emerged as a religious fundamentalist military regime, and the unsuccessful attempt by younger officers against the regime in January 1984, are symptomatic of the differences in ideological perspectives within the military.

25. See Hamza Alavi, 'The Military in the State of Pakistan', paper presented at the Institute of Development Studies and Institute of Common-

wealth Studies Conference, Sussex, England. (Revised version of mimeograph written in February 1974.)

26. Sir George MacMunn, *The Martial Races of India*, (n.d.) p. 233 in US Department of State, Office of External Research, *Security Decision-Making in Pakistan*, by Stephen P. Cohen, (Washington, D.C.: Government Printing Office, 1984).

27. US Department of State, *Security Decision-Making in Pakistan*, chapter 3.

28. Stephen P. Cohen, *The Indian Army* (Berkeley: University of California, 1971), p. 145.

29. U.S. Department of State, *Security Decision-Making in Pakistan*, p. 61.

30. Ibid.

31. Ibid., p. 72.

32. Ibid., p. 73.

33. Ibid., p. 74.

34. Ibid., p. 75.

35. Eqbal Ahmad, 'Pakistan: Sign Posts to a Police State', *Outlook*, 18 May, 1974.

36. 'It is clear that the distribution of national product should be such as to favour the savings sectors.' Government of Pakistan Planning Commission, *The Third Five Year Plan, 1965-70* (Karachi: Government of Pakistan, May 1965). p. 33.

37. 'Savings are a function not only of the level of income but also of its distribution.' Mahbub-ul-Haq, *Strategy of Economic Planning* (Karachi: Oxford University Press, 1963), p. 30.

38. Government of Pakistan, *Third Five Year Plan*, p. 17.

39. For a discussion of inefficiency of Pakistan's industry, see R. Soligo and J. J. Stern, 'Tariff Protection, Import-Substitution and Investment Inefficiency', *Pakistan Development Review* (Summer 1967). See also C. C. Winston, 'Over-invoicing and Industrial Efficiency', *Pakistan Development Review* (Winter 1970).

40. R. D. Mallon, 'Export Policy in Pakistan', *Pakistan Development Review* (Spring 1966).

41. K. Griffin, 'Financing Development Plans in Pakistan', in *Growth and Inequality in Pakistan*, ed. K. Griffin and A. R. Khan (London: Macmillan & Co., 1974), p. 133.

42. Ibid., pp. 41-2.

43. Government of Pakistan, Finance Division, *Pakistan Economic Survey, 1973-74* (Islamabad: Government of Pakistan, 1974), p. 133.

44. See 'The Memorandum of Agreement between the Government of Pakistan and the World Bank, 1980.' (Typescript.) Also see 'Economic Policy Memorandum of the Government of Pakistan for 1981-82', May, 1981. (Mimeograph.)

45. L. J. White, *Industrial Concentration and Economic Power in Pakistan* (Princeton: Princeton University Press, 1972), p. 63.

46. Ibid., pp. 74-5.

47. Ibid., pp. 79-80.

48. Ibid., pp. 81-5.

49. N. Hamid, 'The Burden of Capitalist Growth: A Study of Real Wages in Pakistan', *Pakistan Economic and Social Review (Spring 1974)*.

Pakistan', *Pakistan Economic and Social Review (Spring 1974)*.

50. Griffin and Khan, *Growth and Inequality*, pp. 204-5.

51. For a detailed study of regional disparities within West Pakistan, see: N. Hamid and A. Hussain, 'Regional Inequalities and Capitalist Development', *Pakistan Economic and Social Review* (Autumn 1974).

52. For discussion and evidence on the failure of the attempts at land reform in 1959 and 1972, see A. Hussain, *The Land Reforms in Pakistan*, Group 83 Series (Lahore, February 1983), n. pag.

53. Ibid.,

54. Landowners with 150 acres and above rent out 75% of their owned area to tenants operating 25 acres or less. See A. Hussain: 'Impact of Agricultural Growth on Changes in the Agrarian Structure of Pakistan: 1960-78' (D. Phil. thesis, Sussex University, 1980).

55. A. Hussain, *Land Reforms*.

56. Ibid.

57. A. Hussain, 'Impact of Agricultural Growth'.

58. A. Hussain, *Land Reforms*.

59. Ibid.

60. For a more detailed description of the *Jamā'at-i-Islāmī*, see Aijaz Ahmad, 'Democracy and Dictatorship in Pakistan', *Journal of Contemporary Asia*, 1 (Winter, 1978).

61. Ibid., p. 503.

62. Ibid.

63. Ibid.

64. Ibid.

10. Pakistan's Problems of National Integration

by Feroz Ahmed

Introduction

> [The Muslim League] is irrevocably opposed to any federal objective which must necessarily result in a majority of community rule under the guise of democracy and parliamentary system of government. Such a constitution is totally unsuited to the genius of the peoples of the country, which is composed of various nationalities and does not constitute a national state (resolution passed by the Muslim League in 1939).

The word 'nationality' is acquiring increasing usage in the context of the grievances of Sind and other smaller provinces of Pakistan. While it may be gaining acceptance in some quarters, it still remains a buzz word in many circles, particularly those belonging to the Punjab and the Urdu-speaking people. Many individuals, sympathetic to the rights of the smaller provinces and desiring equality between the autonomy for the provinces, somehow consider 'nationality' an inappropriate term for the ethno-linguistic groups of Pakistan. To them, this word belongs to the lexicon of the enemies of Pakistan who have invented it to undermine the concept of religious nationality as used by the Muslim League to justify the creation of Pakistan.

How this word, with its present connotation, entered the phraseology of Pakistan is difficult to determine. But it is generally established that the solution of the nationality problem in Soviet Central Asia has been a source of inspiration for the backward and oppressed nationalities in South West Asia and that the more commonly referred to writings of this question have been the works of Lenin and Stalin. The latter attempted to formulate a cut-and-dried definition of nation on the basis of the usage of Marx and some non-Marxist European scholars. Stalin defined a nation as 'a historically evolved, stable community of language, territory, economic life and psychological make-up manifested in a community of culture'. Nation was also assumed to be a phenomenon of bourgeois ascendancy, of capitalist development, of integration and delineation of markets.

The term 'nationality' initially came to be applied to ethno-linguistic communities which were in the process of evolving into supra-tribal civic societies and acquiring the characteristics of a nation. Many of these established political states of their own, but were still referred to as 'nationalities' rather than nations because of the low level of development of their productive forces, of their social formations. On the other hand, many ethno-linguistic communities, satisfying the definition of nation and possessing a very advanced capitalist mode of production, continue to be called nationalities rather than nations (e.g. Quebec) simply because they do not possess independent states of their own. In Third World countries, communities referred to as nationalities seem to possess both of these characteristics, i.e. persistence of the pre-capitalist mode of production as well as a lack of an independent state. In addition, usually there is an explicit or implicit desire to exist within a multinational state and to evolve into a larger nation. Curiously, however, any culturally homogeneous community which established its own state has been accepted as a 'nation' regardless of its level of development.

Using Stalin's definition too rigidly, many writers have objected to the use of the term 'nationality' for this or that group because it did not satisfy a particular condition in Stalin's list of minimum necessary conditions. Existence of another linguistic group in the midst of a community has in particular been cited as a proof against that community's claim to being a nationality. Here, it should first be borne in mind that Stalin primarily had European nations in mind, rather than nationalities of the underdeveloped world. Students of ethno-linguistic evolution have for long recognised that it is not uncommon for some secondary languages or dialects to persist even after the emergence and recognition of the lingua franca of the nationality or the national language. Furthermore, one more characteristic that needs to be added to the definition of nation or nationality is its own perception of its identity. If the Brauhi-speaking people prefer to consider themselves part of the Baluch nationality on the basis of their historical intercourse, comon culture and other factors, they cannot be arbitrarily separated from the Baluch just because Brauhi is a Dravidian language — a group apart from the Indo-Iranian Baluch.

Nation or Nationality?

The perception of the Punjabi, Sindhi, Pakhtun and Baluch people as distinct nationalities is not based on the mischief of 'anti-state' elements as Pakistan's rulers would want us to believe. Its roots lie in the thousands of years of history of these peoples. Each of these peoples evolved into a distinct ethno-linguistic community which, in political terms, should legitimately be called a nationality. Organised and vicious anti-intellectualism of the state of Pakistan and right-wing forces cannot alter this historical and academic fact. A. K. Brohi, the military's intellectual in residence, has engaged in a lot of mumbo-jumbo to prove that there is always correspondence between nation and state and that the very mention of the word 'nationality' means a conspiracy to separate from Pakistan. I have dealt with Brohi's 'thesis' elsewhere and need not dwell upon it here.[1]

As far as Sind is concerned, the crystallisation of the Sindhi nationality had taken place as far back as 1200 years ago. Gradually tribal identification had been subordinated to Sindhi national identification. A feudal nationality, so to speak, came into existence, while vestiges of tribalism remained and a number of secondary languages continued to coexist. When the Arabs conquered Sind in the early 8th century, they did so by defeating a sovereign ruler of the long-established state of Sind. The Arabs had no difficulty in recognising the separate national identity of Sind and even considered it apart from 'Hindu' or India proper.

After the lapse of Arab rule in the 11th century, two Sindhi dynasties, Soomro and Samo, ruled independent Sind for nearly 500 years. The Arghuns and Tarkhans, who came from Central Asia, also reigned as more or less sovereign rulers of an independent state. In 1592 the Mughul ruler of India, Akbar, imposed 'direct' rule over Sind. But it did not cease to be a distinct entity. The Mughuls never really attempted to integrate Sind with Hindustan. Despite administrative fragmentation of Sind, they not only considered Sind as one country, but their *subedar*s (governors of provinces) and their *faujdar*s (distinct military commanders) of the *sarkar*s (provinces or administrative divisions) were no more than farmers-general of revenue.

The population of Sind, in a large measure, refused to accept Mughul rule. At least 40 clans were in continuous or sporadic rebellion against the Mughul satraps. The Sameja Unar, Chandio and Nomri were particularly noted for their resistance to alien rule.[2] Finally, this rule came crumbling down, and the later Mughul rulers had to recognise the sovereignty of Sind under the Kalhoro native rule. Although defeats and humiliation at the hands of successive Irani and Afghan rulers had abridged Sind's sovereignty and subjected it to the payment of a tribute, Sind's quest for regaining full sovereignty never ended.

Before the British conquered Sind in 1843, the latter had established itself as a fully sovereign state, ruled by the Talpur Mirs. All the resistance offered to the British, before, during and after the conquest, was in the name of the independence of Sind and no other entity. Commander Hoshoo, who became a hero, raised the slogan of *murvesoon, Sind na desoon* (we will die but will not give up Sind). It does not need much imagination to figure out what nationalism it was that inspired the people of Sind to continue to resist the British colonial rule. Can that national feeling, which fuelled the people's will to regain their freedom, be erased so easily?

Even the British had to recognise the advanced nationality development of Sind. They decreed Sindhi to be the official language to be used in the schools, courts and revenue records. A standard script for the Sindhi language was developed. Sindhi prose and poetry made considerable progress. Even novels came to be written in Sindhi. This literary and cultural advancement was in no way comparable to the backward state of the surrounding nationalities. That is why it is often difficult for many non-Sindhis to understand the Sindhi people's attachment to their language and their refusal to give up their language in the name of 'national unity'.[3]

The Evolution of National Consciousness

It is a common phenomenon in history that subjection to a common alien rule or conflict with a common enemy brings different people closer to one another, develops into a common struggle and produces common consciousness. Many warring tribes of Africa have been welded together into modern nations by their common colonial experience. In the subcontinent of India all the peoples had, sooner or later, been brought under the yoke of British imperialism. This gave them a sense of common suffering, common goals and the will to struggle together. Initially these feelings found their articulation in the movement for the freedom of India. This, consequently, produced Indian nationalism, which continued to thrive despite the persistence of nationalisms of the different subdued nationalities. At a later stage, the question of the rights of the Muslim minority, and subsequently the demand for a separate homeland for the Indian Muslims, was raised. Without going into the details, it should be stated clearly that there were solid material bases for the response that the demand for Pakistan received. In Sind, specifically, the landlord class, with its experience of being a part of the Bombay Presidency, had clearly visualised that an independent India under Congress leadership would not be able to avoid drastic land reforms. The small and emerging Muslim middle class faced stiff competition from the Hindus, who were already entrenched in the government and educational services as well as in other white-collar professions. The peasantry, which was almost entirely Muslim and which was subjected to cruel oppression by the largely Muslim *zamindar* class, was little involved in the Pakistan Movement. Yet it was not opposed to it and even welcomed the creation of Pakistan. The peasants were also pitted against money-lenders who were largely Hindus and who had grabbed nearly 2.5 million acres of land of the peasants as well as of the landlords.[4] The exit of Hindus, the peasants hoped, would provide them some relief.

It is important to recognise that Muslim nationalistic consciousness in Sind was not only based on narrow material considerations but was also of a very short duration — too short to be an effective antidote to or substitute for the long-nourished Sindhi nationalism. Furthermore, any support for Pakistan was clearly conditional upon the 'autonomy and sovereignty' of Sind as envisaged in the 1940 Muslim League resolution and the 1943 Sind Assembly resolution. Concretely, this can be understood clearly from the example of the second *Hur* movement in the 1940s. Few people realise that this movement was the longest and most widespread resistance to British rule in the subcontinent. It manifested the most sophisticated tactics of indigenous guerrilla war. The British imposed martial law in Sind in 1942 and did not lift it until a few months before Independence in 1947. Barbed wires and concentration camps were common sights in Sind. So were derailment of trains, breaching of embankments and ambushing of police parties. Police were brought in from Punjab to assist in the counter-insurgency operations. What is important — and what has been ignored — is the fact that despite the dubious circumstances which triggered this insurrection and despite the crudity of the ideology of the movement, the legitimating idea of the *Hur* movement was independence of Sind. Pir Sibghatullah Pagaro claimed that his ancestors had prophesied that the *gudi nasheen* (successor) in his generation would rule over Sind. Although he sought to establish autocratic rule, he raised the slogan of independence of Sind from the British. As would be expected, it rejuvenated the national consciousness of the Sindhi people. This movement transcended religious, sectarian and caste differences, and a lot more common people participated in this movement than in the Muslim League movement in Sind which was going on simultaneously. Nay, the Pir and his followers did not have much admiration for Mohammad Ali Jinnah, the leader of the Pakistan Movement.[5]

The process of nation-building is always a very complex one, especially in multinational states. For Pakistan, the task was even more difficult than in most newly independent countries. Besides the geographical separation of East Bengal (which had the majority of the country's population) from West Pakistan, each of the five provinces represented a distinct nationality which had had a fully or quasi-sovereign state of its own before the British conquest. Furthermore, these provinces varied greatly in their size, population, resources, level of social development and proximity to power. The transfer of populations, resulting from the partition of India in 1947, also affected them differently. The removal of direct colonial rule led to an enormous concentration of executive power in the hands of the civilian bureaucracy, which consisted largely of Punjabis and Urdu-speaking refugees from India. The ascending economic force was the capitalist class, which again consisted almost entirely of Punjabis and Kathiawari immigrants from India. The landlord class, which was quite powerful in Punjab and Sind, was incapable of exercising political hegemony in a modern state, and its economic power was largely localised. Finally, it was the military which, as a result of Pakistan's alliance with the United States, emerged as the paramount political force in the country by the late 1950s. This institution also consisted mainly of Punjabis, but Pakhtuns have recently acquired a strong junior position. Given this matrix of wealth, power and ethnicity, extreme sensitivity and caution were needed to prevent the alienation of less privileged nationalities.

But the rulers of Pakistan adopted the opposite course. They sought to impose a centralised unitary form of government and subjected the country to the rapacity of the powerful economic and political classes and groups. The state not only perpetrated inequality, discrimination and nationality domination, but it sought to destroy the identities of the nationalities. All legitimate grievances of the less privileged or dominated provinces were construed as acts of treason. Islam, integrity of Pakistan and the Urdu language became the code words for national domination. In the name of Pakistan's unity and integrity, the very foundation of unity was eroded.

Causes of Resentment in Sind

The insensitivity and ruthlessness of Pakistan's rulers culminated in the separation of East Bengal from Pakistan in 1971. Yet, no lessons were learned from this experience, and the Baluch people were subjected to armed suppression again from 1973 to 1977, resulting in the almost total alienation of the Baluch from Pakistan. More recently, when the Sindhi people staged a national uprising against the Pakistan Army, even those who cared to analyse the roots of their discontent went little further than blaming the army for its exceptionally harsh treatment of Sindhis since 1977 and pointed out a few socio-economic indicators of 'disparity' suffered by the Sindhis. No one mentioned that the national oppression of Sindhis is even more severe than that of the Bengalis before 1971 and that the degree of their dispossession may even be comparable to that of the Palestinians and American Indians. That this is not an exaggerated claim can be gauged from the study of the treatment meted out to the Sindhis since 1947. The major events and policies which led up to the current resentment in Sind are summarised below and arranged in four categories for the same of convenience: demographic, economic, polital and cultural.

While the exchange of populations between India and Pakistan made Punjab and NWFP ethnically more homogeneous and did not affect Baluchistan, it dramatically affected Sind, where the number of Sindhis was reduced absolutely and relatively. Nearly one million Hindu Sindhis left for India, and in their place more than one million, largely Urdu-speaking persons from India settled in Sind. With the concentration of industry and commerce in lower Sind there has been a continuous inflow of people from Punjab and NWFP. Recently, several hundred thousand Biharis from Bangladesh have settled in Sind. Due to inadequate census-taking no one knows the accurate figures, but many fear that Sindhis may already have been turned into a minority in their own province.[6] Although Sind is the most urbanised of all provinces of Pakistan (about

45%), in none of its major cities are the Sindhis in a clear majority. While this demographic trend, except during the years of India-Pakistan mass migration, has been a function of the economic domination and exploitation of Sind, it is now being turned into a rationale to justify the perpetuation of injustices and disparities.

More than one-half of Pakistan's industry is located in Sind, but Sindhis have practically no participation in it — whether as owners/managers or as workers. The lucrative commercial, transportation, construction and service sectors, which comprise 55% of Pakistan's gross domestic product, are also located largely in Sind. But Sindhis do not have even a marginal share in this sector. In government service, educational institutions and other white-collar jobs, the Sindhis are represented far below their population proportion, whether it be on an all-Pakistan basis or within Sind itself. A survey conducted by Sindhi students in 1969-70 showed that out of one million workers employed in private industries in Sind, no more than one thousand were Sindhis. Only 250 out of more than 10,000 bank employees in the province were Sindhis. In central government service there was only one Sindhi per five thousand, while in the Sind government the Sindhis comprised less than 40%.[7] More importantly, most of the jobs held by Sindhis were low-ranking and low-paying. The situation improved marginally under the People's Party government when some Sindhis got jobs in the nationalised sector, but the present military government purged tens of thousands of Sindhis from government service and public sector enterprises.

Agricultural lands were considered to be the bastion of Sindhi (landlord) economic power. But since the creation of Pakistan that situation has been drastically altered. The nearly two million acres of land left behind by emigrating Hindus were awarded to refugee claimants rather than being distributed among landless Sindhi peasants. The land (more than a million acres) brought under cultivation by the construction of Kotri and Guddu barrages was also awarded to non-Sindhi military and civil officers or 'purchased' by prosperous Punjabi farmers in give-away auctions. As much as 40% of Sind's prime agricultural land may have already passed into the hands of non-Sindhis, while three-fourths of Sindhi peasants own no land at all. Juxtaposed to the already high concentration of land in the hands of a few Sindhi landlords, this development has further exacerbated the condition of the common Sindhi. Sindhi peasants, more than the landlords, have also suffered from the violation of the 1945 Punjab-Sind agreement on the distribution of Indus water. New irrigation works have been built without the consent of Sind, which have resulted in decreasing the latter's share of irrigation water.

The neocolonial capitalist model of development pursued by Ayub Khan (1958-69) resulted in enormously adverse terms of trade for agriculture vis-à-vis other sectors. Although this policy had an impact on the entire country, because of the Sindhi people's almost exclusive reliance on agriculture there was a definite ethnic differential in its impact. These terms of trade improved somewhat under Bhutto, but the present military regime, under IMF-World Bank pressure, has removed many agricultural subsidies and practised an urban bias.

Recently, oil has been discovered in large quantities in Sind, and the question is already being asked whether it would be used for the benefit of the local population or simply pumped out on the pattern of natural gas in Baluchistan.

The centre-province relationship started on the wrong foot. To get its way the central government disregarded not only legality but also elementary norms of decency. The issues on which it victimised Sindhi politicians and the ruthlessness it manifested in achieving its objectives would today sound unbelievable. But these facts are indeed stranger than fiction. To begin with, the central government, ignoring the Sind Assembly support for Mohammad Ayub Khuhro, appointed Sir Ghulam Hussain Hidayatullah as Chief Minister of Sind. Then it made him Governor and appointed Khuhro as Chief Minister. It wanted Khuhro to instigate communal riots to force Hindus out of Sind and create room for the *muhajirs*. Khuhro refused and punished the goons who had been creating disorder at the behest of the refugee-dominated bureaucracy. Khuhro also refused to part with Karachi. Therefore, the central government dismissed him and threw him into jail. A stooge by the name of Pir Illahi Bux was then illegally appointed Chief Minister. He agreed, in 1948, to deprive the Sindhis of their prime city, Karachi, which was separated from Sind and declared the 'federal capital area'. It put Sind in a ridiculous position of locating its government in a city which did not belong to it because no other city in the province had the infrastructure to host the provincial government. After Illahi Bux had done the dirty work for the centre, the court conveniently declared his appointment illegal. The central government, then, appointed in his place Yusuf Haroon, who was not even a member of the Sind Assembly. Soon he was replaced by Qazi Fazlullah. Then Khuhro was brought back again and dismissed soon after. Then the centre imposed Governor's rule in Sind under a Punjabi lawyer by the name of Din Mohammad. When the centre found a pliable candidate in the person of Mir Ghulam Ali Talpur, it removed Governor's rule. But he too resisted some of the most outrageous anti-Sindhi plans of the central government and was dumped. Then, Pirzada Abdul Sattar was brought from the Central Ministry to head the Sind Cabinet under an unusual set of circumstances. By then, Pakistani rulers' designs to impose dictatorship in the country and erase the identity of Sind had become clear. Under Pirzada's leadership the Sind Assembly passed bills and resolutions which demanded the return of Karachi to Sind and the protection of Sindhi national rights, resisted attempts to award Sind lands to military officers, approved projects to build two irrigation works in Sind, appropriated money for institutions engaged in research on the literary and cultural heritage of Sind and opposed the idea of 'one unit'.

Pirzada also voted in the National Assembly for curtailing the powers of the Governor-General. All this was more than enough to bring upon him the wrath of the central government, and he too was dismissed by the centre. Finally, to push its plans through, the central government brought back as Chief Minister the same Khuhro whom it had dismissed twice, jailed and disqualified from holding public office.

Acting as the centre's hatchet man this time, Khuhro used strong-arm tactics including kidnapping, disqualification and intimidation of Sind Assembly members to bring them around to passing the 'one unit' bill. Thus, in 1955, even the identity of the provinces was erased by amalgamating them into 'one unit'. The post office staff was instructed not to deliver any letter bearing the word 'Sind'. The Rs. 330 million surplus from Sind's account was used to offset, in part, the Rs. one billion deficit of Punjab. After a decade and a half of widening disparities and intensified bitterness among the nationalities, the 'one unit' was finally dissolved in 1970, and the original provinces were reconstituted. But to undo the harm done by 'one unit' was not without dangers. A whole generation of non-Sindhis had been brought up in urban Sind which had no concept of Sind, of the Sindhi language and culture, and of Karachi being part of Sind. The mere arrival of some low-level provincial government servants in Karachi was seen as an invasion of Martians, and the Assembly bill to promote the Sindhi language in Sind was met with riots and killings. While the Sindhis had not even begun to get the crumbs from the table of neocolonial development, a myth of 'Sindhi domination' was created by right-wing forces, just because the Prime Minister was a Sindhi.

In Pakistan's parochial calculus, there is no room for a Sindhi prime minister. Zulfikar Ali Bhutto accomplished the unthinkable. But for that both he and the Sindhi people had to pay a heavy price. Bhutto, both because of his cosmopolitan outlook and his consciousness of coming from a minority province, was extra-cautious in matters pertaining to redressing regional and nationality grievances. Yet because of him there was a resurgence of hope among the Sindhi people, who began to feel, for the first time, that they had a stake in Pakistan. The military coup d'état of General Zia turned that dream into a nightmare.

In the excitement of the Sindhi people's honeymoon with the People's Party government it was overlooked by most Sindhis that the constitution of 1973 did not provide a sufficient quantum of provincial autonomy nor protection for their national rights. A politically conscious and vocal minority, though, was not content with having a Sindhi prime minister and a Sindhi majority cabinet in the province. It empathised with the Baluch struggle and stressed the objective oppression of the Sindhis. Aside from having negligible power in the central government and inadequate autonomy for the province, the Sindhis felt politically dominated and estranged when it came to dealing with government officials on a day-to-day basis. A list compiled at the time of dissolution of 'one unit' in 1970 showed that since 1955, in the interior of Sind, out of 184 postings of deputy inspectors general and superintendents of police only 53 were of native Sindhis. Likewise, out of 150 postings of commissioners and deputy commissioners, only 41 were of Sindhis.[8] In Karachi no Sindhi was appointed to these senior positions. The insensitivity, and even callousness, of these officials contributed a great deal to the alienation of the Sindhi people from the state of Pakistan.

The economic disinheritance, political domination and demographic engulfment of the Sindhi people found their correlate in attempted cultural genocide. First of all, because of the mass refugee influx, the Sindhis in Karachi were turned into strangers in their own town where very few people spoke their language, and they in turn were forced to learn Urdu. No new Sindhi-medium school has been opened in Karachi, and most old Sindhi schools have been shut down since the creation of Pakistan. Soon after 1947, Sindhi students in Karachi were required to learn Urdu, but non-Sindhis were exempted from learning Sindhi. The teaching of Sindhi, however, continued in the interior of Sind. But Ayub Khan, after coming to power in 1958, discontinued that practice by the force of a verbal order, while making Urdu compulsory for Sindhis. The Sindhi Language Bill, passed by the Sind Assembly in 1972, tried to rectify this anomaly by introducing Sindhi as a required subject for all and by making it mandatory for all provincial government servants to learn the Sindhi language. While the former provision was generally implemented only on a token basis, the latter had to be amended, under duress, to allow a 12-year grace period. This period expired in July 1984, when the Zia regime decided not to enforce the language requirement.

Successive Pakistani governments have not only failed to encourage but actually sought to obliterate the Sindhi language and culture. Censorship and suppression of the press and publications have been common in Pakistan, but the treatment meted out to Sindhi publications bears no comparison. First, the government resorts to 'preventive' measures by denying declarations (publishing licences) to proposed Sindhi publications. Then, it carries out a witch-hunt of the existing ones. In 1975, practically all Sindhi periodicals were banned by the government — even the government's own magazine was not spared. At present hardly any groups other than the government and *Jamā'at-i-Islāmī* are allowed to publish newspapers and journals in Sindhi.

While Sindhi writers are denied an avenue of expression in their home country, any Sindhi writer or poet who dares to publish in India is, at once, declared a traitor to Pakistan. Even publishing in India is not necessary for a Sindhi writer to earn the title of an enemy of the state. To promote his language and to depict the sentiments of his people are enough to land a Sindhi writer in trouble. Amar Jaleel, Ibrahim Joyo, Shaikh Ayaz, Tanveer Abbasi, Najam Abassi, Tariq Ashraf and Rasheed Bhatti are just a few of those who have been accused of undermining the ideology of Pakistan. The uproar about Amar Jaleel's short story, *Sard*

Lash Jo Safar, had all the earmarks of a Scope monkey trial. I had first-hand experience of the Pakistan government's paranoia about just anything published in Sindhi when I briefly published the monthly *Saneh* in 1979. Its first issue was precensored, and yet we were fined for using the word *ghotalo* for 'crisis', while the third and final issue — also precensored — led to a tormenting encounter in which the government interpreted its cover as an affront to Zia ul Haq's 'Islamisation' measures because it carried a photograph of a spider and its web against a background of green leaves! Although my Urdu publication, *Pakistan Forum*, also invited the wrath of the government, there was just no comparison between the two publications in terms of the severity of government response in relation to what was printed in each publication.

While the state promotes and finances the exchange of visits between Urdu writers of India and Pakistan, even a false rumour about a Sindhi writer having attended a Sindhi conference in India sets off a hysterical media campaign against 'Indian agents'. The power of the right-wing Urdu press in these matters has been so enormous that in 1975 the provincial government of Sind had to bend over backwards to assure the public that by sponsoring a conference on 'Sind Through the Centuries' it was not undermining the foundation of Pakistan. It was forced to add the words 'A Province of Pakistan' to the logo, and the list of participants was scrutinised by intelligence agencies. Lest he be dubbed parochial, Prime Minister Bhutto decided not to inaugurate the seminar.

Television, which has become the dominant mass medium and principle cultural influence, has only a token place for the national languages of Pakistan. During the entire week, the Karachi TV station, the only one in Sind, telecasts no more than one hour of programming in Sindhi. Radio programming is, likewise, limited. Sindhi music, dances, traditional crafts and art receive no encouragement from the state. The state's policy of 'assimilation' has manifested itself in completely ignoring the historical personalities and folk heroes of Sind while naming streets after Urdu poets who never even migrated to Pakistan. There is a major road in Karachi named after Jigar Muradabadi, but no street of comparable size has been named after Sind's poet-saint Shah Abdul Latif Bhitai. There has never been official mention of General Hosh Mohammad, alias Hoshoo Sheedi, who led the valiant fight against the British. The *Hurs* who fought against the British were treated as criminals by the Pakistan government, and many of them were hanged. Properties confiscated from the *Hurs* by the British were never returned to their owners.

Few countries in the world, barring Nazi Germany, have been as blatant in their policy of cultural suppression as Pakistan. The creation of Pakistan coincided with the decision to set up Sind University in Karachi. The Pakistan government packed off the new university to Hyderabad to vacate the room for Karachi University, which was supposed to be an Urdu-speaking refugee university in which there was no room for even a department of the Sindhi language. While Karachi University remained a more or less exclusive preserve for the Urdu-speaking intelligentsia, no such exclusive policy was adopted in the hiring of faculty at Sind University. Political unrest at Sind University has been used to perpetuate third-rate academic standards in that university. This, then, is used to justify job discrimination behind the myth of the 'merit system'.

How various oppressive and discriminatory practices have affected the cultural development of the Sindhi people can be gauged from the figures on female literacy in the 1981 Population Census: 42.2% for urban Sind (largely non-Sindhi) but only 5.2% for rural Sind (almost all Sindhi).

When a people voluntarily surrenders part of its sovereignty and subordinates its national consciousness for the sake of an identity of a higher order, it expects its interests, its identity and its consciousness to be subsumed by the same of the higher order but never agrees to their obliteration. The economic development of Sind, under the present social system, has largely meant de-Sindhisation of Sind. Living under a military dictatorship amounts to living in an alien-occupied country because the Sindhis have no participation in the military. The ideological legitimation adopted by Pakistan's rulers is seen as an affront to the culture and values of the Sindhi people, who have a tradition of religious tolerance as opposed to the bigotry preached by Pakistani rulers and their ideologues. Herein lie the basic contradictions between Sindhi national existence and the presently constituted state of Pakistan.

In the course of 36 years since the creation of Pakistan, the rulers of the country have done nothing that would bring about a substantial change in the national self-identification of the smaller nationalities. On the contrary, their brazen oppression has forced the nationalities to rely more and more on their historical national identification and has sharpened their national consciousness. Since cultural genocide has been a major tool of the oppressors, it is not surprising that the materially deprived but culturally rich Sindhis have reacted with vengeance. The literature and music of resistance produced by the Sindhis are comparable to those of any people struggling for its national liberation. The torment of Sind is well expressed in the following beginning line of a popular national song: '*Sind ahay amar, Sindh rahndi sada*' ('Sind is immortal, Sind shall live forever').

Structural Problems

Although policies and attitudes of particular governments and particular leaders on the question of provincial and nationality rights may have differed slightly, the problem is basically structural. It is not that the Punjabis have an inherent tendency to dominate others or to usurp other people's rights. It just happens that in a neocolonial country like ours the military and civilian bureaucracies have concentrated enormous power in their own hands, and they are not subservient to the traditional propertied classes and their civil institutions in the manner of the advanced capitalist countries. In these institutions representation of Punjabis is out of proportion to their population numbers. For example, more than 70% of the senior officers and more than 80% of the NCOs and soldiers in the military are estimated to come from the Punjab, whereas Punjabis comprise about one half and Punjab accounts for 56% of Pakistan's population.[9] Even otherwise, Punjab's demographic superiority would continue to pose a problem in the multinational state. Such problems have been recognised in all civilised countries, where checks and balances have been built in to prevent the tyranny of the majority. Only in an ideologically and politically backward country like Pakistan do we hear responsible people talk of the hegemony of the majority. There are two minimum desiderata for the voluntary survival of states like Pakistan: 1) eradication of military-bureaucratic rule and institution of a representative system of government and 2) a large measure of autonomy to the federating units and checks and balances in the federal institutions that would prevent the majority province from riding roughshod over the smaller provinces. These are the minimal requirements only in a theoretical sense. In practice it would require a lot more for the different peoples of Pakistan to live amicably together in a single state.

Many democrats, particularly from the majority province, have come to recognise that the weapons formerly reserved for the smaller nationalities are now being freely used against anyone who attempts to defy the military dictatorship. This includes the so-called 'Ideology of Pakistan'. Yet, most of them still fail to see that the stereotypes made of the spokespersons for national rights and the stigma attached to the very mention of the word 'nationality' are part of the rulers' ideological and psychological warfare against the people. Some of these democrats are as allergic as General Zia ul Haq to the mention of the words 'nationality' and 'confederation'. Tactical avoidance of certain terms is one thing, but an instinctual revulsion to these terms reflects only the extent to which these individuals have swallowed the crypto-fascist ideology of Pakistan's ruling classes. They will have to decide whether they are willing to raise their level of political education and be more sensitive to the problems of the oppressed nationalities or, because of their ideological predilections, whether they would like to join the company of Zia ul Haq and Pakistan's ruling class. The time has arrived that these democrats recognise the organic link between the national oppression of smaller provinces and overall denial of political rights to the people of Pakistan, Punjab included.

Class and Nationality

Many progressive individuals from Punjab, who harbour no prejudice against other nationalities and even sincerely desire equality between the provinces and between the nationalities, often feel disturbed at the use of the word 'Punjabi' in front of the words 'domination', 'exploitation' and even 'military'. It is not uncommon to hear them say 'the military is oppressive because it is military. Why do you have to drag in the Punjabis here?' Or, many are fond of saying that the Punjabi masses are themselves oppressed; they don't exploit the people of other provinces. Of course, the military is oppressive because it is a military holding enormous political power and not because it is predominantly Punjabi. Of course, the vast majority of the Punjabi people are oppressed and exploited. Of course, national domination and national oppression are not the work of the common people of Punjab. But isn't all that obvious! Such friends are missing the essential point and in fact trivialising the issue. Lenin, in his writings, makes the distinction between class and national oppression and even showers the socialists who hide national oppression behind the slogan of class oppression with epithets such as 'scoundrel'. In fact, the nation which subjects other peoples to oppression first exercises class oppression within itself. Therefore, for the progressives of the dominant nationality it would be well worth remembering the famous words of Marx: 'the people which oppresses another is forging its own chains.'

Simply stated, if there is class exploitation within a nationality it does not mean that that nationality cannot oppress other nationalities. Furthermore, once national domination and exploitation do exist, even the exploited classes of the dominant nationality inadvertently benefit from such injustice. Think about the effect on Punjab of spending as much as 70% of the national budget on armed forces. In the methodology of modern social sciences, the effect of a particular variable (such as nationality in our case) or another (which we can take to be economic well-being, political power or social development) can be studied only by controlling for all other independent variables (such as class) which affect the dependent variables. In simple terms, let us compare economic well-being, political power and social development of the same classes of people from Punjab and other nationalities. It will take an incorrigible supremacist to deny the predominant position of Punjab in such a comparison.

For the emancipation of the oppressed classes of Punjab, it is precisely necessary that the power of the classes that oppress them be destroyed. Since these classes also happen to carry out the national oppression of other nationalities, there is an objective basis for unity between the oppressed classes of Punjab and the oppressed nationalities of Pakistan. But before that unity can be achieved it is necessary that the progressive forces in Punjab fully understand that there is class exploitation, that there is national exploitation and oppression, and that the two should not be confused. The fact that the labouring classes of the oppressed nationalities are exploited by their own elite also does not mean that there is only the class question and that the national question is not important. Resort to class in order to deny the national question has become so pervasive among the progressives of the dominant nationality that the people of the oppressed nationalities, particularly their intelligentsia, are becoming increasingly allergic to this sort of rhetoric. They don't need any pseudo-Marxists to tell them that there is something called class. This is another form of national arrogance and superiority which some of the progressives from the dominant groups tend to manifest.

Nationality or Province

Many democrats from Punjab or from the Urdu-speaking group, while recognising the necessity of more regional autonomy and equality between the provinces, argue that the question should be posited entirely within the framework of provincial rights or centre-province relationship. In certain respects treatment of the problem in provincial terms, such as the settlement of the relative powers of the centre and provinces, may be quite appropriate. A provincial framework could also lend itself to protecting the rights of the ethnic groups in the province other than the principle nationality. Other problems could be dealt with in urban-rural terms, particularly in Sind, when it comes to allocating development funds. But the inadequacy of the provincial framework becomes apparent when we look at the figures like the following: Sind comprises 23% of Pakistan's population but contains more than 50% of its industry, consumes 42% of the commercial energy and has a per capita income about 40% higher than in Punjab. What inference should be drawn from such figures? That the Sindhis are the most prosperous nationality in Pakistan or that these inter-province comparisons obscure the distinction between Sindhis and non-Sindhis in Sind? If we insist on such measurements, it is conceivable to have a very highly developed Sind in which Sindhis would be reduced to the status of American Indians. Likewise, the rural-urban approach is also quite limiting. Take, for example, the case of the sugar mill at Piaro Goth in Dadu district. This was a rural area with no non-Sindhi population. But when the factory was located there, all the managerial staff and most workers were recruited from Punjab and NWFP. Even the *imam* of the mosque was brought over from Punjab. It is precisely for this reason that we should recognise that provincial rights are only one dimension of the problem and that attempts to remove disparities in urban-rural terms may fail completely. The crux of the matter, therefore, is the national question. The Sindhis, like the Punjabis, Pakhtuns and Baluch, are an historically evolved nationality. Their decision to be a part of Pakistan cannot deprive them of their inalienable historical rights.

Recognition of national rights does not mean only that discrimination in jobs be ended, that usurped lands and properties of the Sindhi people be returned to them, that the Sindhis and all other nationalities be given a fair and equitable right of participation in a democratic policy, that an adequate quantum of autonomy be granted to the provinces, but also that the historical fact must be recognised that these are distinct nationalities which should have full freedom to develop their culture and national personality and to determine their future without coercion. Only a voluntary and equal association of the nationalities of Pakistan on the basis of their geographical, historical and economic relations, rather than on the basis of the fanciful and coercive Pakistan ideology, has any chance of success. There can be no other basis for a multinational state of Pakistan.

Conclusion

The late Prime Minister Zulfikar Ali Bhutto, who hailed from Sind but who was a Pakistani nationalist par excellence, understood well the dilemma of Pakistan's nation-building. He recognised the need for a theoretical basis for the state of Pakistan and realised that Islam and the Pakistan ideology could not be the cementing force. He stimulated a debate on 'Pakistani culture' with a view to finding in the common civilisation of the different peoples, a real, secular and concrete basis of unity for Pakistan. Even that could not be tolerated by Pakistan's ruling class. It is difficult to see how it would ever stomach the idea of nationalities.

Ghaus Bux Bizenjo, leader of the Pakistan National Party, has formulated a conceptual framework which, while juxtaposing the resolution of the nationality question with the integrity and solidarity of Pakistan, provides a tactical flexibility in terminology. Euphemisms might come in handy in political propaganda, but any serious academic discourse on the problem has to adopt relevant concepts; and 'nationality' is central to it. The vicious response of Brohi to Bizenjo's reasoned arguments is indicative of the degree of intolerance on the part of Pakistan's ruling circles.[10] This intolerance and prejudice are shared by many who otherwise oppose the military regime and even claim to be progressive and democratic. Their refusal to come to terms with relevant concepts cannot simply be a semantic problem. It is symptomatic of the deep malaise in the democratic forces of the dominant nationality.

During the four-month (August to December 1983) civil disobedience movement launched by the opposition coalition, Movement for the Restoration of Democracy (MRD), the strengths and weaknesses of the popular forces became quite apparent. Even though the Sindh masses bore the brunt of the struggle and the feeling of national oppression provided a strong stimulus to their courageous struggle, they made it quite clear by their slogans and actions that they were fighting for the freedom of the entire population of Pakistan. Likewise, few democrats in the other ethnic groups failed to appreciate the character of the movement. There were warm expressions of solidarity with the Sindhi people from all ethnic groups. Many in Punjab proudly put on a Sindhi cap and *ajarak* (hand-printed sheet cloth) while courting arrest. But this was as far as it went.

The obverse side of the coin was that the aggregate response from Punjab was extremely limited and of a very low intensity. Failure of the movement to topple Zia ul Haq and the use of the regular army, amid an anti-Sindhi propaganda blitz, to suppress the movement added all the more significance to this differential response and led to the intensification of national feelings in Sind. It is quite clear that the nationality question will now figure even more prominently in the politics of Pakistan. This throws up new challenges to the democratic movement in the country, especially in Punjab. In the past, Punjab was too slow to agree to the dissolution of 'one unit' in West Pakistan, and it failed completely to sympathise with the grievances of East Pakistan. It remains to be seen how long it takes it to come to terms with the intensified nationality question. This time, while the resolution of the problem requires some fundamental concessions from Punjab's rulers, the patience of the smaller nationalities is wearing thin.

The struggle for democracy and social justice cannot be waged in the ideological framework which is designed to enslave all the peoples of Pakistan. The less privileged nationalities of Pakistan have never accepted this opiate which was sold previously under the labels of 'national integrity' and 'Islam in danger' but which is now being pushed down the throats of the Pakistani people as 'Pakistan ideology', 'Islamic ideology' and 'Islamisation of society'. The time has arrived that the people of Punjab also must cast aside the shibboleths which their rulers use to oppress not only the other nationalities but the Punjabi people themselves. A democratic movement must have a democratic ideology. In Pakistan's context, it must not only be secular but must also incorporate national rights and social justice.

References and Notes

1. Feroz Ahmed, 'Nationality: Refuting Mr. Brohi', *Dawn* (Karachi), 24 and 25 October, 1978.

2. Yusuf Mirak bin Abul Qasim 'Mankeen', *Tarikh Mazhar Shahjehani* (Hyderabad: Sindhi Adabi Board, 1979). This is a reprint of the 17th-century original.

3. Despite fourteen years of official suppression of Sindhi and promotion of Urdu in the schools, the 1961 population census showed that in Sind, for each person literate in Sindhi, there were only 1.4 literate in Urdu. In contrast to this, in Punjab, for each person literate in Punjabi, there were 95 persons literate in Urdu. For Pushto in NWFP and Baluchi in Baluchistan, the corresponding ratios were 1:8 and 1:71 respectively. See Government of Pakistan, *1961 Population Census*. Vol. 3 (Karachi: Manager of Publications, 1963).

4. Figures are based on Sind Assembly records quoted in G. M. Syed, *Sidhoodesh Chho ain Chha Lai* (Ulhasnagar, 1974), p. 125.

5. H. T. Lambrick, *The Terrorist* (London: Ernest Benn, Ltd., 1972).

6. According to the 1981 population census figures on 'languages usually spoken in households', 52.4% of Sind's population spoke Sindhi. Another 7.9% spoke Baluchi, Brauhi and Siraiki. These groups usually identify themselves as part of the Sindhi nationality. Yet another 5.97% of the households were put in the residual category, which includes Rajasthani dialects, the speakers of which also identify themselves as Sindhi. The Gujrati speakers have also been included in the residual category. Some of these identify themselves with the indigenous population, while others view themselves as *muhajirs*. The lingual groups which tend to assert a strong non-Sindhi identity are the Urdu, Punjabi and Pushto speakers, whose respective percentages were 22.64, 7.69 and 3.06. Therefore, the Sindhi-non-Sindhi divide in Sind could roughly be placed at 65.35. Government of Pakistan, Statistics Division, Population Census Organisation, *Main Findings of the 1981 Population Census* (Islamabad: Government of Pakistan, 1983), p. 13.

7. Survey figures are cited, among other places, in Sayed, *Sidhoodesh*, pp. 135-42.

8. Abdul Hai Palijo, *They Ruled Sind for Fifteen years: 1955-1970* (Hyderabad: Sind National Students Federation [National Group], 1970).

9. Government of Pakistan, *Main Findings of the 1981 Population Census*, pp. 5 and 13.

10. A. K. Brohi, 'Appropos of the Wisdom of our Brother Bizenjo', *Dawn* (Karachi), 9 October, 1978.

11. Pakistan's Geopolitical Imperatives

by Mohammad Asghar Khan

Strategic Considerations

A look at the historical atlas of any part of the world will reveal a fast-changing pattern of national boundaries. Except for island states, which have been left relatively undisturbed, these boundaries have been changing more rapidly where a dynamic civilisation has come into contact with a weaker or divided society. In the second half of the 20th century, however, these patterns and pressures have assumed a global dimension. With the super-powers, notably the Soviet Union and the United States, engaged in what they consider to be a struggle for survival, the smaller nations on the periphery are liable to be written off unless they tread warily on the international chess-board. The two giants have too much at stake to be mindful of diplomatic niceties in dealing with situations which appear to them to threaten their security. The record of the Soviet Union in Hungary, Czechoslovakia, Poland and Afghanistan and of the United States in Vietnam, Central America, the Caribbean and the Middle East is indicative of the ruthlessness of their policies, which they tend to pursue with a singleness of purpose that endangers the survival of weaker states.

It is Pakistan's good fortune that it is not — contrary to the belief of many Pakistanis — an area of vital strategic importance to either the Soviet Union or the United States. Its territory, though an area of desirable influence, is not vital for the survival of either of the two super powers. It is not convenient as a springboard for the acquisition of some other territory of greater strategic importance. It is a little out of the way for both the super-powers and could well be left alone by both, unless it goes out of its way to move so close to either that it becomes a danger to the other. For the past few years Pakistan appears to have been doing just that.

The Soviet move into Afghanistan provided the United States with the possibility of engaging it in the type of war the United States had itself fought in Vietnam. Pakistan's shaky military dictatorship found this a God-sent opportunity of getting United States' support for the country's tottering economy, creaking under the burden of mounting non-productive expenditure.[1] The Soviet move into Afghanistan coincided with the fall of the Shah in Iran and the induction of an aggressive Republican administration in the USA. With the Shah gone, Pakistan's military dictator, true to the mercenary traditions of his military predecessors, appears to be the natural choice to act as the watch-dog of United States' interests in this area. Once known as the most allied of United States allies, Pakistan became once more the trusted agent of United States' interests in this part of the world and moved snugly into the United States' fold against Soviet interests in South and South West Asia. Since then it has been drawn deeper and deeper into the United States' camp. Its policy towards Afghanistan leaves it with no other choice. The definition of its Islamic ideology as a custodian of the interests of Muslims all over the world, and its crusade against godless communism towards its north-west, are situations upon which the United States looks with warm approval. There are, however, certain realities of the situation that require a close examination.

Soviet Presence and Interests

Perhaps the most important are those that spring from the geopolitical factors which Pakistan has to live with. Over some of these it can exercise little control, but a better understanding of these factors can help it to steer a safer course in the international field. There are other trends, changing patterns and international compulsions, which, if correctly anticipated, will enable it to adjust its policies to suit its peculiar needs. An understanding of these developments and their timely anticipation are important for Pakistan's security. To the extent that some of these are variable, they offer it the choice of a flexible response. These latter factors are therefore likely to be of great importance to it in the future.

Perhaps the most important of these is the proximity of the Soviet Union and its interests in this area. Broadly speaking these can be described as follows: 1) securing the southern borders of its Central Asian republics and ensuring a friendly Afghanistan, preferably under Soviet influence; and 2) denying the use of Pakistan's territory as a base for operations against the Soviet Union.

Soviet intervention in Afghanistan is seen from two different angles. The pro-Western and rightist lobby in Pakistan sees the Soviet move as brazen aggression against a weaker state, a part of Soviet aggressive designs on a global basis and an attempt on its part to expand its territories towards the oil-rich areas and the warm waters of the Persian Gulf. They encourage a religious approach to what is essentially a geopolitical problem and encourage the promotion of the spirit of *jihad* to deal with the situation. The United States, delighted at the shape things have taken, is anxious to exploit the situation to the full in order to embarrass the Soviet Union. It has therefore been gradually increasing its military and economic commitments in support of the anti-Soviet operations in Afghanistan. Its anti-Soviet line in Afghanistan has succeeded in softening the reaction in Muslim countries to its pro-Zionist policies, and much of what it has been doing for Israel has therefore been forgiven.

A discussion of the long history of Soviet-Afghan relations, the role of Pakistan in pushing Afghanistan further into the Soviet camp and the reasons for Soviet moves into Afghanistan does not belong here. Suffice it to say that a dispassionate look at the problem will show that there are some grounds for the Soviet Union wanting to ensure against moves which in its view endanger its security. The fact that there was no justification for its move into Afghanistan does not alter the truth that the decision could have been influenced by its historical experiences of an unusual nature.

Russia has faced four major invasions during the last 150 years. In the Second World War alone, the Soviet Union lost over twenty million people, and there was hardly a family in the entire Soviet Union that was not affected by this holocaust. Some of its cities were reduced to rubble, and it had to fight desperate battles for survival. These invasions, starting with Napoleon's in 1812 and ending with Hitler's in 1941, were not provoked by the Russians.

Since the Second World War, the obsession of the United States with the need to establish a *cordon sanitaire* around the Soviet Union led it, in south-west Asia, to encourage Iran and Pakistan to adopt measures that would check Soviet moves to increase its influence in this area. Traditionally neutral, Afghanistan had for almost 150 years acted as a buffer between czarist Russia and the British Indian empire. It would, in favourable circumstances, have maintained this neutral status between the Soviet Union and the United States — the successors to the political power of the British raj in this part of the world. Afghanistan's support for the Pakhtunistan demand, and Pakistan's domestic compulsions, prevented it from extending the support that Afghanistan needed to draw it into the Western camp. Moreover, Pakistan broke off diplomatic relations with Afghanistan in 1950, 1955 and 1960. As the United States' influence in Pakistan increased in the early 1960s, pressure was put on it to mend its fences with its neighbour and so help to reduce Soviet influence in that country. By then, however, the Soviets had made considerable inroads into Afghanistan, whose neutral status had begun to erode.

In the 1960s the Shah of Iran, with United States' prompting and support, began to take a greater interest in Afghan affairs, and after President Eisenhower's visit to Kabul in 1959, the United States increased its aid to Afghanistan. In 1964, the Shah mediated in the Pak-Afghan dispute that had led to a rupture of diplomatic relations, which were as a result restored. The Shah's overtures and his efforts to reduce Soviet influence in Afghanistan found a ready response in Kabul, where Daud was beginning to be concerned with the growing strength of the

Khalq and *Parcham* parties. Whereas the Shah tried to counter this with large-scale economic aid, Pakistan's Zulfiqar Ali Bhutto, after his visit to Kabul and his meeting with Daud in 1973, decided to aid the rightist forces in Afghanistan. Gulbadin Hikmatyar of the *Hizb-i-Islāmī*, Professor Burhan-ud-Din of the *Jamā'at-i-Islāmī* and Maulvi Younas of the *Hizb-i-Islāmī* were invited to visit Pakistan and began to receive substantial assistance to strengthen anti-communist forces in Afghanistan.[2] These efforts intensified the East-West confrontation in Afghanistan, which hastened the ouster of Daud.

Whereas these moves can help one to understand the forces at work which led to the communist coup in Afghanistan, they do not provide the Soviet Union with a justification for acting in the manner it did in 1979. Its move into Afghanistan was aggression against a weaker neighbour. Its historical experiences may provide the grounds to understand its actions but do not clear it of the guilt. However, if it can be so sensitive about Afghanistan, it must be equally concerned about the possibility of Pakistan being used as a base for United States' operations against Soviet and its allied territories, whose southern border has now moved from the Oxus to the Khyber Pass. It would therefore be reasonable to assume that, should it seriously believe that such a threat could materialise, it might react in a similar manner, politically or militarily, as it did in Afghanistan to remove this threat. Pakistan must therefore be mindful of the Soviet Union's approach to such problems of its security as could affect Pakistan's interests.

United States' Interests in Pakistan

Since the other world power, the United States, is vitally concerned with Soviet moves and its global and regional postures, Pakistan's importance in the United States' eyes is related primarily to its position and role in US-Soviet relations. It suits the United States to ensure that the Soviet Union does not vacate Afghanistan. It hopes that the Soviet Union's intervention in Afghanistan will weaken it economically and militarily, and also by playing up this invasion of a Muslim country by the Soviet Union, it hopes to rehabilitate its own image in the Muslim World. Clearly its role as a champion of Muslim interests confers some advantages of the United States that enable it to support the anti-Arab policies of Israel better than it would otherwise have been able to do.

The heavy dependence of Pakistan's military regime on economic assistance from the United States, and the inherent unpopularity of a repressive and unrepresentative regime, force the military rulers of Pakistan to act as an extension of United States' policies in this area. And since United States' interests require that the Soviets should stay in Afghanistan, it is in the United States' interests that the *mujāhideen* operations continue. The United States understands that if the *mujā-*

hideen operations were to end and the Soviet armed forces were to pull out, the people of Afghanistan would have an opportunity to assert their traditionally independent status. Much as this would be in the interests of the Afghan people, this does not suit the United States. Paradoxically, therefore, the United States, whose declared aim is the removal of Soviet troops from Afghanistan, is consciously following a policy that ensures their stay in Afghanistan indefinitely. It is even more tragic that Pakistan, understanding this, should be a willing tool in perpetuating the Soviet occupation of Afghanistan, which is its declared aim to end.

The dependence of the West on Middle East oil and the flow of this commodity through the Persian Gulf lend great importance to this area for the United States. Pakistan's proximity to the Gulf and to the Straits of Hormuz therefore, quite apart from Afghanistan, increases its strategic value in United States' eyes. Its long and steadfast championing of the Arab cause in international forums has won it respect in Arab eyes, and it enjoys a position of some importance in the Muslim World. Since Israel is likely to be a permanent responsibility of the US, it is of great importance to the United States to have an effective lobby in this forum of Muslim states and a reliable ally who can look after its interests there. An example of how these interests are projected was the advocacy by Zia ul Haq of Egypt's re-entry into the Islamic conference in the conference of heads of Muslim countries in Rabat in early 1984.

Over the last two decades, the United States has worked assiduously to fill the vacuum left by the British in the Middle East and has built up a military presence, albeit by proxy, in the area. Its pro-Israeli policies have hindered the process to some extent, but it has nevertheless been successful in building up a reasonable arrangement to counter Soviet moves in the area. The fate of the Shah of Iran, the rising level of political awareness among the Arab people, and the corresponding weakening of the position of the monarchies and sheikhdoms in this part of the world, have driven home to the United States the need to bolster its position by increasing its military strength in this area. A carefully planned triangle of United States' interests has therefore been built up with Saudi Arabia as the centre and Egypt, Jordan and Pakistan as its corners. In this arrangement for the containment of Soviet influence, Israel also has a role to play. In spite of its tensions with its Arab neighbours and of its public condemnation by the components of the triangle, it is clearly an extension of United States' military presence in the Middle East and therefore the cement that keeps the triangle together. The strength and influence of the Jewish lobby in the United States compels the United States' government, whether Republican or Democrat, to take effective steps to ensure Israel's security. Without these compulsions the United States could well relegate Israel to a lower priority in its global scheme of things and be reluctant to spend vast sums in military and economic aid on it. Israel is therefore a reason for United States' interests in the area and an added justification for its presence in the Middle East.

The India Factor — The Turnabout

For the first three decades after its independence, until the Soviet intervention in Afghanistan in 1979, problems of Pakistan's security have been dominated by its perception of the military threat from India. The Soviet move into Afghanistan, however, has led it to look at the problems of its defence from a wider angle. While still mindful of the Indian military threat, it is now more concerned with the threat from the west and with this new orientation has sought security in aligning itself more closely with the United States. However, India will continue, at least for the foreseeable future, to be an important factor in Pakistan's defence planning and one it cannot ignore.

There is not much force in the argument that has in the past been advanced by some quarters in India, and more particularly by the government of Mrs. Indira Gandhi, that even limited military assistance to Pakistan poses a threat to India's security. India's industrial potential, its capacity to produce military aircraft, ships, tanks and other sophisticated weapons, the vastness of its armed forces — many times greater than those of Pakistan — and its nuclear capability place India in a position that cannot be weakened or threatened by Pakistan. Moreover, the separation of East Pakistan in 1971 has enabled India to concentrate its military strength in the west and has tilted the balance — if indeed there ever was one — heavily in India's favour.

Centuries of Muslim rule in India and an inbred inferiority complex that has developed as a result in Indian society, however, are factors that cannot be ignored. Whereas a rational approach would show that Pakistan, even if it was infected with a suicidal virus, cannot endanger India's security, it is possible to play on the historical experiences of the Indian people and whip up their fears of Muslim dreams of conquest and domination of the Indian subcontinent.

Unfortunately these fears are relatively easy to exploit, and it is unlikely that those who control the destinies of the Indian people will always be able to resist the temptation. The aggressive fundamentalist religious philosophy of Pakistan's military regime will inevitably encourage this trend, and it therefore appears that the tension which has existed in Indo-Pakistan relations will not easily abate. With the Soviet presence in Afghanistan, the record of close Indo-Soviet relations and United States' involvement in Pakistan, these fears are likely to gain further ground. Pakistan therefore, while facing the west, will have to keep looking over its shoulder at its old adversary, now much stronger and more confident militarily. Keeping in mind the fickleness of public opinion and temptations for Indian leaders of political gains — by using the familiar bogey of a militant Pakistan — it would be unwise for Pakistan to be misled by mere assurances of support or sympathy from its Western friends. They have their own axes to grind in keeping Pakistan on its present anti-Soviet path, and their interests do not necessarily coincide with the long-term requirements of Pakistan's security.

In the present circumstances, Pakistan therefore faces a military threat from the west. A Soviet-supported military move on its western border with an Indian initiative in the east or in Azad Jammu and Kashmir will remain a possibility. Its nuclear installation could also, in the air of mistrust that has been built up, receive India's attention. Its benefactor, the United States, could in this situation give it full diplomatic support and considerable military assistance, but it is unthinkable that it would engage its military forces in Pakistan's defence. Pakistan's limited military capacity, its lack of depth and the heavy odds facing it in such a scenario would, in any case, make such assistance, even if it were to arrive in time, of doubtful value.

Faced with the possibility of such a situation, Pakistan has only two alternatives. The first, and the one on which it appears to be launched, is to maintain its inflexible position towards Afghanistan and seek greater economic and military assistance from the United States and sympathy from its Western allies. The second is to reach a settlement of its dispute with Afghanistan and diffuse the dangerous situation on its western border. The second alternative will automatically lessen the military threat from the east as well, and with the normalisation of relations with Afghanistan, the danger to its security from India will be greatly reduced. With patient efforts and a genuine policy of rapprochement towards India, the ability of elements there to exploit the people's fears and sentiments about Pakistan would be lessened. The ushering in of a civilian representative government in Pakistan is further likely to take the sting out of the argument used to remind people in India of the record of adventurism of Pakistani generals.

The Islamic Factor

If championing the cause of other Muslim countries is welcomed in the Muslim World, the hard-sell approach of Zia ul Haq in projecting Pakistan as a state created for the propagation of an ideology is likely to create some problems. There are only two states outside the communist world that could be termed as 'ideological'. The first is Israel, which has, because of its adherence to an aggressive ideology in the midst of the Muslim World, created problems for itself as well as for its neighbours. The burden placed on its economy as a result is immense, and today it has one of the highest inflation rates in the world. This is largely the result of a high defence expenditure, which in 1979 was 29.8% of the GNP.[3] Its survival would be doubtful if it did not have the full economic and military backing of the United States. The second, Pakistan, was created as a homeland for the Muslims of the subcontinent, in which the majority Muslim areas in the north-west and north-east of India could form independent states. The ideology did not at the time go beyond that, but as time passed new definitions began to be aired. The religious groups, who wanted to establish their supremacy, tried to prove that Pakistan was created as a theocratic state in which they alone would have the right to interpret the word of God. That this concept was quite contrary to what Mohammad Ali Jinnah had in mind is proven by his own words:

> In any case Pakistan is not going to be a theocratic state to be ruled by priests with a divine mission. We have many non-Muslims — Hindus, Christians and Parsis — but they are all Pakistanis. They will enjoy the same rights and privileges as any other citizens and will play their rightful part in the affairs of Pakistan.[4]

The overwhelming support that Jinnah received from the people shows that his definition of Pakistan was accepted by the prople, and the views of those who wanted to turn it into a theocratic state or who were opposed to its creation were rejected.

After the establishment of Pakistan those religious parties that had opposed its creation and had condemned the Quaid-i-Azam as *Kafir-i-Azam* (the Great Infidel) became the advocates of the philosophy behind the creation of the state. The term 'Ideology of Pakistan' was thus born. Two successive military governments arrested the political process, and in the restrictive atmosphere these elements used the opportunity to propagate their philosophy. The public acceptability of this theory was nevertheless put to the test in the 1970 general elections, when some ninety so-called *'ulamā* issued a *fatwa*, defining the 'socialism' projected by Zulfiqar Ali Bhutto as *kufr*, and warned Muslims not to vote for his party. In spite of this, he won a resounding victory at the polls. During Yahya Khan's martial law, obscurantist elements threw their full weight behind his repressive regime and supported his policies in East Pakistan. They were so blinded by the pursuit of their ideological concept that they went all out to Islamise the East Pakistanis, who, they believed, were under Hindu cultural influence. They believed that thus alone could Pakistan be saved. Their misguided efforts hastened the end of a united Pakistan, and Bangladesh was born.

The military regime offers these people yet another opportunity to turn Pakistanis into better Muslims or in other words to strengthen their own political base. Quite apart from the divisive effect of these moves within Pakistan, this process of 'conversion' could have certain important repercussions outside Pakistan's borders which could endanger its security. Oblivious to this, Zia ul Haq has continued his efforts to turn Pakistanis into his definition of true Muslims. The farcical nature of Zia ul Haq's claim is borne out by his statement made while addressing the closing session of the *Majlis-i-Shoora* on 29 November 1983, five and a half years after assuming absolute power. In this statement he said that he had been unable to find 200 good Muslims for the *Majlis-i-Shoora* in a nation of 85 million Muslims.[5]

While he continues on the course that he has charted, Zia ul Haq fails to see some obvious pitfalls which could endanger the country's security. The southern states of the Soviet Union have a large population of Muslim ethnic origin, whose rate of growth is much greater than that of the Slav population of the country. With Afghanistan having entered the sphere of Soviet influence, the proximity of Muslim Pakistan is a matter of added interest to the Soviet Union. It cannot therefore be unconcerned with the ideological offensive launched by the military regime of Pakistan. Similarly India, which is beset with problems of minorities on its extremities in the north-west, north-east and south, cannot be unconcerned with the emphasis on Islamic ideology which is a feature of Zia ul Haq's Pakistan. This aggressive campaign will be watched with interest by India's Muslim population, larger than that of Pakistan and spread all over the country but concentrated largely in Kashmir and in Uttar Pradesh, the heartland of India. Both the Soviet Union and India have the capacity either together or separately to destabilise Pakistan, if they feel that its ideological campaign is beginning to create problems for them. The fact that this realisation has dawned on Zia ul Haq's government is shown by a statement of his Minister of the Interior, in which he is reported to have said that 'so long as the country stayed and stuck to its ideology, the countries against out ideology would continue to send trained saboteurs and it is very natural'.[6] In spite of this, the nature of Zia ul Haq's regime precludes any possibility of his slowing down his almost messianic approach to making ideology and religion the corner-stone of his internal and external policies. This is not so much through conviction or belief as through a realisation that this approach alone confers a justification for his continuation in power and provides him the opportunity to exploit the religious sentiments of the people. That the country may as a result distintegrate is not for him the most important consideration, as in a slightly different context it was not for Yahya Khan before him.

Misuse of Islam and its Divisive Effects

Undue emphasis on religion and the use of the state apparatus to enforce it on the lives of the people are beset with problems in a society as varied even in the religious sense as that of Pakistan. Soon after the early phase of Islam, which lasted for about 40 years after the Prophet's death, Islam became open to a variety of interpretations. These differences merged with dynastic and regional factors and gave unscrupulous rulers and their agents, masquerading as *'ulamā*, an opportunity to exploit religion to the full. The Islam that we see today is therefore a mere shadow of the message of God revealed to the Prophet and preached by him. So far as rituals are concerned great care is taken to conform to tradition. But the substance, wherein lie the true values of religion as these affect the lives

255

of the common people, is conveniently forgotten. With emphasis on rituals, the social and economic aspects of Islam have been placed in the background, and with it the appeal of religion as a unifying force has diminished. Although possessing great emotional appeal, Islam, because of merciless exploitation by the ruling classes and their hypocritical self-seeking religious henchmen, has become a divisive rather than a unifying force. The greater the emphasis on its form by the exploiting class of rulers to suit their own ends, the less is it likely to provide the unifying force it once was.

In Pakistan's peculiar circumstances, the differences between the *Shi'a* and *Sunni* preclude any possibility of the acceptance by the entire nation of a truly religious state with a single religious ideology. In fact the more the state regulates the lives of the people in religious matters to suit its own requirements, the more are the Muslim religious minorities likely to resent and resist this move. Even among the *Sunni*, sharp differences exist in religious beliefs and practices between different sects, the most prominent of these being the *Brelavi* and the *Deobandi*. In practice this means the establishment of separate mosques for the different sects with their own *imam*s. If left to themselves, they can practise their religion according to their beliefs, but whenever efforts have been made to bring them closer together, either by the state or by religious zealots, serious trouble has resulted. The Islamic Centre in Washington, D.C., which because of such differences has remained closed for a long time, is one example, while the perpetual wrangling and disputes in the Islamic Centre in London offer another. Both were meant to provide Muslims of different sects an opportunity to pray in a common mosque. The well-known case when the British police had to use police dogs to separate two warring sects of Muslims in a mosque a few years ago was another disgraceful example of religious bigotry, the exploitation of which will always result in undesirable consequences.

In Pakistan, a serious clash between *Brelavis* and *Deobandi* in Lahore in early 1984 was the inevitable result of Zia ul Haq's policy in religious matters. The irony was that one sect had called a conference in the Badshahi Mosque of Lahore, which it had called the *Ya Rasool Allah* Conference, while the other insisted that the conference be called the *Mohammad ur Rasool Allah* Conference. The clash between thousands of *Brelavi* and *Deobandi* outside the mosque was only controlled after the police lathi-charged the crowd and used tear-gas. A large number of people were injured, little realising that they were making a mockery of the teachings of the messenger of God in whose name the conference was being held. It is unlikely that Zia ul Haq's military regime, which has exploited religion for its own purposes, will as a result of such experience change its approach to this important issue. On the contrary such examples of religious fanaticism are more likely to lead it to want to fan religious differences. It could thus hope not only to divert the people's attention from vital economic and political issues, but by encouraging bigotry in religion, also to muster support for its policies in the domestic and international fields.

Iran's predominantly *Shïa* population and its differences with the Arab world are also factors of considerable importance that affect Pakistan's position in this part of the world. Unless these differences are amicably settled — and the chances are that they will not be — the military regime's emphasis of the definition of Islam is likely to move it closer to the fundamentalism of Saudi Arabia. Already dependent on Saudi Arabia and the Gulf sheikdoms for economic support. Zia ul Haq's religious leanings towards them are likely to create complications for Pakistan, which could prove a destabilising factor in its internal situation. The fundamentalism of Zia ul Haq's regime will before long also bring to the fore the sense of insecurity prevailing in some Muslim sects which, in the eyes of the fundamentalists, are heretical in their practices.

It was undoubtedly a realisation of these possibilities that led Jinnah to state in categorical terms that Pakistan would not be a theocratic state. He realised that leaving people to interpret Islam according to their own beliefs would unify them as a nation, and any narrow definition of the state or its religious character would prove divisive. Although an eminent constitutional lawyer, he did not, because of the need to keep the people united during the dynamic phase of the Pakistan Movement, define the country's future constitutional framework. Nor did he to the end support a place for religion in the state of Pakistan.

Federalism

The concept of Pakistan as put forward by the Lahore Resolution of 23 March 1940 visualised a federal state. It was to be a grouping of provinces with their distinctive historical, social, linguistic, racial and cultural backgrounds. Undoubtedly, religion was a common factor and provided a cementing force of great importance, but it was not the only thing that provided the justification for the creation of Pakistan. If it was, it would have been more logical to have merged the new state, or at least the western provinces, with Afghanistan. If Islam was the only factor, then why insist on national boundaries with Iran? And just as historical factors came to play in keeping the newly emerging state of Pakistan separate from its Muslim neighbours, so the different historical, linguistic, racial and cultural backgrounds of the people of different provinces of Pakistan have to this day come in the way of the removal of these regional definitions.

In its first 25 years, Pakistan saw a tug-of-war between a Bengali parliamentary majority and a West Pakistani political, military and bureaucratic machine. With less than 50% of the population, and

257

therefore in a minority in the National Assembly. West Pakistan had over 95% representation in the armed forces and in the top echelons of the bureaucracy. With the active support of the army, political and bureaucratic intrigue doomed the East Pakistan majority to the status of a permanent minority, and the federation began to disintegrate. The break-up of Pakistan was therefore a logical end to an experiment that was given no chance to succeed. The ties of Islam proved fragile compared with the historical, social, linguistic, racial and cultural factors which the rulers in Islamabad were prone to ignore. When the geographical factor was added to these, the survival of Pakistan could not be taken for granted. Shortsightedness and ignorance of the geopolitical situation tore the federation apart.

Since the emergence of Bangladesh as an independent state, and more particularly since the assumption of power by Zia ul Haq, the stresses in the federation comprising the remaining provinces of Pakistan have increased. From 1972-1977, during Bhutto's rule, the federation operated virtually as a unitary state. This was given formal recognition in the 1973 constitution, which gave complete powers over the provinces to the federal government in Islamabad. There was no provincial list of subjects in the constitution, and the provinces had to carry out the wishes of the central government. This was shown poignantly when the central government, on flimsy charges of a carefully planned conspiracy, dismissed the Baluchistan government. The resignation of the NWFP government which followed regularised a situation that had existed since December 1971, when Bhutto had assumed power. The federal character of the state was thus formally buried. In 1977, Zia ul Haq's martial law further emphasised the unitary character of the state. Military governors of provinces were made directly responsible to the Chief Martial Law Administrator, and the unrepresentative and repressive character of their administration drove home to the people of these provinces the true nature of the regime.

Any unitary form of government in Pakistan must inevitably give an appearance of the rule of the Punjab. When the country is run by a unitary system of government, even though democratically, the elected representatives of the provinces have some voice, albeit inadequate, and therefore they have some sense of participation. When the government is run by the military, the sense of isolation is more marked. 85% of the army and the bureaucracy in Pakistan today is from the Punjab, and when the centre rules the provinces directly in a military regime, it is eventually these people who run the country. Moreover, a lot of water has flowed down the Indus since the 'one unit' was tried and since Bhutto and Zia ul Haq imposed their versions of unitary governments in Pakistan. The sense of deprivation today is more marked than ever before and to an extent that the survival of the federation is at stake. The question is often asked that if the dominance of the Punjab by its military and bureaucracy forced the majority province of East Pakistan to seek separation, how can the same dominance lead to a workable arrangement between the provinces of present-day Pakistan? The closer one looks at it, the more it becomes apparent that unless the provinces are given their rights and made in both spirit as well as in letter equal partners in the federation, the country will not be able to resist the stresses and strains of internal and external pressures.

The 1973 constitution is federal only in name, and its unitary character can be gauged from the face that one province, the Punjab, had a clear majority in the National Assembly, and also the Senate, which had equal representation from each of the four provinces, had virtually no powers. Even when a joint session of the National Assembly and the Senate was held for consideration of certain issues, the Punjab still enjoyed a clear majority over the remaining three provinces together. The fact that political parties have been asking for a return to the 1973 constitution is not because it is a desirable document from everyone's point of view but because, with all its drawbacks, it is still something which was approved by the requisite majority of the elected representatives of the people. Thus with all its failings it has respectability in the eyes of the people, and shorn of this respectability no constitution has any meaning. Unless a constitution has the stamp of approval by the people's representatives, however misguided they may have been, it cannot last. Even when it has that approval it is still a fragile document in countries with a long history of interference by ambitious military dictators. Without it, it is not worth the paper it is written on.

The Human Factor

The territory that is Pakistan today comprises five distinct historical, cultural and linguistic groups. The Punjabi, Pakhtun, Sindhi, Baluch and the Urdu-speaking Mohajir together form the Pakistani nation. Except for the Mohajir, the areas that they inhabit are distinct but contiguous. The Mohajirs are concentrated mainly in Karachi, in the cities and towns of Sind and to a lesser extent in some cities of the Punjab, such as Multan. In the larger cities such as Karachi and Hyderabad they retain a clearly separate cultural entity, but in the smaller towns they are gradually being assimilated in the province of their domicile. Having sacrificed a great deal for the creation of Pakistan, they are intensely nationalistic and impatient of any regional and parochial approach in national affairs. They are, in fact, the true Pakistanis who gave up their homes to travel to their chosen land. They become Pakistanis by choice.

The others were indigenous inhabitants of the provinces that formed the new state, and their historical, cultural and linguistic roots were much older than the concept of Pakistan. Their experience and contacts spilled over to adjoining countries, where people across the borders were in some cases of the same racial stock with whom they had enjoyed social and cultural relations for centuries. These historical contacts could not be written off with the creation of the new state. Thus well-meaning but short-sighted policies of the central government, designed to hasten the process of national integration, tended to create centrifugal pulls that unnecessarily delayed this process and in the case of East Pakistan led to its separation. It is unfortunate that the mistakes of the past are still being repeated, and problems are being created by self-styled guardians of the integrity of Pakistan which are likely to endanger the country's survival.

The largest ethnic group in Pakistan is the Punjabi. Although comprising numerous tribes with linguistic and ethnic variations, it is for the purpose of this chapter considered broadly as one ethnic group. The northern districts of this province provide 80% of the manpower for the armed forces and almost an equal share of the police, civil armed forces and bureaucracy. It has a large landed gentry (a feature common with Sind) which has for centuries been loyal to every ruling class whether Afghan, Mughul, Sikh or British. Since the creation of Pakistan, this class has, true to its traditions, supported every autocratic or unconstitutional government in power. Along with the bureaucracy, the police and the armed forces, it provided the steel frame that governed the country. The old system of strengthening dynastic rule by marriages between scions of the capitalist class, the army's ruling hierarchy, the top bureaucracy and the feudal class has further strengthened the stranglehold of this class of the new 'Mughuls' of Pakistan over the people. Partly because of their cultural, tribal and linguistic affinity, but largely because of the power that they wield and its shameless application, this class has been able so far effectively to control things in their home province of the Punjab. In other provinces, however, their presence and the brash display of power are resented in the NWFP with a slight variation and in Baluchistan and Sind with clear and undisguised contempt and disgust.

The NWFP has over the years thrown up an entrepreneur class which with its dynamism is now involved in commercial and industrial activity in the Punjab and Sind. There are more Pakhtuns living in Karachi today than in Peshawar and all the district towns of the NWFP put together. Thus the Pakhtun of today has a stake in Pakistan and does not think on narrow provincial lines. He does, however, seek his full share of power and responsibility in running the country. His deep interest in, and affinity with, the people across the border are factors that should be borne in mind in any assessment of Pakistan's relations with Afghanistan.

Baluchistan's position close to the entrance of the Persian Gulf, its proud and relatively insular past and the Baluch population in Iranian Baluchistan have for some time fired the imagination of the romantics among the Baluch, who have conjured up a dream of 'Greater Baluchistan'. The ordinary Baluch is economically the most deprived of Pakistan's population, and the military government's efforts to place greater emphasis on development in Baluchistan than has been the case hitherto have so far benefited a few *sardar*s but have not materially touched the scattered population of this poverty-stricken province. The sense of deprivation of the Baluch is natural when he has little participation in running the affairs of either his own province or of Pakistan. Baluchistan, and to a lesser extent the NWFP, will therefore remain areas of political instability until they become full and equal partners in the federation and until they feel that their exploitation by the power clique, whom they associate with the Punjab, has ended.

If the NWFP and Baluchistan have some justification for a sense of deprivation, Sind has more. It had played a leading role in the creation of Pakistan and had accepted a flood of refugees from India who were culturally and linguistically very different from the Sindhis. The interference of the armed forces in politics since 1953, when Ghulam Mohammad, with the army's backing, dismissed the Prime Minister and later dissolved the National Assembly, led to political strangulation, which set the process of national disintegration in motion. The provinces, except the Punjab to which the ruling elite belonged, began to feel a sense of deprivation, and the schism between the ruling hierarchy and the ruled began to grow. This sense of a lack of participation and denial of justice was prevalent in East Pakistan as well as in the smaller provinces of West Pakistan. In Sind, where lands and jobs were given by successive regimes to non-Sindhis, this sense of injustice began to grow. The treatment of the Sindhi language and the move of the country's capital away from Karachi were resented in Sind, and the successive rule of military governments gave the Sindhi a sense of deprivation and neglect. He has begun to feel himself a second-class citizen in a state he had helped to create, and he resents having been reduced to the permanent status of a political outcast. This feeling of the Sindhi and the Baluch and to a lesser extent of the Pakhtun can only grow until they are made the masters of their own affairs and become real partners in running the country. At present they cannot see this happening and are convinced that Pakistan's military rulers have no intention of parting with power.

The future of Pakistan will depend on whether the equally suppressed people of the Punjab will struggle along with the downtrodden people of the other provinces, against an ever-growing exploitative class. This class is not exclusively Punjabi. The *pir*s and *wadera*s of Sind, the capitalist *khan*s of the NWFP and most of the *sardar*s of Baluchistan are today partners in exploitation with the Punjabi ruling hierarchy, and this class knows that its future is safe in the hands of a reactionary autocratic regime. Experience has, however, taught them to keep a lookout for a change in the direction of the political wind. They judged this accurately in 1970, when they joined Zulfiqar Ali Bhutto's PPP in large numbers. The *pir*s and *wadera*s of Sind showed this capacity to survive again in 1983 when they saw that the people of Sind were ready to rise against the military regime. In fact, they were so quick to see this that they appeared to lead and not follow the tide. The capitalist and feudal classes of the NWFP and the Punjab would have followed this example just as promptly if they had seen the beginning of a similar movement in their provinces. The feudalists of the Punjab had lost no time in flocking to Bhutto's banner in 1970, when they had seen that he had considerable support among the common people of their province. A decade and a half later, they could have lost neither their judgment nor their ability to preserve their position in society. Their anxiety to do so is illustrated by a pathetic appeal sent out by a senior leader of a component party of the Movement for the Restoration of Democracy (MRD) from prison to the acting Secretary-General of this organisation towards the end of 1983. In this he expressed the fears of the capitalists and feudalists among the political leadership of the MRD that a continuation of the movement against the military regime would upset the 'status quo'. He explained that his views had the full support of the leadership of the PPP in prison with him, most of which was feudal. Pleading for the preservation of the existing social order, he wrote that the 'equilibrium of this centuries-old socio-economic order — *zamindars*, *batai* system and the wage system — is in the political power being in the hands of the old feudal families'. He went on to say that 'this political power is being challenged today', which in his view was 'likely to disturb the equilibrium and would pose the question of coexistence with the army, which is a matter of grave concern'. He expressed his fears that 'any disturbance of the equilibrium of the socio-economic order would pave the way for radicals and radical politics'. Summing up, he pleaded for the preservation of the existing order and expressed the opinion that 'the present socio-economic order can only survive in the coexistence of the junta and the feudals'.[7]

The poor and oppressed people of Pakistan must therefore understand the real causes of their poverty and beware of subterfuges. It would be in the interest of the Sindhis, the Baluch and the Pakhtun to forge a common cause with the equally deprived and oppressed Punjabi — the landless labourer, the industrial worker and the petty civilian employee — against the tyranny of the ruling clique of oppressors, who will not see reason until they are faced with the might of the oppressed people of this country. This will require a great deal of patience on the part of the people of the smaller provinces, a quality they have shown they possess in large measure but one they may be beginning to feel they have exhausted. The alternative will, however, lead to disaster. Separatist and extremist slogans and talk of a confederation will not help. Even if such moves were to succeed, the beneficiary would not be the common man but a coterie of exploiters. The nationalistic pride of some may thereby be satisfied, but it will not be long-lived. The united struggle of the oppressed in all the provinces is likely to be a more rewarding effort. It is only when the oppressed people of the Punjab rise against the predominantly Punjabi oppressors that they and the people of the other provinces can be liberated from the yoke of an oppressive machine. Without their active participation it will not be a worthwhile undertaking. From the way things are shaping it is clear that, before long, the people of the Punjab will begin to play their part in liberating themselves and the people of the other provinces from the state of slavery that they have tolerated for so long.

Servants, Not Masters

It was 14 August 1947. The first Governor-General of Pakistan was hosting a reception in Karachi to which a large number of people had been invited. Among those present were a few defence service officers. Seeing the Quaid-i-Azam move freely among his guests, these officers moved close to him and, seeing them in uniform, he asked them how they were. Encouraged by this friendly gesture, one of the group, Colonel Akbar Khan, later of Rawalpindi conspiracy fame, sought the Quaid-i-Azam's permission to speak. Receiving a nod he began to expound his views on defence policy. In his eloquent discourse, on matters that in a democratic system are properly the concern of a civilian government, he began to advise the Quaid-i-Azam on how the defence services should be run. He had not finished what he had to say when the Quaid-i-Azam cut him short. Raising his finger and looking at Akbar Khan sternly, the Quaid spoke in low deliberate tones:

> Do not forget that you in the armed forces are the servants of the people. You do not make national policy. It is we, the civilians, who decide these issues, and it is your duty to carry out the tasks with which you are entrusted.[8]

The Quaid-i-Azam's remarks appeared to have a profound effect on those present. But how quickly they were forgotten! Barely four years later, in 1951, Akbar Khan, to whom these words had been addressed, attempted a coup to oust the constitutional government of Pakistan, and in 1953 General Ayub Khan, the army commander-in-chief, by supporting Ghulam Mohammad's unconstitutional act of dismissing an elected Prime Minister and dissolving the Constituent Assembly, directly involved the armed forces in the politics of the country. Once the die had been cast, one thing led to another. In 1954 Ayub Khan was made the Minister of Defence in Mohammad Ali Bogra's Cabinet, a portfolio that had hitherto been with the civilian prime minister. It was significant that he insisted on continuing at the same time as the commander-in-chief of the Pakistan Army.

In Mohammad Ali Bogra's Cabinet, the strongest voice, not excluding that of the Prime Minister, was of the Commander-in-Chief of the Pakistan Army, and there was nothing he could not have done if he wanted to. However, Ayub Khan was an intelligent person. He knew that the prize was his for the asking. With Iskander Mirza as Minister of the interior he had his way until in October 1958 he and Iskander Mirza, then the President, overthrew the civilian government of Prime Minister

Feroz Khan Noon. A few days later Iskander Mirza was ousted, and the de facto control of the army over Pakistan since 1953 was regularised. Martial law had been declared, and Ayub Khan and the army were able to run the country without any pretences or camouflage. In 1962 a constitution, whose real architect was Ayub Khan himself, was enforced, and he continued to rule until 1968 under the controlled democracy which he had introduced. Martial law had been lifted, but the army's umbrella was visible throughout. With Ayub Khan's outster by Yahya Khan the country had another taste of martial law. The elections of 1970 produced a result that Yahya Khan had not foreseen, and he refused to hand over power to the Bengali majority of Sheikh Mujib ur Rehman. Bhutto, not comprehending the consequences of his actions, supported Yahya Khan and his anti-democratic moves, which led to military action in East Pakistan and eventually to the dismemberment of Pakistan.

Bhutto took over the reins of office in difficult circumstances, which were really of his own creation. A demoralised nation and a demoralised army, 93,000 of whom were prisoners of India, had to be rehabilitated. The lesson that the Quaid-i-Azam had given to a group of defence service officers 24 years earlier was to be retaught. Instead, Bhutto tried to outsmart himself and eventually succeeded in doing so. Having failed to secure enough seats to form governments in two of the four provinces — Baluchistan and NWFP — he decided to achieve by force what he had failed to achieve through the ballot. The provincial JUI-NAP government of Baluchistan was dismissed on trumped-up charges, and the NWFP JUI-NAP government resigned. Governor's rule was imposed in both these provinces, and Bhutto thus became the unchallenged ruler of the whole of Pakistan. He had all prominent opposition leaders in these two provinces arrested and began to use the army to quell all dissent in Baluchistan. As resentment grew, the army's area of operation expanded. GHQ, rather than Bhutto's Governor in Quetta, began to run the government in Baluchistan. This was the second time that the army had been used to quell dissent in Baluchistan. The first time was during Ayub Khan's period, when almost for a decade the army had tried unsuccessfully to suppress recalcitrant *sardars* and tribes. However, the intensity of operations then was less than during Bhutto's rule, and the army had felt restricted by Ayub Khan during these operations. With this experience of the Ayub Khan era, GHQ felt confident that the army would, if it was this time given a free hand, sort things out rapidly and re-establish government control throughout the province. It was the classical approach of the army wanting more and more guns to finish an operation, which ends in drawing in more and more resources and in prolonging the conflict. Many wars have been started with the confidence that the political objective would be achieved in a few days, but it has remained unfulfilled even after a few years. The most recent example is the Iraqi invasion of Iran, which Iraq and many in the West believed would bring Iran to its knees in a few weeks. The Iraq-Iran war shows no sign of ending even after five years.

However, Bhutto's military action in Baluchistan restored the army's confidence, which had suffered badly in the Bangladesh debacle. When an army loses a war there is a natural urge to redeem its honour and regain its self-respect, at least in its own eyes. This has happened repeatedly in history, and armies have fought many a war merely to redeem their honour. The Indians hoped to do this in the 1965 Indo-Pakistan War after the Chinese debacle in 1962; and since the 1965 war ended in a stalemate it had to fight Pakistan again to be able to hold its head up and whitewash its pitiable performance against the Chinese. It got the chance it had been looking for in East Pakistan in 1971 and more than regained its lost prestige. After 1971, the Pakistan Army could not hope to regain its honour by fighting any outside power, and the Baluch tribes, ill-equipped and fighting with First World War rifles and in some cases with 19th-century weapons, gave it the opportunity it had been looking for. It was never able to subjugate these people, but it felt that it was able to redeem some of its lost prestige by killing and punishing the militant Baluch tribes in a manner it had not been able to do to the *Mukhti Bahini* in East Pakistan. Both the Bengali and the Baluch spoke a language the Pakistani soldier did not understand, and they had been told that both were against the 'solidarity' and 'integrity' of Pakistan. As the Pakistan Army regained its confidence, misplaced though it was, so did its ambition rise. The humiliated and defeated army of 1971 had by 1977 begun to harbour political ambitions and was beginning to feel that if it could sort out the Baluch and run Baluchistan, it could also sort out others and run the other provinces. It argued that running a vast province like Baluchistan, so ill-served with communications and inhabited by wild and hostile tribes, was far more difficult than running the provinces of the Punjab and Sind, where the conditions were more favourable and the people more placid and peaceful. When Bhutto rigged the elections in 1977 and a movement was launched for re-elections, his obstinacy and faulty political judgment led him to use the army to quell the people's movement. It was only a matter of time before the army, which had already tasted absolute power in Baluchistan, should want to formalise the situation and take over the affairs of the rest of the country.

As negotiations dragged on in Islamabad in mid-1977, Bhutto brought Zia ul Haq and his generals more and more into the political arena. By getting them to brief the PNA's negotiating team, ostensibly to inform them of the 'grave' situation on Pakistan's borders rendering the PNA's demand for re-elections untimely, but actually to impress them of the support of the army that he enjoyed, he gave the generals confidence in their own strength. Bhutto's game of brinksmanship and of using one against the other led to the only logical end. He had created conditions for his own ouster, and 5 July 1977 brought to an end a process he had himself set in motion. The badly bruised army, which had been licking its wounds after its shameful defeat in East Pakistan, saw this as the opportunity of a lifetime to refurbish its soiled image. It mattered little that on 5 July 1977 it had not succeeded in conquering an enemy but its own people. What mattered to the generals was that they had conquered someone. They felt that they had achieved so great a victory and had been entrusted with so great a responsibility that they could now afford to forget the dark days of 1971, when their generals had been stripped of their badges of rank in the *Paltan Maidan* and their officers had been made to crawl on their bellies in the streets of Dhaka. And after all, which country could they have fought to redeem their honour? India was now in comparison much more powerful, and even Afghanistan might have been too tough a nut to crack. The unarmed people of Pakistan were a much safer bet. So Pakistan entered the ultimate in military adventurism — a grip its army would not easily loosen.

The Future

This examination of Pakistan's geopolitical imperatives suggests that there are some problems that are of a fairly permanent nature and some others of its own making. However, even those problems which the people have imposed on themselves cannot be shaken off easily. The organised exploitation of religion to serve narrow group interests, its divisive aspects in a society such as that of Pakistan, the desire to overemphasise the concept of ideology even at the risk of endangering the security of the state, the keenness to become a part of the super-power tussle in the area, the continuance of the supremacy of the military in our national life and the peculiar psychosis that our generals have developed are matters that must be resolved if the country is to survive. Even singly these are sufficiently grave to endanger seriously the integrity and existence of Pakistan. Together these could ensure its speedy end. Time will show whether the Pakistani nation has the capacity to shake off some of these shibboleths and become more realistic in facing the changing requirements of the time. And time does not wait.

References and Notes

1. The budgeted non-productive expenditure of the federal government in 1984-85 was 81.1% of the government's current expenditure. See Government of Pakistan, Finance Division, *Annual Budget Statement 1984-85* (Islamabad: Government of Pakistan, June 1984), pp. 11-13.

2. *Daily Jang* (Lahore), 12 May 1984, p. 1.

3. International Bank for Reconstruction and Development, *World Development Report 1982* (Washington D.C. World Bank, 1982), p. 157.

4. Quaid-i-Azam Mohammad Ali Jinnah's broadcast to the people of the United States of America, February 1948.

5. *Nawa-i-Waqt* (Rawalpindi), 1 December 1983.

6. *Dawn* (Karachi), 13 March 1981, p. 1.

7. Letter of Abid Zuberi, Information Secretary, National Democratic Party to Malik Mohammad Qasim, Acting Secretary General, Movement for Restoration of Democracy, December 1983.

8. The writer was one of the group.

Contributors

EQBAL AHMED is a well-known social scientist and is at present teaching at the New Hampshire College, USA. He is also a fellow of the Institute of Policy Studies, USA. He has specialised in Islamic Studies and Middle Eastern affairs.

SUROOSH IRFANI was educated at the University of the Punjab (Pakistan), the University of Shiraz (Iran) and the University of London (UK). He was taught at the Uromich and Shiraz Universities in Iran and was in that country during the Iranian Revolution. He is the author of *Revolutionary Islam in Iran — Popular Liberation or Religious Dictatorship?*

ABBAS RASHID was educated at the University of the Punjab (Pakistan) and Columbia University (USA). He was taught international relations at the University of the Punjab as well as at the Civil Services Academy of Pakistan. He is currently a senior faculty member at the Society for the Advancement of Higher Education in Pakistan.

ZAFARYAB AHMED was educated at the University of the Punjab (Pakistan) and at the University of Manchester (UK). He has taught sociology at the Agricultural University in Faisalabad (Pakistan) and history at Aitchison College in Lahore (Pakistan).

ZIAUL HAQUE was educated at the University of Sind (Pakistan) and obtained his doctorate in Arabic and Islamic studies from the University of Chicago (USA). He was a senior faculty member at the Islamic Research Institute, Islamabad, and edited the journal *Islamic Studies*. He is the author of *Landlord and Peasant in Early Islam*. Another of his works in the process of publication is entitled *Islam and Feudalism*.

OMAR ASGHAR KHAN was educated at the University of Peshawar (Pakistan), the University of Essex (UK) and the University of Cambridge (UK). He taught economics at the University of the Punjab until November 1983 when his services were terminated by the martial law authorities.

268

PERVEZ AMIRALI HOODBHOY was educated at MIT(USA), where he obtained his doctorate in nuclear physics. He has taught physics at MIT, has been a guest scientist at ICTP, Trieste (Italy), and a post-doctoral fellow at the University of Washington, Seattle (USA).

ABDUL HAMEED NAYYAR was educated at the University of Karachi (Pakistan) and obtained his doctorate in solid state physics from Imperial College, University of London (UK). He was a visiting associate professor at the University of Manitoba, Winnipeg, Canada during 1982-83.

AKMAL HUSSAIN was educated at the University of the Punjab (Pakistan), the University of Cambridge (UK), and obtained his doctorate in economics from the University of Sussex. He has taught economics at the University of the Punjab (Pakistan), the University of Sussex (UK) and the University of California, Riverside (USA).

FEROZ AHMED was educated at the University of Karachi (Pakistan) and obtained his doctorate in demography from Johns Hopkins University (USA) in 1968. He is a well-known political and economic analyst. He founded and edited *Pakistan Forum* until 1979 and is currently the editor of *Pakistan Democratic Forum* published in New York.

Index

ASIA TITLES FROM ZED PRESS

POLITICAL ECONOMY

Francois Houtart and Genevieve Lemercinier
HAI VAN:
Life in a Vietnamese Commune
Hb and Pb

Ben Kiernan and Chanthou Boua
PEASANTS AND POLITICS IN KAMPUCHEA, 1942-1981
Hb and Pb

David Selbourne
THROUGH THE INDIAN LOOKING GLASS
Pb

Hassan Gardezi and Jamil Rashid (Editors)
PAKISTAN: THE ROOTS OF DICTATORSHIP
The Political Economy of a Praetorian State
Hb and Pb

Stefan de Vylder
AGRICULTURE IN CHAINS
Bangladesh — A Case Study in Contradictions and Constraints
Hb

Rehman Sobhan and Muzaffer Ahmad
PUBLIC ENTERPRISE IN AN INTERMEDIATE REGIME:
A Study in the Political Economy of Bangladesh
Hb

Satchi Ponnambalam
DEPENDENT CAPITALISM IN CRISIS:
The Sri Lankan Economy, 1948-1980
Hb

David Elliot
THAILAND: ORIGINS OF MILITARY RULE
Hb and Pb

A. Rudra, T. Shanin and J. Banaji et al
STUDIES IN THE DEVELOPMENT OF CAPITALISM IN INDIA
Hb and Pb

Bulletin of Concerned Asian Scholars
CHINA: FROM MAO TO DENG
The Politics and Economics of Socialist Development
Hb and Pb

Hua Wu Yin
CLASS AND COMMUNALISM IN MALAYSIA:
Politics in a Dependent Capitalist State
Hb and Pb

Ruth and Victor Sidel
THE HEALTH OF CHINA:
Current Conflicts in Medical and Human Services for One Billion People
Hb and Pb

Betsy Hartmann and James K. Boyce
A QUIET VIOLENCE:
View from a Bangladesh Village
Hb and Pb

Rehman Sobhan
THE CRISIS OF EXTERNAL DEPENDENCE
Hb and Pb

Elisabeth Croll
THE FAMILY RICE BOWL
Food and the Domestic Economy in
China
Hb and Pb

W.F. Wertheim and Matthias Stiefel
PRODUCTION, EQUALITY AND
PARTICIPATION IN RURAL
CHINA
Pb

Srikant Dutt
INDIA AND THE THIRD
WORLD:
Altruism or Hegemony
Hb and Pb

CONTEMPORARY HISTORY/
REVOLUTIONARY STRUGGLES

Carmel Budiardjo and Liem Soei
Liong
THE WAR AGAINST EAST
TIMOR
Hb and Pb

Susantha Goonatilake
ABORTED DISCOVERY:
Science and Creativity in the Third
World
Hb and Pb

Olle Törnquist
DILEMMAS OF THIRD WORLD
COMMUNISM
The Destruction of the PKI in
Indonesia
Hb and Pb

Sumanta Banerjee
INDIA'S SIMMERING
REVOLUTION: The Naxalite
Uprising
Pb

Selig Harrison
IN AFGHANISTAN'S SHADOW:
Baluch Nationalism and Soviet
Temptation
Hb and Pb

Musimgrafik
WHERE MONSOONS MEET:
History of Malaya
Pb

Lawrence Lifschultz
BANGLADESH:
The Unfinished Revolution
Pb

Satchi Ponnambalam
SRI LANKA:
The National Question and the
Tamil Liberation Struggle
Hb and Pb

HUMAN RIGHTS

L. Wiseberg and H. Scoble
(Editors)
ACCESS TO JUSTICE:
The Struggle for Human Rights in
South East Asia
Hb and Pb

Permanent People's Tribunal
PHILIPPINES:
Repression and Resistance
Pb

Julie Southwood and Patrick
Flanagan
INDONESIA:
Law, Propaganda and Terror
Hb and Pb

Kimmo Kiljunen
KAMPUCHEA
Decade of the Genocide
Hb and Pb

RELIGION

Kim Yongbock
MINJUNG THEOLOGY:
People as the Subjects of History

WOMEN

Bobby Siu
WOMEN OF CHINA:
Imperialism and Women's
Resistance, 1900-1949
Hb and Pb

Else Skjonsberg
A SPECIAL CASTE?
Tamil Women in Sri Lanka
Pb

Gail Omvedt
**WE WILL SMASH THIS
PRISON!**
Indian Women in Struggle
Hb and Pb

Agnes Smedley
**PORTRAITS OF CHINESE
WOMEN IN REVOLUTION**
Pb

Marie Mies
**THE LACEMAKERS OF
NARSAPUR:**
Indian Housewives Produce for the
World Market
Pb

Arlene Eisen
**WOMEN IN THE NEW
VIETNAM**
Hb and Pb

Elisabeth Croll
CHINESE WOMEN
Hb and Pb

Patricia Jeffrey
FROGS IN A WELL:
Indian Women in Purdah
Hb and Pb

Madhu Kishwar and Ruth Vanita
(eds.)
IN SEARCH OF ANSWERS
Indian Women's Voices
Hb and Pb

Mi Mi Khaing
**THE WORLD OF BURMESE
WOMEN**
Hb and Pb

Kumari Jayawardena
**FEMINISM AND NATIONALISM
IN THE THIRD WORLD**
Hb and Pb

ECOLOGY

Vaclav Smil
THE BAD EARTH
Environmental Degradation in
China
Hb and Pb

Zed titles cover Africa, Asia, Latin America and the Middle East, as well as general issues affecting the Third World's relations with the rest of the world. Our series embrace: Imperialism, Women, Political Economy, History, Labour, Voices of Struggle, Human Rights, Religion, Ecology and other areas pertinent to the Third World.

You can order Zed titles direct from Zed, 57 Caledonian Road, London, N1 9BU, U.K.